After Django

JAZZ PERSPECTIVES

Eric Porter and John Szwed, Series Editors
Lewis Porter, Founding Editor

After Django

Making Jazz in Postwar France

Tom Perchard

UNIVERSITY OF MICHIGAN PRESS • ANN ARBOR

Published in the United States of America by the
University of Michigan Press
Manufactured in the United States of America
♾ Printed on acid-free paper

2018   2017   2016   2015   4   3   2   1

A CIP catalog record for this book is available from the British Library.

Library of Congress Cataloging-in-Publication Data

Perchard, Tom, 1976–
      After Django : making jazz in postwar France / Tom Perchard.
         pages cm. — (Jazz perspectives)
      Includes bibliographical references and index.
         ISBN 978-0-472-07242-2 (hardcover : alk. paper) — ISBN 978-0-472-05242-4
   (pbk. : alk. paper) — ISBN 978-0-472-12075-8 (e-book)
         1. Jazz—France—1941–1950—History and criticism.   2. Jazz—France—
   1951–1960—History and criticism.   3. Jazz—France—1961–1970—History
   and criticism.   I. Title.
   ML3509.F7P47   2015
   781.650944'09045—dc23
                                                                          2014032681

Arts & Humanities
Research Council

Support for this project was provided by the Arts and Humanities Research
Council (AHRC).

To Seymour Wright

Acknowledgments

The bulk of this book was written during the course of an Arts and Humanities Research Council fellowship. I'm very grateful to the Council, and to my department at Goldsmiths, University of London, for making this leave of study possible. Throughout, I was fortunate to be assisted by some sterling librarians and archivists, including Ann Aldridge at Goldsmiths, David Nathan at the National Jazz Archive, Arndt Weidler at the Jazz-Institut Darmstadt, Florence de Coninck at IRMA, and Antoine Provansal at the Bibliothèque nationale de France; my great friend Tom Farncombe expertly traced André Hodeir's scores to a warehouse in the middle of nowhere. Thanks to those who have engaged with me in extended conversations around the topics explored here: Jason Toynbee, Nick Gebhardt, Marc Dooley, Jedediah Sklower, Victor Schonfield, Alyn Shipton, Chris Kennett, Byron Dueck, Andy Fry, Catherine Tackley, Jacques Oger, Gérard Rouy, Jacques Thollot, Caroline de Bendern, Guy Kopelowicz, Martine Palmé and Patrick Wilen. A number of those people also acted as readers for portions of the manuscript, and, even when they disagreed with my arguments, their careful comments improved the work greatly; thanks on this score also go to Roger Magraw, Alan Stanbridge, Eric Drott, Alex Hawkins, Alex James, Pierre Fargeton, Jeremiah Spillane, Steve Beresford, Clifford Allen, Flurin Casura, Anthony Pryer and the University of Michigan Press's anonymous reviewers. I was given invaluable opportunities to present and discuss some of this work by John Stringer and Jenny Doctor at York, Annette Davison at Edinburgh, Tony Whyton at Salford—Annette and Tony also provided valuable readings and advice along the way—Cliff Eisen at Kings College London,

George Nicholson at Sheffield, Stefano Zenni at the Piacenza Jazz Fest, and Trevor Herbert and Jeffrey Nussbaum at the 2012 International Musicological Society meeting in Rome (thanks also to Krin Gabbard for facilitating this). Steve Wilford and Katy Miller were keen, able and efficient research assistants; Lola Reboud provided generous hospitality in Paris. The publishing process has been much helped by Walter van de Leur and, at the Press, Christopher Hebert. Thanks, finally, to the Perchard and Milliard families, and—above all—to Coline.

The text incorporates parts of the following published items. "Tradition, Modernity and the Supernatural Swing: Re-Reading 'Primitivism' in Hugues Panassié's Writing on Jazz," by Tom Perchard, *Popular Music* 30, no. 1 (January 2011): 25–45. Copyright © 2011 Cambridge University Press. Reprinted with permission. "Hugues Panassié Contra Walter Benjamin: Bodies, Masses, and the Iconic Jazz Recording in Mid-century France," by Tom Perchard, *Popular Music and Society* 35, no. 3 (December 2012): 375–98. Reproduced with permission of Taylor & Francis, http://www.tandfonline.com. "Thelonious Monk Meets the French Critics: Art and Entertainment, Improvisation, and its Simulacrum," by Tom Perchard, *Jazz Perspectives* 5, no. 1 (August 2011): 61–94. Reproduced with permission of Taylor & Francis, http://www.tandfonline.com. "Lulu's Back in Town," music by Harry Warren, lyrics by Al Dubin © 1935 M. Witmark & Sons. This arrangement © 2013 M. Witmark & Sons. All rights controlled and administered by WB Music Corp. and B. Feldman & Co., Ltd. All rights reserved. International copyright secured. Used by permission. Reprinted by Permission of Alfred Music and Hal Leonard Corporation.

Contents

ONE

Histories of Jazz in France

There's a notion of long standing that the French, loving jazz perhaps even more than the Americans whose birthright it was, have always offered the music and its musicians safe haven—great, and sometimes weather-beaten African American players above all. Stories of the black artists who had flocked to interwar Paris in search of a creative life free of race prejudice took root around the middle of the 20th century, as did the idea that it was in Europe that jazz was first given the critical scrutiny and celebration that was its due.[1] The Swiss conductor Ernest Ansermet's 1919 article on the Southern Syncopated Orchestra, and particularly its star clarinetist Sidney Bechet, was resurrected by the French jazz press in the late 1930s as proof of the music's early, cultivated European appreciation; Rudi Blesh's classic jazz history *Shining Trumpets* (1946) was only one of the books that soon helped fix this idea for American jazz audiences.[2] Just as important was the famous reverence with which French audiences regarded those expatriates who, at home, had been mere vaudevillians, Josephine Baker and later Bechet most prominent among them. After World War II, popular tales of culture celebrities like Jean-Paul Sartre and Simone de Beauvoir's dancing to jazz in choking subterranean *caves*, and filmic representations like *Paris Blues* (1961)—centering on two jazz musicians, played by Paul Newman and Sidney Poitier, who had escaped American small-mindedness to ply their trade on the Left Bank—helped perpetuate the belief that jazz was better off abroad.

Maybe there was something in it. Even in the late 1960s it was possible for the members of Chicago's experimental, marginal Association for the Advancement of Creative Musicians (AACM) to move to Paris, play to audiences of thousands, and shape a countercultural profile that would have been unthinkable for them in the United States. [3] Nevertheless, numerous jazz musicians living in France knew that the supposed freedoms on offer came with strings attached, and the jazz historian James Lincoln Collier has argued forcefully that serious French enthusiasm for the music neither antedated nor surpassed what was to found in America. [4] Black-and-white memories of jazz in France still flicker in a cultural imagination for which the country—and especially Paris—stands as a fount of taste, romance and untrammeled creativity. Yet that imagination does more work than many jazz musicians could ever find.

That's one meaning of this book's subtitle, "Making Jazz in Postwar France": the study investigates those critical discourses that "made" jazz into an object of fascination, debate, and contemporary culture—and, indeed, which made "jazz in postwar France," since the book also asks how particular historical narratives of the music's life in that country have been constructed. But underneath all that is a more literal meaning and a more straightforward aim. To begin with, the book is a study of the music's French creation between 1945 and 1985. [5]

This is a history that is still underexplored, especially in Anglophone writing, but it threw up practices and trends that demand study: the emergence of musicians who excelled in American styles, the development of musical approaches that tried to pull away from transatlantic example, the cultivation of particularly lively and sophisticated critical discourses (these often as illustrative of the social climate in which they flourished as of the music they addressed). Still, postwar developments built upon an older fascination with black music, and though the tale of jazz's arrival and interwar life in France is increasingly familiar, it needs outlining here.

What would now be called African American music had been heard in the country at least since the 1870s, when touring vocal groups like the Fisk Jubilee Singers had begun to popularize the spirituals. In 1903 the vaudeville stars George Walker and Bert Williams presented Will Marion Cook's operetta *In Dahomey* at the Olympia, Paris's famous music hall; in the same year the cake-walk craze pranced across French society floors. The drummer Louis Mitchell led a band through a residency in the basement club of the Casino de Paris in 1917, and in January of the following year, after the United States' entry to World War I, James Reese Europe's regimental band disembarked their troopship at Brest—these were the Harlem Hellfighters, who would play in some twenty-five French cities and towns through 1918. Those groups mixed novelties, sentimental songs, ragtime, military and dance music; by the 1920s the *chanson* of the Parisian cabaret or the Nice resort had often been replaced by the "jazz band," even if that term could signify nothing more than the presence of a drum, or a dark face.[6] All-black spectaculars followed, most famously *La Revue nègre* which, in 1925, introduced Josephine Baker to the French public. In the latter 1920s and early 1930s, Sam Wooding, Noble Sissle, Lucky Millinder and other African American bandleaders toured and enjoyed residencies at clubs and restaurants in the capital and on the coast.[7] Louis Armstrong and Duke Ellington made their Parisian debuts in 1932 and 1933, and over the course of the 1930s Fats Waller, Coleman Hawkins and many other American jazz musicians, black and white, would also pass through.

The French culturati was, for a time, entranced by the new music, and again and again in their writings the claim was made: a Romantic idea of "art," too distant from 20th century experience to remain meaningful, was being replaced by new forms—jazz, cinema—that fused the creative and the everyday. In his 1926 book, *Le Jazz*, André Schæffner argued that it was because "Negroes perhaps no longer perceive in their culture that hiatus that we seek to maintain between art and the other manifestations of our activity" that jazz was capable of wringing out an "occidental art, saturated with harmony and orchestration."[8] Writing in the surrealist movement's house magazine, *Documents*, Michel Leiris argued that it was precisely because it didn't constitute "an Art proper" that jazz was immune from the "overdevelopment" that plagued "that bastard concept."[9]

This kind of thinking is explored later. But no matter how much jazz was venerated for its pure popular vitality, from its appearance in France the form was met by efforts to cultivate those elements of the rather more polite light classical music that it also contained. This was the style that became known in France and across the world as "symphonic" jazz, a music that emphasized the ensemble elegance of the ballroom or concert stage over the hot brass effects of speakeasy fantasy, and brought jazz into a less dubious, more widely appreciated sphere as a result. Most notable among symphonic jazz's French stars, all of whom followed the extremely successful American example of Paul Whiteman, was Grégor Kelekian. Though the bandleader was an unremarkable musician, like Whiteman he had a great capacity for spectacle, business and talent-spotting, and his highly popular group, Grégor et ses grégoriens, featured many of the best French jazz players to emerge during the 1930s: the saxophonists André Ekyan and Alix Combelle, the trumpeter Philippe Brun, the pianist Stéphane Mougin, the violinists Michel Warlop and Stéphane Grappelly.[10] The "hot jazz" of players like Louis Armstrong, Muggsy Spanier, Bix Beiderbecke, Fats Waller and Duke Ellington inspired great fan devotion in interwar France, and it was soon supported by a dedicated commercial and critical infrastructure. But that music could not compete with the work of (white) American dance bands like those of Whiteman and Ted Lewis, and the local imitations that trailed in their wake. Grégor aside, it was French bandleaders like Ray Ventura, Raymond Legrand, Fred Adison—and their English counterparts Ray Noble, Nat Gonella, and above all Jack Hylton—who were generally understood to represent "jazz" in 1930s France.[11]

Even the most famous of all French jazz groups was only moderately successful on its home territory.[12] In 1933 the young founders of a soon-to-be-important jazz fan society, the Hot-club de France, decided to form an orchestra that would tour and promote both the music and the organization. An early formation featured the Paris-resident Americans Arthur Briggs on trumpet and Freddy Johnson on piano. But the club directors leading these efforts—Jacques Auxenfans, Pierre Nourry and Charles Delaunay—soon resolved to concentrate on promoting local musicians instead. In spring 1934 they set about forming a French group, and by the end of that year a lineup had begun to cohere. Two recording sessions were arranged featuring violinist Grappelly, guitarists Roger Chaput and the brothers Jungo and Joseph Reinhardt, and bassist Louis Vola (Grappelly and Jungo would, sooner or later, become Grappelli and Django). The recordings released on Ultraphone in February 1935 bore the group's definitive name, Le Quintette du Hot-club de France.[13]

Though Grappelli and Reinhardt vied for leader status, in truth the guitarist rendered his colleague undistinguished: despite having famously lost most use of the third and fourth fingers of his left hand in a 1928 caravan fire, Reinhardt had cultivated a mastery of style and thought which, in contrast to the violinist's babbling linework, was always articulated in the clearest terms. Playing the banjo-guitar with musette and tango groups long before he discovered jazz, the young Reinhardt's taste and technique had been formed by exposure to cultures of gestural virtuosity that, in those two musical styles as in early century New Orleans jazz, likely owed as much to European concert music as they did folk improvisation of whatever kind. But by the time of his first recordings in 1934, the trills, octaves and note showers with which the guitarist embellished his melodic inventions often recalled Fats Waller's pianism; Louis Armstrong's clarion arpeggios and deft vocal feints were just as present.[14]

As much as his technical excellence and fluidity, it was Reinhardt's play of ideas that set him apart from his bandmates, and from the preponderance of jazz musicians at home or abroad: the motifs that were stated and then restated, subject to surprising rhythmic shifts each time, or the lines and patterns that, seeming to head for a certain point, continued on to a destination more unlikely but much better. This looping detail stood in relief to the solid motion which the Quintette had perfected by the time it recorded for Decca in London and Paris during 1938–39 (the group would essentially dissolve at the start of World War II). In feel, instrumentation and repertoire this was an absolutely local jazz style, and though in the postwar period musicians and critics routinely pondered how a truly French jazz might be reached, the Quintette had provided one answer early on. A number of groups soon began to work in the same territory, Michel Warlop and André Ekyan's various ensembles prominent among them, and numerous musical and familial associates of Reinhardt's would continue to work in the style that would eventually become classicized as *jazz manouche*, or gypsy jazz (among them Joseph Reinhardt, and later Django's son Babik).

Following the outbreak of war in September 1939 and France's capitulation to the German army in June the following year, the country was divided in two: a German-administered occupied zone in the north and along the Atlantic coast, and in the south a free zone governed by Maréchal Pétain's Vichy regime (which was itself subordinate to German interests). Until the country's progressive liberation by Allied forces from mid-to late 1944, the French were subject to the diktats and whims of Nazi rule and its local interpretation. Hardly the most serious of these was the assertion of control over the performing arts, and it has often been assumed that in France, jazz, a music associated with the Nazis' various American *bêtes noires*, was subject to a blanket ban. In fact the situation was more complex. Jazz was never prohibited outright in France, though Nazi limitations on jazz's diffusion, and measures against the performance of work by American and British songwriters—especially if Jewish—certainly had serious effects on the way the music was played, written about and enjoyed. But some Nazi edicts were ambiguous, and others were not. If names of works to be played during public performances were often required to be submitted to local authorities, and all English-language titles replaced by French approximations, then the performances themselves were still largely permissible; if one of the leaders of the Hot-club de Marseille was sent to a Silesian concentration camp never to return, it wasn't because he was fond of jazz, but because he was Jewish.[15]

The few black American musicians who had not left Paris as war loomed found themselves interned as Americans rather than non-Aryans. French Caribbean and African musicians like Robert Mavounzy and Freddy Jumbo—and the Rom Django Reinhardt—could still perform and tour.[16] The American-born but naturalized French trumpeter Harry Cooper was able to negotiate his release from prison, and went on to perform regularly on the German-run Radio Paris, recording for the jazz label Swing in 1943 even after the introduction of a requirement that all such activity had to be approved by the Propaganda-Staffel. Hugues Panassié was able to broadcast a jazz radio series on national radio in mid-1942, and though subsequent complaints led to the Vichy prohibition of such programming, jazz remained accessible via British and Swiss stations.[17] Members of the German army and occupying government were often no less partial to the music than were the people they policed.

Nevertheless those involved with jazz and its promotion proceeded with caution. Charles Delaunay, de facto head of the Hot-club during the occupation, acted to suppress the organization's public activity, not least because a small resistance network had formed around the club's head-quarters: Delaunay and his fellow club member Jacques Bureau were arrested, and several members of the extended network were eventually caught and executed.[18] Still, Delaunay was able to organize events and festivals in wartime Paris, sometimes making a concerted effort to frame the music offered in terms that would quell Vichy and Nazi anxieties. Before a "Festival de jazz français" at the Salle Gaveau in December 1940, Delaunay distributed to the press a pamphlet that underscored the French cultural heritage of this New Orleans music, and the native excellence demonstrated by the Quintette. "I intended to create a fiction, a sort of myth for better or worse capable of protecting our little concern," Delaunay wrote in a postwar apologia. As Andy Fry has suggested, this was one of the acts of accommodation that, committed yet not fully resistant, cooperative yet not fully acquiescent, characterized French life during the occupation.[19]

But jazz was also the instrument of more dogged and openly articulated positions. Several prominent collaborators wrote on the music during the war, among them Lucien Rebatet and André Cœuroy. The latter's *Histoire générale du jazz*, published in 1942, is an aggressive version of the defensive Frenchification of jazz that Delaunay and others practiced, one which begins with orthography—Cœuroy insists on referring not to the blues, but the *blouze*—and widens to claim the music for France and

Europe. "Jazz is not an isolated island forever cut off from the continent of music," the author writes, instead a "peninsula" jutting off from that continent, one essentially European.

> We have long believed that jazz was specifically negro. The present thesis is quite to the contrary. Jazz has been black only by accident. The principal elements of which it is comprised are owed to the whites, and to the whites of Europe. Through its history, through its materials, jazz is ours; its future is in our hands.[20]

The argument continues throughout Cœuroy's book: whatever the mooted etymologies of the word "jazz," "in reality" it comes from the French word *jaser*, to gossip, which is what a jazz ensemble does; the music reflects far less its African heritage than it does the old European folk music found in the once-French colonies of the south; rhythmic superimpositions thought characteristic of black music could be found in Chopin and even Mozart as well as African sources. The Hot-club Quintette, Cœuroy concluded, had recently won "a victory for the whites in the raging quarrel of jazz."[21] For those 21st century writers seeking to develop an appreciation of jazz's global dimensions, the book is intriguing—and deeply disturbing, since the author's intelligent if impressionistic attempt to expand upon jazz's African/American origins is so tainted by the nationalism and racialism of the moment.

The *Histoire générale* presented jazz in terms that satisfied the Vichy regime's Franco-folkloric obsessions, but the music was also being instrumentalized by a youth "subculture" much more oppositional in attitude. The *zazous* were so-called because of their identification, sartorial as well as musical, with Cab Calloway's well-known vocalization style and stage act. These were lovers of swing music, and the popular, music hall adaptations of jazz made by singing stars like Charles Trenet and Johnny Hess; their dandyism, long hair and hepcat manners were taken as announcing a threat to Vichy and the country. Regime newspapers featured cartoon *zazous* alongside hook-nosed Jews and other caricatured figures of decadent France, and Pétainistes were encouraged to scalp dangerously coiffed swing fans in the street.[22] The *zazous* were shown only marginally less contempt by the fans of hot jazz, who disdained the commercialism and preen of what they saw as an inauthentic music and movement.[23]

This is the story of jazz in France up to the end of World War II, the period most attended to by the limited number of narratives—popular or scholarly, in French or English—accorded the music in that country.

Until the first decade of the 21st century, language barriers—and the pre-occupying richness of American jazz—conspired to reduce Anglophone histories of the music in France to the broadest outlines. Even thereafter, in a period of great growth for jazz scholarship, the French effort could sometimes only merit a footnote or two in general works: Scott DeVeaux and Gary Giddins's 2009 book, bearing the seemingly comprehensive title *Jazz*, hardly for a moment considers the music's life abroad, stepping onto French soil only when Duke Ellington or Bud Powell do; John Gennari's 2006 *Blowin' Hot and Cool: Jazz and its Critics*, a book that purports to tell the story of jazz through a study of its criticism—and that, as far as that work's American history goes, does so very well—pays very little attention to the French writing that constitutes one of jazz's most sustained and serious critical traditions. But the present book makes the case for an expanded notion of jazz history, and it does so in the company of a growing number of works on the style across the world.[24]

Several studies of jazz in France have been published since the end of the 1990s. As noted, this literature tends to focus on the early decades of the 20th century, and, rather than the music and its musicians, on discussions of the cultural and critical discourses into which jazz was incorporated: these are English-language works like Jeffrey H. Jackson's *Making Jazz French* (2003) and Matthew F. Jordan's *Le Jazz* (2010), and Francophone studies like Denis-Constant Martin and Olivier Roueff's *La France du jazz* (2002). Standing somewhat apart—and referred to throughout this study—is Ludovic Tournès's French-language *New Orleans sur Seine* (1999), the only work to examine both pre- and postwar periods at any length (though the author devotes comparatively little space to the years after 1960). The scope, detail and great accomplishment of *New Orleans sur Seine* make it the field's landmark work.

The aforementioned writers are cultural historians rather than musicologists, and their books share a similar goal: to monitor critical debates between those who saw jazz either as a renewal of or a threat to French identity, and thereby to track what is usually referred to as the "acceptance" of jazz into French cultural life.[25] In the hands of a scholar as skilled as Matthew Jordan—who records changes in the terms of jazz discourse which are sometimes broad, sometimes minute, but always significant—this approach gives valuable results; these ideas of identity, refusal and embrace are important, and we will return to them continually. But their common methodological orientation determines that these investigations can do little other than circle that central issue of acceptance, and if these books generally fail to address the postwar period it is because, by that time, quarrels over jazz's legitimacy are deemed settled. Similarly, if they fail to engage with what we (unlike the players themselves) might call musical practices—and those cultural, political and aesthetic debates still being conducted in sound as well as words long after World War II—it is because their authors' disciplinary backgrounds would neither enable nor reward it. So one of the basic aims of this book is to map a body of French music that is not now well known, in or outside France. Though sometimes making use of a small amount of illustrative music notation, this effort is largely verbal, and unapologetically evaluative. The text makes constant reference to recorded musical performances, many passing, but some more concentrated, and in all cases precise track timings are included to render these useful to all readers.

Another important distinction of this study is its concentration on French, rather than American, musicians and works. Much extant and forthcoming Anglophone writing on jazz in France is interested principally in the activities of (African) American musicians abroad.[26] It's a fascinating and important topic. But, as jazz studies begins to expand its focus to include countries outside the United States, it seems vital to tell new stories about the music in its local formulations rather than merely to broaden American jazz's critical stomping ground, and so this book is primarily concerned to understand the ways in which jazz was received and remade by those culturally and geographically distanced from the music's perceived source. Still, it would not do to write out those traveling American musicians' experiences and voices, and two of the era's most prominent players do receive extended treatment here, the significance of Thelonious Monk and Miles Davis's French work and reception still not fully understood. And if the already recounted adventures of some Americans in Paris are given short shrift—Lester Young, Kenny Clarke, Bud Powell and the Art Ensemble of Chicago have only walk-on roles—their music, and the totemic figure of the African American musician at large, lingers throughout.

After all, a book about jazz can't help but be a book about America, even if—especially if—it's set elsewhere. From the moment of jazz's arrival in Europe, the music was made to stand for that newly dominant power; as many of the books discussed earlier have shown, debates around the style's meanings and merits were part of a larger argument around how far old France should cede to modern American influence and industry. Though this exciting but disturbing "America" continually changes shape, it remains a constant point of reference until the end of the period under study here. Representations and fantasies of an exotic blackness, for instance, play an important role in musical and, especially, critical discourses throughout the period; these have been addressed at length by those writing on early century and interwar France, when the cult of primitivism was at its strongest, but no small part of this book is concerned with the postwar continuation of those ideas, and with the problems they caused for white European musicians lacking this apparently essential jazz prerequisite.

A counterweight to "America" is the idea of a particularly European or "French" jazz practice, one that we have already seen emerging with the Hot-club Quintette in the 1930s. While periodically lying dormant, the call for a French jazz would emerge again in the 1950s and, especially, the 1970s. The final identification of an indigenous style makes a tempting end point for any work on jazz outside the United States in the 20th century. But this book is concerned to critique that kind of soft nationalism, which is found in books like Mike Heffley's *Northern Sun, Southern Moon: Europe's Reinvention of Jazz* and Stuart Nicholson's *Is Jazz Dead? Or Has it Moved to a New Address* (both 2005). Evading the nationalist means establishing a critical approach that is capable of identifying and interpreting distinctive French jazz practices without fetishizing them; it also means avoiding making the kinds of revisionist jazz historical claim that the music trumpeted does not always support (in the context of postwar French jazz, the composer and bandleader Jef Gilson has more than once been accorded this kind of treatment).[27] In a good number of cases this study does make the case for the high value of particular, and often little-known, musicians or recordings. But rather than presenting alternative entries for the established (and essentially American) canon of jazz greats, it is primarily concerned to investigate the dynamics of musical creativity and criticism: to think about music in the making rather than to eulogize this or that particular musical product, or to wish into being an autonomous French jazz tradition.

Internationalism was always assured. Not only playing a music identified with the United States, many important "French" musicians of the period were also born outside metropolitan France. These players were Belgian (René Thomas, Bobby Jaspar), Swiss (Daniel Humair, Irène Schweizer) and French Caribbean (Robert Mavounzy, Alain Jean-Marie); others who were more "fully" French nevertheless grew up away from the mainland, or had French upbringings in other ways reflective of the country's colonial and Mediterranean status (Martial Solal, Georges Arvanitas, Jacques Coursil, Jean-My Truong). A number of those musicians brought distinctive musical approaches with them, and that—along with the presence of numerous American expatriates and other visitors—means that in this book's telling, France becomes not so much a nation in which jazz is acculturated, but a center of jazz aesthetics and professional activity that stretched across Europe and beyond. Aside from the singularly "French," then, the study also considers the dynamics of cultural flow, reception and creation in a broader sense, and the historical movements belonging to jazz in France can often stand for patterns in jazz's global spread generally.

Though this book can be read as an overarching narrative of the period, it's formed of discrete studies of important musical or critical practices, and of specific works and issues. These have been singled out because they show particular conversations about, and particular efforts towards, French understandings of jazz, and because in so doing they illuminate trends in local political and intellectual culture. Some of this work, then, examines musical and cultural discourses in toto. But often more attention is paid to the progress of individual "actors"—the musicians and writers themselves—than is the case in those discourse-focused books on jazz in France mentioned earlier.

That doesn't mean the book duplicates the historically and critically naive Romantic-artist biographies of days gone by, in which towering geniuses rise above time and place to point the way for those trailing behind. Instead, it aims to shuttle between individual and collective efforts and trends. Several careers—those of Hugues Panassié, André Hodeir and Barney Wilen—are here followed closely and over their entire span, and this allows us to ask not just how the individual is enabled, shaped or constrained by larger social and cultural forces, but how, as people age, their motivations change, their ambitions and interests grow and subside, their projects are embraced by others and rejected by them. But while some figures are tracked over time, others—Thelonious Monk, Miles Davis, Django Reinhardt, Martial Solal—make appearances as problems as much as people: more than for what it might tell us about the players themselves, their work is examined for the questions it raised for the French jazz world.

The central methodological challenge for this study has been to find ways of making critical and nuanced descriptions of the various relationships that French players and listeners cultivated with (American) jazz during the postwar period. The book's conclusion apart, these descriptions appear in narrative form rather than as theorizations or models of cultural encounter and change. As mentioned, in his history, Ludovic Tournès paints a portrait of what he calls the gradual French "acculturation" of jazz, and at length we will return to that conceptualization. But it will help to proceed from the outset with a wariness towards any notion of historical process that is unidirectional and goal-directed, rather than the repetitious, messy and inconclusive.

Music-making cannot be separated from the political, intellectual and commercial environments in which it exists and which it helps form. Though it touches upon the Popular Front movement and competing, briefly triumphant fascisms of the 1930s and '40s, the book's first half unfolds during Europe's Marshall Plan reconstruction, the early Cold War, and a moment of widespread fascination in front of American superpower; its second half takes in the dramatic events of May 1968, moves through their decade-long repercussions, and ends during the 1980s socialist government of François Mitterrand. Other, quieter forms of cultural politics appear throughout this period of great change and growth—which, its frequent turmoil and OPEC-inspired demise notwithstanding, was famously dubbed by the economist Jean Fourastié "Les Trente Glorieuses," the thirty glorious years.[28] Yet the study aims to avoid the awkward two-step sometimes made when the aim is to introduce "context" to music, or to decorate cultural-political arguments with sound. Where Politics with a capital P is discussed, it is because of its direct relationship with the jazz under discussion, and never—hopefully—as once-upon-a-time scene setting.

The same is true of the theoretical work so readily identified with the French postwar. This was a time of great intellectual excitement, as indigenous forms of existentialism and phenomenology morphed into various kinds of Marxian commitment, or a structuralism at first identified with anthropology and historical studies was answered by the post-structural work that came to characterize the postmodern moment. Numerous attempts to "read" jazz through the works of Merleau-Ponty, Lévi-Strauss, Foucault and Derrida have been made elsewhere (and Sartre's few observations on the form have been wrung dry in the search for hip significance).[29] But, again, this book's loyalty is first and foremost to the music made, and where "ideas" are evoked it is in the service of jazz. These appearances take one of two forms. In the first, seen in every chapter, intellectual writing that directly informed the jazz practices in question is discussed alongside the music and writing it helped shape.

In other places, however, the book brings important concepts together with the jazz that was their contemporary—even if no such identification was made at the time—not in an attempt to validate theory or music, but to recognize concerns shared by musical and intellectual practitioners across cultural divides. To be clear, this is intellectual history, and some of the ideas in play here will be familiar. Nevertheless, these investigations, seen in chapters 2, 4 and the coda, do open up original lines of jazz-historical enquiry; they comprise a series of arguments about the relationship between audiences and the developing mass media, one of the most profound transformations of life in early and mid-20th century France.

Less rarified, and so more often forming this study's terrain, are the changing cultural-industrial settings in which jazz was created and addressed. Most important to this history is the jazz press. Early French writing on jazz is discussed in some detail in the next chapter, but the principal landmarks in the creation of a jazz journalism and criticism were the 1935 foundation of the Hot-club de France's newsletter, *Jazz hot*, which would last into the 21st century as one of the music's journals of record, and the 1954 foundation of *Jazz magazine*, similarly durable and influential. These monthly Parisian publications—which claimed print runs of 15,000 each in the mid-1950s—were joined at the time by a Marseille-based magazine variously titled *Jazz bulletin, Jazz* and finally *Jazz hip*. Whatever its name, this was the third largest French specialist magazine, averaging 3,000 sales at its early 1960s peak. All three magazines generally focused on "modern" jazz, but the traditionalist *Bulletin du Hot-club de France*, published by Hugues Panassié from 1950 onwards, circulated to around 4,000 at that decade's midpoint.[30] The last significant journal of the period was *Cahiers du jazz*, a quarterly published between 1959 and 1968, and which stood apart from the fan magazines even at their most serious: the *Cahiers* featured long, erudite essays and analyses that functioned as an academic jazz scholarship *avant la lettre* ("Jazz and notions of space and temporality" was a typical article title).[31] Jazz was covered in newspapers, too. Boris Vian contributed to the Communist *Combat* from 1946; *Le Monde* and *Figaro* provided occasional coverage; beaux-arts and literary papers like *Arts* and *Les Nouvelles littéraires* also hosted important writing on the music at various times. It's worth noting that it was not its quantity, but its ambition that made much of this work so interesting. For French commentators on jazz as for those working on cinema, literature and the visual arts, criticism was often conceived as a creative practice in its own right, not merely a parasitical or second-order endeavor. The interpretive and intellectual license this allowed French writers rendered such discourses unique, for better and for worse. This work, and these publications, form central primary sources for the present study.[32]

Specialist jazz record labels began to emerge in the 1930s. At first—as in the case of the preeminent Swing, founded in 1937 by Charles Delaunay with support from Hugues Panassié—their aim was often to reissue unobtainable American recordings above producing their own. In 1945 Delaunay launched another central label, Vogue, and four years later Eddie and Nicole Barclay founded Blue Star; changing its name to Barclay in 1957, the label would become one of the country's largest. Barclay distributed recordings made for American labels like Prestige, Atlantic and Verve throughout that decade, and several major French labels employed jazz critics as Artist and Repertoire men towards the same purpose.[33] The end of the 1960s saw the founding of several small but, in the documentation of American and French free jazz musicians, important labels: BYG, Shandar, PALM.

American armies stationed in postwar France brought with them forces radio, though these programs—which could mix Louis Armstrong and Fred Astaire—were largely unloved by purist fans. But Hugues Panassié and the American expat Sim Copans began radio shows soon after, these lasting into the late 1960s and 1970s respectively, and in the 1950s jazz broadcasting blossomed. Over the course of this study's period, the state-run stations France Culture, France Music and France Inter, and the commercial Europe N° 1—which hosted Frank Ténot and Daniel Filipacchi's highly popular *Pour ceux qui aiment le jazz* from 1955—broadcast a number of often long-running jazz programs that included recorded music, live and specially recorded concerts and discussions with critics and musicians. These were important means of disseminating both the music and, often, a particularly sophisticated critical attitude towards it. Also notable was the work of André Francis, who from 1946 to 1996 broadcast on several national stations, for some time at a rate of 200 programs per year. Francis's ubiquity helped his introductory book, *Jazz* (1958), become a favorite for generations of French listeners, and his importance in the documentation of jazz in France was cemented after the introduction of his weekly Radio France concert broadcasts, for which he recorded over 10,000 sets.[34] By contrast, television offerings remained scant throughout the period.

Big-name American jazz musicians had always appeared in theaters and concert venues, especially as part of touring packages, and large-scale (if often loss-making) festivals form landmarks in the music's mid-century French history: Nice in 1948, Paris in 1949, 1952, and 1954, Cannes in 1958.[35] But throughout the 1940s and '50s it was jazz clubs and dance halls that provided musicians with much of their work and space in which to develop, these present across the country but most numerous in Paris and large cities like Marseille, Lyon and Nice. In the early 1960s the jazz nightclub circuit went into decline, and across the West a new concert hall and festival culture began to emerge. Owing to the strength of local organization and governmental support—especially towards the end of the present period of study—in France such festivals proliferated, and often included much noncommercial, experimental music. The increasingly generous forms of governmental funding that began to support these endeavors in the 1970s are described in the book's penultimate chapter.

It should be noted that, at some points and in some ways, the strength of jazz criticism, media and performance in France could be owed to the exceptional efforts of—and powers wielded by—a few significant individuals over and above the institutions they represented: media figures like Panassié, Ténot, Filipacchi, Francis and Lucien Malson were stalwarts whose high visibility and devotion to jazz did not necessarily reflect a wider support for the music. Some, like Filipacchi and Eddie Barclay, parlayed their early jazz activities into large and diverse media portfolios, largely by spotting and exploiting new popular music trends as they arrived in the 1960s.

These were backroom boys, but they still enjoyed high media profiles. The same was hardly ever true of the many women who also worked in the French jazz business during this time. With even standard jazz singing all but ruled out—a much more viable Francophone alternative existed in *la chanson française*—prominent female jazz musicians of any kind were largely absent in France before the 1980s; as they were elsewhere, women players were kept back by the macho culture of jazz performance, the lack of mentors and precedents, and social expectations that pitted the domestic over the professional—the kinds of problems, then, that have conspired to limit women's success and prominence in workplaces of all kinds. Some female players did make careers as performers. Following Josephine Baker and Ada "Bricktop" Smith in the 1920s, the Americans Valaida Snow and Inez Cavanaugh also based themselves in Paris for periods in the 1930s and '40s. In the 1960s, the Lambert, Hendricks & Ross-styled vocalese group Les Double Six—which over time would evolve into the Swingle Singers—was formed by Mimi Perrin alongside fellow-vocalists Monique Aldebert and Christiane Legrand. The drummer Micheline Pelzer (later Graillier) cultivated an international career from the late 1960s onwards.

A jazz historian like Sherrie Tucker would argue that, in order to construct a new jazz history better representative of women's involvement with the music, study should be focused not on already-canonical areas of musical activity, but on those female musicians active in disregarded contexts like "novelty" all-female bands. There is surely much weight to the demand; the relationship of women towards that canonical jazz history is not so different from the relationship of non-Americans towards it. Yet this book does not cast a spotlight on those few female musicians who, though active, were for whatever reason not deemed outstanding (and the same goes for the males: skilled, busy professionals like Guy Lafitte or Roger Guérin were more present to French jazz listeners than they are here). Aiming to produce the first full outline of dominant musical practices in postwar France, the study concentrates instead on those identified and celebrated as leaders of the various French schools.

"Dominance," "leadership," this book is open to the charge that the exclusions enacted in history are inevitably reproduced by a method that does not seek to excavate in any detail the work of people not then framed in those terms. It's important, then, to record some of the names of those women who, even if they were not identified as the music's producers, channeled energy and ambition into roles important to its production. These are figures like Angèle Nourry, mother of the Hot-club co-founder Pierre, and a woman who had a central but largely uncredited administrative role in the society's early days, or Andrée "Daidy" Boyer, who performed similar, even more clandestine work for the club during the German occupation.[36] Marie-Thérèse Ricard, a Resistance member tortured by the Gestapo during the war, would later become the proprietor of the important Parisian club Le Chat Qui Pêche; Nadine Bodenheimer, a gallery owner in Marseille, organized touring logistics for artists like Bud Powell and Thelonious Monk. From the 1970s on, Dolores Cante, proprietor of the record shop Dolo Music on Paris's Left Bank, did much to disseminate music recorded for European labels like Incus and FMP, and, her shop becoming an important meeting place, she often acted as a fixer for musicians and promoters.[37] As always, numberless wives and companions aided and often materially supported their male partners' creative work. Madeleine Gautier cowrote the *Dictionnaire du jazz* with Hugues Panassié and was an important postwar Hot-club figure besides; as we will see, Caroline de Bendern, and later Marie Möör, both partnered and collaborated with the saxophonist Barney Wilen. In the 1970s a number of women—Marion Piras, Geneviève Peyrègne, Corinne Léonet—expanded what had been similar relationships of personal support into careers in jazz management. Important promoter-organizers like Martine Palmé and Marie-Claude Nouy, the latter eventually becoming director of ECM France / Universal, emerged in the following decade.

The jazz media showed glimmers of awareness of that male dominance during the 1970s, and women were better represented there and elsewhere from the 1980s.[38] The bassists Hélène Labarrière and Joëlle Léandre, and the pianist Sophia Domancich—the latter the first female winner of the prestigious Prix Django Reinhardt, by then awarded annually for nearly half a century—garnered international attention through the 1980s. The clarinetists Isabelle Duthoit and Catherine Delaunay, and the alto saxophonist Géraldine Laurent, emerged in the 1990s and early 21st century. But those players, arriving after the end of this book's historical range, still represented a minority of those identifying as professional jazz musicians—90 percent of whom were, in 2004, male—and they still faced many of the same struggles that their predecessors had.[39]

Histories of music-making are usually histories of musicians, and scene-makers, organizers and enablers are usually written out—yet the fullest history of women in 20th century jazz will linger offstage as much as on. Here, though, more far-reaching than any treatment of jazz women is the recognition and discussion of prevailing forms of masculine power as they are encountered in high-visibility French jazz practices and discourses. These include the heroic critical modernism of André Hodeir and the "French" Thelonious Monk, the subjecting gaze and musical speaking-for a female character in Louis Malle and Miles Davis's film work, and the masculine performance cultures of free jazz.

Chapter Summaries

The music and writing of postwar French jazz practitioners cannot be understood apart from earlier critical debates around jazz's meaning and import—and certainly not from the hugely influential work of Hugues Panassié, one of jazz's great European popularizers and the central figure of chapter 2. It was Panassié who most decisively shaped early French ideas of blackness as they manifested themselves in jazz, notions that many others at first adhered to, and later fought against. This chapter examines the critic's writing—which, informed by contemporary, right-wing Catholic thinking, had the future of godless France as its secret subject—then examines the New Orleans revival, before following the writer's postwar organization of the Hot-club de France.

Chapter 3 records the major moments and players in France's postwar bebop movement, and examines in depth the work of the jazz composer and writer André Hodeir. In both music and writing, Hodeir sought to overcome worries about the "inauthenticity" of that postwar French jazz by assimilating the culturally foreign (conceived as jazz improvisation) into the culturally familiar (art music composition). The chapter also looks at the relationship between notions of high art and low jazz as they existed and changed during the French 1950s and '60s. These issues come to the fore in a discussion of the French reception of the pianist Thelonious Monk. By the late 1950s, Monk had become a figure of veneration in French modern jazz circles, the pianist imagined, by those now many willing to ascribe jazz "art" status, as a bebop Beethoven. But in the first years of the following decade, Monk's French critics began to censure the pianist for having ceased to "evolve" as the classical masters had. This chapter puts that French critical trend in context, showing how issues occurring globally in Monk's 1960s reception were revoiced by French writers in the language, and to the ends, of a specific and local debate between jazz writers.

Chapter 4 opens with a discussion of the rash of modern jazz-backed movies made in the late 1950s by young French directors like Louis Malle, Edouard Molinaro and Roger Vadim. It goes on to construct a detailed history and reading of Davis's celebrated music for Malle's *Ascenseur pour l'échafaud* (1958), this study using the most influential French film criticism of the time—André Bazin's writing on realism—to illuminate contemporary understandings of recorded jazz improvisation in general, and this music of Davis's in particular. Critiques of Bazin's phenomenological work made in the latter 1960s and '70s by film theorists informed by the psychoanalyst Jacques Lacan, also discussed here, provide new ways of thinking about the much reinforced "ideology" of immediacy and realism in jazz improvisation. The chapter goes on to discuss jazz and African American music in the directorial work of Bazin's key disciple, and the *nouvelle vague*'s leading figure, Jean-Luc Godard.

Chapter 5 follows the career of Barney Wilen, one of French jazz's most celebrated instrumentalists. As a young and supremely talented tenor saxophone star in the 1950s, Wilen played and recorded with several leading American players, and he was idolized by press and fans alike as the future of the music in France. But in the early 1960s, bored with bebop, Wilen disappeared from view; he returned in 1965 to play an important role in Paris's nascent free jazz scene, mixing free playing with documentary sound on one album, Indian music on another, rock on the next. The arrival of free jazz in France, and Wilen's adaptation of these models, is examined in detail: at the end of the 1960s, and coinciding with the upheavals of May 1968, black American liberation politics became central to jazz discourses in France as they did the United States, and the incoming free music was strongly identified with that politics as well as with the anti-colonial movement celebrated by French leftists.

Chapter 6 examines ideas, ever-present but deemed especially urgent in the 1970s, around an indigenous French jazz. Through that decade, a number of free players began to explore regional French musics and organizational practices; the first part of this chapter examines the work of the multi-instrumentalist Michel Portal, which combined jazz, free improvisation, contemporary composition and various traditional styles. The identification of this kind of eclectic but distinctive mix led more than one commentator to salute the 1970s as the moment at which a properly "French" jazz arrived, and this chapter seeks to test those claims, scrutinizing musical nationalisms and internationalisms in turn. The chapter concludes by sketching out jazz's 1980s—a period during which the music was in some ways "legitimized" through French state investment—and by assessing the achievements of French jazz musicians over the course of the postwar period. A short encore, in which a number of the book's key players return for a final bow, considers the ways that images from French jazz history have since circulated in popular culture.

TWO

Hugues Panassié's Supernatural Swing

Criticism, Politics and the Iconic Jazz Recording

The early French jazz listeners faced something of a paradox: they loved the music's lived coincidence of creative thought and execution—no sooner had Louis Armstrong conceived a melody than it wound its way out of his trumpet—and yet, for the most part, it was only by listening to that melody wind its way up from an Okeh 78 and out of the phonograph's horn, maybe for the tenth time that morning, that Europeans could themselves experience such moments. Though Paris was becoming jazz's European capital and American musicians were not hard to find, and though imported discs were rare and expensive, nevertheless the jazz fans of interwar France were, as the historian Ludovic Tournès has written, "equally, and principally," record fans.[1] So, in an effort to wean his student off the unworthy dance bands of Paul Whiteman and Jack Hylton, Hugues Panassié's saxophone teacher had loaned the boy some *real* jazz, 78s by Bix Beiderbecke, Frankie Trumbauer and Fletcher Henderson. It wasn't long after this, and a few lessons in the music of Louis Armstrong taken in front of the gramophone with trumpeter Philippe Brun, that the young man gave up the commercial orchestras forever. And along with those bands went the saxophone: the mediocre musician had been eclipsed by an increasingly expert *discophile*. When in 1929 Panassié began approaching American jazzmen visiting Paris to request discographical information—"isn't that such-and-such playing clarinet," he would ask musicians of imported discs, these semi-anonymous novelties for which almost no artistic or historical labeling had yet been thought necessary—the visitors, in Panassié's own recollection, would be taken aback by the accuracy of the young Frenchman's ear. "I recognized them," Panassié claimed, "as a connoisseur of painting distinguishes at the first glance, and without risk of confusion, a Marie Laurencin from a Chagall. It was as easy as that."[2]

It wasn't only jazz lovers who were caught in the blare of the new recorded medium, and if some critics bickered about classical music's debasement into *une musique mécanique,* the presence of new magazines like *Arts phonétiques, L'Edition musicale vivante* and *Le Phono* nevertheless signified the extent to which French musical discourses in general had, by the mid-1930s, expanded to accommodate the needs of the discophile. Few writers were as central to this new field as Panassié, who, beginning his critical career at eighteen, soon became the leading European authority on jazz. Having contributed to French dance band magazines from 1930, in 1932 he helped form the influential fan society the Hot-club de France (HCF)—the club's founding declaration, published in *Jazz-tango* that November, included the pledge to "pressure recording companies to regularly release the major American discs"—and in 1934 he became HCF president, a position he held until his death forty years later.[3] Also in 1934 Panassié published *Le Jazz hot,* one of the first books on the music in any language; the long-running magazine *Jazz hot* was inaugurated in 1935, and *The Real Jazz,* a paean to the old New Orleans style that stands as the critic's definitive statement, appeared in 1942. Both books and magazine articles arranged theoretical reflections of one kind or another ("True and False Jazz") around thematic surveys dotted, by way of reference, with record catalogue numbers, and this method served the writer until the end of his life. By that time—in addition to his important concert promotion, record producing and broadcasting work—the critic had written a dozen volumes on the music and compiled almost 250 editions of the *Bulletin du Hot-club de France,* a journal he wrote almost on his own. Panassié, then, was a central actor in what is commonly (if not entirely accurately) acknowledged as a European achievement, the establishment and development of a specialist jazz criticism; although, as we'll see, many French writers of the 1920s had taken an impressionistic, "anthropological" interest in jazz, he was one of the first practitioners of what Matthew F. Jordan has identified as an "idealist" jazz criticism, a writer who, like his friend and colleague Charles Delaunay—the author of the first jazz discography (1936)—attempted to taxonomize his way through the growing body of recorded jazz.[4]

And yet, whether in his books or his regular *Jazz hot* "chroniques des disques," Panassié's record reviews were by no means as disinterested as Jordan's term might suggest. From the middle 1930s onwards, the critic would forever promote black musicians as the singular originators and upholders of jazz style, and of a "primitive" cultural-spiritual purity, while dismissing white musical incursions as either inept or symptoms of the music's commercial degradation; in this he was likely influenced by a new associate, Mezz Mezzrow—a white clarinetist whose attempt to self-transform into blackness was total, and whose anti-white musical dogma formed part of the rejection of his former self.[5] Panassié's 1936 *Jazz hot* review of a disc collection records "the natural superiority of the colored peoples . . . when you have just heard some records by the [white] New Orleans Rhythm Kings and the Wolverines and then play a record by King Oliver, you are immediately struck by the infinitely greater swing of the latter"; a 1938 review of Jimmie Lunceford's "For Dancers Only" occasions a brief reflection on the unity of black music and dance ("not the feeble, anti-jazz dancing of the whites, but the marvelous dancing of the American Negro"); in his assessment of Bix Beiderbecke in *The Real Jazz*, Panassié praises the cornetist for taking inspiration from "the best Negro trumpet players" but chides him for showing in his phrasing the influence of white trumpeters, and, in his composing, the influence of Debussy, all of which separated him from "the Negro spirit," "the only real jazz spirit."[6]

Panassié's interpretive terms were highly influential in jazz circles and beyond—indeed, given his control of the Hot-club and the sole specialist magazine *Jazz hot*, until the end of the Second World War they were essentially hegemonic. But the critic's personal and professional reputation subsequently came under extended attack. Faced in the late 1940s with a music changing in ways he despised—the new bebop, he argued, showed how black musicians had been contaminated by "white" musical theory and technique—Panassié redoubled his efforts in favor of a supposedly simple and pure black jazz style, played by supposedly simple and pure black musicians. Though he never would have used the term himself, these players read like Noble Savages, and in the wake of the war jazz listeners and writers who had previously played along with such exoticism began to think and write about the music otherwise.

Panassié was far from the only jazz writer to have dallied with these primitivist ideas. In an influential study of early jazz criticism, the jazz historian Ted Gioia has identified that body of work as an inheritor of the dubious primitivist legacy of Picasso and the *négrophile* early 20th century Parisian avant-garde. Gioia accuses Panassié and his early colleagues of transposing the Noble Savage into black American jazz as part of an effort to process the sheer, affective excitement the music had introduced to interwar Europe—and which so contrasted with the alleged waning health of that continent's own music.[7]

But Gioia's association of Panassié's racialist ideas and Parisian artistic primitivism does not tell the full story—indeed, if they were better known, the details of his background would only excite more condemnation of the Frenchman's work. Panassié was as much a devotee of the political far-right and of ultra-conservative Catholicism as he was of hot jazz, and his aesthetic was profoundly informed by contemporary rightist ideas. As a youth he was a member of the quasi-fascist group Camelots du Roi (itself affiliated with the anti-Semitic, nationalist organization Action Française). In 1937, he provided the jazz column for the militant rightist weekly L'Insurgé, a journal that campaigned for the installation of an authoritarian government and which, in its first editorial, proclaimed that "the new state must be founded upon the natural realities of soil, blood and history." During and after World War II Panassié would remain close to a number of Vichyistes, some of whom would sit with him on the board of the postwar Hot-club de France.[8] That the black exceptionalist cultivated associations with adherents to a regime that had collaborated so enthusiastically with Nazi Germany might seem surprising, but, jazz aside, it was notions of racial, cultural and spiritual "purity" that formed the common ground.

Still, as will become apparent, rather than specifically secular politics it was from rightist historical and theological readings that Panassié drew the primitivist ideas which defined his, and thus his many followers', conceptions of jazz. For those looking back on his work, the fact that Panassié forever remained an unmatched champion of certain African American musicians may not mitigate the extraordinary arrogance of a critic who would sit in moral judgment on a distant cultural activity, praising jazz when it could be put in the service of his own primitivist ideals and damning it when it couldn't. But where in the 21st century "primitivism" generally signifies some downwards glance, a judgment condescending to a supposed evolutionary inferior, for Panassié all these terms were reversed; where "primitivism" generally implies an encounter fraught with racial ideology, this implication the result of all those downward glances made during the ignominious modern development of European colonialism, racism and accompanying pseudo-sciences, for Panassié the term was not always racially loaded, the pure primitive not necessarily Other, or even human—looking through the skin of those he always called *les noirs*, Panassié's primitivism found its real origin in God. The critic attempted to portray jazz as a thing of sacralized tradition rather than, as was common among other writers on jazz at the time, of technicized modernity, and his work is a window onto mid-20th century French notions of national history and identity as much as the reception of an American popular music.

But the religious primitivist forever remained a discophile, and so this chapter also examines the ways that Panassié framed and employed the jazz record in his writings and public appearances. "Fortunate, indeed, that the phonograph was invented about the same time that the first jazz appeared," the critic wrote in 1936's *Le Jazz hot*, and in the new recording technology Panassié saw the means by which a "pure," sacralized black musical activity could transmit to the French a new and better way of being.[9] The merest mention of early technological reproduction usually summons the ghost of the critic Walter Benjamin, whose contemporary essay "The Work of Art in the Age of Mechanical Reproduction" is ritualistically, if carelessly, invoked in these kinds of contexts. But, as I argue, it's worth bringing these contemporaries into extended contact the better to understand the complexities of the period's aesthetic and political urges. The two men were most probably unknown to each other; their work did not share a "discourse" or form a "debate" as such. But in the 1930s they often shared a city and much else besides. When Benjamin left the Paris lodging house in which, during late 1935, he was drafting his essay on the reproduced artwork's revolutionary potential, it was to crisscross the streets, to wander and observe the crowds and the shop-window phantasmagoria of advanced capitalism; for his part Panassié, if not writing for his newly established magazine at his country seat, could often be found traipsing between the capital's nightclubs and lecture halls, helping promote concerts, delivering explanatory talks on jazz that he would illustrate with the music's mechanical reproductions. Both men were journalist-critics of modernity, their writing on popular culture informed by radical politics; both were thinkers for whom bourgeois aesthetics were, dead, deadening, for whom incoming and technologically borne creative forms would restore sensorial life to Europeans, would ignite action in the body rather than dilettante appreciation in the mind. Of course one was of the left, the other of the right; one saw in film a force that might "innervate" the masses with revolutionary energy, and the other heard at the phonograph how an embodied, orally transmitted expressive practice could reaffirm stability and tradition in a Europe wrecked by reform. As the critics made their cases, all the time

Paris was loud with political unrest. Between the riot of February 6, 1934, when a battle between rightist and leftist groups left fifteen dead, through the rise and quick decline of the Popular Front and on to the German taking of the capital in June 1940, on numerous occasions hundreds of thousands turned out on the streets of Paris to contest France's future. It was amid this volatile political atmosphere that the two writers posed the question that lies behind their works, and which forms another of this chapter's concerns: how could the relationship between individual and society be transformed both practically and politically in front of mechanically reproduced (jazz) forms?

Panassié's activity brings into focus a complex of issues—old primitivism, new technology, debates around France's past and its future—all of them in some way articulated through his writing and speaking about jazz. As these culture-wide concerns cast their shadow over Panassié, so the work of this important, troubling figure cast its own over French jazz writing and music-making in the following decades: there is no way to understand local ideas of progressivism surrounding 1950s bebop, or the radicalism of 1960s free jazz, without first getting around the portly figure who helped define the music for the French in the 1930s and '40s.

French Jazz Primitivisms

At the turn of the 20th century, a Parisian fascination with African art was both preempted by and confused with widely circulating images of African American cultural practices—principally ragtime and the cakewalk. Aspects of both new- and old-world blackness, "American" rhythm and "African" line and form, were assimilated into local media as varied as the piano music of Debussy, the paintings of Picasso or the textiles of Sonia Delaunay (mother of Charles); in adventurous Parisian circles of the early century it was as interesting and modern to be a *négrophile* as it was to dance in the new nightclubs of Montmartre and Montparnasse, in which, for the first time, social classes and races mixed in public, American cocktails in hand.

During the 1920s, French newspaper and music journal commentary on jazz both positive and negative tended to be shaped by two vocabularies, each representing a strand of this local African/American fantasy. On the one hand, jazz was supposed another harbinger of modernity, that vortex of speed and mechanization that had swept in from America to transform traditional French society, and which was the subject of much popular debate. Jazz, the novelist Pierre Mac Orlan raved in 1925, "communicates by admirable jolts linked to the rhythm of our blood and to our nervous systems which finally begin to separate themselves from those old desires which have become impotent . . . It is us today."[10] The increasing Taylorization of French manufacturing was a common subject of concern at the time; arriving simultaneously from the United States and both bearing the stop-time stamp of modernity, jazz and Taylor's machines were often aligned in the Parisian intellectual imagination.

But on the other hand, jazz was represented as that indulgence of the primitive, of the rhythmic voodoo that animated music made even by French initiates. From Ansermet's piece on Bechet through the 1920s and into the '30s, many of these commentators imagined a corps of black American jazz players bringing with them a happy delirium that would enliven a morbid postwar world. But there were others who looked at the approaching, primitive black bodies with a pained squint. The critic André Levinson located in jazz's "bad blood" a "*virus noir*" that would contaminate rather than revivify Europeans.[11] Writing on jazz in a 1935 issue of the respected journal *La Revue musicale*, André Suarès could only see

> [t]he monkey drunk on himself, without morals, without discipline, fallen into the undergrowth of instinct, revealing his naked flesh with every bound, together with a piece of flesh even more obscene, his heart. These slaves must be brought to submission . . . Jazz is, cynically speaking, an orchestra-full of brutes with non-opposable thumbs.[12]

Whether positively or negatively conceived, tropes of primitivism and the ancient were ubiquitous. But the early explorations into jazz that advanced beyond the standard headlines—"this frenzy is contagious"—often constructed for the style a deeper-rooted ethnological profile, and were conducted by the surrealist *hommes de lettres* of Georges Bataille's *Documents* magazine as well as music critics and ethnographers.[13] In his 1926 book *Le Jazz*, musicologist-ethnologist André Schæffner posited a historical and pancontinental *musique nègre*, of which jazz was merely the latest expression.[14]

In jazz discourse, then, the nonintellectual machine and the supposedly preintellectual black musician were superimposed to create the image of a para-artistic music, motorized by timeless urges; a collage of available images, both primitivist and modernist, helped writers make do with the paucity of actual experience they had of the black American music.[15] And as much as it was their subject, for many of these early writers, jazz—meaning America, dark skin, machine—was an object of reflection, in which could be seen the future of Europe and, specifically, of France.

Negrophilia, and primitivist, racialist critical tropes, surrounded jazz's early reception in countries like Britain, too.[16] But in France more than anywhere else, these jazz-inspired redefinitions of local selves and foreign Others were playing their part in a contest around national status and identity—one which Hugues Panassié would now join. Panassié had grown up in a country riven by disputes over the far-reaching secularization of state and education enacted during the early decades of the Third Republic, some of these new laws designed in response to the Dreyfus affair and the wave of anti-Semitic nationalism to which it had given rise. Very much opposed to such reform, even before his teenage encounter with jazz Panassié had autodidactically arranged rightist notions of God, nation, monarchy and tradition—and those ideas' opposites, all embodied by the secular, democratic modern state—as the fundamentals of his intellectual self. Although coming into focus alongside contemporary *négrophilie*, the young Panassié's conception of jazz was largely owed to his religious readings, and, in his own work and that of the many writers he influenced and published, discourses around American music and French politics would continue to intermingle.

In his late memoir, the critic recalled that this thinking was first inspired by a reading of Léon Bloy. Aged fourteen, recuperating from the polio that left him forever dependent on a walking stick, Panassié—then only lazily observant—began to read the works of this author whose polemical, prophetic tone made him the extremist counterpart to the turn-of-the-century French Catholic writers latterly led by Charles Péguy.[17] Bloy, Panassié recalled, "spent his time knocking heads," smearing his attacks on the clergy, the state and the bourgeoisie with images of shit and vomit, symbolic results of decadence and the secret unmentionables he wanted dumped at the doorstep of modernity. The railing against a modern world and its corrupt institutions (including a weakened and reforming Catholic church), the continually professed faith in the ancient order of God and monarchy, the tone of condemnation—all of Bloy's concerns and tactics would be mirrored in Panassié's writing, whether overtly or through the cipher of black American jazz; Bloy's self-righteous crusade against self-appointed authority, one made in the name of God and those forsaken by power, forms a pre-echo of Panassié's own campaigns, made against what he saw as empty or corrupt commercial or critical powers and in the name of *les noirs*.

Panassié credited Bloy with bringing about his return to active religious observance, as well as inspiring his "furious study" of the Church fathers and "the entire history of Catholicism."[18] The most affecting intellectual figures the young man discovered were the occultist René Guénon—of whom, more later—and the Thomist philosopher Jacques Maritain.

In his widely read book, *Art et scolastique* (1920), Maritain had described how artistic "habit"—a devotional activity, never an end in itself—was to be embodied through practice and practical instruction, the kind of participatory, oral-manual tradition which, in evading the intellectualization of the theorist and the individuation of the "genius," evaded the technical and canonical degradation that characterized modern art. For Panassié, it was jazz musicians' distance from such modernisms—in his imagination *les noirs'* musical skills and excited bodies were always roused by sacred impulse—that meant jazz danced through black American lived experience in a way classical music did not for Europeans.

Maritain's influence can be seen in the book Panassié authored eight years after his adolescent religious awakening, *Le Jazz hot* (1934). Here, the writer begins what would become a long-running argument against classical music, reified to death, and in favor of his beloved, vital, creative jazz. Where classical musicians were unthinking automatons, Panassié claimed, improvising jazz players were true "creators"; where classical instrumental techniques were stunted in unmusical ugliness by institutionalized teaching, jazz musicians' personalized, vocalized techniques were "warm and emotional"; in contrast to the modern, bureaucratic conservatoire system, jazz pedagogy was one of noninstitutionalized, practical master-apprentice relationships, just like "the guild apprenticeship which existed long ago in France."[19]

The contrast between living jazz and dead classical music made periodic reappearances through the 1930s in *Jazz hot*, the magazine that the authoritative Panassié edited into critical uniformity; "[w]hile the great operas are performed in front of empty minds," Panassié's friend Louis Bayard wrote in a 1938 issue, "hot music, through swing, returns to that rhythm which is at the base of all music, of every dance."[20] But the argument's fullest expression was given by Panassié himself in *The Real Jazz*, published in 1942 (the book appeared in the United States in English translation three years before the publication of *La Véritable musique du jazz*). Here, the idea of jazz's Maritainian oral-traditional embodiment was extended to include the music's audience, and its participation in both musical and social creation.[21] "Many feel it is ridiculous for Negroes to clap their hands, dance in their seats, sing and cry when listening to an orchestra," Panassié wrote.

But to me the most ridiculous spectacle is the sight of a concert hall filled with hundreds of spectators who sit statue-like in their seats listening with a lugubrious expression to solemn music which is served up to them in massive doses . . . it is only normal for our bodies to translate the sonorous language which our ear receives, to dance in our seats if nothing more than that. Yes, jazz is dance music and this is precisely its greatest attribute.[22]

The concert-hall presentations that visiting stars often gave in France were thus not ideal: the banalities of commercialism and professionalization, and the lack of a dancing public, rendered stage presentations creatively and energetically impoverished. Even outside the context of dance, a bodily musical participation of the kind forgotten in Europe—not just individual kinesis, but a full, socio-musical incorporation—was vital.

Panassié had already begun developing a method for jazz's sounding public presentation that aimed to retrain the French body.[23] From the mid-1930s onwards the critic had toured his *conférences-auditions*, during which he would play and explicate jazz records for an audience, each meeting devoted to a particular instrument, player or style. In following the taxonomies that Panassié's print criticism set out, these demonstrations gave fans both structured insight and wider access to American hot jazz discs that remained expensive commodities, and in this, the *conférences-auditions* were not much removed from the many "rhythm clubs" that were springing up in America and Europe. But Panassié also developed for these talks a strange gestural performance that aimed to materialize the abstract practice of jazz improvisation for those present, a performance that he can be seen making in later filmed interviews: always knowing by heart the solos and arrangements he played, the critic would mime a juggler throwing balls into the air in time to a leaping saxophone phrase, or sneeringly wag his finger along to a chiding, nasal trumpet line.[24] Ludovic Tournès suggests that this method served to give fans with no musical background a point of entry into the music, Panassié identifying the instrument in play as he mimed a sliding trombone, following as he did so Maritain's dictum that artistic practice be demonstrated rather than explained.[25]

But this is not fully convincing: while Panassié was surely thinking of Maritainian habit as he waved his arms around, the non-instrumentalist was in no position to pass on a craft to audiences many of whom themselves did not play. Rather than the superficial performance conventions of the music itself—this is a trumpet, these are drums—the primary educative purpose of Panassié's gestural show was surely to teach the French, as a collective of listeners, to experience this traditionary jazz groove somatically rather than intellectually. In this Panassié was following what he himself had learned to be an authentic practice of active listening and bodily translation among *les noirs*. In the earliest of a number of similar accounts, Panassié describes a 1933 listening session by the phonograph with Freddy Johnson, a black pianist resident in Paris and hired by the writer and his associates for one of the early HCF concerts.

> To listen to a disc with Freddy was the most riveting thing in the world. His ear always alive to everything, he translated his pleasure in mimicry, gestures so expressive that it was almost impossible not to shake along with him and the music being listened to.[26]

Panassié attempted to communicate the somatic essence of swing in religious-ritualistic prose, too: in 1943's *La Musique de jazz et le swing*, the critic constructs a dialogue between a "profane" and a "swingfane," the master explaining to the bodily incompetent novice how to feel the accent on the weak beat.[27] But it was in the public *conférences-auditions*, given across the country over the course of decades, that Panassié most effectively conveyed what he had learned to be the "authentic" *noir* practice of bodily groove and disc-audition. The public playing of records was in the service of an aesthetic and spiritual project in which the individual listener's body would, through verbal and gestural ritual, be incorporated into the body of an incoming, black American tradition at the same time that it accessed an old, socially embodied European music practice: "[f]ar from representing 'the nerve-wracking life of our century,' 'the noise of the machine' and other foolish theories which have been brought forth from time to time," the Maritainian jazz critic wrote in 1942, inverting the commentary of earlier jazz-age sensationalists, "jazz represents the reappearance of such a primitive musical conception as had arisen many centuries ago among the people of Europe and elsewhere."[28] To be sure, Panassié's adored music did not need technological reproduction in situ. But in France, largely barren of live "real" jazz, it was via the turntable that the critic would attempt to teach the French body to recover the Thomist groove. The presidents of local HCF chapters began to illustrate their own *conférences-auditions* with gestural performance rituals: in the 1950s the Bayonne chapter would stage an initiation rite for hopeful new members, the applicant being required to sing successfully a clarinet passage from Fletcher Henderson's recording of "Down South Camp Meeting" while the existing adepts stood and sat, singing and miming the brass backings.[29]

Panassié contended that jazz had been something strangely intriguing not because it belonged to an unknown future, but to a forgotten past; at least at first, he believed that a sleeping Western primitivism, musical and perhaps otherwise, could be awoken by a hot jazz '/8. The critic's thinking here was indebted to another of his key religious influences, René Guénon, that scholar of "traditionalism" and the occult. Guénon, one of many writers of the 1920s influenced by Oswald Spengler's *The Decline of the West* (1918), continually portrayed a moribund modern Western civilization whose only hope of cultural and spiritual renewal lay in its potential assimilation of eastern metaphysics.[30] Guénon's work was a touchstone for Panassié: in one of many articles exploring black America's cultural corruption by what he called "le cancer blanc," the writer would recommend *Orient et occident* (1924) to his readers, and would in his late memoir quote liberally from *La Crise du monde moderne* (1927).[31]

In that once-popular book, Guénon railed against the notion of progress, upon which Panassié too would also come to be furiously focused. That the world progresses for the better is an inversion of reality, Guénon wrote, as truth lies at the beginning, with God and pure spirituality, and the longer truth inhabits the human world the more it is corrupted; the passage from the proto-capitalist disruption of the feudal system, through Renaissance humanism and the Reformation, showed the West beginning "to turn away from the heavens under pretext of conquering the earth."

> [O]wing to its desire to reduce everything to the measure of man as an end in himself, modern civilization has gone downwards step by step until it has ended by sinking to the level of the lowest elements in man and aiming at little more than satisfaction of the needs inherent in the material side of his nature.[32]

The historian Mark Sedgwick writes that this Platonic ladder, on which a godly ideal, once issued, descends a worldly order of increasingly inferior instantiations, was the cornerstone of 19th century "perennial philosophy," the conflation (and what was perceived as the mutual confirmation) of pagan philosophy and Christian belief.[33] Indeed, though fashionable at the time, decline narratives such as Guénon's and Spengler's had been a fixture of philosophy and theology since antiquity. The stoics held that man had an original kinship with the laws of nature, and that these were sullied by those of human society. And man himself had been corrupted when the sensual (*aisthesis*) was preferred to the intellectual or moral (*nous*); later transposed into Christian tradition—Eve taking the place of *aisthesis*, and Adam, *nous*—this narrative, in which every generation away from creation and every movement away from nature would further corrupt, constituted a continuous tradition of anti-decadent primitivism spanning several millennia.[34] When, in his 1942 *Real Jazz* polemic against Western art music, Panassié had written that such music had become too complex, too elaborate in musical conception and performance—"[a]n excess of culture atrophies inspiration," he wrote, "and men crammed with culture tend too much to play tricks, to replace inspiration by lush technique under which one finds music stripped of real vitality"—the critic was consciously participating in and extending the reach of this tradition.[35]

By the time of his 1946 memoir, though, Panassié admitted that while he had in the 1930s imagined it possible to convert the French public to the cause of jazz's primitivist, musico-traditional practice, it had become clear that this project was "chimerical"; familiarity with jazz had not caused a culture-wide revelation, but had led instead to the music's debasement.[36] As early as 1942 Panassié had seen that not only classical music, but also the jazz he deemed "real" was in likely permanent decline. "To be astonished would be naive," he wrote, following the anciently ordained narrative, "for all primitive music is destined to lose its character little by little as it comes into contact with the civilized world." Jazz's fall from innocence mirrored classical music's own because it was owed to the same pernicious modernism: in the early 1940s, jazz was being ravaged by the modern forces of commercialism, giving rise to swing, and by the technical excesses inherent in any autonomously conceived art.[37] Rather than Guénon's prescription for cultural rejuvenation, it was that writer's damning of Western decay that Panassié would now prefer to celebrate; even though it was written before the arrival of what Panassié would dismiss as the artified "pseudo-jazz" bebop, *The Real Jazz* functions as a eulogy for the music it pretended to herald.

> [W]hen jazz orchestras began to appear in theatres as "an attraction," when the magazines and reviews began to speak of jazz as an art, and when white musicians, conscious of artistic theories, began long discussions on the nature of jazz seeking to establish its relationship to other musics, the Negro musician became increasingly aware of his own importance, or at least of the importance of his music. That mu-

sic which had been up to then an amusement took on the aspect of a fine art. And the inevitable occurred. These musicians who had infallibly played in a perfect manner, and had never digressed for an instant from the pure tradition of their art as long as they blindly followed their instincts, now rejected their tradition and began to reason and to "improve" their music. Of course they fell into innumerable errors.[38]

The uncultured but sublime black musician, only corrupted when brought into contact with white society, artistic "theories" and ideas of "progress": it is unsurprising that Panassié's critics have long accused him of grounding his idea of jazz history in the Noble Savage myth. But so too is Panassié's adoption of the figure unsurprising, as something similar can be found in use by numerous commentators, from the theologians of the medieval period, through the new world explorers, to 18th century *philosophes* like Jean-Jacques Rousseau, who wished to critique their own West European society's failings by way of comparison with unexpectedly virtuous Others.[39] He did not use the term himself, but Panassié was only the latest European—indeed, only the latest Frenchman looking towards the Americas—to use the idea of the Noble Savage to help define a political project at home.

And the role to be played by Panassié's imaginary, uncorrupted black jazz musician was one constructed in opposition to, and, as the historian of early French jazz Denis-Constant Martin has observed, "outside modernity." For Panassié, Martin writes, *le noir* "incarnated a model of natural purity and spontaneity," the condition of childhood. Martin lists the infantilizing adjectives that Panassié was apt to attach, by way of praise, to black musicians he had encountered: where whites were tense, worried, boring, blacks were cordial, stimulated, natural, candid, gay, nonchalant, lighthearted, happy-go-lucky, pure, gifted with vitality, at ease, full of *joie de vivre*, were childlike, pleasant.[40] In Panassié's late memoir, readers were assured that Louis Armstrong could act excitedly "like a child," and then, a few pages later, that Django Reinhardt—not black, but a "natural" musician nevertheless—"loved games like a kid." "He was a primitive, in the good sense of the word. He was a gypsy, he had their characteristics."[41]

The infantilizing of Others, whether to praise or to ridicule, is a familiar kind of racism. But it is not to excuse this racism to note that, once more, Panassié's childlike primitive was born of old philosophy as much as contemporary condescension. For medieval Christian "primitivists" (as for Panassié), moral and cultural purity always came from a closer proximity to God and godliness—that is, to man in his original condition before the fall. The nature of this original condition had been a perennial subject of Christian theological dispute, religious theorists needing to explain the pre-fall presence of temptation in Adam, who had been created in God's image and had therefore, supposedly, been wholly good. In this debate—one which clearly anticipated the Enlightenment's Noble Savage discourse—the Christian primitivists commonly argued that Adam's lust for knowledge was no sin, his godliness not contradicted, since before the fall he had been child-like, innocent, therefore beyond reproach. George Boas has written that the pre-medieval assertion that childlike innocence was man's ideal paved the way for Christian anti-intellectualism, "the *docta ignorantia*" according to which the true Christian,

> in becoming like a child, returns to the state of Adam before the Fall. This state is "communion" with Heaven, which may be interpreted as "direct knowledge" of Heaven, the kind of knowledge which a child in the Platonic myth of reminiscence might be supposed to have.[42]

A 1936 *Jazz hot* piece by Panassié's associate Georges Herment, "Hot—sixième sense," made extended use of this Platonic idea (and, elsewhere, of the ancient Greek image of the body as cosmos). "Hot jazz gives us yet another proof of the existence of the Unknown," Herment wrote.

> How can we acquire and strengthen this feeling for Hot music? It is certain that everyone has it within him, more or less atrophied by the ideas of Art, Beauty and Culture which people force themselves to inculcate us with from our birth onwards. Once purified of all these atavisms, of all these bad habits, this lost sense, however little of it remains, however meager it may be, will reappear. Hot music is childhood.[43]

Before anything, it was direct and nonintellectual knowledge of and communion with heaven that the profoundly committed Catholic Panassié desired, and which he claimed to find in the music; the critic's work of the mid-1940s sought to explore and demonstrate this above all. Certainly Panassié's work was already saturated with religious language and thinking prior to the five-month trip he made to New York in 1938–39. But it was in that city that Panassié would experience a revelation that would deeply mark his subsequent work, one that would for him definitively join jazz and the godly.

The Supernatural Swing

At half-past midnight on January 10, 1939, Panassié and his party sat in Harlem's Savoy Ballroom, watching as Chick Webb and his band took the stage. In an account given in 1947's *Cinq Mois à New-York*, the critic described his watching the drummer-bandleader as the music began.

> During the first chorus—the exposition of the theme—he stayed inside himself. But from the moment the orchestra attacked the second chorus, he set about playing with an incredible power, establishing a tempo that exploded from the cymbal. My breathing stopped. Hardly had he started to play in this way than enthusiastic "oohs" escaped the mouths of Milton [Mezz Mezzrow] and *les noirs* sitting around me. It wasn't a banal cry of satisfaction. It was a cry literally *snatched* from them by the intensity of Chick Webb's swing. The reaction of these people instantaneously augmented the force of my own. By the way they shouted, by the moments at which they shouted, I glimpsed that Webb's playing gripped me exactly as it did them, and the simultaneity of these reactions made them grow in intensity without cease. Here we were no longer concerned with the "refined artistic emotion" such as conceived by more or less degenerate intellectuals, no more than by the "sensual music" babbled on about by other cretins even more degenerate, it was a question of an inexplicable joy, an *empty* joy that left room for no image, no reflection of the spirit; it was a question of a *jouissance* as simple as that of a plant before the sun. I felt that I was about to reach for the first time the heart of this music and, neglecting at last every secondary element (color, style, sonority, etc.), to meet the *essential*, the essential that could never be expressed, explained: one lives it or one doesn't, and that's it. I suddenly understood, with extraordinary acuity, the irremediable imperfection of *intellectual* knowledge . . . intellectual arguments are powerless to give faith to those who haven't received the grace. The love of God, the only way by which to know Him, is the supernatural equivalent of that which I had just experienced in front of Chick Webb.[44]

"An empty joy that left room for no image," a swung ascent up the Platonic ladder to pure knowledge and pure godliness, nonintellectual knowledge recovered—and all this by the grace of Chick Webb, a black, "hunchbacked" drummer, a double outsider whose supposed wretchedness would in biblical tradition almost guarantee his proximity to the sacred.[45]

Already in *Le Jazz hot*, Panassié had warned against the "common error" of judging jazz according to the principles of classical music.[46] But now in New York—even if he'd been led there by a primitivist fantasy—the critic, checking his responses to Chick Webb's swing against the "authentic," intragroup responses of (black) audience members, had begun to enter into something like the contemporary anthropological "native's point of view," and had begun to clarify for himself and his French readers an understanding of swing that had until that point been clouded by formalist approximation or adjectival mess. "I realized how poor my work had been up to that time," Panassié admitted while reflecting on his New York experiences in 1947.

> When writing in my book or my articles that, for example, such a musician didn't have the defects of another who overloaded his solos with notes, I had tried to form people's taste, but that which we can call "external taste" . . . [However], what is important, before everything else, is that the musician is *in the groove*, and a musician that makes a few rapid strokes in his solos and is *in the groove* is worth more than one who constructs his phrases in a manner more perfect—apparently—but is not *in the groove*. This is what most jazz fans, except those who are black, only come to understand with difficulty and which I myself took long to learn. And yet all of jazz is in *this*.[47]

Born "in the field" was a new understanding of the limits of the "idealist" taxonomic critical project, as part of which Panassié—despite his readiness to identify and to validate what he perceived as inherently black playing styles—had necessarily assessed the music according to the rather European, and rather earth-bound, criteria of refinement, balance and control. The political impulse behind it was still foreign, racialist, the religious language in which it was swaddled was still primitivist. Yet Panassié's attempt to strip his responses to jazz of the last vestiges of an aesthetics he now saw as European, Romantic-modernist, corrupt yet still normative, formed an important moment, one not recognized as such in jazz historiography.

The Savoy revelation allowed Panassié to conceptualize a social swing, or groove, that had been unknown to him in Paris, listening to records or fish-out-of-water visitors. This feeling, Panassié now wrote, was a current of energy, a perfect equilibrium that was achieved through a communal microadjustment of tempo—this community including musicians, dancers and listeners—and as such was a "mysterious quality" contingent upon the coincidence of numerous factors: skill, luck, environment.[48]

Groove was of primary importance in music as in life, because "this ideal tempo is no different from the interior and exterior rhythm upon which depends the harmony of the world itself"; a healthy heart beats in time, Panassié suggested, an untrammeled mind understands everything it studies with ease. So when jazz musicians attained this transcendental swing, they were achieving "participation in the rhythm and the order of the universe."[49] Once more Panassié could consolidate his religious and music-theoretical ideas, cementing the cosmic order, linking Harlem to the heavens, swing time to eternity.

And once more, this religious project would be advanced by way of the jazz recording. Having returned to France, Panassié passed the occupation revisiting his many prewar experiences, and—as in *Cinq Mois à New-York*, excerpted earlier—the books he published at the war's end consolidated and reinterpreted his 1930s experiences at home and abroad in a manner equally demonstrative of the writer's religious and discophile obsessions. *Douze Années de jazz* (1946) contains numerous long-winded reports of Panassié's studio work as supervisor for HMV and Swing, the label he had in 1937 helped establish with Charles Delaunay, while *Histoire des disques Swing* (1944) consists almost entirely of descriptions of sessions Panassié conducted for that label in New York during his 1938–39 visit. In the course of this 117-page itemization, the writer describes his tracking down half-forgotten heroes of the "real" jazz style—Tommy Ladnier, James P. Johnson and Sidney Bechet were the recordings' lynchpins—going on to detail the positioning of musicians in the studio, providing diagrams of each microphone setup, giving take-by-take descriptions of studio rehearsals and performances, narrating his visit to the production plant to collect test pressings.[50]

Commenting on this writing, Ludovic Tournès has argued that Panassié was not only participating in the music's creation, but also "realizing the dream of every discophile, to enter into communion with the artist at the moment the latter was in action. For music lovers, the aura of the recording studio owed much to the fact that it was one of the privileged sites of such an encounter."[51] The gesture is towards Walter Benjamin's ubiquitous essay, "The Work of Art in the Age of Mechanical Reproduction," published in 1936. There, Benjamin famously argued that the technological reproduction of artworks—he focused on images, but also mentioned music—stripped art works of their authentic, singular "aura": just as authentic, singular, auratic icons had served as the focus of religious devotion, so quasi-religious art icons in the museum had attracted aesthetic devotion. But, Benjamin wrote, mechanically re-

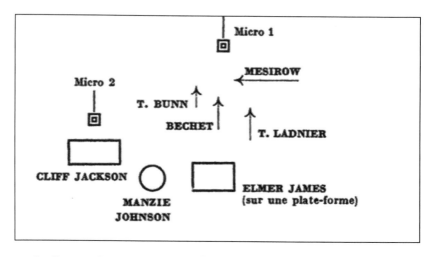

Studio setup for Panassié's *Swing* session of November 21, 1938. (From Panassié, *Histoire des disques Swing*, 20.)

produced forms like film, the "artform" of the moment, had no original and so did not attract the fetishism of the authentic object, were produced by a series of technical operations rather than by a mystical genius, and were characterized by montage techniques designed in the style of modern life—thus exciting their audiences through electrified "shock effects" rather than inviting awestruck and thoughtful contemplation. So in claiming the discophiles heard an "aura" coming into being in the studio—this Benjamin's site of anti-auratic art production *par excellence*—Tournès challenges this theory; the historian writes that the sonic quality of electric recording, and the reportage of Panassié and his ilk, produced a "reconciling of the listener and the work," rather than "the estrangement feared by Walter Benjamin."[52]

But this is a misreading of the German writer's argument: Benjamin did not "fear" the estrangement of audience and the traditional, auratic artwork, but, seeing such quasi-religious aesthetics as a central fixture of corrupt bourgeois ideology, welcomed it; what Tournès identifies as the reconciliation of audience and recorded work, Benjamin recognized as the power of technologically produced art to circumvent interpretive mediation—by clergy or art historians—and as the anti-auratic force that would ultimately lead the massed audience, given the right kind of inspiration, to "detonate" in socialist revolutionary action. If, after all this, Tournès's discophiles perceived an "aura" in Panassié's jazz recordings—

"Panassié's" in so far as he was producer and chief promoter of jazz in France—then it was not just because of the illusion of "closeness" guaranteed by electric fidelity and prolix reportage: it was because so much of the critic's practice contrived to take that seemingly immediate new music further away, constructing transcendence around those musicians caught in the recorded sound image.

Benjamin's hopeful thesis on mechanical reproduction was aimed against social authority in the name of the left, so it might not be surprising to find an interpretive authority on the right acting in the name of a competing idea, constructing the disc as something capable of giving rise not just to bodily retraining (as we have seen), but also to the sublime-auratic unity of beholder and universe—exactly what Benjamin identified as an oppressive social ordering disguised by mystique. In his 1944 book-length report of the New York recording sessions he had supervised, Panassié placed much emphasis on the recording of "Weary Blues," the first moment at which the assembled musicians found what the critic called "the tempo" necessary to access this cosmic impulse.

> Jazz musicians only attach such importance to the "groove" because, when they find it, they feel this sentiment of plenitude, of beatitude one might dare to say, that man can feel once he succeeds in living in perfect harmony with the rhythm of the universe, in living intensely, *fully*. In this interpretation of Weary Blues, the musicians rose to achieve this perfection.[53]

The final take of this song, its music thus cosmified, was available for contemplation by jazz fans wanting, via the recording, to enter into this now-structured relationship of belief and art. To be sure, the mechanical reproduction of such a moment was not preferable to its real-world experience: though in *The Real Jazz* Panassié assures his readers that "one can rely on [recordings] in the majority of cases without fear," there and elsewhere he suggested that it was indispensable to hear musicians "in the flesh."[54] But, as the critic well knew, this was not possible for most French jazz listeners most of the time, and in providing a second-order image of auratic art—a reproduction of the lived moment—Panassié's cosmic-auratic jazz recording became something like a portal to this distant, otherworldly musical practice: it became an icon. The theological arguments were only implicit in *Le Jazz hot*, but, in his writing of the 1940s, Panassié was moving towards what we will see to be an openly sacralized critical and organizational practice, one dependent upon the mobilization of this iconic jazz recording.[55]

For well over a decade, the religiosity and primitivism of Panassié's own dogma exerted an extraordinary hold over even his most senior and able colleagues. As is confirmed by his 1939 book-length mélange of jazz boosterism and philosophical platitude, *De la vie et du jazz*, Charles Delaunay was an energetic promoter, organizer and discographer rather than a notable writer or thinker ("LIVE to LIVE and not to DIE").[56] Nevertheless, until the end of the war, when Delaunay did articulate his views on jazz it was often in the Panassié style.[57] André Hodeir, who would soon become France's leading jazz writer—and whose work is examined in the next chapter—began his critical career in earnest with *Le Jazz, cet inconnu* in 1945, and that book was similarly defined by self-acknowledged primitivism: for the young Hodeir, jazz was "the image of the black man: simple, naive, dynamic, sensual, sometimes comic, always brimming with a fervent sensibility that reveals all of a sudden an unsuspected profundity."[58] Many of those close to Panassié would retain this frame of reference for good. But the elder writer's attempt to formalize a French jazz inculcation, through print and sound, could not prevent a critical attitude from arising among some of the Hot-club's members; eventually, the musical and discographic sensibilities that Panassié had helped develop so that members could identify "real" (black, pure) and "false" (white, commercial) jazz would exceed that project's own ideological limits.

Schism and Revival

For much of the 1930s Panassié had been holed up in the Aveyron, communicating by letter suggestions and rulings to the Hot-club leadership in Paris. He remained in the *zone libre* throughout World War II, there passing a relatively quiet war, although he was accused of collaboration during and after the Vichy period.[59] Certainly in promoting a music full of folk genius and blood-and-soil traditionality, Panassié was in step with what would become the prevailing cultural policy of the Vichy regime— and during the occupation he would give a *conférence-audition* at Vichy to a room full of German officers—but in choosing a music that was product of both culture industry (however much Panassié affected to detest jazz's commercialization) and, moreover, black America, his interests diverged significantly from the Pétainist line.[60] Nevertheless, following liberation, suspicions over Panassié's wartime sympathies added to a growing distrust of his aesthetic project among the critic's colleagues, and this at a time when, borne on a second troopship-inspired wave of enthusiasm for jazz, the HCF was expanding dramatically: growing from twenty-nine local chapters in 1944 to seventy-seven three years later, at its peak the club incorporated an estimated 5,000 members.[61]

For his part Charles Delaunay had stayed on in the capital, organizing concerts and amateur tournaments even throughout the occupation. So Panassié's authority was in question among many old hands and unknown to the many new, and it was in this context that a debate began over incoming recordings of the new bebop style—anathema to Panassié and his acolytes, the sound of a brave new beginning to a society faction now led by Delaunay. The growing tensions within the HCF were represented in the pages of *Jazz hot*, the club's then-official organ.[62] The argument would in October 1947 cause a decisive schism within the club. The few chapters loyal to Delaunay, including Paris's, split to form a rival, pro-bebop federation with international aspirations (and with which the magazine *Jazz hot* remained associated); Panassié retired to lead a traditionalist HCF from Montauban, the provincial seat at which he would remain.[63] Yet almost at the same moment, the music and musicians Panassié had for years been promoting were taken up by a new generation of players and listeners, and the New Orleans style propelled to a level of popularity never before seen.

As the jazz historian Alyn Shipton has pointed out, the sessions that Panassié supervised in New York during 1938–39 were some of the first documents of what would become known as the New Orleans revival. Panassié had been only one of several late 1930s producers minded to enlist older musicians and invite their harking back to an earlier—and in some eyes, more "authentic"—jazz style. At the time of the Frenchman's trip, Milt Gabler had just established his Commodore label, its first sessions being led by Eddie Condon's Chicago-era group; the British guitarist Vic Lewis was even then making his own pilgrimage to New York, sitting in and recording with players like Pee Wee Russell and Zutty Singleton; and George Avakian was about to embark on a series of recordings for Decca that would, like Gabler's, attempt to re-create the Chicago style of a decade earlier.[64] The work done by these men, European and American, helped give impetus to a musical movement that would soon acquire a global reach. The early 1940s saw the formation of groups like Lu Watters's Yerba Buena Jazz Band in California, Graeme and Roger Bell's various groups in Australia, and in Paris—directly inspired by an encounter with Panassié's New York discs—Claude Abadie's band with Boris Vian.[65]

The arguments being marshaled by Panassié against the new jazz styles were not unique to French jazz discourse. As the revival spread, similar lines of ideological demarcation were drawn in the American jazz press confrontation between "moldy fig" critics and their modernist opponents; Rudi Blesh's 1946 book *Shining Trumpets*, shot through with noble savagery, was countered by the work of bebop progressives like Barry Ulanov and Leonard Feather.[66] But while the discursive tropes drawn upon in Anglophone debates sometimes recalled those of Panassié's work, there, traditionalist and modernist cliques were not so simply aligned with right or left politics as they had come to be in France—indeed, when such alignments were made, Panassié's favored style was often championed by leftists, not those on the right. Likewise, the religious impulse from which Panassié's dismissal of evolution and progress drew its strength was a strictly French phenomenon—and, despite that theory, Panassié still championed swing players that many other New Orleans purists would reject. The international movement towards jazz history, then, was a disparate effort, and if the musicians and listeners who marched under its banner were of numerous political persuasions or none at all, then their attitudes towards the cultural politics of their music also varied: "tradition" might have been the watchword, but such was understood in several ways. By the early 1950s, British revivalists—and the large general audiences their music now attracted—could choose between Ken Colyer's purist reframing of New Orleans musical history and Chris Barber's constructivist mélange of rags, blues, marches and Ellingtonia.[67] Faithful re-creations of the old music were everywhere to be found in postwar France, too, but there was no doubt that the greatest star of the time saw it as his task to refashion his own, performed musical history in the image of the country in which he now found himself.

Having arrived in France alongside Josephine Baker in 1925, Sidney Bechet had ranged across Europe with *La Revue nègre* before ending up back in Paris. In 1931, after serving a prison sentence handed down after a gunfight with another musician, he was deported to the United States. Performance and recording work became increasingly sporadic for Bechet over the course of the 1930s and '40s, but a turning point was reached when, in 1949, Charles Delaunay invited the soprano saxophonist and clarinetist back to France to perform at the Paris international jazz festival.[68] Following Bechet's success there Delaunay arranged a French tour, and, his opportunities at home seeming limited by comparison, the musician subsequently relocated to France, where he remained until his death in 1959. Bechet's last decade was spent as a star: in Paris he worked in the booming jazz basement clubs (or *caves*), but he also toured the country appearing in concert and on mixed music hall bills. The breadth of the audience he cultivated meant that his most famous record, 1949's "Les Oignons," would sell over a million copies during the 1950s.[69] In 1955, 3,000 people, many teenagers, crammed into Paris's Olympia to hear Bechet play; the same number, outside and unable to gain entry, started a riot instead.[70]

Bechet was revered as a singular representative—a living icon—of a past time. What he had already recognized as his stylistic isolation meant that he took his role as an educator seriously. At home he had trained the young saxophonist Bob Wilber, and in France the traditionalist bands with which Bechet worked—led by Claude Luter, André Réwé-liotty, Maxim Saury and Michel Attenoux, all young reeds players—where drilled mercilessly in the music and its presentation, amateurs transformed into professionals whether they liked it or not. The quality of those players remained variable, and Luter's own measured delivery was not always reflected by the musicians in his group (many of whom also appeared in the other aforementioned traditional bands). If the tuning and ensemble passages could be rustic, especially on the many slow, romantic ballads that now appeared in Bechet's repertoire, then it wasn't there that the real purpose of the endeavor lay: these bands gave solid accounts of up-tempo, New Orleans-style collective improvisation, their good-natured noise enveloped by the power of Bechet's own musical personality. That character is the focus of hit records like "Marchand de poissons" and "Les Oignons," the latter's constantly repeating folk-tune a blank canvas for Bechet's brilliant, brief solo and final flourishes, melody and swing reduced to a few whip-crack gestures. Bechet's exciting and unending insistence on the rightness of it all endures on record, and can only have been more thrilling in performance.

Indeed, an important component of Bechet's wider French success was precisely his refusal to act as a museum exhibit, his desire to play music that keyed into broad and vital French popular music trends. Bechet's saxophone playing was full of subtleties, like the notes dotted here and there around longer lines, which, given a different timbre, were the swallowed syllables that gave his horn such a vocal quality. But the strident projection, nasal tone and wide vibrato were not only the player's most striking features: they were also the characteristics that reverberated most strongly within a contemporary French chanson style. The ballad "Petite fleur," a hit first recorded in 1952, sounds like the kind of piece that the concurrently popular Charles Aznavour could have come up with (indeed, he would later record it), and is delivered in a style not dissimilar to Aznavour's own; already popular French songs like "Mon homme" were also incorporated into the repertoire.

Other pieces played and recorded recalled the Caribbean ("Lastic," 1950), early Ellington ("Summertime," 1952), and, as signaled in "Les Oignons," the Crescent City's old jazz style. But even that notionally original jazz was available for (imaginary) Frenchification. Andy Fry has shown how Bechet was ever keen to present not just his own contemporary music, but New Orleansian jazz *tout court*, as a hybrid in which elements of traditional French styles had always been present. "The rhythm came from Africa," Bechet once said, "but the music, the foundation, came from right here in France." Fry argues convincingly that a Bechet-inspired critical identification between jazz and French forms like the bourée allowed French critics and audiences to indulge a kind of "feigned familiarity" with the musician and his music—imagining their positive responses as resulting from Bechet's accordance with, rather than difference from, local traditional practices.[71]

That, of course, had been Panassié's line: jazz was not appealing because it was foreign and exotic, but because it resonated with an old, occluded European primitivism. Nevertheless the critic professed distaste for Bechet's postwar music, which he denounced as a commercialized betrayal of the original New Orleans style. The saxophonist recognized that Panassié's disdain was owed to the fact that his new manager was the critic's rival, Charles Delaunay (that Bechet was Creole rather than *un noir* might not have helped).[72] Yet no matter how disingenuous, Panassié was correct to see Bechet not as an "authentic" New Orleans jazz phenomenon, but as a fixture in a wider, French popular music world. As the next chapter shows, those modernist critics who rejected the "new" traditional jazz did so on the grounds that even the best revival players would never be as good—would never create music as charged with urgency—as the originals.[73] But that was missing the point: those French New Orleansians who thought about such things could have claimed with good reason that, in listening to a group of Frenchmen interpreting local popular songs alongside an American jazzman, they were indeed participating in the contemporary development of jazz, albeit a development not made according to modernist standards of technical innovation.

Of course, many among Bechet's huge audience would not have given much thought to the burden of jazz history: they simply wanted to have a giant musical authority erupt in front of them and to be swept away because of it. And while there were still many listeners who remembered the New Orleans style from the first time around, the revival audience—especially in the wake of the 1955 Olympia riot—was widely identified with a rowdy youth culture.[74] If not the rowdiness, then certainly the youth was borne out by the reader and listener surveys periodically conducted by the jazz media (borne out too was Panassié's gleeful and often-repeated assertion that his "real jazz" remained more popular than the modern jazz style). A 1959 poll of listeners' favorite French jazz musicians, conducted for the Europe N° 1 radio station by the critic-presenters Daniel Filipacchi and Frank Ténot, put modernists Barney Wilen and Martial Solal in first and second place, but the rest of the top ten was occupied by players identified with New Orleans and swing (or what in France was by then referred to as "middle jazz"): Guy Lafitte, André Persiany, Claude Bolling, Claude Luter.[75] In the same year, a *Jazz magazine* survey found that its readers were largely concentrated in the fifteen–twenty age bracket, were often students who had been interested in jazz for three or four years, and, overwhelmingly, had become interested in the music via New Orleans, Sidney Bechet and Louis Armstrong.[76]

These kinds of responses were typical, and had not changed significantly even a decade later, when a *Jazz hot* poll found that New Orleans was still a favorite style among more than twice as many respondents as was modern jazz (though, showing the eclecticism of the readership by that time, R&B, spirituals and pop music were the most preferred genres).[77] Second-wave groups like Les Haricots Rouges and Les Hot Peppers de Marseille, and instrumentalists like the trumpeter Irakli de Davrichewy, continued to emerge during the 1960s; Irakli would claim to interpret Louis Armstrong "as others do Chopin," and, as Gérard Conte reported of the trumpeter's noted opening performance at a 1965 Armstrong concert, while Irakli's playing was exceptionally faithful to the Armstrong of 1924–27, his phrases were not copies of Armstrong's own, instead statements that Armstrong might have made.[78]

But Conte's appraisal of Irakli's music described both the highest aspirations and the limits of a classicizing jazz project (one which would be much in evidence in the jazz of the latter 20th century). Idiosyncratic "hybridizers" apart, most revivalist players could not hope to transcend historical pastiche, however skilful, and as a result those modernist critics Panassié had by the 1960s taken to calling the "jazz mafia" often deemed New Orleans music—and the critic's favored swing styles—part of a nostalgic sideshow, one irrelevant to more vital developments taking place elsewhere in the jazz world. In light of the older forms' popularity, traditionalist French fans and musicians had reason to feel neglected by the specialist jazz press, which during the 1950s and '60s gave overwhelming precedence to the (American) stars of modern jazz: while debates around developments in postwar jazz were nothing if not involved, coverage of the New Orleans revival was too often limited to reports from amateur tournaments. But that popular music was not apt to be framed by its participants or critic-supporters in intellectualist or even sociohistorical terms, and such meant that the style's on-stage sounding did not easily find an echo in print discourse—especially since the workings of the musical practice itself had been comprehended and digested so many years previously.

Indeed, the lingering, reactionary presence of the author of so much of that critical work, and the nature of the intellectualism that he *had* accorded prewar jazz, contributed much to postwar traditionalist/modernist sectarianism. Even the musical sympathies Panassié and the French traditionalist musicians shared were compromised by the critic's fascination with a blackness those players lacked: Panassié and his project were far from universally revered by a New Orleansian fraternity that, in Maxim Saury's words, could see its own "LIVING French music" marginalized in favor of the authoritative direction "towards the buying of this or that American record."[79]

That was the lot of Hot-club members through the postwar period. Continually multiplying, freely circulating, circumventing any singular critical authority, a now-abundant recorded jazz—traditional and modern—was escaping whatever ideological strictures Panassié's interwar efforts had successfully imposed upon it. And so the critic had redoubled his efforts to bestow the legitimacy of the authentic upon particular "iconic" records representing particular musical practices; during the 1950s, while the wider French jazz discourse moved beyond the racialism and religionism of previous decades, Panassié retreated into a more distant Churchly past, facing as a result a problematic of copy and control that belonged to an earlier period in the history of art.

Institutional Control and the Iconic Jazz Recording

As much as the commandment delivered against them and recorded by Moses, it was the ease with which religious icons multiplied and evaded churchly authority that caused early Christian theologians so much worry. Having ceded to the icon's realpolitik adoption—in a time of general illiteracy icons were a useful tool for the teaching of the Christian story, and after 869 they were recognized as a medium of revelation equivalent to the Scriptures—the Western Church attempted to assert some kind of control over their use by means of stylistic and symbolic reduction; the "diversity of visual experience" found in Byzantine icons, the art historian Hans Belting has written, was in the West "reduced to a canon that suited the church-controlled cult image … The reduced but universally valid canon of forms reflected, in the icon, a superordinate canon of values, which was safeguarded by the centralized church." But, in religious as in jazz contexts, the image's very reproducibility militated against such control. By the Middle Ages, use of private, portable iconic images had spread to all European classes, and no longer did veneration of the icon have to take place as part of a public ritual, focused on an authentic, original object, mediated by the clergy. With the domestication of the image came its release from aesthetic bonds—the new, portable (and eventually, reproduced) images "served up one modernism after another," Belting writes—and the distance between the beholder and the sacred once imposed by tradition, priest-led ritual and a formalized visual vocabulary could now be traversed at leisure, worshippers entering into an unsupervised personal dialogue with whatever saint was represented by the object of their devotion.[80]

The Church had responded in the only way possible, by swathing its relics in stories and the aura of the original.[81] And as both jazz recordings and uptake of the unapproved new bebop style became more widespread, so Panassié's role shifted from prophet to priest, his task becoming, and remaining, the distinguishing of the original jazz word, distant but brought close by its authorized image, from a heretical modern form. The arrival of that "pseudo-jazz," the inactivity or deaths of many of Panassié's most admired musicians, France's geographical and now historical distance from the musical object of attention: with the New Orleans revival being of distant secondary interest to the critic—and despite frequent visits to France by surviving stars of the pre-bop period—after World War II all these things combined to make Panassié's "real jazz" a thing of the unreal, an archaic, auratic recorded phenomenon above all.

Panassié's inadvertent opposition to Benjamin's theory of mechanically reproduced art would now take its final form, the German writer's ideas developed in negative: in the name of ideological power, Panassié's jazz records were accorded the status not just of reproductions of a magical, authentic moment of music, but of authorized icons which, fixated upon in both ritual and private study, would function as guarantors of that authenticity, as media of revelation of the authentic "word," and as the image props of an authorized interpretation—Panassié's own. On seeing Panassié's bodily accompaniment of a Louis Armstrong disc at a 1946 *conférence-audition*, André Hodeir would later write, "I knew that I was participating in a ritual ceremony, of which the man gesturing on the platform was the officiant."[82] But Panassié had made the connection between clergy, disc and sacred authority much earlier. From the critic's 1938 New York diary:

> 23 October. In going to mass with Helen Oakley, I hear an incredible sermon during which the priest . . . compares himself to a phonograph needle reproducing the word of God.[83]

Panassié's ideological positioning of the jazz recording coincided with an attempt to restructure the Hot-club's organization: the HCF statute established after the 1947 schism showed a reformed organization bent on the prevention of dissent and divergence within its ranks.[84] New members had now to be nominated by two existing affiliates; a definition of "real jazz" was given, making it possible to enact an exclusion of "all propaganda in favor of bebop in the heart of the HCF"; such exclusion was made simpler by the establishment of a new, comprehensive disciplinary mechanism. Apart from adherence to or promotion of bebop, excommunicable offences included the demonstration of racial prejudice, particularly "vis-à-vis the *noirs* of the United States"—a more-or-less abstract moral position perhaps, but one whose nuances were consistent with the past of some board members. (When Panassié wrote in 1947 that "clearly, race prejudice doesn't much exist in France," he was forgetting that five years earlier the Vichy regime had sent over 70,000 French Jews to the concentration camps, and that his close friend and ongoing HCF colleague André Doutart had served Vichy's commissariat on "Jewish questions.")[85]

At its establishment, the new HCF board ordered a "general liquidation of doubtful elements" in the society's ranks, and clearly Panassié had designed the post-schism HCF as an institution of singular identity, impervious to difference, one that would create and disseminate a program of cultural-ethical inculcation and uniformity.[86] It's the workings of these mechanisms of power and pedagogy—in which an iconic medium of revelation would serve to bind together what the critic now thought of as "an elite" of saved jazz lovers—that forms the focus of this chapter's closing section.[87]

In *Reproduction in Education, Society and Culture* (1970), their famous, Francocentric study of the field of modern education, Pierre Bourdieu and Jean-Claude Passeron offer a study of educational structures which, formed in the Church, over time migrated to the secular world. In the sociologists' analysis, individuals or organizations seeking respectability and influence ("propagandists, publicists, scientific popularizers") but lacking what the authors call "pedagogic authority"—educational posts institutionally granted and guaranteed—tend to usurp the practice of those institutions in possession of such. That authority is created, at first, in formalizing a priesthood or its secular equivalent; religious or secular messages can only become doxa when dispensed not by the individual, but by the office that the individual inhabits. Specific kinds of authorized information are conveyed—and the unauthorized prohibited—so that pupils can reconvey them, first to their examiners and then, once ratified as authorized themselves, to the next generation of pupils; pedagogic communication is thus shaped by "the necessity of producing the conditions for its own establishment and perpetuation." Occupants of pedagogic office preserve these conditions and exercise their authority through their ability to enact "symbolic violence" against unauthorized activity, ranging from a cross in a schoolbook to expulsion. In this way, pedagogic action becomes "the chief instrument of the transubstantiation of power relations into legitimate authority."[88]

Such creations of office, maintenance of doctrine and enactments of symbolic violence characterize Panassié's postwar, post-schism HCF career. President of a society endowed with "pedagogic authority"—in 1953 the HCF was authorized by the Ministry of Education as an *Association d'éducation populaire*—through the authoring and publication of the club organ, the *Bulletin du Hot-club de France,* Panassié would until his death work to reinscribe continually the musical workings and moral values of "real jazz." A reading of the *Bulletin* in the 1950s and '60s shows this ideology, as well as the regulatory and disciplinary apparatus of the society itself, in both energetic establishment and sclerotic decline.[89]

Launched in October 1950 and addressed largely to HCF members, the *Bulletin,* which was published at the rate of ten a year, sometimes featured contributions from other members of Panassié's circle. Yet many of the 7,500 pages that made up the magazine between 1950 and the critic's death were written by the critic alone. The *Bulletin* thus functioned as a relentless, monological reinscription of the HCF's foundational values, which were, without fail, those of Panassié himself. Articles—whether by Panassié or others—were limited in subject matter to the evils of "progressive" thinking in music and the world. Musicians were also drafted in to provide support for this message, their proximity to Panassié routinely vouched for by the reprinting of signed and dedicated publicity photos directly linking musician and HCF sovereign, guarantor of the interpreter's proximity to his sanctified source. Interviews were presented as articles authored by the musicians themselves, as in "Bebop is Not Jazz," by "Louis Armstrong, Président d'honneur du Hot-club de France," in which the silent interviewer could be detected leading his subject through familiar themes: the absurdity of the idea of bebop as "progress," black music as expression of the popular genius.[90] In one edition Révérend Père Louis-Marie de Saint-Joseph was allotted two pages to give a Thomist analysis of how Tommy Ladnier's recordings captured the trumpeter's musically expressed godliness.[91] As the profile of gospel rose through the 1950s, the devotional lyrics of Mahalia Jackson and Sister Rosetta Tharp songs were printed without comment. Indeed, fully fledged religious figures were also presented in epigram and aphorism, by the 1960s such maxims regularly dotting the *Bulletin*'s pages: the words of Léon Bloy, Simone Weil, St Felix and numerous others were printed in boxes, cited apropos of nothing but the ongoing project.[92]

Other sections included news from America, and a review of the press, always devoted to the rebuttal or ridiculing of "modernist" critical writing in *Jazz hot* and later *Jazz magazine*. Accounting for over half of each issue, though, the most important element of the *Bulletin* was its record reviews, for it was these that fully described and delimited the HCF's musical doctrine. The space allocated reflected the relative worth of each musician in Panassié's personal historical narrative. Dominating were the legendary, long-careered and much-reissued Louis Armstrong (around 400 separate reviews between 1950 and 1974) and Duke Ellington (just over 300); each reviewed on average more than once per edition, even their slightest rereleases were never passed over, one or both artists practically always listed in the "best discs of the month" and opening the review section. Count Basie followed (reviewed some 200 times) and members of a second-rank "traditional" cadre (Lionel Hampton, Erroll Garner, Django Reinhardt, Fats Waller) were represented by around 150 different reviews each. Meanwhile, other classic texts from the 1920s were frequently reexamined (Jelly Roll Morton, King Oliver, Kid Ory and Johnny Dodds' reviews numbered around 50 each). Once in a while Panassié would set up a John Coltrane, a Miles Davis or a Bill Evans as a straw man so as to reaffirm the traditional faith, and it was only the leading half-dozen modernists (the above joined by Thelonious Monk and Charles Mingus) whose records made even a couple of appearances in the 243 *Bulletin* issues Panassié edited.[93] Rarely did a musical "canon" so embody that term's original, churchly meaning.

In their detail these reviews were not often explicitly programmatic. But their collection always described the limits of the acceptable, and, in a great many instances, discs were put to pedagogic use. Over the years, numerous "discothèque de base" series visited the same core works of the authorized style.[94] Feature articles on particular historical areas collected catalogue numbers, artist biographies and ideological insinuations.[95] And some of Panassié's reissue reviews made an extended (and musically sensitive) attempt to lead the neophyte listener through the details of an iconic performance, this practical knowledge later "reproduced," in Bourdieu and Passeron's terms, by HCF member apprentices: prizes for "best listener" were awarded at HCF meetings.[96]

Almost every issue of the *Bulletin* showed an effort to reinforce the practices and security of the institution and the control of its membership. Forcefully worded warnings on elapsed club memberships or *Bulletin* subscriptions appeared routinely. Readers were informed that blue HCF pins could not be worn after June 1, 1951, and that new green ones could be purchased for 100 francs (though these were to be worn only by "1. Personal members of the HCF, 2. Members of clubs legitimately affiliated with the HCF").[97] In March 1952 club members were required to submit details of their profession, place and date of birth.[98] But it was exclusion, the ultimate symbolic violence, that defined the postwar HCF as an institution. Errant members were publicly ejected almost monthly, continuing adherents threatened to boot: alongside an announcement of the exclusion of two members in 1952, readers were advised, "in their own interest, to deal no longer with messieurs Duhamel and Anache."[99] In December 1955 the entire Strasbourg chapter was announced as excluded for having organized a Chet Baker concert.[100] The immutable doctrine and culture of excommunication was ridiculed by modernist critics who saw Panassié's sacralizing project for what it was. In a long 1954 denunciation of Panassié's methods, André Hodeir wrote that the elder critic's repetitive texts were to be read like a psalm: "these sentences don't speak to reason, but flatter some inclination towards the magical."[101] Boris Vian often referred to Panassié as "le Pape," or "mon Père"; in a 1957 *Jazz hot*, Vian wrote of the "Ote-club," the removal club, "so called because its members are all expelled one after the other by M. Panassié."[102]

Seen with changing postwar ideas of consensus and tolerance flowing around them, these structures of belonging and exclusion seem increasingly shaky, as risible as Vian and other modernist critics thought them. But such had been absolutely in keeping with the sociopolitical landscape of interwar France from which Panassié's project sprang. Then, membership and ideology was not a game, and the fatal clashes that occurred in the Paris streets between supporters of Hugues Panassié's right and Walter Benjamin's left were accompanied by massive increases in membership of political parties.[103] This culture of joining extended beyond party politics: in contrast to fascist Germany and Italy, where every activity was organized by and subsumed into the state, political and cultural activity of the French mid-1930s was in many ways defined from below. Julian Jackson has written that the leftist Popular Front movement "was born out of, and gave rise to, an extraordinary efflorescence of committees and associations . . . There seems to have been almost no activity for which a committee was not formed in these years." The right had been banding together too, and though it would be absurd to characterize the 1930s HCF as a "rightist" group—whatever the leanings of some of its leaders—the society grew out of a context in which the (quasi) politicized organization of leisure activity was widespread.[104]

At that time, armed with libraries of both records and reactionary tracts, removed by geography and historical circumstance from the viscerality of the everyday lived encounter between white and black in America (or even Paris), Panassié could luxuriate in a theoretical, textual, auditory relationship with fantasy primitives. But as we've seen, the critic's primitivism was not one simply comparable with the *négrophilie* of his early Paris milieu, additionally informed as it was by a long cultural heritage—and by cultural insecurities—quite distant from modern European encounters with blackness. And this primitivism signified not just a condescending pleasure taken in the gifts of a simple Other, but also a loathing for the "same": Panassié borrowed from Bloy, Guénon, Maritain and their informing primitivist sources a decline narrative in which "black" jazz was sometimes simply deployed as the vehicle of an argument directed at "white" society.

It was nevertheless a bargain always made to that society's advantage. As James Clifford has argued, 20th century Western attempts to treat "the primitive"—the art of Picasso or Gaugin, Levi-Strauss' *pensée sauvage* or Lévy-Bruhl's *mentalité primitive*—often professed an interest in a shared humanity while masking their enabling, colonialist realities, and what Clifford calls "the restless desire and power of the modern West to collect the world."[105] There was no better example of such a "collection" than the records that lined Panassié's walls, and the reviews he provided of them; by ascribing the shellac-imprisoned Other a depersonalized, limiting set of cultural characteristics—no matter whether positively or negatively portrayed—Panassié's primitivism rendered the black unknown "known," exalting it as ideal so as to neutralize the kinds of instability it engendered among most of the critic's rightist confreres. That the fictive, desirable *noir* might have had the upper hand in this worldview of Panassié's did not change the fact that the *noir* was being used, imagined, for the benefit and definition of a hoped-for European self: one which would spurn modernity and return instead to timeless, sacred truths and traditions.[106]

Panassié's own program had inverted Walter Benjamin's ideas exactly, the Frenchman's newly auratic jazz recording serving as the means of unification between individual body and cosmic mass under the sign of "traditional" godly and governmental authority. But through the 1950s and '60s Panassié's phonograph needle was reproducing the word of God from a record worn increasingly crackly, his attempts to initiate the youth of the "*Trente Glorieuses*" into an aged aesthetic order ever more forlorn. From 1963, the critic ran weeklong summer *stages d'éducation* at his Montauban record library. By 1969 these were being advertised in the *Bulletin* almost as package holidays, prospective vacationers reminded of the region's famous wine and fruit as well as Panassié's 20,000 records.[107] Even if they nowhere felt the godliness Panassié preached, later generations of jazz listeners might have found something like the aura of the distantly close in their imaginative engagement with those historical recorded moments. But to those never called they would have seemed like so many stacks of plastic.

THREE

Jazz between Art and Entertainment

André Hodeir and Thelonious Monk

The first Dizzy Gillespie and Charlie Parker discs had been circulating in Paris since 1946, and the trumpeter Alan Jeffreys, trombonist Jack Carmen and drummer Benny Bennett—players who arrived in the capital with Don Redman that year and stuck around after their leader departed—had in summer 1947 tried their luck as the Bebop Minstrels, recording a few sides alongside local musicians similarly grappling with the new style.[1] The Hot-club split itself in two over the modern music a few months later. So the concert given by Dizzy Gillespie's big band at the Salle Pleyel in February 1948, often remembered as marking the arrival of bebop in France, was for many a moment of confirmation rather than revelation. Still, the music must have been disorientating: in the course of a number like "Oop-Pop-a-Da," the Gillespie band juxtaposed broad comedy and extreme drama, the arrangement's scattershot rhythm and cracked-mirror harmony surely outside the firsthand experience of any local jazz listener. At least pieces like that one belonged to a recognizable popular tradition. An extended version of George Russell's "Afro-Cuban Suite" featured Gillespie accompanied only by Chano Pozo's hand drums and vocal calls, these, like the other bandmembers' chanted responses, delivered in a language distinctly African. A recording of the concert shows the audience frenzied at the end of each piece, the turmoil palpable. Gillespie was mobbed afterwards. "Back to Timbuktu," called one member of the crowd. "Learn some French, you half-savage [mal blanchi]."[2]

Over the next five years, many of the stars of modern jazz would make their first (and sometimes only) visits to France. Charlie Parker, Kenny Dorham, Miles Davis and Tadd Dameron came for Paris's first Salon du Jazz in 1949, Parker returning the following year. Thelonious Monk and Gerry Mulligan arrived for the Salon's third edition in 1954, and Chet Baker followed in 1955. Stars in the making came somewhat incommunicado: Zoot Sims made his first visit as a member of Benny Goodman's band in 1950, and Clifford Brown, Gigi Gryce and Quincy Jones appeared as members of Lionel Hampton's orchestra in 1953. As ever, some American visitors stayed on, for months, years or occasionally a lifetime. Don Byas, like those Bebop Minstrels having arrived with Don Redman in 1946, passed much of the next two decades in France before moving to the Netherlands. Kenny Clarke was resident in Paris from 1948 and James Moody from 1949, both staying until 1951. Quincy Jones spent eighteen months as director of the Barclay label's house band from April 1957. Donald Byrd spent long periods in Paris from the late 1950s to the mid-1960s, both working and studying with composer-teacher Nadia Boulanger; Bud Powell lived in the capital from 1959 to 1964.[3] But of the bebop players who spent a significant amount of time in France, it was Kenny Clarke who was the most visible, and, in terms of his involvement with developing French modern jazz practices, the most important. Having passed the first half of the 1950s in the United States (where he had been a founding member of the Modern Jazz Quartet), Clarke returned to Paris in 1956 to join Jacques Hélian's commercial big band. In the latter 1950s he worked as the house drummer for Barclay's label, before leaving to take up the same role at Paris's Blue Note club. Settled permanently in the Parisian suburb of Montreuil, Clarke recorded, performed and toured with numberless players, French, American and otherwise, before setting up a drum school in 1967, which he ran until shortly before his death in 1985.[4] Attracted by the city's now-historic jazz reputation, American players—second-generation bebop musicians like Nathan Davis, Phil Woods and Mal Waldron, and later the free jazz musicians discussed in chapter 5—continued to move to Paris in the 1960s, '70s and beyond.

Though this changing cast of expatriates would continue to mingle freely with local players, it would be some time before American and French competencies were aligned. Nor did French audiences show much understanding towards European players who struggled to adapt to bebop's new and pitiless technical demands. Following Gillespie's first Paris success, in May 1948 a "Grande semaine du jazz," spanning

New Orleans and bebop, took place at Paris's Théâtre Marigny. The weekly journal *Arts* reported that trumpeter Howard McGhee's performance, even if "extremely dissonant," was "fascinating," and that even unforewarned sections of the audience responded enthusiastically. But the journal also took issue with those in the crowd who had whistled French players—like the popular Harry James–style trumpeter and bandleader Aimé Barelli, who was heckled when he imitated Cootie Williams and Dizzy Gillespie—and asserted that even though there was a great difference in quality between American and French players, visiting stars like Coleman Hawkins had applauded the efforts of their French counterparts. (The journal didn't report that, during Hawkins's performance, Percy Heath had emerged from the wings, taken the hapless Emmanuel Soudieux's bass from his hands, and begun to play in the Frenchman's stead.)[5]

The first French bebop recordings would be stylistically as well as technically uneven: with new kinds of expertise and new practices emerging, such inconsistencies were—indeed, always are—inevitable. The American discs that had in 1945 captured the style at its moment of emergence had been the same. There, younger players fully committed to the new music (Parker, Gillespie) had found themselves alongside older musicians shaped by and embodying the styles bebop would render passé (Slam Stewart, Sid Catlett); the supercompetent (Max Roach) found themselves next to their distant inferiors (Argonne Thornton). This developmental moment was repeated three years later in Paris, when the excitement generated by the new music saw labels recording Americans like McGhee in the company of local players, most of whom had previously been active in different stylistic contexts—though some had altered their approach to suit, and some had not.[6] The youthful Fol brothers, altoist Hubert and pianist Raymond, each described one of these tendencies. Hubert had begun with Claude Abadie's New Orleans group, but was an early adopter of Charlie Parker's example. His 1947 recordings with the Minstrels show a sense of line that has caught the gist of bebop, but also a violin-like glide that reminisces over an earlier style. The saxophonist's powers grew quickly, and by the time of a 1949 session with Kenny Clarke his language is more intricately involved with Parker's, his sound singing and relaxed (though he still lags intellectually, pausing, weighing up and then attacking each harmonic strain like a show jumper progressing around a course).[7] While the alto player quickly became one of the most capable French bebop players, his pianist younger brother Raymond, even though present on a number of bebop sessions, had not yet given up an adolescent method that bolted Ellington and Gershwin together in rickety kitsch. As in America, rhythm section players were often slower to adapt to the new sensibility than their horn-playing counterparts, and Raymond Fol's late 1940s playing continually drags his colleagues' music down rhythmically, as well as back stylistically, even bebop swing undercut by his dotted-eighth bounce (though none of these descriptions would hold by the time of his 1955 Paris sessions with Chet Baker).[8]

The most high-profile adaptation to the new style was made by Django Reinhardt: if, over time, elements of the bebop vocabulary would seep into the work of all kinds of musicians, the French guitarist was almost alone among the leading swing players in attempting a thoroughgoing, bebop-inspired transformation of his playing. Out, firstly, went the Quintette-style groups of acoustic strings. Reinhardt had played an electric guitar on his unsuccessful 1946 U.S. tour with Duke Ellington, and not long after his return home he adopted the instrument for good; from the end of the decade until his death in 1953 the guitarist preferred to work with a standard rhythm section and one or two horns (including Hubert Fol, and the trumpeters Roger Guérin and Bernard Hullin). The early bebop recordings of Charlie Parker and Dizzy Gillespie were pastiched, and sometimes quoted, in Reinhardt compositions like "Babik," and—along with a new, Gillespie-like approach to rhythm and phrasing—several already standard bebop harmonic devices now made an appearance in the guitarist's improvisations ("Double Whisky," May 1951, 1:11–35).

As Benjamin Givan writes in his Reinhardt study, the musician's late period recordings represent a sometimes uneasy and idiosyncratic assimilation of bebop, and the security and nuance of Reinhardt's pre-bebop acoustic playing is often missing—an absence perhaps caused as much by the new instrument as by the intention to overhaul a too familiar way of working.[9] The payoff was music with an admirable sense of daring, and, indeed, moments of total bebop mastery ("Troublant boléro," January 1952, 1:25–45). Yet, as Givan notes, Reinhardt was likely predisposed towards bebop because so many of its priorities, particularly harmonic, had long been his too;[10] the guitarist's most astonishing "bebop" playing can be found on recordings he made years before that style or its musicians had been heard from.

In his book *The Birth of Bebop*, Scott DeVeaux singles out Coleman Hawkins as a key figure in the prehistory of the form: the tenor saxophonist was preoccupied with harmonic innovation above all, and his techniques were communicated to an interested generation of musicians by record and in person, Hawkins employing emerging players like Thelonious Monk and Miles Davis. The tenor player lived in Europe from 1934 to 1939, and, though recorded documentation is scant, DeVeaux suggests that Hawkins's decisive investment in what would become bebop's characteristic harmonic approach might be dated to around 1937. Examining recordings made in Paris for Delaunay's Swing label, the writer shows Hawkins making new use of passing chords and the tritone substitution, the kinds of materials that he would be fully exploiting by the time of his return to the United States and his highly influential 1939 recording of "Body and Soul."[11]

In describing Hawkins's playing, however, DeVeaux does not find anything nearly as harmonically or historically incongruous as the substitutions that Django Reinhardt was using at the same time; the author does not consider whether it is important that it was during the period in which the saxophonist was in close contact with Reinhardt—and lesser, but still harmonically adventurous musicians like André Ekyan—that Hawkins's new approach took shape. Both those musicians play alongside Hawkins on the Swing recordings, but they are inaudible to DeVeaux who, seeing bebop born American, can only imagine its parents as American, too. Yet a solo on "Chicago," recorded with the Hot-club Quintette two days before the Hawkins session, shows the guitarist progressing through a series of increasingly delirious harmonic visions that paint jazz's future in colors brighter than Hawkins had yet managed on disc. The solo begins with a paraphrase of the theme, this rounded off with the striking jazz use of a classical-Romantic augmented sixth chord (0:44). But something more "modern" is soon to come. Among those bebop gambits that Givan identifies as being incorporated into Reinhardt's playing in the late 1940s is the widely used melodic line that passes from the #9 to the ♭9 of chord V and has as its target the fifth degree of the subsequent chord I (here, E♭, D♭, C); Reinhardt now introduces this device to his solo, a decade too soon. Having anticipated that element of bebop language, Reinhardt immediately passes to a melodic idea that seems strikingly Gillespie-like in both its rhythmic assertion and its inclusion of the "bebop" ♭5th.

This late 1930s performance already full of apparently mid-1940s devices, Reinhardt peels off a chord substitution that would have sounded striking in the 1950s. Here, a suggested V-I progression in F is seemingly overlaid by a V-I in the entirely alien G♭, and though this superimposition is different from that which would become the standard bebop "tritone substitution"—less smooth, more odd—that G♭ arpeggio does in turn suggest itself as a tritone substitution for the V chord (C7) implied and awaited at this point in the song's structure:

More dissonant linework follows, another allusion to the song's theme disrupted by a wild motivic displacement whose tonal disjuncture could suggest a lurch into the post-bop world (1:45). This startling recording was rejected for release by HMV (though the specialist-run Swing would put it out); in light of this, and the fact that the Quintette's first recordings had also been passed over for being "too modern," it's useful to ask how far recording and broadcasting company mediation led to the toning down of Reinhardt's magnificent musical imagination. Even though he is routinely described as a genius, a U.S.-focused jazz history, too, tones him down, allocating the guitarist a position on the European fringes of jazz, an inventor of the "gypsy jazz" style perhaps, but not a player in the thick of what would turn out to be an important developmental moment for the music's core technical resources.[12] The point is not to replace one "great man" with another, but to suggest that the lines of jazz's development were multiple, collaborative; nevertheless, it's true that in his late music Reinhardt embraced what were unambiguously American bebop models and formats, rejecting the old Quintette style that he had helped found and which for many had become synonymous with French jazz.

That music was still part of the stylistic collision found in early French bebop recordings. Claude Laurence was a violinist who, as a twenty-one-year-old, had emerged onto the Paris circuit in 1942; with Stéphane Grappelli in wartime exile, he had become a fairly well-known player in the manner ordained by the Quintette's coleader. Laurence worked with Reinhardt, Ekyan and others during this period, recording a disc for Swing under his own name on which he demonstrated a Grappelli method stripped of Grappelli glitz.[13] The violinist's playing had not changed significantly before he made a series of recordings with Kenny Clarke and other bebop players in 1948, and here modernist repertoire met an indigenous but already rather tired approach. With Clarke's group in May, Laurence's phrasing of themes is all wide, Grappellian quarter-note triplets, his solos simple scalar ascents and descents, a thin-toned prattle that shows little appreciation of the new bebop methods of line construction. Recording under his own name in October, the player makes a formal announcement of the bebop standard "Hot House"'s theme, ill-advisedly attaching classical ornamentation to it as he does so.[14] The art music allusions don't finish there: both "Hot House" and another piece recorded at the same session, "John Payne Was Here," feature fugato ride-out choruses, the ghosts of J. S. Bach and New Orleans meeting awkwardly amid a mass of jazz counterpoint that anticipates the West Coast and Third Stream music of the 1950s.[15] These recordings hardly suggest as much, but in his first book, *Le Jazz, cet inconnu* (1945), the young critic and composer André Hodeir had remarked upon Laurence, a musician "of whom we can expect much."[16] Hodeir was apt to be familiar with Laurence's work: they were one and the same person. By the time of his recordings with Clarke, Hodeir would later recall, he had all but abandoned the violin for composition; after these first arrangements were dispatched, so was Laurence, and the musician reverted to a name that would become identified with some of the most important French jazz writing and music of the postwar period.

Important, because as his early arrangements for Kenny Clarke suggested, in formation and outlook, Hodeir was positioned with unusual equilibrium between classical music and jazz worlds; in the wake of bebop and through the 1950s, jazz, though still a popular, "commercial" music, would take on more and more of the trappings of "art" proper, and Hodeir would emerge as a key figure in the local attempt to translate jazz practice into an extant system of bourgeois artistic values. The same was soon to be seen across Europe and in the United States, where jazz would, in the 1960s, begin to be framed as the country's own classical music.[17] But in France, where institutionally cherished notions of cultural worth could be more inflexible than in the Anglophone world, the battle was fought all the more keenly, in music and print—much of it written by the composer-critic Hodeir.

Unlike earlier squabbles over jazz's merit, this contest was not so much between jazz's promoters and detractors as it was between different pro-jazz camps. Alongside a continuation of the traditionalist-modernist battles begun in the 1940s, the period also saw modernist critics beginning to range against bebop musicians who, by the end of the 1950s, were often thought to have reneged on what they had first seemed to promise: to elevate jazz from humble pastime to the height of those venerable art forms the French critics had learned to appreciate during their aesthetic education. As jazz seemed to hover undecided between art and entertainment, a central problem emerged—that of improvisation, a method both heralded by the French writers as jazz's great innovation and distrusted as not fully compatible with familiar standards of artistic durability. In André Hodeir and Thelonious Monk this chapter examines two players in this episode, the former a protagonist and the latter the subject of a French discourse that, uniquely expressed and nuanced, said almost as much about changing French conceptions of cultural value and ownership as it did about jazz itself.

Bilingualism

Those contrapuntal choruses recorded with Kenny Clarke were an outgrowth of the studies that Hodeir had recently undertaken at the Conservatoire de Paris. The student's academic career proceeded at the same pace as his critical and performance activities: he won first prizes for harmony in 1944, for fugue in 1947—the same year he began a four-year tenure as editor of *Jazz hot*—and for music history in 1948. Hodeir joined Olivier Messiaen's famous music analysis class shortly thereafter, studying alongside Pierre Boulez. Both students had it as their goal to compose, but while Boulez's earliest work explored twelve-tone technique, when Hodeir left the Conservatoire and began writing for theater, chamber and symphony orchestra it was in the neoclassical style of Stravinsky and Honegger. These works were soon withdrawn.[18] Around this time, Hodeir also began to take film music commissions, which required him to work in a different mode. The "ballet for fish" he wrote for Jacques-Yves Cousteau's *Autour d'un récif* in 1949 was largely Ellingtonian, if clad in lead boots (Don Byas and Kenny Clarke could do little to save the recording); the music for Paul Paviot's 1953 short *Saint-Tropez* showed the composer to be a skilled pasticheur, again of Ellington, but also of Gerry Mulligan and others.[19] This soundtrack work continued into the early 1970s, Hodeir eventually scoring over sixty full-length and short films. In contrast, a parallel career as a commercial arranger was begun and almost immediately abandoned, a set of overwrought orchestral arrangements completed for a 1951 James Moody session putting Hodeir off such jobbing for good.[20] The early 1950s, he later recalled, were difficult years, during which he struggled to clarify his creative relationship towards jazz on the one hand and art music traditions on the other. The commercial was seemingly beneath him; the neoclassical was behind him; the serialism of his sometime composer colleagues, though intriguing, was beyond a composer who was finally driven by jazz more than anything.[21]

Yet Hodeir retained his links with Boulez and other modernist Conservatoire students and composers. Through the jazz broadcaster André Francis, in 1951 he joined a training course at the Radiodiffusion Française studio of Pierre Schaeffer, the leading composer and theorist of *musique concrète*. Alongside Boulez, Jean Barraqué, Yvette Grimaud and others, Hodeir experimented with the use of tape in composition, realizing the piece *Jazz et jazz* in time for performance at a May 1952 festival that was one of many CIA-sponsored Parisian cultural events of the early Cold War era.[22] Alone on the stage, a piano soloist—Bernard Peiffer—played along to a tape featuring sounds provided by trumpeter Roger Guérin, bassist Emmanuel Soudieux and drummer Richie Frost, the recording's sped-up trumpet lines and backwards drum breaks absolutely modern and knowingly comic. But, like Boulez, Hodeir abandoned the concrète method immediately, and the latter played a minor role in the foundation of the former's group Domaine Musical, which produced concert series of the musical avant-garde from 1954 to 1973. In 1957 Hodeir would present some of his jazz pieces at the Donaueschingen new music festival, a stronghold of serialism; in the early 1960s Hodeir's Jazz Group de Paris would take part in a Domaine Musical performance of Barraqué's piece . . . *au delà du hasard*.[23]

These musical alliances, both personal and aesthetic, were lasting but uneasy. Hodeir's works were never performed at the Domaine Musical concerts, his use of a low popular music like jazz beyond the pale for most of the modernists. (Boulez was known for his disdain of the music, though that didn't stop him drawing on its cool sonorities for his important 1955 chamber piece, *Le Marteau sans maître*.) Writing barely any "serious" work in the early 1950s, Hodeir was instead pondering how to reconcile his art music and jazz interests. This was, he later recalled, a "bilingual" period, experienced as a "living hell": "[l]ike all young musicians of my generation I was sensitive to atonalism and fascinated by the twelve-tone row. This jarred with my aesthetic ambitions regarding jazz. For a long time I was in complete disarray."[24] It was after the Belgian tenor saxophonist Bobby Jaspar commissioned Hodeir to write a twelve-tone piece, "Paradoxe" (first recorded on Jaspar's 1954 Swing album *Bobby Jaspar and his New Jazz, Vol. 1*), that the composer finally recognized the two approaches as incompatible. This was the paradox signaled in the work's title. The through-composed, two-and-a-half-minute experiment—on this first recording featuring Jaspar, trombonist Nat Peck and a three-piece rhythm section—is relatively melodic, its tone row used thematically in the classic, Schoenbergian style. But Hodeir's serialist contemporaries disdained this old approach, instead mining their rows for anti-thematic structural possibilities. to them, the piece would have seemed technically antiquated as well as stylistically compromised.[25] Hodeir was hardly any more pleased with the result, though the experience was an important one, as he recalled in 1961.

> I realized that my "truth" lay in this form of sensibility coming out of Parker, and that, as a result, I would have to completely abandon so-called "classical" composition and try to create this world of jazz composition that didn't yet exist, except in Ellington's work.[26]

Though Hodeir's background and compositional methods would often lead him to be identified with the Third Stream school which, led by the American Gunther Schuller, emerged during in the mid-1950s, in the Frenchman's mind the difference between his efforts and those composers' was clear (the 1961 magazine interview quoted earlier was headed "I don't belong to the Third Stream"). In wrenching himself away from "so-called 'classical' composition," Hodeir had also disavowed the Third Stream's attempted hybrid of jazz and art music, one that would see composers continue to attempt the marriage of twelve-tone technique and jazz material, as in Rolf Liebermann's 1956 Concerto for Jazz Band and Orchestra, or Schuller's 1960 *Variants On A Theme Of Thelonious Monk*. Not classical, not hybrid, by 1954 Hodeir had decided that without fully rejecting the principles and techniques he had learned at the Conservatoire, his work would be shaped by a jazz aesthetic above all. And what a "jazz aesthetic" was he had just come to define, in what would soon be recognized as one of the most important single critical works published on the music.

Hodeir had repudiated his early writing *à la Panassié*—including the book *Le Jazz, cet inconnu*—after hailing Dizzy Gillespie and Charlie Parker in 1946.[27] As a writer and editor of *Jazz hot*, he had, in the late 1940s, become a leading voice among Panassié's hated *progressiste* critics, those who argued that bebop, rather than being anti-jazz, represented an "evolution" of the jazz tradition. That the most recent developments in jazz were most demanding of interest was self-evident to the modernists, but anathema to Panassié, for whom "evolution" was literally blasphemous and "progress" the watchword of a decadent, deluded West. Hodeir's status as a standard-bearer for the *progressistes* was cemented with the 1954 publication of *Hommes et problèmes du jazz*, a book whose orientation was signaled by the title of its 1956 English translation, *Jazz: Its Evolution and Essence.*

The book commences with a long and methodical attack on jazz criticism, and fanaticism, in its Panassiéiste form. This writing Hodeir takes to task for its amateurishness, its lack of musical learning, and its replacing of critical insight by an enthusiasm which "transforms the love of jazz into a kind of metaphysical crisis," making of Jelly Roll Morton and Tommy Ladnier "legendary heroes or saints."[28] In place of this simple, indeed ideological "enthusiasm," Hodeir aimed to construct a formalized jazz aesthetics supported by analytical musicology. "What I should like," he wrote modestly, "is for this book to become, in its small way, the *Discourse on Method* of jazz."[29]

The evocation of Descartes was significant not only in its signaling of what Hodeir would repeatedly contend was an "objective" analytical project—the full title of Descartes's philosophical masterpiece made clear that the method in question was of "Reasoning Well and Seeking Truth in the Sciences"—but also in its construction of a high-European frame of reference through which jazz history was to be interpreted. Throughout the book's opening section, the history of Western art music is presented as a comparative case against which developments in jazz practice are measured and comprehended, and by way of which Panassié's stationary stylistic purism is refuted and ridiculed. Hodeir's detailed and practical knowledge of this European musical past allows him to posit a theory of "progression" that is considered and nuanced; his art music tradition is not totalized or homogeneous. Still, the use of Western art music history as a yardstick is hardly innocent, and as Hodeir uses it to construct a model of jazz development so he continually implies the existence of a set of artistic values in some way transferable between the two musics, an issue to which we will return.

The historical and ideological program set out, Hodeir proceeds to a series of close studies. The critical skill on show in many of these passages has often been admiringly noted, and rightly so: their musical-technical insight was almost without precedent (in popular criticism it didn't have much in the way of subsequent, either). Hodeir brings an intimate musical knowledge, pertinent analytical tools and acid-clear critical thinking to bear upon music that he either celebrates or—and this is an essential part of the nonenthusiast's "objective" plan—condemns for having fallen short of one jazz ideal or another. Not usually commented upon, though, is the quiet presence of what, in later interviews and writings, was to become Hodeir's grand theme: the loss of appetite for jazz. The trombonist Dickie Wells is the unfortunate target of one extended rumination on the gradual decline of the improvising artist. "[D]oes life begin at forty?," Hodeir asks at the chapter's outset. "The jazzman does not bear out this optimistic philosophy, for it seems that his life—his musical life, of course—usually comes to an end around that age."[30] Hodeir was thirty-three in the year of his book's publication, but he was already writing with an older man's jadedness; from time to time the writer—who was shortly to begin work on a group of compositions that he called *essais* (and who had, after all, already owned up to modeling his work on Descartes)—seems to be trying for the sagacious and reflective tone of the first great essayist, Montaigne.

> Some pieces of music grow old; others stay young. At times we can hardly believe it possible that once we actually enjoyed listening to a page of music or a chorus that now seems overwhelmingly long on faults and short on merits. To make up for this, some works seem more and more attractive to us as time goes by. For one thing, we are more difficult to please at thirty than we are at twenty. Instead of liking a hundred records, we no longer like more than five or six; but perhaps we like them better.[31]

Panassié had charged that bebop was marked by its incorporation of "white" musics and theories, and Hodeir's critical work, parading its European intellectual orientation, does little to challenge that perception.[32] Indeed, Hodeir counters that, since the elder critic's favored prewar styles were evidently hybrids of African and European music, it was surprising that purists like Panassié "accept everything jazz borrowed from the whites until around 1945" but "now refuse to allow jazz the right to keep on borrowing."[33] This importing of materials did not lead to the disfiguring of jazz tradition: "[u]ndoubtedly the essence of jazz lies partially in a certain *Negro spirit*," Hodeir writes, "which is the only thing that could have oriented these continual borrowings in a single direction."[34]

While Hodeir's mature critical work was not generally given to racial mythification—at least by comparison with earlier French writing on jazz—it had not escaped the pull of such ideas entirely. While a slightly younger writer like the recent sociology graduate Lucien Malson would portray jazz in culturalist terms, Hodeir remained trapped in the metaphysical language of "spirit" and "essence" that had so suffused that earlier Panassiéiste literature.[35] A discussion of jazz's essence thus takes up much of the second half of the book, and, as the English-language publishers realized in naming their translation, along with the opening tract on evolution it is this investigation that characterizes the study— and which is key to understanding Hodeir's goals, overt and covert.

So another master of method (and student of essences), the phenomenologist Edmund Husserl, is invoked in both name and procedure. "What we have to do," Hodeir writes, "is distinguish between the vital center of jazz and the part that is just connected with it," to identify the music's essential and accidental features.[36] At length, Hodeir decides that the blues' "melodic language" is not essential, finding none, for instance, in Coleman Hawkins' famous 1939 recording of "Body and Soul."[37] Improvisation, too, is deemed inessential, since some works or arrangements were through-composed but could still only be called jazz.[38] What were still called "hot" techniques, like the trumpet growl, were lacking from "innumerable" recordings, and could therefore not be essential.[39] Hodeir is not even keen to retain the idea of swing, noting that different eras of jazz demonstrate different notions of what this constituted, preferring instead to think in terms of tension and release and building its description from a language that would not have been out of place on the pages of the soon-to-be-launched serialist journal *Die Reihe*. "The rhythmic phenomenon," Hodeir argues, "is not simply a question of *time values*; the succession of *attacks* and *intensities* is also an important part of it"; the critic writes of swing's reliance upon, among other things, conjunctions of "Infrastructure" ("tempo and accentuation") and "Superstructure" ("the rhythmic construction of the phrase conceived in terms of the infrastructure").[40]

Hodeir's final and emphatic definition of jazz's essence is of "*an inseparable but extremely variable mixture of relaxation and tension* (that is, of swing and the hot manner of playing)."[41] Extreme vagueness apart, it's not immediately clear how the "essence" of jazz might comprise "the hot manner of playing," an element already deemed inessential, and this is not the book's only example of confused argumentation. But rather than engage in the debate around jazz's "true" essence—an argument that would hobble on into the 21st century—it may be more productive to ask why, in the French 1950s, the definition of the "essential" was such a vital and lively prerogative.

It's evident by now that in attempting to (re)define the essence of jazz, Hodeir was engaging in a local battle, trying to wrest critical authority and musical validation away from a school of New Orleansians who had claimed the jazz-essentialist high ground. Yet he was also participating in a longer "European" tradition of philosophical essentialism, and the critic's importing of jazz into that tradition—by way of his referencing of great thinkers and their methods—was just as important a part of the attempt to win for jazz a new kind of bourgeois validation as was the juxtaposition of jazz and European art music histories. Tony Judt has written that this essentialist thinking flourished in post-Enlightenment France more than anywhere.

> [F]rom Rousseau and Helvétius and before, we find the essential privileged over the contingent. The object was always to construct systems of thought whose innermost fundamentals would be invulnerable to criticism, the latter always deflected onto secondary or accidental features which were dispensable. Hence the proliferation of *categories* in French discourse, with the object . . . of preserving the core of a theory by rendering almost indefinitely flexible the periphery of the argument. Originally employed for distinguishing between nature and society (or, earlier still, between forms of godly creation), these distinctions served stoutly in the years from 1945 to preserve a notionally "essential" Marxism from its (contingent) errors and sins.[42]

At the moment that leftist intellectuals in France were poised to turn away from the Soviet gulags and towards what Judt calls the "metaphysical Marx" so as to keep the essential truth of Marxism alive and separate from worldly ruination, Hodeir—sharing with those thinkers an intellectual heritage if not a political inclination—was enacting a similar maneuver in a different sphere.[43]

Though the critic described his work as "objective" and analytical of actually existing jazz, in the latter stages of his book Hodeir made a half-concealed argument for the possibility, indeed the necessity, of an entirely personal musical project, and this subtext was always missed in both dazzled and critical appraisals of Hodeir's musicological insight. His argument was formulated in the same essentialist terms as Panassié's, but Hodeir's aim was diametrically opposed to that of the elder critic. Panassié's essentialism, focused on musicians, tied jazz to black America; Hodeir's essentialism, focused on music, allowed jazz to be seen apart from that context and, preserving only an abstracted core of "relaxation and tension," to be promoted to the universal.[44]

What was being elevated, though, was jazz in its ideal form. Throughout the book, Hodeir states and restates his disappointment with the music ("[t]o me," he admits at one point, "the riches of jazz, however precious, cannot for a moment match the riches of contemporary European music").[45] Hodeir is preoccupied not with what jazz can do, but with what it can't: a music based on spontaneous creation, he argues, can never achieve the formal "rigor" and "perfection" he finds in the best art music composition.[46] In another writer's hands, this gambit would have enabled the confirmation of Western art music as superior to jazz. But for Hodeir, the "bilingual" composer-critic, it instead points the way towards a music in which what he calls jazz's "emotional content" would be newly enveloped by that formal rigor—a method, that is, in which imperfect improvisation would become perfectible composition.

> It would seem that jazz can expect to speak a perfect collective language only if it is worked out by individuals (this paradox is more apparent than real). And if this is what were required for jazz to attain a higher level of expression and be truly contrapuntal—if, in other words, jazz had to become more and more like music that is composed "purely," by being written out—then it would be up to the creators to let their thought take the place of the performers', and the performers, as Don Byas has observed, would have to make the listener think he was hearing improvised music even when he wouldn't be doing so at all.[47]

Though a black American improviser was given the lines to speak—Byas, perhaps making his remark at the recording session for Hodeir's early *Autour d'un récif*—their author was surely the composer himself. The methodological demotion of both the blues and improvisation to "nonessential" status, the mooted transformation of the soloistic style into composition, the removal of a musical "essence" from the American site of its birth: as his musical work would soon make clear, Hodeir's critical writing was not "objective," but designed to clear a pathway into jazz for the interested European composer. One like Hodeir himself.

If not completely uncritically, *Hommes et problèmes du jazz* was received with warmth and respect by the modernist French critics: Jacques B. Hess and Boris Vian published tributes in the specialist magazines, and the book soon became a constant point of reference for a postwar generation of French writers—Lucien Malson, for instance, reproducing in his own work the unabashed intellectualism that he saw playing a vital part in Hodeir's "pleading for an elevated conception of the music."[48] The book was published in English by New York's Grove Press in 1956, and its Anglophone reviews were more mixed. In the United States, Nat

Hentoff heralded the work, and Wendell Otey called it "ingenious" and "brilliant."[49] But Billy Taylor objected to Hodeir's downgrading of the blues, and Dan Morgenstern pilloried Hodeir's "great white father" condescension.[50] Though not named, Hodeir's work seems to have been one target of LeRoi Jones's 1963 polemic published in *Down Beat* as "Jazz and the White Critic": neither jazz sound nor black-cultural meaning, Jones wrote, were graspable by the "musicological analysis . . . which has come into favor recently"; nameless, white, "middle-brow" European critics of the 1940s had been guilty of forcing jazz into "that junk pile of admirable objects and data the West knows as *culture*."[51] For several years, the French critic's work was at the center of an international conversation between those interested in—or offended by—a new kind of "cultivated" jazz criticism and analysis; at the end of the 20th century, Hodeir would again routinely be cited in scholarly critiques of what had come to be seen as a disreputable, "Eurocentric" approach to understanding jazz.[52]

Whatever the book's ulterior motives, whatever its appeals to the dubious authority of the European cultural canon, Hodeir's work was far from a simple act of bad faith. Nor was the most important part of its reception to be found in the thrust-and-parry of the specialist press, since by 1962 it had sold 30,000 copies.[53] This was the first fully realized product of Hodeir's "bilingual" classical and jazz training: critical work that constructed an aesthetics that, however far removed from (African) America, nevertheless helped a large, international jazz audience towards a new musical cosmopolitanism; writing that, beyond the fetishism and enthusiasm of old, insisted that the music of black Americans be taken seriously above all. That bilingualism's second product, music that led off from those critical speculations—and even further away from American jazz sources—would soon follow.

Essais

"Classical" composers, American and European, had been making use of ragtime and jazz elements since the 1910s, and, as Wendell Otey wrote in an early study of Hodeir's music published in the short-lived American quarterly *Jazz*, the idea of "transforming jazz art through sophisticated technique" was one that had been shared by many on the other side of the divide, from Jelly Roll Morton and Fletcher Henderson to Jimmy Giuffre and Johnny Carisi.[54] In France, Christian Chevallier was in the mid-1950s emerging as a composer-arranger who had expertly assimilated the complex big-band techniques of American writers like Gil Fuller and

Shorty Rogers (these eventually demonstrated on the much-heralded 1956 disc *Formidable*). But such bandleaders and jobbing writers did not fully occupy the role of "composer" as Hodeir understood it. Even the venerated Ellington, whom the Frenchman sometimes described as the closest to a jazz composer precedent, was not an example to follow. If in "a few, rare instances," Ellington's work had shown the way forward, then the suspicion remained that even he was usually too much the arranger, someone who slotted blocks of unrelated material into preexisting formal molds, or twisted it to preordained formal ends.[55] For Hodeir, schooled in Romantic-modernist organicism, the "composer" was that singular intelligence who would manipulate and develop a musical idea in whatever direction it might take, a piece's structure and shape usually emerging at the same time (AABA be damned). If Hodeir would reject the Third Stream, then in this concern for form he certainly shared some of that music's ambitions. So much had been announced in Bernard Peiffer's foreword to the French edition of *Hommes et problèmes du jazz*, in which the pianist quoted one of Hodeir's favorite maxims: "We must expand jazz so that we never have to leave it."[56]

To this end, and having rejected art music ensembles and formats, in 1954 Hodeir formed the nine-piece Jazz Groupe de Paris. Between October and December that year he set about composing what he dubbed a first book of *essais*, which, as the name would indicate, were experimental compositions that—free of the demands of the visual image, and the commissioner-client—explored the problems of jazz form and developmental technique that Hodeir had been pondering for several years.[57] A second set of pieces was completed and recorded in 1956. Looking back a few years later, Hodeir said that although he was increasingly sure of his handling of orchestration at this point, "at the level of form (which I'd started to realize was the most important), I was still in the dark, and each piece constituted an attempt to fix this indefinable thing that is the 'musical becoming.'"[58] Though his aspirations in this area outstripped those of any forebear, the composer acknowledged that the terms of the Jazz Groupe's project had been set by Miles Davis' 1949–50 nonet recordings for Capitol later collected as *Birth of the Cool*, and, as Wendell Otey pointed out, piano apart the group's instrumentation mirrored that of Tadd Dameron's ensemble of the same period—two trumpets, a single trombone, alto, tenor and baritone saxophone, vibraphone, bass and drums. This was a setup that was small and flexible but that allowed the composer an amount of contrast between brass and reed choirs, and a registral spread wide enough for complex and weighty chord voicings.[59]

Otey delighted in the academic devices he found in the Jazz Groupe recordings: Hodeir's fellow composer wrote that "pedal point, canon, point of imitation, atonal counterpoint, hocket, interpolation, expansion, elimination, inversion, retrograde motion, rondo form, and the use of 3/4, 5/4, or simply no-meter floating effects" were all employed underneath a stylistic umbrella identifiably "jazz" in its timbre and swung-rhythm basis. (Hodeir maintained that a largely constant swing feel was necessary, as without it jazz's characteristic syncopation was impossible, this steady pulse providing the base for asymmetrical superimpositions.)[60] Many of the techniques Otey cited were ancient, but rather than facilitating baroque or classical pastiche—as they often did, for instance, in John Lewis's music of the time—in Hodeir's books of *essais* their use followed that of more recent interpreters. The mirror harmonic plan of "Esquisse 1," in which a chord progression proceeds up to the piece's central point and is then reversed, is reminiscent in different ways of Schoenberg or Messiaen's methods; the hockets of Jordu and Bicinium sound like Webern's.

The first pieces were recorded for Swing, and a 10-inch album released as *Essais d'André Hodeir*.[61] On that record, the heaviness that dragged *Autour d'un récif* down is sometimes still present, in several pieces the orchestra's lower register overburdened with contrapuntal activity and misconceived harmonic daring.[62] At drummer Jacques David's insistence, the rhythm section swings between truculently stiff and laxly flexible, and neither Hodeir nor his horns seem to have arrived at a collective agreement as to how, between precisely even and lightly swung, the reams of eighth notes he had written should be articulated. One piece, though, is an unqualified success: "Paradoxe II," the quasi-modal, Orientalist scale-work and gauzy harmonic sense of which gesture towards the Messiaen of *Poèmes pour Mi* (1936), those clouds clearing at intervals for an ever-varying game of repeated entries on the same note (0:52, 1:33, 2:33).

Both composer and band had much developed by the time a second collection of "essays," *Le Jazz Groupe de Paris joue André Hodeir*, was recorded for Vega in 1956.[63] The album includes several small masterpieces of arrangement, most notably Duke Jordan's "Jordu," which is subjected to many of the formal and contrapuntal techniques in Hodeir's repertoire. But Hodeir's original compositions are the most impressive pieces, now stylistically coherent and technically assured, and yet still open, provisional. These are études on single ideas. "On a Scale" sets up a theme that, as the title suggests, meanders up and down a scale of Hodeir's devising in original, varied and then transposed forms. This line—the top line in the following example—is given a shimmering, clustered harmonization, with all the group's winds packed closely to each other in a way that, while strikingly original, still recalls several different coloristic traditions: the *klangfarbenmelodie* of early Schoenberg, the parallelisms of Debussy, Satie and other turn-of-the-century French composers, and the thick ensemble writing of a figure much influenced by that French school, Duke Ellington.[64]

The interest is formal, too. Following this eight-bar opening theme and its partial variation is a vibraphone solo, and then a development of two ensemble ideas: a first homophonic passage develops the opening theme's scale and harmonization idea, a second gives a single-line ensemble "improvisation" on the theme, and then these two passages are then combined in dialogue, a solo trombone working on the single line, the other winds responding with a further development of the homophonic variation. A closing recasting (rather than repeat) of the opening theme is broken up by free statements from the solo bass, this perhaps alluding to the ending of Dizzy Gillespie's famous 1940s big-band pieces "One" and "Two Bass Hit." Underlying this surface of thematic development is a harmonic progression equally subject to variation. As with the solo and homophonic variations that emerge in the winds, two different chord progressions, the one a variation of the other—the first the original theme's underpinning, the second an adaptation often moving at half the original's harmonic tempo—are alternated (and internally varied), giving the piece a sense of flux; moving quickly at the start, the harmonic drive lessens during the vibraphone solo, increases through the central game of variations, and then, somewhere near the "golden section," comes to rest on a tonal plateau that, in a "key" distant from the tonalities previously in play (G♭ rather than G, both major and minor), creates a feeling of indecision before the original theme and harmonic ground come back into view.

A similarly successful application of notionally "classical" technique to jazz materials permeates other pieces.[65] In Hodeir's second set of works for the Jazz Groupe, the art music compositional prerogative of material integration, continual development and formal unfolding are glimpsed in a new, jazz environment; the craftsmanship of the writing is neat, clever, the resources and forms gesturing towards two very different contemporary musical practices and incorporating them without pretentiousness or preciousness.[66]

There is little suggestion in the French press of the time that this music caused much popular excitement, and none of these records sold in great quantities. Hodeir was, however, respectfully regarded by his jazz writer colleagues, and he was waved off with some pride when, in spring 1957, he traveled to the United States to discuss the follow up to his highly successful book of criticism and to rerecord the first *essais* with American players: the Savoy label had expressed an interest in the composer's music, but was reluctant to release the original recordings (the label did release the second album, retitled *The Paris Scene*, and Epic published a non-Jazz Groupe album originally on Philips, *Kenny Clarke's Sextet Plays André Hodeir*).[67] The composer was also regularly allotted magazine interview space in which he could expound on his method and its importance. Talking about his music just before his 1957 departure, Hodeir said that his dominant recent aim had been

> to find a form that allowed the integration and exposition of the theme, the variation of this exposition and a variation on that variation, more and more free, arriving progressively at complete freedom [liberté] in relation to the harmony of the theme.[68]

So much had been partly realized by a piece like "On a Scale." But the short works written for the Jazz Groupe had only been able to dally with these formal concerns, then still delimited—as Hodeir's comment suggested—if not by jazz chorus structures, then by a related idea of theme and variation, and, often, by a juxtaposition of solo foreground and developing background figures.

Now, though, with works like the *Jazz cantata* and *Le Palais idéal*—longer pieces written in 1958 for short films by Michel Fano and Adonis Kyrou, respectively—the composer began to envisage what he would in 1961 describe as "a 'grand form' permitting the musical becoming to escape the perpetual rolling-out of choruses."[69] So *Le Palais idéal* is fixated upon the demonstration of its formal "unity" by way of the constant reiteration of a central motif (which includes an awkward tritone and altogether spans an even more awkward major seventh), treated at first with Gil Evans–style orchestration, here loud in the brass, there hidden in the bass, sometimes squeezed into sleazy swing time like a gumshoe into an ill-fitting suit (whatever Hodeir's formal aspirations, the walking bass and shakes in the brass summon TV and cinematic idioms before they do thoughts of organic purity). Like Hodeir's thematic use of the tone row, this development out of and around a constantly revisited motivic kernel would have seemed outmoded to the contemporary serialists: often taking their cues from contemporary physics rather than the organicism of the Darwinian 19th century, they tended to aim at material "integration" by constructing complex systems of pitch interreaction rather than audible lines of motivic relationship.[70] But Hodeir had already rejected the structural thinking of serialism after "Paradoxe," and this kind of obvious motivic unification would soon be dropped too: the musician having decided that he was a jazz composer working within a jazz tradition, the formal identity of his 1960s music would be determined by its advertised adherence to a jazz prerogative of continually developing improvisation—albeit of an unusual kind.

Simulated Improvisation

The formal development of his pieces, Hodeir said in 1957, was to resemble a spontaneous unfurling, to be arrived at "in an improvised style." This meant that traditional chorus structures were to be renounced. But that in turn militated against actual improvisation, since, the composer assumed, soloists used to playing over repetitive, four-square chord progressions would be thrown off balance now these were dissolved into more fluid formal movement. The difficulty of improvising across an unusual and uneven harmonic space—especially given the limits of rehearsal and performance time available to a noncommercial proposition such as the Jazz Groupe—had meant that, tenor Bobby Jaspar, vibraphonist Fats Sadi and pianist Martial Solal apart, Hodeir's musicians had sometimes been presented solos to play: where once there would have been only empty chord progressions left to the the players' devices, the demands of this new music, Hodeir reflected, meant "it was necessary to provide a kind of writing." This the composer would come to call "simulated improvisation."[71]

Where possible, "improvised" solos were written by Hodeir in the soloist's "own" style, this allowing the improviser "to look at himself or herself from another perspective."[72] But just as the composer's solo retained the improviser's playing characteristics, so, rather than letting the improviser alter the creative terms of the piece, Hodeir retained the characteristics of mood and material implied or demanded by the composition at that moment. This meant circumventing what the composer would later call "a very serious danger"; namely, that the soloist "wouldn't do what I wanted. Given the risks that I had taken in terms of the unity of the work, I couldn't assume those of others as well."[73] If simulated improvisation had at first been deployed largely to override soloist weaknesses and difficulties, by the end of the 1950s it had also been made to take on more fully the responsibility of securing structural and stylistic coherence—as per Hodeir's ruminations in *Hommes et problèmes*. The opening of the *Jazz cantata*, then, features a duet for Christiane Legrand's soprano voice and Hubert Rostaing's alto saxophone, and while the gestural spontaneity of their music suggests jazz improvisation in the classic sense, both musicians make use of the same motivic materials, and their lines are more neatly interwoven, mutually referential and tightly organized than two improvised statements could ever be.[74] Whether this was improvisation perfected, or merely nipped and tucked, was open to question.

If the appeal to developmental "improvisation" was made in the context of jazz, then it was a method that had been adopted and validated by composers as different, and as similar, as Debussy and Boulez: Hodeir's application of the rhetoric of spontaneity in a nonspontaneous compositional context was not as new as all that. Nor was it always convincing to contemporary critics. Commenting on the 1961 Fontana album *Jazz et jazz*—which, along with the title piece, included the *Jazz cantata* and *Le Palais idéal*—Aris Destombes argued that such "integral" composition was "the negation of jazz," Hodeir's simulated improvisation a violation of what had long been jazz's collaborative code.

> In my eyes, it's spontaneous creation and improvisation, by a soloist working upon a harmonic canvas, that gives jazz its specific artistic value and its musical depth. Jazz is a multicreation. It's unthinkable, for me, that it could be the work of one person alone, executed by others, as is the case for classical music. The soloist must be an author before an executant.[75]

Hodeir was keen not to align himself fully with that kind of composerly authority, suggesting throughout his career that the jazz composer's ideal would not be to deliver scores to an orchestra of anonymous professionals, but to be surrounded by, and to compose for, the members of what he would call a "creative workshop—very much like those of the Renaissance painters—in which a community of thought reigns, around a master composer."[76] (If his example was rather curiously drawn from the European painting tradition, Duke Ellington or Charles Mingus's groups were the most obvious jazz precedents.) But the Frenchman admitted that, far from attaining his workshop ideal, his relationships with the players of the Jazz Groupe and the New York scene had often remained strained, and verbalized ideals could not obscure the hierarchical reshuffling enacted upon jazz in Hodeir's scores.

Indeed, to observers of Hodeir's early career it might have seemed remarkable that a man so impressed by jazz and improvisation could have shared both training and professional space with those composers who, like Boulez, caustically denounced the limitations of the style. But by the end of the 1950s, Hodeir's views and methods were striking not in how they differed from that attitude, but in how much they reflected it.[77] Ideas of the unfixed and unforeseen had been introduced to avant-garde European music circles by John Cage, whose works were well known and much discussed from the American's 1954 European concert tour onwards. Influenced by his Zen Buddhism studies and keen to remove the compositional constraints of what he always referred to as "taste and memory," Cage had developed a technique in which materials and their placement in the score were arrived at by chance procedures, including the tossing of coins and sticks. At first Boulez was drawn to Cage, both the composer and the man. But in 1957 he wrote an essay polemic that ranged against Cagean chance for its resignation of composerly responsibility; these ideas Boulez developed in a 1963 article in which he took pains to differentiate such supposed composerly abdication from his own work now using indeterminate methods—notably the Third Piano Sonata (1955–57, revised 1963), in which separate, fully composed modules could be performed in different orders. The composer described that piano piece as a response not to Cage, but to a European tradition of artistic indeterminacy, one represented by canonical authors James Joyce and, especially, Stéphane Mallarmé, whose idea of a book with loose and infinitely recombinable pages Boulez made much of. If, as George Lewis has persuasively argued, Cage had written jazz out of his theory of musical spontaneity—always positioning Zen as chance's forebear—then Boulez wrote out Cage, straining to find a European high-cultural precedent for composition in-the-moment, jazz remaining maligned, the composer remaining all-powerful.[78] The text-based scores Stockhausen would write in the latter 1960s would be subject to the same complexes.[79] In light of this, Hodeir's refusal to accept what he called the "risk" posed to his works' structural and stylistic unity by his performers' multiple musical imaginations seems of a piece with the thinking of his art music contemporaries: for all concerned, the challenge was to square the use of unfixed methods of creation with the traditional authority and overview of the individual composer.

Hodeir Hero

The 1950s was a time in which composers could be much given to bold and authoritative stances. None was more outspoken or influential than Boulez, who, among many other cultural-historical imperatives, famously pronounced that "any musician who has not experienced—I do not say understood, but truly experienced—the necessity of dodecaphonic language is USELESS. For his entire work brings him up short of the needs of his time."[80] In Europe (and to a lesser extent in the United States), a powerful clique of highly self-conscious modernist composers spoke continually of such needs, the need to press ahead, to make musical history by rejecting standard practices in favor of technical innovations of whatever kind. In his 1961 book-length study of leading contemporary art music composers, *La Musique depuis Debussy*, Hodeir's unkind judgments of figures like Schoenberg resembled Boulez's own.[81]

Working in this climate, and arriving at the technical innovation of simulated improvisation, Hodeir—and those critic friends who wrote appraisals of the composer—simultaneously cultivated the image of a jazz artist unbound by convention, concerned only to forge ahead. As Lucien Malson noted in one of several thoughtful pieces on the composer written at the turn of the 1960s, this self-understanding was much informed by Hodeir's appreciation of Nietzsche's heroes, "overmen" like Napoleon who had created a new world of values to escape a philistine present. "He knows," Malson wrote of the composer, "that moral authenticity equates free life at its highest intensity, negation of the dead past, and the constant creation of the self." Here and elsewhere, Malson's Hodeir was "un solitaire," alone on a path towards an envisaged jazz composition. In the writer's description of a conversation between the two men, discussion of Nietzsche turns to the problem of Hodeir's "audacious project": "how to insert oneself into the course of history, or rather how to enter into it in order to reroute it."[82] Explicitly, this rerouting entailed the transferal of formal and aesthetic conceptions of composition from art music practice into jazz; implicitly, then, it would also seek to transplant jazz's creative center from an imagined (African) America to an imagined Europe. The rhetorical, essentializing strategies of *Hommes et problèmes*, and of the composer's subsequent recasting of improvisation as composition, must be seen as a part of an honest attempt to make room for a European contribution to a music that was, after all, long global in its reach. But as we will see, this "audacious project" was increasingly governed by an attitude that, having at first inspired an argument for the incorporation of local technical traditions and concerns, could goad its adherents on to a fantasized appropriation of jazz's future in general.

It was not accidental—though hardly Hodeir's fault—that some of the composer's contemporary interpreters presented his work in thinly veiled terms of racial attributes and deficits. Such ideas were unthinkingly reinforced even by Malson, an avowed and sincere anti-racist. In a 1959 piece, Malson had written that the rhythmic revolutions so regularly enacted by black American jazz musicians, most recently Elvin Jones, were simply beyond a French musician like Hodeir, who could only be "un jeteur des idées," an ideas man making use of his head, not his body.[83] This division would be brought out in the several pieces devoted to Hodeir and published in the French jazz press of the second half of the 1960s by another of the musician's most committed (if unwanted) supporters, Gérald Merceron, himself a composer.[84] For Merceron, Hodeir's work stood opposed to the "vulgar sexuality still so current in the many forms of jazz traditional and modern," music that was characterized by its "infantile" level of compositional sophistication. The familiar portrayal of blacks as emotional and untutored, and whites as rational and learned, was emphasized in Merceron's disavowal of improvisation in the name of jazz composition à la Hodeir. Having alluded to the fine improvising "sensibility" of Charlie Parker, Louis Armstrong, Miles Davis and Lester Young, Merceron wrote that, "unfortunately,"

> when one possesses only sensibility there is a certain level that one cannot surpass: none of the great jazz musicians I have just mentioned could have written Paradoxe II, a marvel of construction that could only be born of a mind that had progressed through the stages of culture [franchi bien des étapes de la culture]! One can write a Paradoxe II only when one is capable of aesthetically and historically situating a musical fact, of or outside jazz, when one is able to reject certain routines as undignified complacency or easy way out, when one can only make the most noble choice—that implies the possibility of resisting "first movements" born in the euphoria of discovery—when one has, finally, the courage and the patience to think, rethink, destroy, begin again, examine oneself with severity, reconstruct a hundred times, a thousand times, a hundred thousand times if necessary![85]

Published later, the second part of Merceron's excited paean suggested that improvisation would disappear from jazz in a future in which such primitive sensualism had been left behind by what were assumedly more fully sentient musical beings. As had been the case at least since the 18th century anthropological classifications of Linnaeus, Kant and others, blacks were imagined functioning on intuition, Europeans on rational thought; as it had been at least since Hegel, the division of racial endeavor was enacted by the phenomenon of writing, the capturing and reworking on paper of thought or events that would otherwise be transient, floating free of that which Hegel's "Africans" lacked and Hodeir's fellow modernists worshipped: History, with a capital H.[86]

To be sure, Merceron's reformulation of Hodeir's own stated motives was eccentric (and, lest his words be thought a simple indictment of French racism, it should be noted that Merceron was not a white metropolitan Frenchman but a mixed-race Haitian; the interrelations of race, musical practice, cultural value and France's postcolonial heritage were complex indeed).[87] If Hodeir's own notion of jazz's composerly future allowed the music somewhat less room for improvisation, he certainly did not express the rejection of one practice and the embrace of another in such racialized terms. Nevertheless, what Malson called the "elevated conception" of jazz that Hodeir was trying to construct entailed the creation of a new audience—for if a formerly popular music was to be elevated to the level of art, who was it to be elevated above, if not the general populace. Following a Jazz Groupe rehearsal one night in 1958, Hodeir and Quincy Jones had adjourned to a café on one of Paris's grand boulevards, where they sat talking, until two in the morning, about the future of the music. In Hodeir's later retelling, the musicians agreed that the old chord progressions and forms were worn out and that composers would become more important in the development of new, innovative jazz material. Of course, said Jones, that won't make any money—one has to make music for people with no ear. But you'll never manage that!, he joked to his earnest French colleague.[88] The conversation, and Jones's comment, stayed with Hodeir for decades, and little wonder, since it represented such a pivotal moment in his self-understanding: on the one hand, the composer's decisive analysis of the task ahead and subsequently pursued, an analysis assented to by one of the most prominent of the young, black American jazz musicians; on the other hand, the moment when the music—abandoned in favor of vulgar popularity, even by the most prominent of the young, black American jazz musicians—seemed poised to be taken up by a method, aesthetic and perhaps institutional world hitherto serving only the great Western art traditions. This was to Hodeir the point at which jazz, so scorned and contained by crass American populism and show business, might find a new, more productive home in Europe and a cultural space cleared by Nietzschean authors of history like himself.[89] "Europe," of course, didn't simply stand for hostile, racialized cultural takeovers. But given Hodeir's continual invocation of the canons of post-Renaissance thought and art, perhaps it shouldn't be surprising that, whatever the composer's own intentions, the discourse around his audacious project only loosely concealed centuries-old binaries that had been erected precisely to divide a newly "Enlightened" Europe from the savage rest: the rational and the sensual, composed and felt, white and black, artistic and popular.

Toward Art

A rather too reductive telling of jazz history sees the music begin to migrate from low- to high-culture worlds during the 1950s, bebop always being made to articulate a break between jazz in its popular and recherché incarnations. Certainly, during this period jazz began to gain more regular access to concert halls as well as nightclubs, an intellectualist as well as trade-based criticism, patronage as well as ticket sales—access, that is, to a new kind of symbolic capital, exchangeable throughout the West. But in France at least, the "artworld" towards which jazz was headed was homogeneous in neither its material nor imaginary conceptions, and notions of the high cultural were undergoing significant changes at this time; rather than one rising to meet the other, a better account of jazz's 1950s progress would see notions of both jazz and "art" meeting amid a new middlebrow culture.[90]

The development of this culture, and of jazz's profile and status, can be tracked across the postwar pages of *Arts*, a weekly newspaper that in the 1940s was an arbiter of bourgeois, beaux arts taste: appreciations of Balzac, Picasso, Debussy and Louis XV furniture fill issue after issue. In the latter part of the decade, only the very occasional mention of Django Reinhardt, or a chanson star, would break up the music page's review of Paris's classical concert life.[91] The 1948 concert arrival of American bebop musicians hardly transformed this situation, though a piece by Claude Chamfray, written following the Semaine du jazz festival at Marigny, suggested the way that the new style would be brought into a discourse also including art music: in its rhythmic fragmentation and inner conflict, Chamfray wrote, bebop might offer a way forward for all music (he meant "classical" composition).[92] The tasteful, non-snobbish ecumenicalism Chamfray exhibited would come to dominate the journal. So, from the early 1950s, Ingres and Henry Moore were joined by features on fashion and, especially, cinema; dense pages of text made room for cartoons and publicity shots of smiling stars, and news of Wagner productions appeared next to write-ups of Dizzy Gillespie and Ella Fitzgerald records. As Theodor Adorno might have commented, jazz's 1950s meeting of "art" music proper owed much to the synchronizing of those two fields under the banner of a new cultural consumerism (rare, at first, was the mention of jazz that was not linked to a record review—"Jazz and the disc," Boris Vian wrote in a 1954 issue, "are inseparable").[93] Against what was estimated at the time (perhaps optimistically) as a combined monthly jazz press readership of somewhere around 30,000, *Arts* sold some 50,000 each week, and the paper represented a channel of written communication between specialist critics and a general audience of unparalleled size; it would host some of the most important postwar critical work on jazz outside the specialist press.[94]

Jazz had not yet cultivated the kind of mature, knowledgeable, and—especially important for patron-seeking artists—financially established audiences that classical music could claim to enjoy and to which *Arts* seemed often to appeal. Since its arrival in France, the music had largely remained an adolescent obsession, its listeners often resigning their interest at some point in their twenties, their places taken by a new clutch of young *amateurs*.[95] To critics like Vian, Hodeir and Malson, all of them addressing this issue in *Arts* between 1954 and 1960, the jazz audience's eternal youth was one of the great obstacles to the music's evolution as art. For them, it was not encouraging but embarrassing that young jazz fans blazed with enthusiasm for idols soon discarded: embarrassing, and indicative of a passion that was social rather than musical (in constantly returning to this problem the writers were perhaps making a play for the journal's readership, assumedly sharing those qualities of establishment and education missing among the denim-clad). Youth was yoked to mass popularity, and the concern lasted into the early 1960s, this the high point of both modern jazz's cultural presence and *Arts*' coverage of the music, by then under the stewardship of Lucien Malson.[96]

If some of the modernist critics writing at this peak moment saw the general, all-too-immature audience as one not to celebrate or court but to leave behind, others were not so pessimistic. In April 1958, Jacques B. Hess cheered modern jazz's new presence, writing that "in the last four years"—a period matching the music's extended coverage in the journal—jazz had in Europe won over radio programmers (who devoted hundreds of hours to the music every week), great concert hall crowds (which now welcomed musicians with solemn respect rather than partisan whistling) and a last, ill-defined but valuable group, "the intellectuals." Most important for Hess was his perception that this new, large, thoughtful jazz audience was not a *grand public* of the kind that had recently attached itself to Sidney Bechet: instead, it was a group of knowledgeable amateurs, able to appreciate and welcome the new, able to lead the way for an even wider audience "which draws itself around the audience of connoisseurs like a halo."[97] Jazz was now an art form, but a modern one, present in concert halls but also in broadcasting, not confined to an elite but enjoyed by a broad, cultivated crowd.

Hess, however, was responding to a piece by Hodeir, who had replaced Vian as *Arts'* jazz correspondent at the end of 1955. In stark contrast to his predecessor's work, Hodeir's articles were marked by their extremely stern tone: the critic chose to use his access to a large mainstream audience not to praise jazz as it existed, but to bury it. Here, under the title "Three Accusations Against 'The Greats,'" the critic-composer skewered Louis Armstrong and other stars for having ceased to create in the moment—this failure brought about by a surfeit of the popular acclaim that Hess celebrated, but which in Hodeir's view led musicians to stop evolving and to stop challenging their own earlier work. This was now Hodeir's main theme. Many of the more substantial pieces the critic published in *Arts* went to make up *Toward Jazz*, a 1962 English-language stopgap published by Grove Press in New York while the firm waited for the follow-up to Hodeir's earlier publishing success, and, in the introduction to that book, Hodeir explained his new project. The writer claimed to have shed the supposed "objectivity" of his previous critical study in favor of something more self-consciously engaged: whereas the "exhausting reappraisal" of jazz aesthetics needed at the time of *Hommes et problèmes* had "required a Cartesian skepticism," he wrote, "the task at hand today calls for the visionary outlook of a Nietzsche."[98] (Hodeir had not lost his sense of grandeur, nor developed a keener sense of the ridiculous.) It was urgently necessary, the writer argued,

> to reappraise the individual jazz musician, examining both his strengths and weaknesses. The greatest jazz artists have, at times, displayed attitudes toward their audience which would have been despised by a Beethoven, a Van Gogh, or a Kafka. So far no one has ever set forth the motives for their behaviors with any conviction.[99]

It was, again, the Nietzschean artist-hero, disdainful of the public and driven only by personal vision, that Hodeir meant to laud—or rather, it was the absence of these heroes in jazz that he once again set out to bemoan. In *Arts* and then *Toward Jazz*, major figures like Duke Ellington and minor ones like Trummy Young were brutalized in the service of a single goal, to show the jazz musician forever unable to reach the level of overman because forever content to revisit past glories, the improvised hardening into the routine, the demanding softening into the servile. As we will shortly see, this was influential writing, and the ideas Hodeir expressed were soon taken up by other jazz critics.

Read in *Toward Jazz*, these articles are bitter, vituperative. But it's crucial to consider this writing in the context in which it was first designed to appear. Across French cultural discourses, all serious creative forms were periodically beset by what were usually called "crises" (popular forms, by contrast, didn't face such problems: they were easy, after-work solutions). The 1950s pages of *Arts* and other journals are thus fraught with worry—over French theater, French cinema, the disc, television—such angst sometimes too transparently manufactured in the interests of copy. Jazz's tentative entry to this level of discourse had come in an August 1954 issue of the journal, in which Frank Ténot and Hess engaged in a full-page debate as to whether jazz was still a "un art nègre."[100] Not quite constituting a fully fledged crisis, that debate appeared under the page heading "Problèmes"—the word, of course, also appearing that year in the French title of Hodeir's first book, similarly intended to raise the level and importance of jazz critical discourse. Hodeir's subsequent work for the journal, characterized by its sourly gleeful rejection of those popularly taken to be jazz's "greats," aimed to clear a space for jazz in a wider critical culture in which an art form was not vital—was not really an art form—if it was not in a state of uproar; in a cultural world in which the film criticism of François Truffaut and the musical polemics of Boulez castigated establishment artists and demanded the total remaking of their creative fields, meek critical applause was hardly the order of the day.

This, then, was not so much a moment of high-cultural arrival for jazz as it was of high anxiety. At the moment of the music's greatest popularity, modern jazz's French critics, following Hodeir, would become preoccupied with the concern that formerly innovative artists, faced with large audiences clamoring for their favorites, could not continue to develop according to their own ideas. The arts, artists, progressed continually, while popular forms, popular entertainers, did not. Which was jazz, and what path would its musicians take? No one was more subjected to this question in the French critical discourse than the musician who had become a symbol of all that was forward looking, Thelonious Monk. Because Monk was a figure of such importance, scrutiny of his work was intense, and the next part of the chapter is similarly forensic: in examining Monk's reception and his music in close detail, we see how an idea of improvisation's simulation, presented as innovative in Hodeir's composition, could play quite the opposite role in the French reception of an African American musician.

Thelonious Monk Meets the French Critics

In 1954 Thelonious Monk traveled to Europe for the first time to appear at Paris's third Salon du jazz. During those concerts Monk's strange playing and stage manner made little impression beyond bafflement, but over the next few years the American's French reputation was won—in his absence—through imported records and sober magazine discussion.[101] The pianist became a figure of fascination in French modern jazz circles, and when he returned to the country, as he did almost annually from 1961 onwards, it was accompanied by great fervor. Once they had been converted, what most intrigued the critics of *Jazz hot* and *Jazz magazine* was Monk's distance from the instrumental and rhetorical fluidity that had characterized modern jazz. "Only in Monk's music do asymmetry and discontinuity enhance one another," Hodeir wrote approvingly in a celebrated *Jazz hot* appreciation of 1959; it was because of this anti-beauty, Hodeir suggested, the pianist was "to be hailed as the first jazzman who has had a feeling for specifically modern aesthetic values."[102]

Yet in France as elsewhere, Monk's day in the critical sun was all too short. The concern that the pianist's music was becoming routine, first voiced in the United States at the very end of the 1950s, grew the world over as the 1960s progressed.[103] Most jazz writers expressed their weariness in workaday terms, but in France the problem would be philosophized and incorporated into the debate we have seen ongoing, around the nature of jazz as art (or entertainment), as related (or not) to the established cultural canons; even after Monk had become the subject of great French critical praise, he had not escaped the strictures of progress and evolution so dear to the modernist critics, and he still formed a figure in the critical rhetoric that routinely, frowningly situated present success in a context to come. Hodeir's *Arts* writing on the ossification of the jazz great loomed large in this work: "[t]oday more than ever shines a light in Monk," wrote Raymond Mouly at the end of glowing 1961 concert review, "a light without which jazz is only rhetoric or chore. How much longer will this giant who consumes himself permit it to shine?"[104]

The prophesy began to fulfill itself. Michel Delorme, at Paris's Alhambra Theatre to cover one of Monk's February 1964 concerts for *Jazz hot*, had canvassed audience opinions after the performance: "It was bad, wasn't it?," asked one. "Monk has gentrified himself," said another. "Have you noticed he never takes risks any more?"[105] Delorme finished his article by suggesting that Monk visit France less often. The following year, Claude Lenissois had previewed Monk's forthcoming French tour in *Jazz hot* with a reflection on those poorly received performances; revisiting the crisis, and echoing Hodeir's earlier writing, the writer placed Monk's work in a cross-cultural, cross-continental *longue durée*. "Will Monk always be able to renew himself?," Lenissois asked.

> Even if he may disappoint the public, the artist must not be afraid to surprise, only to repeat; experience proves that we pardon error much quicker than complacency. Examples aren't rare. Debussy always refused to give what we expected of him; after *Pelléas*, *La Mer*, and after *La Mer*, *Jeux*. Erik Satie noted, when he became aware that his *Princesse Maleine* would repeat *Pelléas*: "Nothing more to find here. Find other things." Rimbaud preferred to disappear rather than to outlive work he couldn't surpass.[106]

Monk, wrote Lenissois, was subject to this problem as much as any of these great French artists, and it was at this moment—at which, after years of difficulty, the pianist had finally won a large critical and public following—that the danger of ossification would be most acute. These concerns were not confined to Monk, but increasingly applied to bebop in general: in the pages of the mid-1960s jazz press, both critics and fans occasionally but performatively advertised their boredom with even the best hard bop musicians, Art Blakey, Sonny Rollins, Max Roach, Freddie Hubbard and others coming in for such treatment.[107]

Lenissois's artist—one he could only envisage after a decade of critical work in which jazz was interpreted by way of the European genius—would surprise the public even if it meant disappointing them, striking a Romantic-modernist pose radically at odds with that of the entertainer, American or European. "The concerts of two years ago remain unforgettable," wrote the critic in 1965. "Yet the reform [of 1964] was too minimal for the risks run to be profitable."[108] His years of struggle finally rewarded by the international tour and the concert hall, Monk was caught between profitable routine and profitable risk, subjected to demands to reshape his composition and improvisation for every next season, asked constantly to push forwards. But this was not the only direction in which his music faced, and, to fully force open this rupture between Monk's practice and French critical attitudes towards progress and repetition, it's instructive to focus on Michel-Claude's Jalard's sophisticated, nuanced, but problematic 1964 *Jazz magazine* critique of the pianist.

"Certain artists accommodate themselves to routine," wrote Jalard, in the early 1960s one of that journal's most stylistically ambitious young critics. "There comes a moment when their art seems to have made all its choices and fixed all its strategies."[109] Writing in the wake of Monk's 1964 Paris concerts, Jalard listed Armstrong, Clayton, Basie, Hawkins, Ellington and Gillespie as players whose music, though improvised, was by this time so fixed, so secure, that on stage they had simply to "entrust" themselves to their own styles. But such a strategy, Jalard argued, was not available to Monk, "because his style is, in its very essence, insecurity, and for him to reiterate is to negate the style." "Let me explain," the writer continued, before launching into the kind of prose that could only have appeared in a French jazz journal.

> If there is a logic to the Monk style, it is a logic of challenge and dispute, not of discourse—by which I mean rhetorical affirmation, narrative improvisation. Monk's silences are real silences, Monk's sounds are real sounds, not relational elements that organize into a language. This truth diverts Monk from the fictional that applies to all languages, and ceaselessly reintroduces him into the instant, into history; it forces him to throw the dice, and as soon as he gathers them up, to throw again.[110]

Monk's genius, Jalard went on, had always lain in the pianist's resistance to the musical gesture or expression that would "degrade," or had already degraded, into a sign of itself, or to rhetoric: in Jalard's estimation, Monk had never been a player to rely on the learned, and it was this spontaneity that accounted for the pianist's "lived poetic of sound."[111] Jalard's Monk did not merely progress through a piece by dutifully spelling out its formal scheme—by which he meant the underlying chord progression—articulating faithfully every passing chord as did a bebop musician like Bud Powell. On the contrary, Monk's improvisation had been defined by its attempt to resist the formal scheme, an attempt bound to passing success (as Monk ignored one chord, revised another, imposed a harmonically foreign cluster upon the next) but ultimate failure, as the cycle of chords was never really departed from, only defaced; in this way, Jalard wrote, the underlying form would be "constantly affirmed by its constant refusal," rendering Monk's a "poetry of affirmation-negation, which is constituted in the instant, and which the instant constitutes."[112] This poetry was antithetical to cliché, preconception, routine.

> [I]f there is a routine of expression, there cannot be, by definition, a routine of refusal, only its simulacrum. The simulacrum is not a repetition. In a certain manner, it is even repetition's opposite: it's a fraudulent repetition, which articulates the opposite of that which it suggests. In his recent concerts, Monk was content to rely upon memories of past improvisations: this meant that he renounced his lived poetic of sound, which defines his creativity.[113]

The Paris appearances of February 1964—in which, as Jalard suggested and recordings confirm, Monk performed with uncommon fluency—had not only marked the moment of crisis, long foretold, in which the pianist's music would cease to move towards the future; worse, Jalard argued, they signified a betrayal of what Monk had played in the past.

> He presented us with something resembling himself which differed radically from that which he was actually doing: such is the simulacrum. To achieve this simulacrum, he used a pseudo-language constituted of memory and habit, turning away from this lived protest that is the essence of his art: such is the disowning.[114]

Here was an idea with a history stretching back to Plato, and one about to be revivified by a generation of theorists living in a world newly inundated with media images. The simulacrum had been an important figure to the French painter and writer Pierre Klossowski (indeed Jalard's piece may have been influenced by Klossowski's 1963 *Critique* article on the concept in Georges Bataille's work); it would be taken up in 1967 by Gilles Deleuze.[115] But it was Jean Baudrillard who, in the 1970s, would become the theorist most identified with the idea, and it is the moralistic perspective of Baudrillard's slightly later reading that, even if gently anachronistic, best illuminates what lies beneath the jazz critic's philosophical speculation and modernist language: not just a judgment of taste, but a profound aesthetic, even ethical insecurity.

Just as for those other theorists, for Baudrillard the simulacrum is no imitation: instead it is a machine that perfectly describes "reality" but at the same time "short-circuits all its vicissitudes."[116] Likewise, for Jalard, Monk did not feign improvisation, but presented a sign of improvisation that was ontologically distinguishable from the actually improvised only in that it removed from the process risk and therefore failure—a failure that was paradoxically constitutive of the practice's authentic contingency and imputed "success"—and instead merely presented that process's previous successful results.[117]

So, as Baudrillard writes, while *imitation* "leaves the reality principle intact"—reality (truth) and pretense (imitation) maintaining their oppositional relationship—*simulation* replaces reality with a sign of itself. To feign an illness is to pretend that the illness exists, but if, in simulating an illness, a person brings about the illness's actual symptoms, it makes no sense to ask whether the illness is real or not.[118] "What can medicine do," Baudrillard asked, "with something which floats on either side of illness, on either side of health, or with the reduplication of illness in a discourse that is no longer true or false?"[119] In this case the "medicine" is criticism, the "discourse," improvisation: Jalard's concern seems to be not only that an inauthentic Monk was feigning for his audience the creative condition of the improviser, but also, results remaining the same yet the processes giving rise to it entirely transformed, that Monk's music had become something about which the distinction between authentic and inauthentic was no longer meaningful.

As has been glimpsed already, this insecurity in the face of the supposed simulacrum was not new among jazz's French observers, such being the symptom of a new proximity to the music in "real" life—as opposed to its recorded, imported, idealized icon form. For some years, modernist-minded French jazz critics had looked up to distant stars, awestruck by their improvisations as long as they were transmitted by radio and phonograph—an image of assumedly improvised creation—only to be disappointed when, later, with the stars before their very eyes, music emerged from the jazzmen's horns the same old scratched phonographic copy. In 1948, Boris Vian wrote of hearing Louis Armstrong in Nice: "Last night was a triumph for him, tonight will be another. You cannot really find fault with Louis. He is the same Louis you hear on record. In fact you sometimes have the impression that his records are playing, not him." Vian related these reservations to one of Mezz Mezzrow's sidemen, Jimmy Archey, the musician in response yanking down the curtain to reveal magical improvisation's mechanical workings, all bulbs, levers and trapdoors to be called on for effect: "He said to me: 'Of course! This is the road, you want to be sure.'"[120] The improviser's art was rejected in the name of the touring showman's routine.

Certainty, fixity, the absence of the idea: these were anathema to the French jazz critics who had supposed jazz's verity and value were guaranteed by the authentic presence of musical thinking in the moment. Vian's 1940s criticisms of Armstrong, and Jalard's 1960s concerns over Monk, suggest that this wasn't simple disappointment, a case of visiting heroes failing to live up to their earlier standards; instead, these critics forecast the deep cultural malaise found in Baudrillard, a writer who would come to see a modern world saturated with simulacra as a place in which truth of meaning, reliant upon now-extinguished difference, was a void concept. How could those listeners who had valued jazz for its unique access to authentic meaning—what they had believed to be the "truth" of improvisation, the idea realized as it was conceived—continue to comprehend, enjoy or believe in a music that had turned out to be full of inauthentic meaninglessness, of creative realization in the absence of creative impulse?

The improvised vitality and directness of jazz had seemed to so many European writers like the antidote to the played-out Western classics. And yet, as we will see, this understanding of what authentic jazz improvisation should have been—of the remedy—was formulated according to precisely those classics, to the illness itself. These worries over authenticity and the simulacrum were not born with Jalard's writing, or even Vian's. Instead, they formed the central concern of Western classical music practice, one that began to make an appearance in writing on jazz as the modernist critics continued to claim for their music the status of an art.

Werktreue/Manntreue

The figure of the simulacrum circulated on the pages of a philosophical literature and the French jazz press, but it was an idea that had in this instance been inspired by a staged spectacle and had been glimpsed inhabiting an actual body: Monk's body, one which announced its interposition between musical idea and execution with sometimes disturbing vehemence. The English writer Raymond Horrocks had reported on the first of Monk's 1954 Paris concerts for *Jazz Monthly*.

> Fingers poised stiffly, stabbing rather than touching the keys, legs thrashing wildly beneath the piano, searching for the pedal, missing it, banging the floor, body swaying, grunting audibly, arms stretch-

ing and bending as he felt for unusual chords, all but disguising the theme . . . he struck chords with his elbow, and at one point thrust his hand into the piano and flicked hammers onto the strings. Flash bulbs exploded.[121]

In African American aesthetic tradition, the performer's bodily attitude has often been regarded as all-important in the fulfillment, or else the denial, of the performed musical authentic. But more rarely acknowledged is that the same has always been at least true of Romantic-modernist European aesthetics, the system to which Jalard and his colleagues were (unknowingly) in thrall. The "French School" of pianism, for instance, stretching back to the performers and teachers of the mid-19th century, held technique and execution to be all, and deemed "interpretation" taboo; the school's adherents were characterized by their *jeu perlé*, the "play of pearls" that was identified, Charles Timbrell has written, by "rapid, clean, even passagework in which each note [was] bright and perfectly formed, like each pearl on a necklace."[122] In the service of such technique the French School pedagogues proscribed any movement of the wrist, elbow, shoulder or torso (exactly those movements that would distinguish Monk's playing). For them, the body was to be as unbodylike as possible, as unremarkable as possible, the fingers functioning not as the limits of the body but as the conduit between ideal music and its real sounding.

But that stood for an entire modern Western art music tradition, this being the central problem for performers beholden to the dominant Romantic notion of *Werktreue*, fidelity to the work. This ideal doomed all performances to at least partial failure, as the pianist Artur Schnabel described: Schnabel, like all performers and aestheticians of his tradition ranking the composition supreme and its performance merely derivative, gave the performer the goal to "become one with the music," a goal that would be achieved when an inner picture of ideal music coincided, if only momentarily, with its ideal execution, when "the conception materializes and the materialization redissolves into conception."[123] In the same way another great pianist of the age, Sviatoslav Richter, disparaged those performers who would "contaminate" a work with their own personality, rather than, again, "dissolving" into the piece; "[i]f he's talented," Richter argued, the performer "allows us to glimpse the truth of the work that is in itself a thing of genius." But this could happen only when the musician performed "*all* the performance markings," carried out "the composer's intentions to the letter"—because this truth, this thing of genius, was to be accessed via the score and the score alone.[124] Absent music, then, would be made present only when the present performer achieved bodily absence, and the score was opened like a door to another world: the séance beginning, the concert pianist would lay his lifeless hands in front of him and wait for contact; the real and the spectral would swap places at the piano bench; the music would appear.[125]

There was no need for Monk's French critics and listeners to be adepts of either French School pianism or Romantic-Platonic philosophy in order to have themselves been formed by the culture of composer veneration to which these traditions gave rise. After all, for those thinkers in jazz aesthetics sufficiently removed from this world of composers and their scores—and Michel-Claude Jalard was certainly one—it was a performance's *distance* from a composed or recorded original that was to be celebrated, and that spoke of a music-spirit summoned; it was the *visibility* of the performer's body, achieving music however and through whatever gesture the sound might arrive, that was the guarantor of jazz's own truth. Jalard's "lived poetic of sound" was one formulation of the idea that, to a great extent, the personal, charismatic jazz touch vouchsafed the presence of the authentic spirit: Western art music *Werktreue*, fidelity to the work, was countered by the African American "Manntreue," fidelity to the person.[126]

Monk would have concurred. "Technique," the pianist deadpanned to the British critic Les Tomkins in 1965, "is a very technical word," and if the technical was the standard, the universal, there was little of that about Monk's playing.[127] "I don't think anyone can imitate me," the pianist told François Postif in Paris, 1963. "Because I have my own way of putting my fingers on the piano, of making it sound, of leaning my body to one side or the other to get this or that effect . . . it's those kinds of things that make you inimitable."[128] But if in the mid-1960s Jalard was concerned that Monk had resorted to presenting the simulacrum of past improvisations, it was precisely the absence of such idiosyncrasy—and the presence of a spectral performer newly skilled in the classical style— that proved to the writer that he had a case.

> It's not surprising that, in the shadow of an absent Monk, there appeared a Monk more of a pianist he ever had been. It wasn't Monk who was playing, but Thelonious who played Monk.[129]

A year previously, Postif, perhaps giving voice to the disquiet of those other Parisian critics, had asked Monk if he was always improvising when he played. "Have you ever seen any scores on my piano?," Monk responded rhetorically, and—since he was being accused of organizing his music into writing in memory rather than on paper—not a little disingenuously.[130]

At first these classical and jazz ideals of mid-20th century Europe seem opposed. But if Monk's modernist French critics—those so concerned with "evolution" and "progress," equipped with a clear teleology of past, present and future—were asking how much Monk was improvising, or else how much he had become something like a concert pianist, it was because while claiming for jazz a kind of art music prestige they nevertheless understood jazz improvisational practice as the pure negative of classical "recital": while the classical ideal found authentic music arriving from the past when the performing body disappeared, the jazz ideal found authentic music arriving from the future when the performing body was most present. Yet despite their differences—or rather, because one was the negative image of the other, the *Werktreue* and the *Manntreue*—these ideals shared an excluded, or perhaps merely repressed, middle: the entertainer's routine, that simulacrum of authentic musical presence that was so thoughtlessly reproducible from place to place and occasion to occasion.

This local construal of jazz as an inversion of the cultivated Western form interpreted one style by way of the conceptual system of another. That maneuver, characteristic of many encounters across cultures, had not always been problematic; as we have seen, it had also heralded a new attitude on the part of Europeans willing their society to take seriously the music of African Americans. Yet the uneasiness displayed by French writers like Jalard in the face of the mid-'6os Monk betrayed a growing realization that this operation had not been fully successful, that Monk, transplanted into the Western art music body, was being rejected, the pianist found incompatible with the system's requirements. In 1963, Lucien Malson could thunder that Monk had "crushed the argument of those who, judging as they have been conditioned and being proud of their limits"—he meant Panassié—"confine jazz to the domain of entertainment [l'art de distraction]."[131] But their renewed worries over the pianist suggest that the modernist critics who had been formed by bitter squabbles over jazz's status may have begun to think that, in Monk's case as in many others, they may after all have been dealing with a trouper and his act.[132]

If this giant was, in fact, all routine, then the reactionary Panassié would have been proved right: jazz was an entertainment. But more than that, if Monk was a simple entertainer, then those secure structures of modernist dogma around which the critics had modeled the pianist—artistic truth, value, progress—would have started to crumble. Beyond judgments of taste, a much wider system of both personal and cultural self-beliefs was at risk.

But how far was Monk still improvising, and how much was composition, entertainer's routine? However florid Jalard's rhetorical performance, his application of the idea of simulacrum brought a new dimension to the critical problem of repetition in jazz. And yet, as we have already seen with Hodeir's work, this debate was not only the province of writers working with words but also that of musicians working with sound: Monk, too, was saying something new about composition, improvisation and the nature of jazz as art and entertainment. To find out what, we will return to Paris along with the pianist for the first concert of his 1966 European tour.

"Lulu's Back in Town"

"We are in the wings of the Mutualité," says the TV announcer to those watching at home on Friday, March 18, "awaiting the arrival of the Thelonious Monk quartet for what is indeed the artistic event of the evening."[133] The transmission recording shows a hall full of cameras, listeners and journalists, one of whom would in his write-up comment on the striking presence of the Monkish jazz body: "Monk played extremely well this evening, insensible of the crowd and of his accompanists, striking sometimes his fingers, sometimes his hands and sometimes his elbows against the piano in the course of an hallucination that his eyes no longer betrayed."[134]

The band begin to amble through the opening measures of its first piece, "Lulu's Back in Town," a 1935 composition of Harry Warren and Al Dubin's; this was the first time the group had been captured playing the song in concert, though Monk had in 1964 recorded the piece in the studio with most of the musicians present here (Charlie Rouse, tenor saxophone, Larry Gales, bass, Ben Riley, drums).[135] The song's already concise AABA form is rendered short-winded by the chord substitutions Monk is using, which pit the melody's descending chromatic line against another kind of chromaticism, a jagged crop of harmonic ground that is several times encircled. While the throng is still wandering into the hall, Monk sits rigid at the piano, his posture so different from the concert pianist's relaxed suppleness—if those players stroke the piano and seem to want to melt into it, to become both instrument and music, Monk

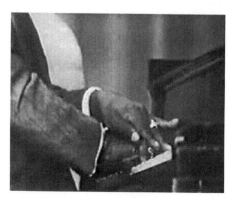

prods and pulls at each key as if to dramatize a tussle between body and sound. The TV cameraman fixes upon Monk's accompaniment of Charlie Rouse's melody, the pianist's elbows flayed out as he jabs the chords, his left hand—or rather two or three fingers of his left hand, the index and the middle especially, the middle sometimes curling underneath the index—stamping out the bass notes of chords spread over two or three octaves. But Monk does not limit the left hand's territory to the left side of the keyboard, and as Rouse begins his solo, Monk has his left hand (or again, a couple of fingers of his left hand) pounding out high notes while his right arm crosses under to voice the rest of the chord.

This crossed-hand passage lasts a few bars, concluding with a rat-tat-tat figure punched at hard, at which point Monk withdraws his arms and with his left hand twists the enormous ring on his right's little finger so that the stone is again facing upwards. Everything seems contingent, of the moment: the desire to touch the keyboard with a certain force—jewelry knocked out of place by exertion—actions conceived as they are executed. After a chorus of this, Monk stands, surely surprising some of his audience, and moves away from the piano, beginning to dance, shifting from foot to foot, describing a circle, looking at Rouse while the saxophonist solos; Rouse plays his last phrase, and Monk jumps back onto the bench to begin his own statement. There the film of this Friday performance ends.

But touring Europe over the course of April, the band would play "Lulu's Back in Town" almost every night, and transcriptions of Monk's playing on various recordings of the song—performances caught in Oslo, Copenhagen and Manchester, as well at a second Paris concert—allow us to turn the music into a sign of itself. Whatever the limits of musical transcription, this allows us to see whether, as Jalard charged, Monk had already done the same, and to identify more precisely the division between what the French critics thought progressive improvisation and regressive repetition.[136]

Jalard's ideal Monk made music out of "real" sounds and silences, these resulting from the pianist's every "throw of the dice," and the bodily drama shown in written reports and film of the Friday Paris concert might suggest as much. Yet this ideal improviser would have been hard-pressed to live his nightly performances in such free fall; Jalard's complaint that Monk had, in 1964, allowed his playing to degrade to a "pseudo-language constituted of memory and habit" might seem to demonstrate a naivety towards not only the real demands placed on Monk's creativity by a career on the road, but also towards the way that jazz worked.

Whatever the apparent spontaneity of each performance, comparison of multiple performances reveals music that, seeming to be conceived as it is executed, is in fact far from the magical plucking of notes "out of thin air," as Paul Berliner has described common perceptions of jazz improvisation.[137] Jalard apart, perhaps, no one familiar with jazz practice and pedagogy would have expected Monk's 1966 performances of "Lulu" to show anything else: like all jazz improvisers of his stylistic

Pathways

© 1935 M. Witmark & Sons. Reprinted by permission of Alfred Music and Hal Leonard Corporation.

period (and most after), the pianist's playing is indeed supported by a pseudo-language of memory and habit, one that refracts a piece's harmonic form (rather that "negating" that form, as Jalard would have it). So in chorus after chorus of solo after solo, Monk approaches the jagged chromatic crop of harmonic terrain shown here—bars 2-3, 10-11 and 26-27 of each chorus, where that ground drops from E7 to E♭7 to D♭7 (and similarly in bars 4-5, 12-13 and 28-29, where the E7-E♭7 leads to A♭6)—and finds before him a number of paths that over time have been cleared through a thicket of possibilities.[138]

The similarity of the strategies Monk employs in this patch of terrain leap out: the melodic curve and note choices used to traverse the D♭7-B7 chord change, the chromatically falling thirds in the next bar, the characteristic whole tone run that sometimes follows, along with a number of other details of chord voicing and voice leading.

This is post-bebop jazz improvisation. But maybe we are looking at a symptom of Jalard's problem: we can't tell "real" improvisation from its simulacrum because jazz effaces that distinction—a distinction the modernist critics relied upon to validate their tastes and values. Nothing here is an "original," nothing a "copy," because those object concepts are not the right ones to describe what is a practice rather than a thing. Each moment shown here describes the retaking of a certain path, constituted not just in or of the moment but by a fast rewind that goes outside the solo (if there is an "outside the solo"), back through all Monk's previous performances of "Lulu," all his years of articulating chromatically descending seventh chords at the piano. Transcription, the reduction to sign—by analyst on the page or musician in the mind—finds Monk's improvisation existing between new and old, and that, finally, seems to be Jalard's worry. The impossibility of isolating an original or its copy, a difficulty precisely constitutive of both improvisation and of the simulacrum, renders Monk's playing—might render *all* jazz improvisation—the summary presentation of a learning and performing process that has taken place before. A simulacrum if one wants to call it that, standard jazz procedure if one doesn't: but, formed by their now-inverted classical ideals, grasping for an as-yet nonexistent critical vocabulary to describe a half-understood music, looking for the authentic unheard rather than the routine replayed—and taking pleasure in their own, creative intellectual conceits—a modernist French writer like Jalard would be apt to seize upon the former.

Yet these paths of Monk's are not simulacra in the sense of repetitions mechanically reproduced, because they present themselves as possible routes for movement across this or that bar, not as images of that movement as once and ever-more carried out. And transcription reveals Monk's playing as undecided at a subtler level, not one of "material" as such, but of execution. Any observer of Monk's Friday night concert at the Mutualité also present on Sunday at the Maison de l'ORTF concert would have seen the band twice opening with "Lulu," Rouse twice opening the solos, Monk twice accompanying the saxophonist's first chorus with the long sequence of dense chords stamped out cross-handed; a fast-forward to the performance of April 15, filmed in Oslo, and to that of April 17, filmed in Copenhagen, catches exactly the same routine in progress. Monk's cross-handed gesture seems like a showman's attention-grabbing gimmick, and no doubt that was part of its appeal. But however often repeated, it also seems like a technique calculated to produce an element of incalculation, the movement to jab at the high register with bunched middle fingers of the left hand apparently designed to produce a hard, splashing sound, the somewhat approximate percussiveness of which was evidently valued over fully previsioned pitch "control."[139] What a contrast, technical and ideological, with the *jeu perlé*: Monk's gesture allows an element of sonic indeterminacy, fingers and sound (and jewelry) to an extent doing what they will, a lived poetic indeed.

In fact, indeterminacy abounds. Monk's method of attacking the keyboard from high above, fingers flat, ensures that notes are often struck not in isolation but along with their neighbors, giving the bare, blunt major seconds and the sharp semitonal clusters that are always cited as characterizing Monk's harmonic approach. The presumably intended—those second-heavy voicings so often present in the same form—merges into the presumably unintended, as in the opening bars of Monk's solo on "Lulu" at Manchester, a month after the Paris concerts, in which the

Major seconds

© 1935 M. Witmark & Sons. Reprinted by permission of Alfred Music and Hal Leonard Corporation.

right hand's seconds, seemingly arriving in error, are of a piece with those of the left hand, a series of jabs seemingly purposeful in both their harmonic function and their being placed in series (but who knows).

The indeterminate nature of the practice makes a fully determined interpretation impossible, but this passage, and the examples below, strongly suggests that in Monk's playing, certain "mistakes"—notes aimed at and missed, or neighboring notes accidentally hit—come to be indivisible from the successes, the "wrong" not always "different" from the right.[140] The peculiarities of Monk's flat-fingered technique produce a dissonant result which is nevertheless in consonance with his style as a whole.[141]

Whatever Jalard had feared in 1964, two years later the lived poetic of sound, that technique in which the sounds Monk produced were unpredictable from moment to moment, still flourished. Not only that: it was the very nature of this poetic technique of Monk's that the improvised (the truly unforeseen) and the re-presented (the elements of a vocabulary) were not fully distinguishable. Examined close up, Monk's playing does not merely show how untenable is the opposition of simulacrum and poetic, or, recast in terms other than Jalard's, of the inauthentic routine and the authentically improvised; instead, it shows that the pianist delights in the collapse of one into the other.

And this collapse also comes to envelop and efface the boundary between composition and improvised performance, text and context. In these performances of "Lulu," Jalard's "reduction to language" certainly does exist in the form of concretized clichés, licks—fragments not unique to "Lulu"'s form, not appearing here alone—which Monk uses in something like bebop's usual constructivist style, forming from them lines or cadences.[142] But in several performances during the tour, of "Lulu" and of other pieces—indeed, in his playing in general by this time—Monk will at some point interpolate licks that have been so expanded that they appear not to link ideas, or cross from chord to chord or bar to bar, but to function instead as blocks of "composed" music dropped into an otherwise "improvised" solo. These blocks are associated with, and their appearance essentially limited to, particular pieces in the pianist's repertoire. Monk's tendency towards this quasi-textualization had begun some time earlier: privately made recordings show some of the central songs in Monk's small performance repertoire beginning to attract their own distinct "textual" solo elements in the late 1950s.[143]

Still, by the mid-'60s, this practice of Monk's had become more formalized. Performing "Lulu," Monk visits these blocks like landmarks on

Opening melody paraphrase

Bridge paraphrase

Sixteenth note sequence

Melody quotation

© 1935 M. Witmark & Sons. Reprinted by permission of Alfred Music and Hal Leonard Corporation.

the way from one end of the solo to another and generally in the same order: from an opening loose paraphrase of the melody, the pianist progresses through paraphrases of the tune at the bridge, to a sixteenth note sequence, to statements of the melody in octaves. If those pathways of Monk's hover between the fluid and the fixed, then this imposition of form at the larger scale would seem to show an "improvised" process more firmly set.

Paris, 8'02"

Oslo, 5'27"

Copenhagen, 7'18"

Manchester, 6'51"

Opening of crossed-hands chorus

The space for improvisation is now drastically limited, with only the A sections of each chorus left free for the non-"textual," every bridge of every chorus of every solo marking a return to the original melody, in the old manner—the same manner in which Monk had recently treated two more songs associated with Fats Waller, "Dinah" and "I'm Confessin'," on the recording that marked Monk's full (re)submersion into this stride tradition, *Solo Monk*.[144] And each solo on "Lulu" ends with what sounds like a piano reduction of a big-band shout chorus, this the crossed-hands passage that also functions, on every occasion, as Monk's single chorus of accompaniment for Rouse before he stands to dance.

Jalard had complained about Monk's apparently newfound melos, those preconceived lines that simulated spontaneity. But for Monk these blocks are evidently conceived as both solo materials *and* materials strongly imbued with "Lulu"'s textual identity—they are not used outside that context—and so stand as neither "composition" nor "improvisation" as such. Multiple recordings of other songs played on the tour show something like this to be the case across the pianist's repertoire. If there is any "simulation" in this method it's one of period style, because what characterizes Monk's use of these blocks in "Lulu" is an antique attitude: these are repetitive, "textualized" statements of fragments themselves often repetitious, an image of the stride practice of pianists like Fats Waller, Willie "The Lion" Smith and James P. Johnson, in which such fragments would be chained together at speed, glinting over a deep, dark left hand continuously leaping from bass note to chord.

Monk's attraction to that pianistic tradition was well known by 1966. Listeners and critics, especially in France, would not generally have been aware that the young Monk had studied stride with a teacher in his neighborhood and had learned part of his craft at private jams and cutting contests with Johnson and Smith among others.[145] Yet as early as 1948 a *Down Beat* reviewer had bemusedly noted the Waller-like left-hand passages in his Blue Note recording of "Thelonious."[146] And though the solo recordings Monk made in Paris in 1954 do not betray the influence of players like Waller, Smith, Johnson and Herman Chittison, by the time he made *Thelonious Alone* in 1959, the style, or Monk's version of it, had begun to creep gingerly back into the pianist's playing;[147] in the years immediately preceding the stride-filled 1965 release *Solo Monk*, the pianist had performed full-blown solo stride pieces in live and TV performance, both in the United States and Europe.[148]

But for the most part, Monk was playing in a group setting and a post-bebop style, and those modern formal conventions had obscured the extent to which Monk's music was, by the mid-1960s, shaped by the old. Twenty years previously Monk had reported to Billy Taylor that he liked the idea of a music that would be formed of bebop and stride at the same time.[149] But it seems not to have been until much later that Monk's "bebop" playing fully took on the radical constructive repetition of the stride pianists' music, in which those chains of fragments occupied two-, four- and eight-bar blocks, each strain sectioned off from the next. Again, this was an amplification of tendencies always partially audible rather than a break of any sort—similar sectioning off can be heard in Monk's solo on his 1947 "In Walked Bud"—yet in these 1966 performances of "Lulu," Monk enunciates and differentiates these divisions with total clarity, conceiving and executing his solo as a series of eight-bar statements. The A, A, B and A of each chorus are generally kept separate by single bars of silence or by sharp affective, textural or textual distinctions, as was de rigueur for the stride pianist; turnarounds are rarely exploited, choruses and ideas rarely linked, tessitura never traversed as was de rigueur for the bebopper.

Indeed the music of Johnson and Waller is in some ways the text for Monk's recitals of the piece, both live and in the 1964 studio version, which Monk opens with three minutes of solo stride that layer the comic and the serious just as they layer the jumping bass and (very Johnsonian) metrical reshapings of "Lulu"'s melody;[150] comedy and stride apart, present in both Monk and the elder pianists' playing are extended, tinkling high passages, crisp dotted-eighth swing, blue note appoggiaturas in right-hand chords, and, most of all, the entertainers' reluctance to depart from the original melody for long.[151] All of these things had, in "evolutionary" terms, been essentially redundant since the early 1940s and so could be confusing to the modernist critics of the '60s; "[w]hen you improvise, why do you stay close to the theme?," Monk was asked in Paris in 1964. "That way I know what I'm playing!," the pianist responded, or sidestepped, but his true purpose may be better explained by Waller, who once recalled what Johnson had taught him in the 1920s about how to be an improvising entertainer (and an entertaining improviser): "[y]ou got to hang on to the melody and never let it get boresome."[152] Robin D. G. Kelley's Monk biography has numerous instances of Monk guiding his band members along the same lines, chiding them for improvising on chords rather than songs, for thinking harmonically rather than melodically.[153]

By 1966, then, Monk had incorporated into his practice a fuller kind of "textual" fixity. In a way, the spatial divisions and textual references in play on "Lulu," a return to earlier jazz principles of structure and purpose, only emphasized Monk's original resistance to melos and rhetoric, that discontinuity that Jalard had heralded in 1960 and eulogized in 1964. But Jalard's ideal Monk replaced bebop's discourse, or rather discursive simulacrum, with a lived poetic of sounds, sounds that were found in the moment; indeterminacy apart, this actual, disdained Monk had come to replace that discourse, not with more authentic improvisation, but with more "text." The effect of discontinuity had been recovered, but the method that had led to its realization was further from improvisation, from the "negation" of the form, than ever before; and it was Jalard's distrusted, routining jazz entertainer—the brother of Artur Schnabel's interpreting classical phony—who had taken center stage. The Monk caught on recordings playing "Lulu" during March and April 1966 is one radically at odds with the searching, idealized artist figure Claude Lenissois and others wished Monk to be, one like Debussy or Satie or another canonic Frenchman; "even if he may disappoint the public," Lenissois had written, "the artist must not be afraid to surprise, only to repeat," and though Monk may have been disappointing audiences and critics—and increasingly he was—it was not by being ahead of the times, nor by being stuck in an eternally repeating procession of simulacra as Jalard had feared, but by being behind them, by letting old-fashioned reiteration appear as the central figure of his performance rather than as surprise's intermittent failure.

The critics were at least partly wrong, and Monk had in some ways "renewed" his playing: now more than ever, and even playing in the post-bebop manner, the structural concerns of a premodernist style shone through. If Monk, the bebop line player of 1964, had presented what was seen as the simulacrum of improvisation because that's how the learning and performance of the style worked, then—whatever the critics may have thought—he surely escaped that modernist figure when bebop notions of "line" were abandoned, and with them the unidirectional development and stylistic teleology so fetishized by the neophile French critics; Monk escaped the modernist simulacrum when he embraced, via Waller, Johnson and the rest, another concept, that "repetition" which James A. Snead famously claims as the central figure of African American cultural countermodernity, an unraveling of the grand, progressive narrative.[154]

Playing "Lulu," Monk shows himself to be neither the idealized improviser the modernist French critics wanted him to be nor the idealized, simulating concert pianist Jalard accused him of becoming. Instead he is something closer to an improviser-interpreter, or a recomposer-performer, a musician for whom finding the absolutely "new" is distantly secondary to another aim: the reworking and rearticulating, more or less animated as the mood dictates, of a limited number of materials, in a limited improvisational space, in a limited textual repertoire. Indeed, the ambiguities Monk finds between composition and improvisation, the present and absent, historical and contemporary, serious and ironic, articulate a profound relativism that stands against the "ideal" and the "authentic" in whatever form. Whichever type of material Monk is exploiting—from the more evidently improvised to the more evidently textual—no hierarchy of meaning or value between the types is ever evident; the meanings (and soundings) of Monk's materials are not fixed, singular or comprehensible as such, and he offers an expression neither unmediated by distance, time or sign nor supermediated by much dialogue with his co-performers; his "lived poetic of sound," that collection of improvised statements uniquely present and directed from one to another, is not more authentic or more true than those elements of "language" or "text" that make up so much of these performances of "Lulu." In emphasizing the song's fictive score and the "transcribed" historical, Monk offers up the repressed or excluded middle of supposed ideals classical and jazz, European and African American: the "written," the remembered, the routine, absent forms of presence that are effortlessly and autonomously reproduced from place to place and occasion to occasion, because that's entertainment.

And yet in this adoption of something like a new textual fixity, and his relative downplaying of improvised creation in favor of "improvised" re-creation, Monk was making a music not entirely removed in method from André Hodeir's own composition. It's this similarity that makes a juxtaposition of the two figures intriguing: both musicians were, in their forties, returning to youthful certainties, for one the prerogatives of art music composition, for the other, pre-bebop piano performance. Equally striking, though, is the disparity of critical response the two men received for their efforts. While Hodeir's "simulated improvisation" was respectfully appraised for the progress it made towards a concept of composed jazz art, Monk's improvisational simulacrum was worriedly dismissed for its regressing to jazz diversion. Certainly it was Monk who continued to enjoy by far the greater reputation, both public and critical, but the differing terms in which the pair's music was framed nevertheless showed how, once again, notions of the "artistic" and of the racialized jazz performer were neither fully separable nor compatible.

By 1966, though, the efforts of Hodeir and others to translate art music values into jazz, and vice versa, were contested from all sides. During the latter part of the decade, Hodeir would make one last affirmation of his vision of a new jazz art, before resigning from what he would finally recognize as a failed project to relocate the music to a new, European, compositional home.

Anna Livia Plurabelle

The Jazz Groupe had continued to give very occasional concerts in France and Germany through the latter 1950s, playing Hodeir's music alongside works by Gil Evans, George Russell and John Lewis.[155] But, working so little, the group was difficult to keep together—at one concert, six of the nine players were deputizing—and while some of its key players would remain associated with the composer, the ensemble's activity fizzled out at the start of the 1960s.[156] Hodeir turned towards different forces. Two pieces had already been written for the Modern Jazz Quartet to play alongside the Jazz Groupe ("Ambiguïté I" and "Ambiguïté II"); in 1960, Hodeir composed "Around the Blues" for the Quartet and accompanying symphony orchestra. Recorded for Atlantic under the direction of Gunther Schuller, this was Hodeir's only real contribution to the Third Stream idea. These were ad-hoc arrangements, though, and in the early 1960s Hodeir attempted to form a more lasting organization with Martial Solal. At first this took the form of a septet—which saw some activity in 1963—and then, in 1964, a larger group, for which Hodeir provided scores markedly less tonally anguished and contrapuntally wrought than his work for the Jazz Groupe had ever been. These pieces were hailed in the same terms by Jean Tronchot and Claude Lenissois, both critics commenting on the new "warmth" of Hodeir's writing.[157] But Hodeir was eager to move beyond this kind of repertoire and to concentrate his efforts on a new compositional challenge: "I realized I had hit a ripe age," he remembered of this time a few years later, "and that I had spread myself too thinly. I'd played with some ideas, dripped some ink around, but realized a true work—no."[158] This, then, would be Hodeir's masterpiece, the summation of the theories and techniques he had been developing since the early-1950s.

When a commission for such a large work arrived from the ORTF, the piece began to take shape. Since the late 1950s Hodeir had talked of developing a writing style for voice neither spoken, scatted nor sung—a jazz equivalent of Schoenbergian *sprechgesang*—and, having found a text that lent itself to such treatment, he proceeded to make this the piece's primary element.[159] The text, which gave Hodeir's piece its name, was the story of Anna Livia Plurabelle, from James Joyce's appropriately prestigious *Finnegans Wake*. Anna Livia comes to symbolize the River Liffey in Joyce's Dublin tale, and Hodeir later wrote that the idea of flow was important for the piece's formal conception (the work opens, Hodeir wrote, "at the frontiers of atonality," progressing towards what will be a tonal conclusion).[160] A few rhythm section directions apart, there is not a bar of open improvisation in the work—Hodeir wrote Jean-Luc Ponty's violin solos in Ponty's style as the composer had found it on record—but, true to his earlier ideas, he nevertheless conceived the work as "a grand improvisation," with composer as improviser. Hodeir soloed at home for nearly a year.[161] On its completion, the fifty-minute piece was recorded and broadcast by ORTF; the recording was commercially released in 1971, and the work was rerecorded under the direction of Patrice Caratini in 1994.

The craftsmanship of the piece, its lightness of touch from moment to moment, is remarkable (and the use of speech and scat in such an "orchestral" context may well have given Luciano Berio an idea for his celebrated 1968 *Sinfonia*, for which the Italian composer employed Hodeir's

Swingle Singers associates, including Christiane Legrand). As late as the pieces written for the Hodeir-Solal group, the composer had made use of devices taken from contemporary art music—the clustered brass swells that climax "Transplantation 1" surely belong to Stockhausen's *Gruppen* (1957)—but these are gone from *Anna Livia*.[162] Instead, it is the influence of Gil Evans that predominates, the American's late 1950s style as strong an influence here as his late 1940s work had been in Hodeir's first nonet pieces. Simulated improvisations for (Ponty's) violin appear throughout the piece, and, during "And Then She'd Esk to Vistule a Hymn" (Hubert Rostaing's) clarinet is given a mini concerto that, despite its post-tonal harmonic ambiguity, can't help but recall Ellington's feature writing for Barney Bigard or Jimmy Hamilton.[163] In contrast to the always graceful instrumental writing, the solo parts for mezzo soprano and contralto suffer from beatbound rhythmic profiles and timebound vocalese semantics ("shake it up, shake it up, *do-do*").

Here is the fullest realization of Hodeir's improvisational technique. Soloistic writing does not just stand in for improvisation: instead, pseudo-improvised phrases elaborate themselves across the ensemble and come to constitute the musical whole. A passage from "First She Let Her Hair Fall" (beginning at 0:32 on the Caratini recording)—this a section that Hodeir was particularly proud of—shows this texture unfolding, and how these lines derive from and constitute their "unity" with the broader musical structure: an opening trumpet and alto sax arpeggio motif, immediately developed and inverted by trumpet and clarinet, goes on to appear in numerous different forms over subsequent minutes; the octave leaps appearing in the clarinet and trombone parts are improvisations on the same gesture made at the section's opening by the solo voice.[164]

There was little new in this approach as such: in their chamber music especially, European composers had for centuries been writing counterpoint that aspired to both formal unification and a dialogical, improvisational character. Hodeir's achievement here is to render this mix in genuine jazz colors, to arrive at a jazz contrapuntal technique that transcends the efforts of the 1950s, whether cod-Brandenburg or cod-Darmstadt. On the recording's release, Alain Gerber called the work "a masterpiece of sensuality." The reliably hyperbolic Gérald Merceron wrote in *Jazz hot* that *Anna Livia* showed Hodeir, with his immense technical and organizational skills, to be "the Gesualdo of his era," the piece arguing with eloquence the case for an "independent" European jazz.[165]

Yet critical and public response was otherwise very much limited, because in truth the piece had come too late. While Hodeir may have aspired to the timelessness of an anti-popular music, the work he had produced announced and still announces its belonging to the 1950s at every moment, its supposed formal daring no match for its sonic safeness, its historical nature accidental rather than radical like Monk's. This is *haute* light music: the elegant Gil Evans–style sound world speaks of Miles Davis's 1950s bachelor-pad concept albums more than it does a jazz given new and various kinds of velocity by the same Miles Davis, or by John Coltrane, Archie Shepp; the notated swing time that underpins most of the music is a polite version of what had, in the hands of Elvin Jones, Tony Williams and Sunny Murray (or French players like Jacques Thollot, Daniel Humair and Eddy Gaumont) by 1966 become something much more multidirectional, polyrhythmic.

Indeed, it's because each passage is accompanied by steady swing tempo—as noted earlier, Hodeir thought this a prerequisite for the essential, superimposed syncopation—that the piece is unable to breathe formally or texturally, each section instead simply panting either slow, medium or fast. Although Hodeir plays games of metrical superimposition from time to time, this regularity of pulse means that the music cannot flow, cohere and dissipate in the manner that composers working with large and potentially inflexible musical structures had, for more than a century, found imperative. So despite all Hodeir's talk of openness and improvisation, the problem is one of too-fixed form: the piece is constructed of twenty-six separate "numbers," and though the composer was at pains to argue that this signified nothing—that unlike an 18th century number opera each of these sections blended one into the other—the claim was a meager one (especially since some sections, like no. 25, have internal ABA forms as simple as those employed in such operas). *Anna Livia* was a piece passé by the standards of both jazz and Western art music.

Not just the method, but also the intent of Hodeir's interlinked musical and critical projects had been overtaken. Hodeir had put his chips on composition, but by 1966 it seemed that jazz's future—at least, most of its present—lay in improvisation. This wasn't just an accident of technical preference. As we will see, the turn to free jazz was in part interpreted as a radical rejection of the bourgeois Western aesthetics and art tradition that Hodeir had since the mid-1950s billed as jazz's next stop. The great promoter of jazz composition was naturally antipathetic to free jazz, and he came to believe that *Anna Livia*, his masterpiece, had been overlooked in favor of what he never quite called, but clearly believed to be, a sham style.[166] Hodeir knew his values were in the descendant. On the back foot and pressed by Philippe Kœchlin to give his position on the new music in 1966, the one-time aesthetic absolutist gestured towards a new pluralism (a common maneuver on the part of outgoing absolutist regimes). "Why should we still talk about jazz [de jazz]," Hodeir asked. "Shouldn't we talk about jazzes [des jazz]?" The composer, now claiming he did not think composition was the only way forward, suggested his method was one among other possibilities; somewhat deviously, he finished by aligning the recently completed *Anna Livia* with the spirit of free jazz: his piece, he said, could be thought of as "'composed free jazz,'" totally removed from the new form, but nevertheless "linked by the spirit of improvisation."[167]

Yet Hodeir was less and less interested in defending his position. As the long-delayed "subjective" follow up to the "objective" *Hommes et problèmes* developed over the course of the 1960s—and as the lone jazz composer's stance in the face of history began to look hopeless—so his creative ambitions shifted away from music and towards literature. From the beginning of the 1970s to his death in 2011, Hodeir would devote himself to writing novels and children's books, often with a musical theme, and *Les Mondes du jazz*, when it finally appeared in 1971, was a mix of resentful, solipsistic reflection on a lost love for music and extended literary pastiche.[168] In 1972 Hodeir completed his final piece of music, for eight Swingle Singers and jazz quintet. Again a Joyce text was pressed into service, this time the last words of *Finnegans Wake*. The piece bore a title that seemed to describe Hodeir's tired, frustrated retirement from the jazz world: *Bitter Ending*.

In his 1961 review of *Jazz et jazz*, Jef Gilson had written that, some of Martial Solal's efforts and a yet-to-be-unveiled Jean-Claude Fohrenbach project apart, Hodeir's was the only French oeuvre engaging with the problem of jazz composition.[169] Gilson, the onetime student of Hodeir, was modest enough not to mention his own activities, but Hodeir might not have thought of Gilson's music as part of the same project anyway: reflecting on his work at the end of his life, Hodeir said that none of his pupils had made the years'-worth of effort needed to master compositional technique. "So, on the route I had traced for myself," he said, "I turned round—and I realized I was alone!"[170] Of course, in the thick of the Nietzschean battle against mediocrity and wrong-headedness in the 1950s, Hodeir had seemed to relish that solitude. Looking back, his work having had little lasting impact, his example not taken up, a late reflection might have been expected to contain more humility. And yet for the composer, speaking in the 21st century, it was everyone else that was wrong.

> I still see myself as the last jazz musician, that's to say he who closed the history of jazz, with written works that are the culmination of jazz's whole history. In continuing thereafter, with free jazz and so on, jazz committed a kind of suicide, to my way of thinking.[171]

Just as his old adversary Hugues Panassié had proclaimed bebop to be anti-jazz, Hodeir seemed unable to countenance the supersedence of the jazz style current at his moment of musical maturation, except by describing it as jazz's negation; the developments in jazz composition that followed in the 1970s and '80s—in work by musicians like Michael Mantler, Anthony Braxton, Carla Bley, Henry Threadgill, Julius Hemphill—may as well have not existed.

Indeed, though the cultivated, universalist terms of Hodeir's criticism have allowed that work to retain a place in the canon of respected jazz letters, the work is hardly less driven by an agenda of exclusion than that of Panassié, to whom such a place is not often accorded. The elder writer might have enjoyed the prospect of his former acolyte being left behind by just the kinds of musical "evolution" and "progress" that Hodeir had once trumpeted. But if the composer-critic was right to engage in that battle, he was thereafter undone by his picking what could only ever be a losing fight with History. He was hardly the only cultural commentator of the period to confuse his own preoccupations for sweeping historical imperatives, but Hodeir would seem to have had no real need to raise the stakes of what he called his "formidable wager" so high: surely, in order to be able to pursue his jazz composition project, he didn't need to argue that improvisation was done for, that the great (black) improvisers were complacent to a man, that jazz would henceforth have to be subsumed into a European art practice. As John Gennari has noted, Hodeir's earlier writing was an influence on the American critic, Martin Williams—a leading American critic of the 1950s and '60s, and, in terms of his dedication to the critical construction of jazz as a fully fledged art form, a similarly motivated one—yet Williams was much more given to the appreciative reading of his subjects' music, and much less to ventriloquizing what he took to be the demands of the epoch.

But Hodeir's pronouncements on that score were practically required of an ambitious man who had emerged into a postwar Parisian musical world, and critical discourse, in which experiments and ideas were only ever framed in the language of historical necessity. Hodeir's writing had to take on the condemnatory tone of Boulez's own: as he labored at his desk to promote the thing of his passions from tawdry cabaret stage to an aesthetic and social status worthy of his own education and vision, the former Claude Laurence must have felt on his back the scornful glare of his volatile composer peer—a man of vastly higher profile and influence, but one similarly driven by modernist doctrine.

Writing on jazz in the mid-1960s, Pierre Bourdieu suggested that the music, like cinema, by then occupied the middle ground in a hierarchy of bourgeois cultural canons—neither beyond the pale nor fully legitimate, but poised as "legitimizable."[172] The discourse around both Hodeir and Monk's 1960s music similarly shows jazz stalled between art and entertainment, between transient popular style and more durable structures of prestige. On the project's own terms progress of a sort had been made, but, for now at least, the attempt to transform jazz into an art form in the classic sense remained unrealized.

FOUR

Cool Going Cold

Miles Davis and Ascenseur pour l'échafaud

"Cool": long muttered in jazz-world conversation, the term was picked up at the music's American marketing desks and press offices in the first years of the 1950s. French musicians and writers didn't lag much behind. The pianist Henri Renaud's article "Qu'est-ce que le jazz cool?" appeared in the April 1952 issue of *Jazz hot*, and André Hodeir's *Hommes et problèmes du jazz* featured a chapter on the new tendency two years later. Hodeir defined the approach in attitudinal rather than technical terms.

> Even when the performer seems to be letting himself go most completely (and cool musicians, as we shall see, cultivate relaxation), a sort of reserve, by which we do not mean constraint, marks his creative flight, channeling it within certain limits that constitute its charm.[1]

It was an apt description, particularly of the Lester Young-derived "Four Brothers" saxophone style that was so popular among French players in the early and mid-1950s—most notably Jean-Louis Chautemps, who would tour with Chet Baker in 1955, and Bobby Jaspar, who, similarly associated with Baker, was one of the most gifted players in European postwar jazz. Born in 1926 in Liège, Belgium, Jaspar gained early professional experience on both clarinet and tenor saxophone as a member of a local but renowned swing group, the Bob Shots (alto saxophonist Jacques Pelzer and guitarist René Thomas also played with the band at various times). Having encountered and absorbed bebop, in 1950 Jaspar moved to Paris, and, his playing soon reflecting the influence of Warne

Marsh and Stan Getz, within a couple of years he had cultivated a reputation as the leading modern saxophonist working in France. Around 1953 the cool scene was centered on the Tabou and Ringside clubs, where Henri Renaud often led groups including Jaspar, the American expatriate guitarist Jimmy Gourley and the drummer Jean-Louis Viale; for better or worse these players accompanied Jaspar on a number of the tenor player's 1950s recordings.[2]

Cool models were formal as well as improvisational, both poles of the new American practice represented in the settings Jaspar was assigned: Francy Boland's septet and octet arrangements for the Swing albums *Bobby Jaspar's New Jazz, Vols. 1 and 2* (recorded in 1954) take on the pseudo-baroque counterpoint and default mezzo piano of West Coast writers like Jack Montrose and Gerry Mulligan, while a four-track EP recorded in the same year, *Bobby Jaspar plays Henri Renaud*, features skillful pastiches of the (East Coast) Miles Davis nonet by Christian Chevallier. Similar inspirations shaped the work André Hodeir contributed to the *New Jazz* albums (and, as seen in chapter 3, the Jazz Groupe de Paris, of which Jaspar would be a founding member).

It didn't matter that these pieces were composed in direct imitation of the American style, since Jaspar's playing was world-class. On record, true to the cool ethos, his talent sounds quietly but profoundly. There is great subtlety in the kite-flown phrasing of his melody statements ("Sweet and Lovely," 0:00-1:16), the bursts of notes that fountain, hang and fall ("Mad About the Boy," 2:12-19; 2:34-42), the long lines that spin off in all directions, following the currents around them, never smelling of stale practice room air ("You Took Advantage of Me," 2:03-08; "Awevalèt," 1:46-54). By his 1955 recordings Jaspar's virtuosity of thought and execution is even more developed. On "There's a Small Hotel," from that year's Swing album *Gone with the Winds*, Jaspar delivers a solo that is remarkable in its thematic invention and tenacity, a play of triplets beginning in the melody and continuing, a guitar interlude aside, for almost three and a half minutes. With his wife, the American singer and pianist Blossom Dearie, Jaspar left for New York in 1956. There—as he worked with J. J. Johnson and Miles Davis, among others—his playing took on hard bop toughness while his health weakened; he died of a heart attack in 1963, aged thirty-seven.[3]

In the music of André Hodeir we have already seen how a cool aesthetic was developed in French jazz. But the "sort of reserve" described by Hodeir in his writing on cool was more than musical: it was an expression of what commentators on both sides of the Atlantic were describing as a new way of being in the world, one peculiar to postwar youth. In his study of the development of cool as an identifiable, and, at first, identifiably American "emotional style," the historian Peter N. Stearns argues that Americans of the (supposedly repressed) Victorian period had commonly believed that the expression of passionate emotions—anger, jealousy, grief—was healthy, leading either to competitive advantage or to inner balance and equilibrium. But in the latter 19th and early 20th century this began to change, and American authorities and sections of the public alike—Stearns presents materials from manuals for parenting and for management, men's and women's magazines, popular literature and diaries—became disinclined to encounter, reveal or acknowledge these emotions. Such were now to be avoided, or else "ventilated" before they could materialize; this was the background to the uniquely American attitude of cool that, the historian argues, became so important in the post–World War II period, both at home and around the world in the form of American cultural-industrial exports (of which cool jazz was but one).[4] Now though, cool was to be at least superficially subversive of the social ordering project that Stearns describes: as much was pop-culturally represented by the shadowy and suave black musician appearing with a trumpet on the cover of Miles Davis's *Birth of the Cool* album in 1957, or the street gang members who were compelled to calm self-mastery in the *West Side Story* number "Cool" in the same year.

Whatever the context, the concerns of postwar cool were usually the same. Scott Saul's study of the hipster figure in the American 1950s thus sets Lenny Bruce and Jack Kerouac alongside sociologists and writers of the day such as Daniel Bell and Isaac Rosenfeld. Bell identified a postwar youth wedded to "irony, paradox, ambiguity, and complexity," Rosenfeld a generation that was "passionless, 'cool' . . . exposed, but uncommitted, to many worlds [but] *au courant* in them all."[5] Saul details the attempts of prominent commentators like Anatole Broyard to come to terms with the new climate of masterful nonengagement. Broyard called coolness a self-defeating "attempt to move from the performer to the omniscient and superior spectator," this figure "a pacifist in the struggle between social groups—not a conscientious objector, but a draft-dodger," one who seemed to suffer from some psycho-sexual malaise, an all-consuming sense of "impotence."[6] As we will see, a kind of "cool" functioning exactly according to Broyard's terms was to be found in jazz-tinged French popular culture.

Yet French onlookers—consumers and then practitioners of American ideas and cultural forms—did not simply copy the new American way of being: the conceptual relationship was reciprocal, Broyard and other American writers on the trend, including Bernard Wolfe, cowriter of Mezz Mezzrow's *Really the Blues* (1947), having been directly influenced by a widely discussed Parisian existentialism (Wolfe had even published on jazz in Sartre's journal *Les Temps modernes*).[7] An American attitude of ambivalence found analogues in a local culture also fraught with alienation. In France, presses, professions and authorities were preoccupied with the question of youth morality throughout the late 1940s and 1950s. The effects of war and the occupation, a 1947 survey of health workers and educators concluded, could be seen in a generation defined by its "promiscuity, moral obscurity and insecurity."[8] Countless cases of juvenile criminality and wantonness were discussed in the papers during this period; many novels and films, most notably François Truffaut's autobiographical debut as a director, *Les 400 Coups* (1959), dramatized what was sometimes described as an unbridgeable gap between prewar and postwar generations.

But while base criminality was often portrayed as the province of working-class and underclass youths, the educated, metropolitan middle classes had their own means of detachment from accepted social values. In the decades since, smoky clichés of an urban, literary French youth cult reared on the existential amorality of writers like Sartre, Camus and Genet have wafted through the popular imagination. Doubtless actually lived experience of this writing and thought could not match the homogeneity of its subsequent representation, but this image was powerfully present at the time, too. The characters in Marcel Carné's film portrait of a generation, *Les Tricheurs* (1958), are defined by their disbelief in the meaninglessness of bourgeois social convention, and by their resultant removal of all emotional contact and commitment from what they understand to be already vapid lives. For these young adults, jazz enables both hedonism and withdrawal: they twirl about to Jazz at the Philharmonic records as the music's fans long had, but they sprawl around the *électrophone* to listen to Gerry Mulligan and Chet Baker's cool jazz in moody silence. Music was a central part of the transmission of a new attitudinal code, central to which—however various its forms—was the idea of removal: removal from a social or moral world whose inauthenticity the clear-sighted wanted no part of, removal from the site of emotional overcommitment or risk. On both sides of the Atlantic, types of what we might think of as "cool" represented the supposed rejection of hegemonic ideologies, of petty bourgeois conformity.

We've seen that *Les Tricheurs* wasn't the first French film to be soundtracked by small group jazz; indeed, Sidney Bechet's late, reflowering French stardom had been amply aided by the cinema, the saxophonist appearing in eight different films through the 1950s. Yet it's possible to track a trend in which, during the latter 1950s, French directors increasingly turned to jazz, usually of the modern variety, in order to form for their work a certain moral climate. Jazz of one kind or another is heard in Roger Vadim's *Et Dieu . . . créa la femme* (1956) and *Sait-on jamais . . .* (1957), the latter featuring music by the Modern Jazz Quartet. But it was the 1958 success of Louis Malle's *Ascenseur pour l'échafaud*, with its music by Miles Davis, that inspired a rush of original jazz "scores"; the trend peaked with films released the following year, fading thereafter.[9] In 1959, Art Blakey and the Jazz Messengers could be heard in Edouard Molinaro's *Des Femmes disparaissent* and Vadim's *Les Liaisons dangereuses 1960*, the latter also featuring Thelonious Monk and Duke Jordan; Molinaro's *Un Témoin dans la ville* had music by a small group led by Barney Wilen (present on *Ascenseur*, and also guesting with the Messengers on *Les Liaisons dangereuses 1960*); Jean-Pierre Melville's *Deux Hommes dans Manhattan* featured a big-band score by Christian Chevallier with Martial Solal; André Hodeir provided the music for Claude Bernard-Aubert's *Les Tripes au soleil*. Solal also composed for Jean-Luc Godard's *A bout de souffle*, released in 1960, collaborated with Hodeir on Bernard-Aubert's *Match contre la mort* the same year, and scored Melville's *Léon Morin prêtre* in 1961.

In all but the last of these films jazz is associated with transgression, hedonism and moral ambivalence, these associations borrowed wholesale from contemporary American film (and television) convention.[10] An early and particularly bold example of jazz and black music's signifying power is contained in Vadim's dismal *succès de scandale, Et Dieu . . . créa la femme*. Brigitte Bardot's character, Juliette, dedicated only to her own (sexual) pleasure, is soundtracked by jazz, mambo and swing-pop. In the film's climatic scene she dances wildly with a group of mambo-playing black musicians while her meek husband looks on, her furious gestures and proximity to blackness leaving no doubt that we are watching the primitive sexual urge well up. For once the husband is driven to fury, and he assaults her; in the film's final shot the husband is seen dragging Juliette home and slamming the front door shut. Now, for the first time, the soundtrack swells to the strains of a full symphony orchestra, cadencing conclusively in the classical style: otherness and rebellion (sexual desire and jazz-blackness) have been removed, order and obedience (Western art music) are restored. Meanwhile, in *Des Femmes disparaissent*, Blakey's tom-toms introduce a pulp story about white slavery; Hodeir's music for *Les Tripes au soleil* soundtracks a prurient take on interracial attraction; Chevallier's work for *Deux Hommes dans Manhattan* is as sordid and overexcited as the New York nightlife it represents. These are second-, third- and fourth-rate films, and however common their elements were to cinematic convention of the time, none of them could match the style and intelligence of the main subject of this chapter, Louis Malle's *Ascenseur pour l'échafaud*—the only jazz-backed movie of the French 1950s to have achieved a lasting reputation.

Here, in Malle's film, is a cinematic attitude whose insouciance and texture speak of a famously innovative era in French film, and of that postwar attitude described at the outset; wry and withdrawn, the film nevertheless ties together love, politics, murder and fast cars. Julien Tavernier (played by Maurice Ronet), an ex-paratrooper and veteran of France's ongoing colonial wars, is now working in Paris for Simon Carala, an arms dealer with whose wife, Florence (Jeanne Moreau), Tavernier is conducting an affair. The film opens with the lovers plotting, by phone, to meet and elope that evening after Tavernier has assassinated Monsieur Carala. Telling his secretary he does not want to be disturbed, Tavernier shuts himself in his room, climbs out of his window, rappels up the side of the building, enters Carala's office, shoots the man, descends and leaves for the night as normal along with the other staff. Just about to drive off, Tavernier glances up at the office building and notices that he has left his rope and grappling hook dangling from a railing. He darts back into the building to recover this incriminating evidence, and is in the elevator when the superintendent, closing what he believes to be an empty building at the end of the day's business, shuts off the electricity. Tavernier is trapped. Meanwhile, outside, a leather-jacketed teenager, Louis, eager to impress his girlfriend, Véronique, hops into Tavernier's car and the two drive off, finding a camera and a gun stowed in the vehicle. Florence Carala, waiting in a café for Tavernier, sees her lover's car speeding past, a woman in the passenger seat; she assumes that Tavernier has not followed through with their plan and has taken off with someone else instead. Florence spends the night walking the rainy Paris streets, looking in at all her lover's haunts in search of him. Having left the city in Tavernier's car, the teenagers arrive at a motel and spend the evening there with a middle-aged German businessman and his wife, taking photos of the party on Tavernier's camera, Véronique dropping the film off at the on-site developer. Later, Louis is about to steal the Germans' sports car but, surprised in the act, he shoots the couple dead with Tavernier's gun. The teenagers return to Paris, arriving at dawn, and try to com-mit suicide by swallowing Gardenal. The power in the office building switched back on, Tavernier makes his escape from the elevator, but the police, having found his belongings at the scene of the Germans' double murder, are looking for him, and he is quickly picked up. Under interrogation, Tavernier is unable to deny the murders since his alibi would only implicate him in the assassination of Carala. Having enquired at the police station and learned that Tavernier has been arrested for the motel murders, Florence suddenly realizes what has happened: she traces Véronique to her apartment and finds the two teenagers groggy but alive. Louis realizes that, were it not for the images caught on the film Véronique had left at the motel to be developed, he and his girlfriend would be in the clear; he speeds to the motel on a moped, with Florence in pursuit, and they arrive at the developer's lab just in time to watch the photos incriminating Louis, Véronique, and Tavernier and Florence—caught together elsewhere on the roll of film—in their respective crimes. A policeman is on hand to make the arrests; Miles Davis's somber music hovers and ends.

Malle's debut feature was immediately successful on its release in France, garnering generous reviews as well as the prestigious Prix Louis Delluc.[11] Miles Davis's soundtrack won the Prix de l'Académie Charles Cros in 1958 and was nominated for a Grammy in 1960. Yet while the film's critical success was widespread, it was not universal. Writing in *Les Temps modernes*, Raymond Borde castigated those who had responded enthusiastically to the movie. "*L'Humanité-Dimanche* headlined: A Young Auteur is Born," he complained. "In *Les Lettres françaises*, an enthusiastic Georges Sadoul cited Mallarmé . . . A sort of collective hallucination has taken over my colleagues." Borde's dissention, made in postwar France's most engaged arts journal, was not based on an aesthetic judgment alone: the critic charged that *Ascenseur* was so "perpetually obliging to the dearest fantasies of little rightwingers" that it was, "in every sense of the word, a fascist film."[12]

What might seem to most 21st century observers an untroubling cultural production was shot through with reactionary local politics of more than one kind. The signifiers of wealth and status that surrounded some of the action—cars, champagne, "offices as long as naves"—Borde sniffed at (these had been remarked upon by other reviewers, too).[13] But it was the figures of Julien Tavernier and Horst Bencker, the German tourist eventually murdered by the young Louis, that for Borde plotted the young Malle's political coordinates. Bencker, the critic wrote, was related to characters in Vadim's *Et Dieu . . . créa la femme* and *Sait-on jamais . . .* , rich Germans who, having done well out of the war and its aftermath (including the establishment of the Common Market), were now presented as worldly and charismatic, "at once father substitutes and heroes of a neo-Nazi romanticism."[14] Similarly reactionary for Borde was the figure of Tavernier, the ex-parachutist veteran of colonial conflict, admired by his colleagues, pointed out in the street ("that guy, he's covered in medals . . . and he's got such style").[15]

One of the first aims of this chapter, then, is to fully divine the sociopolitical undercurrents shaping (and shaped by) *Ascenseur*. If these meanings have been almost entirely lost to later audiences, it's because the nature of such contemporary meanings, together with the young Louis Malle's social and creative affiliations—the real cause of Borde's ire—have been forgotten as the director's first film, and the nocturnal, jazz-infused Parisian 1950s, has hardened into a cool ideal. That image, unalterable by the 1980s, we will return to in the book's coda. To be identified here, though, are the ways that those now-obscure political tendencies formed part of what we have seen to be a new, postwar transatlantic attitude of removal and disengagement otherwise known as "cool," and the ways that such tendencies were articulated via a set of American cultural signifiers already branded in that way. Miles Davis' music included: Hodeir's piece on cool identified the trumpeter as "a kind of leader" of the cool movement.[16]

This was not just a game of symbols, though, and a close reading will show how Malle's visuals and Davis's music act out strategies of disengagement in formal terms. There are other musical issues. That Davis's Parisian experiments helped him towards the modal innovations of his 1959 album *Kind of Blue* has become a critical commonplace, but in this study we will see that *Ascenseur* was important to Davis's development in ways other than the strictly technical. The working methods both director and musician employed, the musical performance role Davis assumed, the critical presentation that the French media gave Davis's music: all these directly impacted on the trumpeter's self-presentation and subsequent work. Equally important, I'll argue, was an anxiety around gender, the film and its music gazing at and containing a feminine object and power. After all, the cool and the disengaged were always bound up in the act of looking on, of exerting control without much acting; in this the American trumpeter's methods shared much with those of Louis Malle.

Malle was born in northeastern France in 1932, and, his mother being a member of the Béghin sugar dynasty, grew up amid great wealth. The boy was enchanted by music from a young age, going "very quickly from Beethoven to Louis Armstrong and Charlie Parker at the age of fourteen, fifteen and sixteen."[17] But having decided as an adolescent that he wanted to direct, Malle attended the Institut des Hautes Etudes Cinématographiques (IDHEC) for eighteen months—*Crazéologie*, a Theater of the Absurd–styled short made there in 1954, has a character repeatedly smashing Charlie Parker 78s over his knee—leaving before graduation to work with Jacques-Yves Cousteau. With Cousteau, Malle codirected and photographed *Le Monde du silence* from 1954 to 1955; during this period Malle also worked as an assistant to Robert Bresson on *Un Condamné à mort s'est échappé* (1956).[18]

Through his work on *Le Monde du silence*, Malle became close friends with Pierre-Antoine Cousteau, brother of the Commandant (the young filmmaker even provided a blood transfusion when the elder man became critically ill). P.-A. Cousteau was an unreformed wartime collaborator who claimed he had wanted a German victory "because it represented . . . the last chance of the white man, while the democracies represented the end of the white man."[19] He had been editor of the far-right newspaper *Rivarol*, and it was via the Cousteaus that Malle was introduced to other figures of what was a shriveled postwar literary right: *Rivarol* cofounder Antoine Blondin, Action Française insider Lucien Rebatet, and the man who would write *Ascenseur*'s screenplay, Roger Nimier.[20] Nimier and Blondin were part of a group of young writers who, after Nimier's novel *Le Hussard bleu* (1950), had been dubbed the Hussards. The group's work was characterized by a set of drearily familiar rightist obsessions—disgust at the descent of bourgeois modern France into decadence, the shame of France's World War II and its failing colonial project—and by a resultant, poeticized nihilism.[21] There's little doubt, though, that Malle was drawn to these anti-Semites and would-be fascists for reasons removed from their artistic program or political beliefs. The director was proud to announce late in life that he had "never made a so-called political film," yet he was perennially attracted to questions of political alignment, at various times in his career taking an interest in the right (the Hussards) and the left (petitioning with Sartre on behalf of the suppressed Maoist newspaper *La Cause du peuple* in 1970).[22] The Malle scholar Hugo Frey argues persuasively that these ambivalences characterize the director's work, and that, rather than outright political sympathy, what likely drew Malle to the Hussards was an intellectual curiosity, a desire to explore the psychological makeup of these self-styled radical outsiders.[23]

So *Ascenseur* and *Le Feu follet* (1963), both of which starred Maurice Ronet, an actor who shared the Hussards's attitudes and politics—and the latter of which was based on a story by the Nazi collaborator Pierre Drieu La Rochelle—engage with postwar France on what Nimier and his colleagues had established as their own terms. The male leads, ex-paratroopers who ought to be men of action, are alienated and neutered, hemmed in by a world of bourgeois mediocrity, of corrupt and absurd authority figures: in *Ascenseur* these are Carala, the arms-dealing businessman Tavernier kills, and the police inspector who preens in front of journalists at the German tourists' murder scene. Indeed, it is the reduction of a supposed active masculine ideal and impulse to either imprisoned inactivity or ejaculatory, adolescent confusion—and that reduction's inevitable corollary, a projection of ultimate blame for this masculine malaise onto a woman, and by extension, women—that must form part of a reading of *Ascenseur* if its full cool significance is to be understood.

That rightist "politics," then, informs *Ascenseur*'s moral mood rather than lending it anything more programmatic. And even if the Hussardian viewpoint was Malle's own, his filmic examination of contemporary French morality was not made in isolation. Those young men who, having begun as critics working for the journal *Cahiers du cinéma*, would shortly make the leap into direction and define French film's "New Wave"—Truffaut, Godard, Rivette, Resnais, Rohmer—were also much concerned by such questions: rejecting the otiose style and subject matter of the French cinematic *tradition de qualité*, they venerated instead a select few Hollywood directors (like Alfred Hitchcock) and Italian neo-realists (chiefly Roberto Rossellini). At their best, it was thought, these schools held a mirror up to society and ethics in a way that French film did not.[24] In the suspense genre the French had dubbed *film noir*, sheen and glitz were often secondary to some stylized moral quandary; Italian neo-realist movies were shot in everyday locations, often with nonprofessional actors, the classic cinema's extraordinary technical and narrative elements rejected in the name of experiential authenticity. This was an attempt to "get to know human beings as they really are," as Rossellini put it to *Cahiers* in 1959, a project that helped authorize for young directors not only a mobile, improvisatory approach to planning, shooting and soundtracking, but also an interest in the quotidian that would lead to the importing of documentary techniques into fictional frameworks.[25] *Ascenseur*, as I will show, was among the first French films to be formed by this kind of approach, one in which ethical, practical and aesthetic concerns were intricately related.

A tempered regard for genre, realism and America was present in *Ascenseur* from the beginning, and if the half-ironic adoption of American codes would be exploited to the fullest by Godard in his 1960 debut, then, as Frey points out, the classic New Wave statement that is *A bout de souffle* has much in common with Malle's film of two years earlier. In both, American film-noir conventions are restaged in contemporary Paris; both are concerned with the nature of criminality and youth rebellion; both have male lead characters who have been deeply affected by their fighting in France's foreign wars; both are blanketed with ennui and cynicism, and have since come to be thought of as unassailably cool. The "morality" of the New Wave was one that more often than not pitted itself against normative bourgeois understandings of that term, and did so via appropriation of stylish and exotic American genres.[26]

Both those films, of course, also made use of jazz in their soundtracks, that music a central signifier of amorality in Hollywood's genre code. But joining Hollywood in *Ascenseur* was a Bressonian filmic rhythm and a neo-realist-inspired examination of contemporary values that sought simply to observe its subjects in action. Or inaction: Jim Hillier notes that the *Cahiers* writers and New Wave directors were obsessed with the possibility of agency in the face of a stifling postwar rectitude—a particularly masculine agency at that, one in which violence and social rejection figured highly—and even if their political sentiments often belonged to the left, here too *Ascenseur* was entirely of its moment.[27]

The Making of *Ascenseur*

While Malle's film, shot at the end of 1957, contains a number of formal and stylistic elements that identify it as the inheritor of the *tradition de qualité* the *Cahiers* critics railed against, it nevertheless forecasts the climate of subversion that would break over French cinema during the next couple of years. The film's innovations are thematic, as with the often ironic appropriation of Americana, but they are also technical: the Paris streets would become a favorite New Wave setting, and *Ascenseur*'s most distinctive and most often recalled scenes were made possible by Malle's adoption of Kodak's then-new Tri-X film stock. Tri-X, the direc-

tor remembered later, meant that "suddenly it was possible to shoot in the street, to shoot in real interiors, with very little light, which means a smaller crew, much smaller budgets, and it gave us the freedom to work infinitely closer to reality than the older generation."[28] Tri-X gave a grainy result and was spurned by established directors because of it, but that only added to the definition of a quasi-documentary attitude that, soon to be developed by Godard, Jean Rouch and others, makes one of its first entries to French cinema when Jeanne Moreau's Florence wanders a rainy, nighttime Champs-Elysées, illuminated only by shop windows and street lights.[29]

The ambitious Malle wanted to enter his first film for the Prix Louis Delluc, but with the film shot there were only a few days remaining before the prize's submission deadline in which to record and edit the music. Even if he couldn't have foreseen the direction that Miles Davis was to take, the prospect of a jazz soundtrack—whose demands of composition and arrangement would, owing to jazz musicians' embodied improvisation skills, be far fewer than any orchestral alternative—had already occurred to the director.[30]

Davis had arrived in Paris in late November for a concert at the Olympia, a three-week stay at the Club Saint-Germain and a short European tour. Exactly a year earlier the trumpeter had toured Europe backed by René Urtreger (piano), Pierre Michelot (bass) and Christian Garros (drums).[31] On his return, Davis insisted on replacing Garros with Paris resident Kenny Clarke, and the trio was also supplemented by the local

rising tenor star Barney Wilen, then twenty years old. Urtreger remembered the Saint-Germain gig with great fondness, but there was clearly
an amount of tension between Davis and Wilen. During one of the saxophonist's solos, the trumpeter would tell Wilen to "stop playing those terrible notes" (to observers the headstrong Wilen seemed unconcerned);
Urtreger suggested that Davis was "not too gentle" about Wilen's acting
"'the great tenor player,' with cool attitude, dark glasses."[32]

Recollections of the approach to Davis differ. Malle recalled enlist-
ing Boris Vian, then-Artist and Repertoire man at Philips and a friend
of Davis' since the American's 1949 visit to France, to help convince the
trumpeter—who was reluctant to record, having arrived in the country
without his own musicians—to come and watch a rough cut of the film.[33]
Marcel Romano, promoter, fixer and booker at the Club Saint-Germain,
was also a go-between, Urtreger suggesting that it was Romano's encounter with one of Malle's jazz-loving assistants that enabled the meeting.[34] (Another account suggests that several of the tour dates Romano
had tried to arrange had fallen through, and that the film session was
thus offered to Davis as a sop.)[35] For his part, Davis claimed to have encountered Malle through Juliette Greco, a memory that may have owed
more to Davis's professed infatuation with his Parisian *idée fixe* than fact.
Davis (or his ghostwriter) also claimed unlikely credit for the hiring of
the Poste Parisien studios on the band's night off from the Club Saint-
Germain: "Since it was about a murder and was supposed to be a suspense movie," the trumpeter is reported as having said in preparing his
1989 semi-autobiography, "I used this old, gloomy, dark building where
I had the musicians play. I thought it would give the music atmosphere,
and it did."[36]

What is agreed upon in Malle, Davis and Romano's accounts is that a
meeting took place at which the trumpeter watched the film, twice; Romano provided a simultaneous English translation for the trumpeter.[37]
Davis had a piano installed in his hotel room, and, according to Urtreger, he took some sketches along to the Club Saint-Germain gig in
the days following. Malle has caused confusion among commentators
by claiming that the music was "completely improvised; I don't think
Miles Davis had had time to prepare anything." But in jazz, preparation
is relative—and by the time they arrived at Poste Parisien on December
4, Urtreger recalled, they were "not entirely uninitiated," having an idea
of the harmonic material that they were to work with.[38]

Like the film's narrative—and this accounts for at least some of the
session's reputation—recording took place over the course of a single

night, from around 8:00 p.m. to 4:30 the next morning, this preceded by an hour's worth of cocktails, a press conference and a photo session, the publicity machine in motion even before the work's completion. The large studio was lit only by three standing lamps, Barney Wilen reported, this lending the proceedings "a quasi-mystical ambiance."[39] Urtreger recalled that director Alain Cavalier and Malle's assistant François Leterrier, an actor and later a director in his own right, were at the session, as was Jeanne Moreau, who served the drinks; Boris Vian, who described the scene in his liner notes to the French soundtrack release, was not present.[40] (Urtreger was also sometimes absent from the session, to Malle's anger; "I was waiting for somebody and I was out in the staircase of the studio," the pianist later remembered somewhat shamefacedly, his habit long ago kicked.)[41]

Malle's team screened selected scenes on loop, and Davis's musicians played along as they watched. The working method was not unheard of. Numerous early jazz performers had been employed in cinemas to improvise along to images during the silent era, and Django Reinhardt had improvised soundtracks to short films several years earlier.[42] An even more direct precedent, one of which Malle may well have been aware, lay in André Hodeir and Henri Crolla's music for a 1955 short film by Jean-Jacques Languepin, *Neige*: with most of the music already scored, the composers put trumpeters Roger Guérin and Fernand Verstraete in front of images they had not seen and asked them to solo along.[43] Nevertheless, to those present the situation was unfamiliar enough to inspire a particular interest in Davis' technique. Kenny Clarke described the procedure.

> [Miles] said, "wait a minute, right here! Stop! Right here." And he'd say, "we play this, and this right here"—'cause this seemed really to go with the scene and it was really well thought out. And we did the music to the film right then and there . . . It turned out beautiful. Miles really put it together wonderfully. And I mean, it happened on the spur of the moment, you know.[44]

Malle interjected, explaining what was happening in each scene and making certain musical suggestions: Pierre Michelot remembered that the director wanted the music to work in counterpoint to rather than servile support of the image. "This obviously explains how he came to use certain takes for sequences other than the ones they were recorded for in the beginning," Michelot commented, and these elements of directorial intervention and postproduction—though apparently not extensive—suggest that any reading of the group's musical response to images as heard in the finished film must be made with care.[45]

In 1960 Malle contributed an interview-article on *Ascenseur*'s music to *Jazz hot*, and the piece is in large part a diatribe against the elaborate, synchronized, "symphonic" constructions of many film scores: "one has, on the one hand," Malle argued, "the dramatic, spatial construction of the film image, and, on the other, a musical construction, and ninety-nine times out of a hundred they don't work together, or else they work together too much." Instead, the director suggested, film image and music should seek more complex ("complementary, contrary and commentary") relationships.[46] What Malle later called *Ascenseur*'s "detachment" of music and image was consistent with what Royal S. Brown has identified as an emerging, and more general, New Wave taste for the disconnection of the seen and heard. So too was it consistent with Malle's ethos of detachment in its moral senses.[47] But this was not the whole story, and in the ways it was conceived, produced and interpreted at the time, Malle's film—and, especially, its soundtrack—was also indebted to a contemporary theory of realism that emphasized not the disjunction, but the unity of image and sound. The reading that follows will try to pick apart these differing aims and influences, to establish the ways that music and action both relate and don't: the constructed relationship between the two media, between sophisticated, internalized emotion and its external nonarticulation, is in large part responsible for what, for decades afterwards, still resonated as "cool."

Sound and Image

Malle's suggestion that *Ascenseur*'s music was to contrast with rather than reinforce the image is certainly borne out by the soundtrack's relative lack of "Mickey Mousing," that common technique whereby onscreen motions are given a precise analogue in the accompanying music. In the bar where Florence seeks her missing lover, for example, a woman remarks that she has seen Tavernier, and this dramatic moment of hope, visually translated by Florence's desperate lurch towards the girl, is unrecorded in the underlying jazz, which—supposedly issuing from a jukebox, as attested by some background extras' toe-tapping—patters on without interruption. This strategy, in which soundtrack music, though hyperrealistically forward in the sound mix, appears in and bears the same relationship to the characters' lives as it would any jukebox or radio user, appears elsewhere in cues titled "Sur l'autoroute" and "Dîner au motel"; when music is used in this way it is fittingly unreflective, up-tempo bebop.[48]

There are, however, moments in which music and event are tied to-gether, and sound serves to heighten on-screen drama. This music, in which the trumpeter is often absent, is fully modal, though its defining characteristics are primarily rhythmic. "L'Assassinat de Carala" has bass and piano chime a pedal note in time with Tavernier's steps as he walks the length of Carala's office, approaching his boss's desk before the mur-der. (Davis had problems making the same synchronization during Flor-ence's night sequence: "The bitch didn't know how to walk in rhythm," the charmless trumpeter told a girlfriend upon his return to New York.)[49] "Julien dans l'ascenseur" (this cue closely related to "L'Assassinat"), "Evasion de Julien," "Visite du vigile" and the interrogation-scene music do similar work.[50] Nevertheless, music that is diegetic or illustrative of onscreen events is cast in a distinctly minor role (indeed, music accom-panies only eighteen of the film's ninety minutes).

These background bebop and action-enhancing modal cues are of much lesser importance than the para-modal pieces that, all based on the same material, come to be identified as Florence's music: it's this mu-sic that characterizes the soundtrack, and, as many viewers' statements suggest, the movie as a whole. Davis had been fascinated by Alex North's music for Elia Kazan's *A Streetcar Named Desire* (1952): "Fuck jazz!," he said to his brother. "Alex North is the man."[51] In that film, themes sometimes entail an amount of soloistic jazz improvisation (or its imitation) over an atmospheric orchestral bedding; in addition, the Varsouviana that ap-pears whenever Blanche DuBois remembers her tragic first husband—in the original theatrical production as in the film, this is represented by the traditional tune "Put Your Little Foot Right Out," recorded by Davis in May 1958 as "Fran-Dance"—provides a direct link to the trumpeter's music for Florence Carala. In both films the music illuminates its charac-ter's psychic workings, reinforcing the spectator's gaze into and compre-hension of that figure.[52]

All the music associated with *Ascenseur*'s main female character fea-tures a cellular chord progression that continually self-replicates rather than leading elsewhere, and a bridge or contrasting tonal area that is itself revealed as suspended and ambivalent, dominant-tonic movement to an extent eschewed and with it a strong sense of tonal direction (es-pecially since some of René Urtreger's "dominant" chords are them-selves revoiced as directionless suspended fourths).[53] The Florence cues hybridize hard bop and modal techniques: "Générique," "Florence sur les Champs-Elysées," "Au bar" and "Chez le photographe" all make use of a harmonic plan in which either sixteen or twenty-four bars of a circling, repeating "progression" in D minor (Dm7, Dm7/F, E7♭5, A7♭9) is followed by a four-bar B section "in F" (formed of a floating C7 or Csus13 chord) and an eight-bar recap of the A section.[54] Urtreger recalled that in advance of recording he and Davis played around with such "ambience" chords—as the pianist called them—at the keyboard. At Davis's request, these chords were then voiced close and relatively low in register and volume, creating an unobtrusive but mood-laden harmonic pad upon which the trumpeter could improvise—and often, improvise "modally," ignoring the chord progression's implicit voice-leadings.[55]

This expansive, indirect music helps furnish the sense of cool languor that characterizes the film as a whole. In his *Cahiers du cinéma* review of *Ascenseur*, Eric Rohmer criticized a film that, for all its suspenseful story line, for him tended towards "a slowness, or, more specifically, a certain *inertia* that the rapidity of movements and the frequency of short cuts cannot shake."[56] Nathan Southern identifies this *lenteur* as a carryover from Malle's former employer, Robert Bresson, and surely this mismatch of classic French filmic poetics with contemporary Hollywood thriller and noir style works to recontextualize and ironize those American references.[57] Narrative *lenteur* is most obviously generated by the inaction that becomes the fate of the two lead characters, Tavernier and Florence, the two lovers who are forever separated, never meeting on screen, indeed not interacting at all beyond the telephone conversation they share in the film's first scene and the photograph they share in its last. Florence's despondent, nightlong search for the missing Tavernier dominates the middle of the film, and it is this sense of hiatus that lingers; if specific actions are not matched by the music, then such an atmosphere is certainly developed by the indolent immobility of Davis's music for Florence, neither fully modal nor fully driven by tonality's goal-directed motor.

On occasion this music is synchronized with the on-screen action. During Florence's forlorn nocturnal walk, a side-on shot changes to a midshot, taking in the character's full face as the music changes "key" into the major. During this scene Florence has only one word of dialogue, "Julien!," muttered hopefully as a car resembling Tavernier's pulls up and parks; while the man gets out of the car, the audience in suspense, the music is cut—this a postproduction rather than performance decision—and once the man is revealed to be a stranger, the tension passed, it fades back in. But it is in this music, more than in any other part of the soundtrack, that Davis most decidedly spurns external action, entering instead into an interior world, Florence's, disavowing identification not just with onscreen action but with any other character apart from the female lead.

Commentary on *Ascenseur* has not noted that Davis's open trumpet is reserved almost exclusively for the Florence music: the full, singing sound is identified with her alone.[58] That sound, in which a pure breath air rush is sometimes a feature, speaks of a human voice. Over the "Florence" material, Davis (and, apart from in its sole mid-tempo appearance in the bar scene, Davis alone) performs a number of solos that closely relate, making much use of a A♭-G-F "blues cry" motif (Davis may well have chosen D minor for this music, and, in 1959, for *Kind of Blue*'s "So What," because the trumpet allows the flat-fifth A♭ a particular vocal quality when the valve is half-depressed). If the trumpeter's unending use of this motif or some variant attests to music's "linguistic" poverty—Davis telling us over and over again that Florence feels the kind of emotional pain that the blues cry had come to stand for—then more subtle semiotic work has been done in postproduction: the reverb added to the trumpet after recording, further intensified on the original soundtrack release, gives this internal voice of Florence's an acoustic space congruent with the streets she will cover, as if the music we hear is a projection of the character's psychological state onto the city that, though sounding, only we film spectators can hear, a sonic ghost at the banquet. On all the other cues, those soundtracking Tavernier and other characters, Davis plays with a mute, his sound tight and almost always unvocal.[59] In *Ascenseur*, Davis's dominant musical persona is Florence's—his voice, even if it doesn't sound externally, is hers—and what he and Malle inscribe is music that seeks to expunge, through instrumental or postproduction technique and thematic consistency, any distance between the music and what is internal to the image, to the character.

Similar "audio-visual" constructions of persona can be found throughout the history of opera, music theater and film. But there is a long-standing critical perception that the presence of improvisation—no matter how manipulated after the fact—gives *Ascenseur* a unique place in that tradition. In a 2004 study, Colin Nettlebeck wrote that

> through its deep emotional connection with the rhythms and emotions to the images, the music actually probes and lays open the more reflective and personal elements of Malle's work, clarifying and liberating what otherwise might have remained latent. In this sense, Davis does not add music *to* the film, he plays *with* it, as if it were another

musical instrument. The final version of the film is almost like the recording of a jam session duet between jazz and cinema.[60]

Nettlebeck's is one of the fullest expressions of what is usually present in appraisals of Davis's contribution: an idea that, through improvisation, the trumpeter's music penetrates the image to access, and gain unity with, some kind of interior psychic content. But to fully understand the provenance and importance of this kind of thinking we need once more to return to the critical discourse that surrounded French filmmaking in the 1950s.

The *Cahiers* critics' rejection of contemporary French cinema was no simple father-slaying. An important figure among these writers was André Bazin, the group's elder in both senses, and here, in Bazin's critical writing, was another basis of the contemporary belief—or posture—holding that technical decisions reflected moral and philosophical positions. These Bazin found in Jean Renoir's films above all others. Bazin valued the great director for his use, in prewar masterpieces like *La Règle du jeu* (1939), of depth of field. In contrast to, say, Hollywood's concentration on close-up and soft focus, Renoir's technique made background and middle-ground setting and event as much a part of the composition as the foreground. These deep focus shots were allied to long wandering takes rather than routinely subjected to the procedures of montage that were the norm for Renoir's American contemporaries; but, following World War II, and the moment that American films once more became available in Paris, Bazin praised directors like Orson Welles and films like *Citizen Kane* (1941) for a use of depth of field and long traveling shots that, owing to American technical advances, were sharper and more assured than the French director had managed.[61]

In various writings of the first half of the 1950s, Bazin distinguished two trends broadly accounting for cinematic practice between 1920 and 1940: the one, as practiced by Renoir, characterized by directors who "put their faith in reality," and the other by those, epitomized by Sergei Eisenstein, who "put their faith in the image"; in other words, "those that relate to the plastics of the image and those that relate to the resources of montage."[62] For Bazin, montage meant "the creation of a sense of meaning not objectively contained in the images themselves but derived exclusively from their juxtaposition"; realist techniques allowed objects to present their inherent "meaning" relatively untroubled by directorial intention.[63] It's clear why this is relevant to the reception of (improvised) jazz, and of Davis's soundtrack: here is a critical idea, and valorization, of the spontaneous and indeterminate translation of reality into a recorded medium. In 1960, after all, Malle called Eisenstein and Prokofiev's joint efforts "too systematic"—not for the French director the traditional score, with its carefully designed, unspontaneous editorial support of the fiction, its Mickey Mousing of narrative meanings.[64]

Bazin outlined what was for him the ontology and particular power of the mechanical image in his famous article "The Ontology of the Photographic Image" (1945). He writes that, since the dawn of man, the meaning of painting had been to "have the last word in the argument with death by means of the form that endures."[65] But the advent of photography had rendered redundant any second order artistic representation of that which would die; now, the object itself was captured by the lens, objectively—Bazin puns here on the French word for lens, *objectif*—the thing and its mechanical representation not mediated or interrupted by interpretation, the thing's ontological identity at the moment of filming sealed into the image for all time.

> The photographic image is the object itself, the object freed from the conditions of time and space that govern it. No matter how fuzzy, distorted, or discolored, no matter how lacking in documentary value the image may be, it shares, by virtue of the very process of becoming, the being of the model of which it is the reproduction; it *is* the model.[66]

Realism was then for Bazin not simply a disavowal of artifice in the name of "realistic" subject matter or look—rather, it was an artificial representation of the world that invited subjective thought and investment in a way that the everyday could not.

It would be wrong to suggest that this critical theory might simply explain any one filmmaking practice, and if, unlike Godard's, Louis Malle's work rarely dallies with such theoretical preoccupations, then it does bear the traces of these highly influential ideas regarding the filmic real and controlled directorial indeterminacy (ideas in which Miles Davis was very much implicated). Hugo Frey writes that, throughout his career, Malle's preference was for a "naive" visual realism—the supposedly naked portrayal of an unadorned reality—that aimed to remove directorial technique from the viewer's gaze and concern. But this is only one approach on display in *Ascenseur*. Frey also notes that another unifying concern in Malle's oeuvre is an attachment to the techniques of documentary, and what was at the time of *Ascenseur* becoming known as *Cinéma direct*, "a cinema of the instantaneous" as Malle would comment approvingly, "a work of constant improvisation, where the choices are made constantly by the camera . . . the *mise en scène* is constituted by a series of choices, but they are made at the moment of filming. Afterwards, one asks oneself, during the editing, why one did it that way at that moment."[67]

Embryonic documentary "realism" is present in *Ascenseur* during Florence's nocturnal sortie, caught by a small crew working quickly in the street with rough-and-ready Tri-X—the results harking back to a neo-realist classic like Rossellini's *Rome, Open City* (1945), shot at the end of the war using handheld cameras, nonprofessional actors, available light, and whatever fragments of film stock the director could lay his hands on (multiple visual textures resulting). But it was also an improvisatory, semicontrolled directorial decision of Malle's to request Davis to provide his jazz score: "what really excited me," the director said in 1960, "was not so much the fact that it was jazz, but that with Miles we reached the idea of absolute improvisation."[68] And the musical performance that followed built another layer of happenstance into the film's form and, as it turned out, its mythology. The myth of presence and happy chance—the momentary act kept alive by the filmic medium so firmly ensconced in the contemporary cinematic imagination by Bazin's work—was perfectly suited to jazz and vice versa, and much publicity surrounding *Ascenseur* presented the story of the music's recording in unacknowledged deference to this ideal. Such is seen in a short promotional film for which Davis, Malle and an interviewer acted out the recording session scene. The Frenchmen sit in a control booth, looking out at Davis as he mimes along to his own music in front of the projected film.

INTERVIEWER: What's happening here exactly?

MALLE: Well, the American musician Miles Davis is improvising on images from my film *Ascenseur pour l'échafaud*.

INTERVIEWER: You mean to say that he's watching the images, and he plays the trumpet in response to the images?

MALLE: Yes—that's to say, he's knows the images well since he's seen the film, and we've discussed what he might do, but then, with his group, we project the images and record.

INTERVIEWER: So he hasn't written a score?

MALLE: Absolutely not.

INTERVIEWER: He plays as it comes to him.

MALLE: As it comes to him.

INTERVIEWER: If he'd done it the day after it would have been different.

MALLE: Yes. Even from one take to another it's different.[69]

Such is present, too, in Boris Vian's often-cited liner notes for the original soundtrack release.

> One may note on the piece "Dîner au motel" a strange sonority in Miles' trumpet. This happened when a fragment of skin came off Miles' lip and became stuck in his mouthpiece. Just as some painters sometimes owe the plastic quality of their touch to chance, in the same way, Miles willingly greeted this "unheard of" element of music ("unheard of" in the literal sense).[70]

No matter that René Urtreger described this story as "bullshit."[71] The nexus of meanings established by the film's images, music, promotional materials and mythologizing worked together in tight concert, and continued to do so. Into the 21st century, when *Ascenseur* has been discussed by critics—Anglophones especially—then so has its soundtrack, and the story of the soundtrack's production. "With Barney Wilen, René Urtreger, Pierre Michelot and Kenny Clarke in tow," begins one entry in this hyperformalized field,

> Davis rolled up to the Le Poste Parisien studio on December 4. With minimal prep, barring a truncated preview for Davis and a short outline of the film's plotline for the band, the quintet improvised the entire soundtrack live as they watched the film unfold before them . . . *Ascenseur Pour L'Echafaud* is something beyond a movie accompaniment; it's a story told in sound. The somnambulist stroll of Nuit Sur Les Champs-Élysées conjures Jeanne Moreau, moodily skulking the dark streets of Paris, the cry of Davis's trumpet arousing the pain of her heartbreak every time it sounds.[72]

A story told in sound for this reviewer in 2011, a sonic revelation of the image's embedded meaning for Nettlebeck in 2004, even for the French film revue *Positif* in 1958 Davis's music constituted a film within a film (and the trumpeter's was better than Malle's, *Positif*'s reviewer concluded).[73] Over the decades, and in newspapers, magazines and jazz histories alike, this bundle of tropes has been repeated almost without end, serving to reinforce the myth of the film, of Miles Davis, and of jazz improvisation.[74] What has struck many general listeners about that musical technique is its immediacy; what has struck many of the film's viewers is that, by dint of the music's peculiar recording process, in using such a creative method Davis was able to give literally immediate responses to the image of Florence, to actualize in music a narrated psychological state—this, after all, is what is assumed to be the nature of the relationship between a jazz musician's own thought and execution.

And that was a belief of long standing. In his 1939 book *De la vie et du jazz*, Charles Delaunay had, like Hugues Panassié even before him, counterposed the immediacy of jazz improvisation with the creative mediation of classical composition and its alienated execution.

> In jazz, what we could call the *interior note*, that's to say the note felt by the artist and *the note emitted* by the instrument, can only be one. A single and same vibration must run through the musician, from his heart to the bell of his instrument. His whole being primed, one can say he becomes the horn. This explains in part the preference of jazz musicians for wind instruments . . . jazz is a form of expression that is direct, total and definitive . . .[75]

From its early framing and publicity department mediation to its looping contemporary reception, *Ascenseur*'s soundtrack's celebrity rests upon a similar, tantalizing possibility of a magical materialization of thought and being in sound, but one now framed by an interest in the postwar plastic rather than the prewar mystic; that this operation unfolded in real time, at the mercy of accident, gives *Ascenseur*'s music a "realism" of a piece with dominant Bazinian ideas of the late 1950s, and with more contemporary (mis)understandings and culture-industry renderings of musical improvisation's workings.

Davis perfectly understood the lust for total presence that these accounts betray, for a subjective reunification born of the perfect correspondence between (sound) image and (improvised) object. Especially after *Ascenseur*, he understood the ways that informal recording methods could inflame those desires. Throughout the middle part of his career, the trumpeter constructed commentaries that would enforce such ideas around his work and invited them to be constructed by others. Such can be heard in the results of the 1956 Prestige sessions that resulted in *Cookin'*, *Steamin'*, *Workin'* and *Relaxin'*, where numerous performances are framed by Davis's comments to the engineer and the band ("when you see the red light on everybody's supposed to be quiet"), his unusually hoarse voice recalling his unusually breathy trumpet tone, two trademarks that attempted to signal full presence, full vocality, full corporality, even in their recorded form; it can be heard in the promotional chatter surrounding *Ascenseur*'s recording, fascinated commentary that must have reinforced the trumpeter's idea that he was on to something; it is seen in the well-known liner notes for *Kind of Blue*, in which Bill Evans

rhetorically overstates the ephemerality of the music and its creation in front of our very ears; it is present in tales of the recording of *In a Silent Way*, *Bitches Brew* and other albums made at the turn of the 1970s in which composition was heard, simultaneously, both in the moment and in its tape-manipulated form. Davis's genius, developed through his encounter with Florence and on his behalf by those producers and writers playing along with the master, lay in his understanding of the ways that stories of his working practices could be made to coincide with the musical semiotics of voice and breath to produce myths of total musical, emotional and personal presence that were asserted even as they were denied—over and over again, yet, tantalizingly, never conclusively—by the nature and fact of their recorded medium.[76]

There's one more piece of contemporary promotional material that signifies this kind of immediate relationship between Davis's music and Florence's mind: a much-reproduced photo call image that shows the trumpeter playing his instrument directly into Jeanne Moreau's ear. Given the instrument's potential volume, a lingering sense of worry, perhaps a threat of male-female aggression, hangs over the picture. But, as I will show, so it does over *Ascenseur*.

The Look and the Voice

A recurrent theme in commentaries on Malle's work—one grounded in Malle's self-admitted ambivalence and disengagement—concerns a kind of looking that amounts to directorial voyeurism. Nathan Southern finds much of this in *Ascenseur*. From the first scenes, Southern writes, Malle focuses our attention on Tavernier's preparation for the assassination, "from the most significant to the most inconsequential aspect, frame by frame," while almost entirely avoiding "look shots" that would show us the world from the characters' perspective. Southern argues that the viewers' objective regard of the unfolding murder works to undermine any developing empathy with the characters involved, though, equally, the audience is not moved to despise the narrative's players—Tavernier's assassination of Carala is not shown so as to maintain this ambivalence. Similarly the noncommunication of the characters, particularly the leading couple that never appears together, means that no sense of passion or involvement is generated in the on-screen world or among us, its off-screen observers. It is, Southern writes, the simple outcome of the story that interests spectators put in such a position, not the fate or well-being of its players. This amoral voyeurism is a standard element of the relationship between the typical film noir narrative and its audience.[77] But such an attitude can also be seen as directly reflective of Malle's putative political ambivalence at the time: fatalistic and uninvested, both authoritarian leanings and directorial technique betray a will to controlling omniscience.[78]

In *Ascenseur* the camera looks, without engagement, on our behalf, and the character it often looks at—Florence—in turn rarely engages those who surround her: enacting one of what Southern calls the "paper thin" romantic and noir conventions present in the film, Moreau's character walks across a street and is nearly run over by a passing car, continuing on oblivious as befits a woman sleepwalking, in search of absent love. A twist on this appears in the final scene; having seen the images incriminating her and Tavernier develop, Florence glances straight towards the camera, in a monologue telling herself and her spectators that her active life is, for all intents and purposes, over. In fictional film, the look at the camera often functions as a Brechtian breaking of the fourth wall, all of a sudden acknowledging the presence and participation of the spectators, undermining their hitherto secure sense of control.[79] This can be deeply unsettling for an audience engrossed in a fictional narrative, but Florence's look does not work in this manner. Instead, it reinforces both her own blindness and the all-powerful vision of the viewer: her words full of self-reproach, she looks not at but straight through us, as if through a two-way mirror.

Not only spied upon by us Mallean voyeurs, not only caught by Tavernier's camera, Florence was watched throughout by another—by Miles Davis, who, of course, gave (internal) voice to the character as, during the recording session, he watched her roam by night. The workings of these spectatorial gazes were to be much explored by the generation of film theorists following Bazin. From the end of the 1960s, realism was attacked for its mysticism, its religiosity, the most strident criticism found in the writings of Jean-Louis Baudry, Jean-Louis Comolli and others working on what became known as "apparatus theory": here, critical investigation identified not the filmic capturing of essences and truth but the full range of technical operations required of mass market cinematic production required to present the "real," examining the ways that such techniques produced and reproduced sociopolitical meaning and capitalist "ideology," trapping viewers within this mechanism (we see later that Comolli was as important as a jazz critic as he was a film theoretician).[80] Out of this work developed a school of feminist film criticism, led in the 1970s and '80s by Anglophone writers like Laura Mulvey and Kaja Silverman, which was concerned with the ways in which gendered social roles and behaviors were established and reproduced in mass-market movies.[81] In a now-canonical 1973 piece, Mulvey argued that in "classic" cinema women had not usually functioned as full (if fictional) subjectivities, rather as objects, gazed at by both camera and (male) spectators. In these films, Mulvey wrote, women were usually mute or immobile icons around whom action was conducted by male characters. Camera, narrative and spectators took voyeuristic pleasure in onscreen femininity and, specifically, femininity's constraint; it was through these narrative and visual methods that an ideology of coherent and all-powerful masculinity was constructed, both on the screen and in the stalls.[82]

Whatever the criticisms that have since been leveled at Mulvey's argument, the scholar's mute women and active men can be seen in countless films across cinema's history.[83] And aspects of her analysis certainly apply to *Ascenseur*, a film, of course, that makes much of classic Hollywood convention. Florence, almost never during the film having a dynamic, fully voiced conversational exchange with any other character, is nearly motionless even when moving, hands by her side, gaze directed at some far-off point in front of her. During the titles, on the telephone to Tavernier, Florence is haloed in soft-focus fuzz—since Mulvey noted that women onscreen are reduced to "icons," the halo is appropriate—just as she is later when sitting motionless in the café waiting for her lover, and in the film's final shot when she announces to the camera that her life, to be spent motionless in prison, is over.[84] The pleasure Malle and his narrative seem to take in condemning Florence at the end of the story was noted by Mulvey as another film noir commonplace.[85]

But one of the film's points of interest is in the ways that it mounts such sexist conventions only to subtly undercut them. Tavernier, trapped in a lift for most of the film's duration, is a poor match for Mulvey's active male hero, who supposedly courses through and commands the three dimensional stage in which action takes place.[86] And whereas Mulvey's spectators were supposedly given to identify with bounding male protagonists, the film's soundtrack makes it clear that Miles Davis—famously, one of the film's first spectators, and certainly, handed a trumpet and a microphone during his viewing, the spectator granted greatest critical agency—seems over and over again to identify with Florence, mute but unmuted, and to spurn Tavernier. *Ascenseur*, like Malle's 1963 *Le Feu follet*, in which Maurice Ronet this time plays an ex-paratrooper driven to suicide by a complex of postcolonial and postcoital insecurities, is unable to successfully perform what it knows should be its own masculine role: in this Malle is faithful to the themes of disgust and impotence that preoccupied Nimier and his fellow Hussards.

The directorial enclosures of *Ascenseur*'s female lead work on another level too—and it is there that Davis's music is most implicated. Writing in the late 1980s on the female voice in film, Kaja Silverman extended Mulvey's critical feminist project to argue that, in classic cinema, female voices had been used in ways that enforced patriarchy both inside the cinema and out. Whereas male characters' voices and utterances were usually externalized, driving the narrative, female voices were internalized, contained by the narrative.[87] Such voiceless interiority became in Hollywood "a synonym for femininity," Silverman wrote, and such removal from narrative determination placed women "definitively 'on stage'"; silent women were often only given voice when, "on command," they externalized a certain kind of psychic reality usually more immediate than language—a scream, a cry.[88]

A silent cinematic woman available for physical inspection: think of diegetically silent Florence, her inner voice enunciated by the trumpet, barely engaging in conversation throughout the film, wandering Paris, watched. Beyond "the discursive impotence of the female voice," Silverman argued, "is projected the yawning chasm of a corporeal interiority," and in Florence's case this chasm is filled by Davis's playing until, on command, Florence herself delivers a monologue accompanying a shot of her motionless, expressionless face describing what is to be a lifelong trauma.[89]

As Colin Nettlebeck would have concurred, the trumpet voice that Davis gives Florence being internal, the musician doesn't so much speak for the character as give the audience X-ray vision into her psyche. But this enacts on behalf of the spectators a rather male fantasy of total, and perhaps controlling, comprehension of the interior female subject, and here might be the point of absolute origin for the realist fantasy concerning Miles Davis's brilliant translation of the image, and character personality, into meaningful sound. In some ways following those earlier critics of realism, Silverman suggested that realist theories such as Bazin's identified the image of the object filmed with the object itself in an attempt to fantasize into being an experiential wholeness.[90] Theories of realism—and theories of Davis's music as what has been described as "a story told in sound," an unmediated summoning of Florence's psychic landscape—constantly make such a unificatory attempt even though the object of their regard, whether cinema or recorded music, constantly "disappoints" it in the announcing of its own recorded medium.[91] Still the desire for this music to *mean*, to fully and fixedly disclose, to have a total ontological congruity with its creating psychic impulse—an impulse that within the confines of Malle's fiction is Florence's, but outside is Davis's own—must be the same desire that leads to the Bazinian identification of image and object: the desire for a total completion and security of meaning that will always escape us.

And yet it wasn't the case that Davis simply ascribed subjectivity to Florence: she ascribed it to him, too.[92] As suggested at the outset, it has become routine for critics to suggest that *Ascenseur*'s recording led directly to *Kind of Blue* (1959), these arguments hinging on the works' shared working methods and materials, sketches and modes.[93] But an equally strong connection between the soundtrack and several years' worth of Davis's subsequent work lies in the trumpeter's switch into a "female" voice, inspired by the effort to represent Florence. However cool his bebop had been, it was with his music for Malle—immediately followed, as the trumpeter is reported as having reminisced, by further conscious attempts to mimic the female voice on his recordings *Porgy and Bess* (1958) and *Sketches of Spain* (1960)—that Davis found the identity that became so canonically ensconced and critically validated.[94] Following this recasting, Barry Ulanov's famous, negative 1953 critical appraisal of Davis's "feeble" "eggshell trumpet" was transformed into numberless positive critiques founded upon the same terms of fragility, emotional vulnerability.[95] Davis' playing had now, according to Charles Fox, "a quality of introspection akin to T. S. Eliot's early poems or the novels of Proust," was "like a man reading aloud from his diary"; Whitney Balliett commented on Davis's "Young-Werther ruminations . . . a view of things that is brooding, melancholy, perhaps self-pitying, and extremely close to the sentimental."[96] Writing on *Ascenseur* for the *New York Times* in 1989, Peter Watrous noted that the Paris recordings "are brave: th[is] sort of emotional exposure, where he allowed an extraordinary amount of tenderness to infuse his playing, was at odds not only with standard jazz practice, but also with conceptions of how men should express themselves."[97] These post-*Ascenseur* critiques reference sensitive males, but they are of a player who had constructed a full musical identity via a female Other.[98]

André Hodeir's consideration of a reserved jazz playing style described a "cool" much more decorative than the self-destructive and nihilistic inaction that infected, and defined, the rightist litterateurs with whom Malle associated around the time of *Ascenseur*. But music working within those cool dynamic limits was absolutely appropriate for the director's visual style and narrative design, one that so fulfilled the tenets of a transatlantic culture of disconnection: the voyeuristic observation that refused to give way to participation, the keen knowingness that refused to make anything of its knowledge, the sociopolitical stance that was constituted not by critical engagement with society or its politics but by the supposed evasion of those forces and the establishment of compensatory aesthetic concerns. Like the French *Cahiers* critics and their films, like the American bebop musicians and their strategies of withdrawal, Malle directed his early work against the supposed conformity of the postwar establishment, and with an attitude of insouciance that—like Miles Davis's own—was underpinned by new formal techniques of easy mastery.

But no matter how much it was advertised, this sense of limit and detachment was undermined by still-powerful contemporary theories of unifying filmic realism and by a related fascination for the ways in which music might open up an image's meaning. That mystical interpretation of Davis's improvised realization persists into the 21st century, and it does so because the culture-industrial framings that, preceding and accompanying the music's production, support that reading—the photo call, the sleeve-note narratives, the staged documentaries—have been replayed time and again, the myth rewound and rebooted almost as often as the movie itself. The relationships between sound and image, between Davis's playing and Florence's (musical) persona, were anything but mystical: instead they were shaped by Malle and a brilliantly imaginative, commercially canny trumpeter whose real instrument was the idea of presence.

Going Cold on Cool

By the mid-1960s, it seemed to many on both sides of the Atlantic that cool could not last. However supposedly subversive of petty-bourgeois norms, its position was staked out between the markers of exotic and idealized American (cultural) industries—the music, the movies, the automobiles. While in France new modes of consumption were strongly associated with American influence, and while for many this initially formed a bone of contention—local Communists talked of "coca-colonization"—what were understood to be the great improvements to the French standard of living brought about by new mass production and consumption were increasingly appreciated.[99] Film played its part in these changes, and as Raymond Borde's *Temps modernes* review complained, *Ascenseur* was one of those French productions to show this value system being internalized. Kristin Ross has written that

> the postwar screens of Europe were filled with an illustrated catalog of the joys and rewards of American capitalism; all the minutiae of domestic life in the United States, its objects and gadgets and the lifestyle they help produce, were displayed as ordinary—that is, the background or trappings to convincing, realistic narratives.[100]

In *Ascenseur*, the "rewards of American capitalism" are there for all to see. Yet once again the film subverts the ideology it purports to display, subverting its Marshall Plan model. Here (consumer) technologies are responsible for the downfall of both principal couples: Tavernier is trapped in the newfangled lift of his modern office block, Louis is seduced by Tavernier's desirable car, Véronique implicates both couples by using the little camera of Tavernier's that she was so impressed by. In this book's final chapter I argue that this ironic relationship towards (jazz) consumerism would later develop in decidedly unsubversive ways. In the 1960s, though, a much more thoroughgoing critique of Americanized consumer culture could be seen developing across Jean-Luc Godard's work. As suggested earlier, Godard's breakthrough *A bout de souffle* (1960) shared *Ascenseur*'s complicated fascination for all things American. Yet having undergone a political radicalization following Vietnam and May 1968, Godard would reflect that his generation's critical and creative valorization of the "little gangster film from Hollywood" and its trappings was not as self-determined as all that: "What was really going on," he suggested, "was that we were living under the mythology of the American cinema."[101]

The critique of such mythology, one that for Godard stood as much for American cultures of expression as it did cultures of consumption and international politics of aggression, would be articulated by the film-maker's changing framing of what were, to leftist French intellectuals at least, some of the most potent symbols of the mid-century United States. If Martial Solal's music for *A bout de souffle* plays on American jazz and cultural codes, then it does so without any sense of "criticality." Similarly, Michel Legrand's Gil Evans-infused scoring is breezy for *Une Femme est une femme* (1961), dark and rich for 1964's *Bande à part*—that film also featuring several bursts of barrelhouse jazz band—but never invested with any amount of commentary significance. By this time jazz's moment of widest popularity had passed; in line with French cinematic use in general, jazz's sounding signifiers now became much rarer in Godard's work. And yet, in the director's unusual case, these were sometimes replaced by jazz and black music's verbal signifiers insofar as these pertained to an increasing radical politics. For 1966's *Masculin féminin* Godard filched a monologue from LeRoi Jones's play *Dutchman*, which was being staged in Paris as the director filmed. It was now in the Paris métro rather than the New York subway that a black man told his white female companion that Bessie Smith's music could mean nothing for whites—except that they could "screw themselves"—and that, if Charlie Parker could have killed the first ten white people he had come across, he could have thrown his saxophone in the sea and never played again. In 1968 Godard was invited to London to film the Rolling Stones during the recording sessions for what was to become *Beggars Banquet*. The director's response differed somewhat from the producer's visions of profitable counterculturalism: in one of several testingly long, single-shot scenes, a group of West Indians and African Americans sit in a Battersea scrap yard, surrounded by the dead hulks of cars, reading excerpts from a Stokely Carmichael speech, Eldridge Cleaver's *Soul on Ice* and LeRoi Jones's seminal black music history *Blues People*. As we see in the next chapter, that 1963 book of Jones's would, following its 1968 French translation, become a central text for the leftist French culturati, the author's words encouraging a new critique of the ways in which black cultural expression had supposedly been traduced by mainstream capitalization. In its original African American usage, Jones had written, "[t]o be *cool* was, in its most accessible meaning, to be calm, even unimpressed, by what horror the world might daily propose," the term "never meant to connote the tepid new popular music of the white middle-brow middle class. On the contrary," Jones concluded, "it was exactly this America that one was supposed to 'be cool' in the face of."[102] *One Plus One*'s juxtaposition of radical African American voices with footage of the Rolling Stones' pseudo-seditious R&B highlights just this cultural trajectory, Godard's presentation of issues of music, blackness and tried-on cool rebellion now as critical as his presentation of the automobile. The final reckoning for that token of Americanized modernity came arrived in 1968's *Weekend* and its ten-minute tracking shot of a gory pileup on a *route nationale*.

Godard's methods were, at the height of the black liberation movement and the Vietnam War, of a piece with a wider trends in leftist French anti-Americanism, anti-colonialism and anti-capitalism, and his renouncing of positive interest in American mass culture resembled that of other French cultural figures.[103] On his visits immediately after the war, Jean-Paul Sartre, too, had been fascinated by the United States and by its jazz, but by 1965 he would refuse even to set foot in the country; the journalist Claude Julien had lived and worked in America before writing his 1968 book, *L'Empire américain*, an updating of that favorite French literary genre in which developments in the New World were presented as dangers for the Old. Julien's work focused not on the mass production that caused so much worry in the 1920s but on the mass consumption of the modern era and the violence that trailed in its wake.[104]

The hostile intellectualist attitude towards a new commodity culture identified as American—but increasingly just as French—linked that consumption to passivity. As they long had done, numerous French sociologists and journalists, not only on the left, lamented the dissolution of traditional bonds of class and community among those modern French who had become "home-centered," seeking entertainment and security in what they watched or purchased; dead-eyed acquisition was satirized in Georges Perec's celebrated 1965 anti-novel, *Les Choses*, "Things."[105] As the *événements* of 1968 would prove, the cool detachment of old was too close to this passivity to be the favored mode of sociopolitical being for a young generation of left-leaning, educated urbanites.

In France as in the United States, jazz musicians, too, were redefining their relationships toward their surroundings, the 1950s cultivation of distanced superiority ceding in the 1960s to a variety of attempts to connect with "the people." In taking another pass through those decades, the next chapter explores this change in more detail—and from the vantage point of one of the musicians standing alongside Miles Davis at the Poste Parisien studio, that famous night they recorded the music for *Ascenseur*.

FIVE

Barney Wilen

Phantoms and Freedom

Some scenes from one life in (and out of) the French bebop business: a young saxophone star, 1958, shouting down the phone to Germany in between sets at the Club Saint-Germain, trying to make himself heard above the din as he negotiates a gig fee; a confused musician in hiding, 1964, listening to Ornette Coleman's free jazz in New York and wondering what on earth he was going to do with his own playing, now rendered so out of date; the same man, 1975, smuggling medicines around a Niger wracked by violence and famine, the saxophone rarely to be seen, but a tape recorder on hand to capture whatever music-making he comes across.[1]

They belong to one biography, but if the camera draws back and pans around these images turn out both to illustrate and to form movements that affected the French jazz world of the 1950s and '60s in its entirety. And not just the jazz world: the cool bebop star at Club Saint-Germain figures in the French fascination with postwar American cultural superpower; the man listening in New York will shortly have to decide what the radical black liberation politics attaching itself to this new free jazz could mean for a white European; the actions of the traveler in Africa, musical and humanitarian, are those of someone spun around in the commotion of May 1968 and plunged into the internationalism of the postcolonial era. No single life can act as a simple, paradigmatic description of what it was to be a French jazz musician, and there was rarely a player as singular as Barney Wilen. Yet every twist in the saxophonist's unusual career mirrored the actions and concerns, aesthetic or otherwise, of countless others—not least those musician peers who, according to the changing tenor of the times, made jazz that sometimes celebrated and sometimes wrenched itself away from the American music that had once been so uncomplicatedly enchanting.

The Making of Barney Wilen

Bernard Jean Wilen, "Barney," was born into a wealthy Nice family in March 1937. His mother, though French born, was descended from an aristocratic Russian family; his American father was a dentist and inventor, the holder of valuable patents for goggles, harpoons and other accoutrements of coastal amusement. The couple were friends with a number of artists and literary figures, such as the poet Blaise Cendrars and the painter Kees van Dongen, and Wilen remembered his youth as unfolding "right in the middle of that F. Scott Fitzgerald French Riviera scene."[2] But it was a youth interrupted by the outbreak of war, and in 1939 Wilen's Jewish father presciently removed the family to the United States, where, for seven years, they lived with a succession of relatives on both coasts. In America the seven year-old Wilen took up the alto saxophone, the horn a birthday gift from an uncle, and he was soon excelling in school bands, music—Wilen recalled much later—the French boy's way of integrating himself into American school life.[3] Among many American teachers the adult Wilen recalled a Mr. Sperry, who put the young player to work on popular tunes as well as traditional exercises; Wilen believed that an intimate relationship with that music gave him an advantage over his French contemporaries that showed when he later came to be hired by visiting American stars. "They had to research the chord changes," he said, "but I could speak the same language the others did."[4] Throughout his career, Wilen and his feature-writing journalist collaborators would evoke this sojourn in the United States, and the encounter with Sperry and the American songbook, shaping a story of a young man uprooted to and yet in some ways born of jazz's native land, formed by its melody and popular song above all.[5]

Following the family's return to France in 1946, the saxophonist—now known to admiring friends as *l'Américain*—formed a group with a number of cousins, which played at parties in the Nice area. As well as stock dance-music arrangements, the band played riffs derived from Louis Armstrong records while Wilen did his best to imitate Sidney Bechet.[6] This experience, and the saxophonist's encounter with Bobby Jaspar's Bob Shots at the Nice jazz festival of 1948—"I said to myself, these Belgians can play this black American music, so it *is* possible"—prepared the ground for an epiphany: both as a young star in the late 1950s and a battered, semimythical figure twenty years later, Wilen would tell interviewers that it was at the age of thirteen that, listening to the radio, he suddenly perceived that jazz was an art, and that he woud dedicate himself to it. "I knew at that moment that I would never do anything else."[7]

Wilen was taken under the wing of a slightly older pianist, Pierre Franzino, who helped develop his friend's knowledge of modern jazz. With Franzino and another young southerner, the bassist Paul Rovère, the saxophonist formed a group that won an amateur tournament in Paris in 1953 (recently struck by the records of Lars Gullin and Gerry Mulligan, Wilen was now playing baritone). While he was in Paris, his nights were spent jamming at the Tabou club with Henri Renaud and Jimmy Gourley.[8] Those players shaped Wilen's existing interest in Lester Young—which was a reaction, the onetime altoist said later, to a first, terrified hearing of Charlie Parker—into an investigation of Al Cohn, Zoot Sims and other saxophonists identified with the American West coast. Once back in Nice to finish his schooling, Wilen dropped the baritone, now deemed "too heavy"; before long the tenor replacement was itself dropped down a flight of stairs and its lower register obliterated, obliging the saxophonist to play light and high for six months and no doubt helping along the cool style Wilen was developing.[9]

Thanks to his professional Paris contacts, Wilen and his group were working with a cutting-edge American jazz repertoire and style, musical information culled firsthand from visitors rather than by way of discs: out performing for pennies, the saxophonist apparently popularized "Bernie's Tune" on Nice's seafront promenade before Gerry Mulligan's famous recording was made. Inevitably excluded from local, Panassié-associated Hot-clubs on stylistic grounds, the band set about finding a place of its own in which to play. On the rue Masséna an old wine cellar was located, stripped and painted; the club, Wilen said later, was full every evening from 6:00 p.m. to midnight, and a 1954 *Jazz hot* report on the local success story described 100 "blue-jeans" aged between fourteen and twenty-five singing along to the cool jazz favourite "Tasty Pudding."[10] The *Jazz hot* piece noted the currency of the Gigi Gryce and Al Cohn–associated pieces in the band's repertoire while criticizing most of its players—though not Wilen, who was praised at length and granted a separate interview profile. A teenager who had triumphed in the capital and now attracted national press attention, in Nice the seventeen-year-old Wilen was an autograph-signing star.

The saxophonist interrupted his schooling in the autumn of 1954 to rejoin Renaud in Paris; he was immediately featured in a *Jazz hot* survey of tenor players in France as a name to watch, his playing belonging to the new, Bobby Jaspar–headed school of cool French tenors.[11] In October, Wilen attended his first recording session as part of a group under the nominal leadership of the drummer Roy Haynes and featuring Renaud, Gourley and Wilen's American-born, Nice-resident baritonist friend, Jay Cameron. The group's ten-inch Vogue release shows Wilen's fleet and easy rhythmic ability, his predictably light (if slightly tart) tone, and his ability to cast off long, gliding phrases that only sometimes fall to earth with a bump. It's playing that has proceeded by feel before rigor, and "Minor Encamp"'s bridge of quickly cycling chords poses some challenges to which Wilen is not yet equal. But the fact the teenager was playing the piece at all was indicative of the expert training he was receiving: this was the Duke Jordan composition that, obtained from Jordan in New York by Renaud, would become famous as "Jordu" in Clifford Brown and Max Roach's yet-to-be-released recording. Wilen's own abilities and efforts, then, were being brought out by his early mentors, well-connected French musicians and American visitors alike.[12] But these musical efforts were given a spur by the genuine popularity of a music that, appealing to the saxophonist's teenaged peers as much as it did adults, provided both abundant performance opportunities and communities of critical eyes in front of which it was important to excel and impress.

In January 1955, Wilen was summoned home to finish his baccalauréat.[13] Following a fraught period—the saxophone was confiscated, bedroom windows were climbed out of, the musician eventually thrown out of the family home—Wilen passed his exams at the second attempt and was free to embark on his career proper.[14] The saxophonist's celebrity grew through 1956, Wilen appearing at the San Remo festival in Italy, leading a group through a long stay at Paris's Club Saint-Germain, and recording with John Lewis and Sacha Distel (*Afternoon in Paris*, Atlantic). But it was the following year that the saxophonist's career took off.[15] Now under the management of the resourceful Paris scenemaker Marcel Romano, Wilen's activities grew more numerous and high profile, his every move reported monthly by a jazz press keen to sell a young French star to its young French readership.[16] A three-year, nine-album contract was signed with Vogue, in January yielding *Tilt* (in fact the only album to result from that deal).[17] During the spring, Wilen recorded *Barney Wilen Quintet* for Guilde de Jazz, and in the summer two long,

Romano-written *Jazz hot* features preceded the saxophonist's winning the Prix Django Reinhardt for best French jazz musician. Press attention arrived from Germany, Britain and Poland, Chinese whispers of a European jazz phenomenon building one puff piece at a time.[18] Wilen enjoyed another residency at the Club Saint-German (leading Martial Solal, Pierre Michelot and Kenny Clarke), and was booked to tour beach resorts and the Côte d'Azur through summer, Spain and Italy in the autumn.[19] At the end of the year, the excitedly reported (and Romano-manufactured) relationship with Miles Davis, which led to the *Ascenseur pour l'échafaud* recording and European concert tour detailed in the previous chapter, cemented Wilen's position as France's leading modern saxophonist.[20]

If the points of reference for Wilen's early playing were largely located on America's West Coast, then by 1957 and his arrival proper the saxophonist's style was much more reflective of the hard bop generally associated with black, East Coast musicians. The division and opposition between those two schools, enforced in the United States by critics, musicians and listeners alike, certainly reflected local race politics as much as it did musical reality. But even in France, in the apparent absence of those antagonisms, such conflict was acted out. Wilen's turning towards the deep-toned, chewily articulated approach then being cultivated in the United States by players like Jimmy Heath, Hank Mobley and, especially, Sonny Rollins was recorded in the French jazz press as a switch of allegiance, "a return to *l'école noire*" and its more "virile" approach, as one of Romano's *Jazz hot* articles had it.[21] Stylistic attributions were sexualized in France as they were in the United States, and other perceived race characteristics were projected onto musicians white and black, too. Played a Jimmy Giuffre record in a December 1957 blindfold test for *Jazz magazine*, Wilen was unmoved: "I prefer tenors with more shout. This is a bit too restrained." In contrast, Wilen could "only just believe" what Sonny Rollins was able to accomplish on "Strode Rode" (from *Saxophone Colossus*, 1956).[22] In fact, the Frenchman had been so overwhelmed by his early encounters with Rollins's records that he had already contributed a laudatory article on the American tenor to *Jazz hot*; there Wilen had written that it was "the genius of nuance" that he most admired, the Rollins who could "jump from a misty sweetness to the blinding clarity of his infallible attack," or "lounge around a chorus with no concern for the passing chord progression, and then launch into an incredible arabesque of harmonic virtuosity."[23]

This enthusiastic (and insightful) analysis might give a clue as to the French player's own musical values, and though the Barney Wilen of 1957 hadn't fully assimilated the flexibility of mood and approach that he found in Rollins, some of the punch lines heard in the American's more profound comedy had nonetheless been jotted down, their delivery mimicked. There is a Rollins-like extroversion to Wilen's playing on the debut *Tilt* that is barely heard on any of the saxophonist's subsequent albums, a joyful mischief that sees him begin a ballad solo with a piercing, long-held high note ("Nature Boy," 2:12), interpolate incongruous quotes from "Chicago" and Offenbach's "Cancan" ("Night in Tunisia," 3:13; "Hackensack," 1:01), and throw his rhythm section utterly with on-the-spot elaborations of "Misterioso"'s theme. The act has duds as well as zingers, the saxophonist's desire to project like Sonny giving his sound a slight shrillness, the perceived obligation to add a personal stamp to a melody leading him to manhandle "Nature Boy"'s wistful theme. Still, this exuberance is shared by the saxophonist's partners, and it makes *Tilt* one of the most exciting documents of bebop in France. Each side of the record features a different rhythm section; it's the less experienced band, featuring Charles Saudrais on drums, Bibi Rovère on bass and Jack Cnudde on piano that tackles a sequence of Thelonious Monk pieces on side 2.[24] Saudrais's clattering, Art Blakey–derived fills often threaten to destabilize the band without ever quite doing so, while Cnudde's hymnal comping and ultra-sparse solo lines sound like one oddly original pianist's tribute to another. When, on "Blue Monk," Wilen dares his band to follow him into a double-time passage they do, forcing a hand-brake turn to get out of it, the performance almost crashing to a halt: this is a group alive to idea and deaf to professional routine, players working at the edge of their techniques—techniques that would have seemed rudimentary twenty years later, but that are heard here in the heat of their making, the filing of blades rather than of fingernails.

The general approach is Rollins-like—as a comparison of Rollins's own recordings of several of *Tilt*'s pieces, made in the company of Monk during 1953–54, will show—but Wilen's vocabulary is just as Parkeresque, a number of the altoist's licks turning up again and again. The first passage in the following example, from the album's opening blues, appears twenty seconds into Wilen's solo, almost verbatim thirty seconds later, and then in fragmented form twenty seconds after that; the second excerpt, from the same performance, shows in one blow a number of Wilen's favorite enclosures and diminished arpeggios, these the Charlie Parker–derived conjunctions that formed such an important part of bebop's lingua franca.

These often-used licks, a few scattered examples of formulaic line-building among many, are much in evidence across *Tilt* and the follow-up *Barney Wilen Quintet*. Of course, Wilen's peers were in the same boat, as the *Quintet* album well demonstrates. Here, Hubert Fol's own Parker licks are articulate enough to answer much of the repertoire's demands, though confronted with a difficult chord progression or unfamiliar bridge the altoist is still momentarily struck dumb; at the piano, Nico Buninck wrestles with but is often constricted by the serpentine example of Bud Powell's lines. But if none of the musicians caught on these recordings is in the process of designing a truly new approach, then the tenor player still stands out: rather than material originality or its lack, what is remarkable is the nineteen-year-old saxophonist's artless sequencing of those common-or-garden bebop phrases, the authority and failsafe fluency that emerge from a surrounding of unswung note splurges and wrong-chord clangers.

And yet, whether caught on a less inspired day or increasingly wary of risk-taking for its own sake, there is already on this second record the slightest hint of a musician turning in on himself, playfulness of thought and rhythm swapped for something surer but in some ways less involved. Why this might have been is not clear.[25] But as Wilen's playing grew more polished—his recorded use of rote formulas and passages decreased through 1957–58, a much more sophisticated style of line construction emerging—so Romano's ambitions for his charge developed. It was popular stardom that Romano envisaged, the manager later recalling that he had wanted to put Wilen "on a pedestal," and a certain reliability and comportment were called for. Those early, thrown-together albums were to cede to more considered productions, the jobbing jazz musician to become something different and more modern: a recording artist.[26]

Wilen is the picture of fully rounded professionalism on one of this project's few resultant products, *Jazz sur Seine*, a February 1958 recording on which the saxophonist is backed by three-quarters of the original Modern Jazz Quartet (the group then at the height of its international celebrity). In one of his gushing, interest-conflicted *Jazz hot* article tributes to his client, Romano had written that Wilen was "what we've been waiting for since the death of Django" and was "the continent's only jazzman capable of effectively transmitting his personality by way of his music."[27] Wilen was on board: "this was my Django Reinhardt period," he recalled in the mid-1960s: "I was trying to make French music . . . a bit naively."[28]

As is suggested by the album's punning title (Jazz-on-the-Seine / jazz center stage), much of the record's repertoire is strongly identified with the French tradition of jazz-inflected popular music that Reinhardt had helped create. The guitarist himself is summoned by way of "Swing 39," "Nuages" and "Vamp," and Charles Trenet, the giant of 1930s chanson, is represented by four of his hits.[29] An anti-blowing session full of carefully arranged and rehearsed tracks—all short and radio friendly, varied and audience-building—the album is a considered, cleanly executed attempt to link still-popular prewar jazz and music-hall traditions with bebop, all this under the control of a singular musical personality. And Wilen occupies those old French melodies in an entirely unironic fashion: his shaping of "J'ai ta main" is jolly and expansive, delivered with a wink and one arm outstretched, Trenet style. The saxophonist's love for and identification with popular melody, above and sometimes beyond even jazz, is allowed to develop here for the first time.

Romano's search for a mainstream audience, and his film-world contacts, delivered Wilen a commission to write the soundtrack for Edouard Molinaro's *Un Témoin dans la ville*, a suspense movie that fails to deliver on an already unimpressive premise involving radio taxis; the resultant, functional music was recorded in spring 1959 with Kenny Dorham, the trumpeter and saxophonist at that time also recording a live album, *Barney*.[30] On this document of two nights at the Club Saint-Germain Wilen's playing is slick, combed and set, but still sometimes shown up by Dorham's inventive stylishness. While the record was sold by Raymond Mouly's back cover notes as Wilen's "first big album," sales were disappointing, Romano's projected image of Wilen the star already blurring.[31] And a creeping sense of disenchantment is, indeed, increasingly audible in the saxophonist's playing. Wilen spent part of the summer in the United States, appearing at Newport and briefly filling in as the Jazz Messengers' tenor saxophonist to record another Romano-fixed soundtrack, this time for Roger Vadim's *Les Liaisons dangereuses 1960*; again the music is doled out by the minute.[32]

That was partly a consequence of the film's demands (though Wilen had seen first hand how Miles Davis could shape hackwork into something more complex). But the saxophonist was coasting, sounding more bored than professional. On record, at least: two further pieces would be recorded with Art Blakey and the Jazz Messengers at a jam session at Paris's Olympia theater that December, and these suggest that live, Wilen could be another player. The Frenchman appears on alto, his regular register given over to Blakey's new recruit, Wayne Shorter, and there is an elastic, ecstatic quality to Wilen's earliest horn that is completely at odds with what had become his rather deadpan tenor. Wilen's give-and-take with Blakey is quick and assertive ("Bouncing With Bud," 5:26, 5:44), the comparison with an incessantly exuberant Lee Morgan and an already off-kilter Shorter suggesting no hierarchy at all. The Frenchman is at his most animated, excited by bebop, it seems, one last time.

Perseverance

Plaudits had continued to arrive. In May 1959, Wilen won a listeners' poll conducted by the radio station Europe N° 1; spots in television variety programs and entertainment magazines upheld a popular profile of the sort that would soon be largely beyond jazz musicians; a 1961 *Jazz magazine* interview began by praising the saxophonist as having arrived at the stage whereby he was, like "Django Reinhardt, Stéphane Grappelly or Martial Solal, a French musician whose personal style owes only a spiritual debt to the great American jazzmen."[33] And yet the saxophonist was beginning to tire of the music he was playing. In 1965 he would tell Philippe Carles and Jean-Louis Comolli that he had begun to feel "at a standstill with bop" just after recording the music for Vadim's *Liaisons dangereuses*. "I had the impression that everything was coming out of the same mould," he said.[34]

That 1961 *Jazz magazine* piece was titled "Barney Wilen, or, perseverance," and it was this quality—and perhaps his own doubts as to how much of it he held in store—that occupied the saxophonist. Significantly, the article reported Wilen's address as Switzerland, the saxophonist having installed himself, his wife, Doris, and young son, Patrick-Charles in a Basel suburb. Despite the happy domestic scene the piece presented—and these lifestyle features were one of the journal's jazz press innovations—the short marriage was almost over. Wilen's withdrawal from Paris had not been made by choice. Doris had removed herself and her son from the city when, returning home from the hospital after giving birth, she found an overdosed Wilen laid out, close to death. The flight from Paris was an attempt to escape from heroin addiction as much as an exhausted style of music.[35]

The new location was pragmatic in other ways. Wilen said he had an eye on the nearby, and active, German and Italian jazz circuits (the saxophonist visited these countries in the company of musicians like Bud Powell and George Gruntz, recording in Milan with the drummer Gil Cuppini and the guitarist Franco Cerri in 1961). To stay busy, after all, a French jazz musician had to be a European jazz musician. What's not apparent is how far Wilen wanted to keep working, or to push his bebop playing any further: on the January 1962 recording of George Gruntz's soundtrack for the film *Mental Cruelty* he sounds badly out of practice. Still, gigs were occasionally undertaken away from the gaze of the Parisian public; at the very end of the Belgian misadventure in the Congo, for instance, Wilen traveled to that country alongside the Belgian saxophonist and fixer Jacques Pelzer and teenaged drummer Jacques Thollot to play a series of concerts supported by the national airline Sabena.[36]

The saxophonist was evidently beginning to develop new, if tentative, approaches during this period. In a long and collaboratively credited report on a festival appearance at Marseille in 1963, Roger Luccioni, Alain Delaye and Florimond Delannoy—local enthusiasts writing for the local enthusiasts' magazine, *Jazz hip*, a journal not beholden to the hype machines and face-to-face familiarities of the Paris jazz world—remarked that the fluid Wilen style so well known from recordings had become disrupted by what the authors called the conjured-away bursts of notes of a Coltrane, the carved-up phrases of an Ornette Coleman. But these new incorporations were judged somewhat cosmetic: "Barney surprised us in a way that could have won us over," the critics wrote, "if only he had known how to take his reasoning to its logical conclusion . . . That wasn't always the case, alas!"[37] In contrast to the almost universally admiring tone of Wilen's critical reception up to this point, the writers identified in Marseille a kind of reticence and noncommitment—one removed from the attitudinal playacting of the cool jazz Wilen had grown up with— which, though it had helped define much of the saxophonist's work, had not previously been remarked upon by a press looking only for positives.

It seems we've expected too much of this young man, formidably gifted but disappointing his admirers with a certain lack of consistency, of thickness. Barney has gained some weight. He isn't and probably never will be a player of the lumberjack variety (Monk, Blakey, Rollins), but the force of affirmation that he has lacked—for our taste alone, let it be said—suddenly seems significant.[38]

The Marseillais finished their article by wishing that they weren't mildly disappointed every time they heard Wilen, and that they could will him on like a fan, twisting in his seat, wills on a favorite boxer. But that wasn't the case. The saxophonist likely concurred. "There wasn't much left to discover," Wilen reflected a few years later. "In fact, I was very bored, I didn't know what to do."[39]

"My direction is . . ."

Wilen resurfaced in March 1964 to give a brief interview to *Jazz hot*'s Philippe Kœchlin. He had left Paris, the saxophonist related, because there was no one he wanted to play with. More darkly, the saxophonist admitted that he had "had urgent, personal business to take care of," code that jazz fans versed in bebop drug lore would likely have been able to decipher. "On the coast I found tranquility," he said. "There are too many distractions in Paris." [40] This allusion was attached to what was becoming another increasingly common jazzworld complaint, both in Europe and the United States. While, as we have seen, the music was increasingly associated with elite culural values, those were often not reflected in the exhausting and precarious working lives of musicians touring an ever-shorter circuit of smoky and dirty clubs, and by the mid-1960s many jazz musicians were articulating their disaffection, calling for government funding of the sort classical music habitually received.[41] Having largely resigned a public and peripatetic career in favor of a quiet life by the sea, Wilen couldn't earn a living from jazz in Nice; he was, he said, merely "getting by" on his record royalties, occasional concerts abroad, and radio and television appearances. In light of those scant professional prospects, it was significant that Wilen claimed to be "concentrating on the problem of integrating classical music and jazz."[42]

This integration, it seems, Wilen saw as taking place at the level of melody.

> I haven't really worked on the instrument, I'm worried about having too much technique. Melody, for me, is everything . . . I tried to get away from it, but it isn't possible. Coltrane and Ornette Coleman are experimenters of genius, and they are going in certain directions, but

mine is towards the classic. It's that marriage that interests me. Jazz is a hydra, it absorbs everything, you can throw anything at it.[43]

If Wilen, formed by his early exposure to the American and French popular song, was self-aware enough to admit that he remained a player of melodies above all, then it's unclear how the saxophonist saw this top-line sensibility as being compatible with an imagined synthesis of jazz and "classical" music: as discussed earlier, many European art music composers of the postwar period had thoroughly repudiated melody in favor of complex structural ideas. Yet Wilen's might not have been an aesthetic ambition first and foremost, the mooted "synthesis" of jazz and classical primarily driven by a desire to access institutional riches. So much was clarified when the saxophonist was asked about his immediate projects: "get to work on the public institutions. There's no private sponsorship any more. Only the Ministry of Culture can work on jazz's behalf now. It has to do something." Somewhat like André Hodeir before him, Wilen suggested that America, home of entertainment and the all-powerful market, would fall from jazz dominance as Europe, now the home of state-supported art, began to intervene.[44]

Nevertheless, in the same year Wilen returned to the United States, called, he said shortly afterwards, by a personal "phantom"; the saxophonist having "lost his way," this spirit called him back to the home of jazz and the site of his earliest musical experiences "to be nourished, or to nourish me. I didn't know if it amounted to a reality, a need, an offer or a demand."[45] Attempting to find out, Wilen spent six months assessing the state of the art, listening especially to the emerging free jazz and being disappointed, he said, by almost everything. Including himself: he found only Ornette Coleman interesting, and Coleman's example had inspired a realization of "all the work I was going to be obliged to do to arrive where I wanted."

> At root, my disappointment was the reaction of a lazy man. It made me sad to realize that I'd wasted my time playing a certain style, in a certain way, and that everything was to be demolished and rebuilt, to be forgotten. Fortunately, I have a terrible memory.[46]

Wilen's candid self-appraisal, and the ruminatory feel of the *Jazz magazine* interview that drew it out, were a world away from the confident statements and celebratory articles of the late 1950s, the brash young musician now a man seemingly trying to find the effort needed to remain interested in something once so important to him. But Wilen would find the energy to adapt to the new style just as he would find playing partners among the new generation of French musicians who, a revolution ahead, had been formed not by bebop, but by what was becoming known locally as *le free*.

The Arrival of Free Jazz

Free jazz, the "new thing," trickled into France in dribs and drabs; the sequential documentation of the music's early development—from Ornette Coleman's *Free Jazz* (1960) through Albert Ayler's *Spiritual Unity* (1964) to John Coltrane's *Ascension* (1965)—was identifiable and, outside the United States, easily available to listeners, only after the fact. The pianist François Tusques, by mid-decade one of the leading French free musicians, later recalled that while in the early 1960s he and his associates in Nantes had "known something was going on in the States," they had not had full access to it; like Joe Harriott in Britain—the saxophonist had been attempting to develop what he called a "free form" at roughly the same time as Coleman had in America—Tusques claimed to see his music as a parallel rather than subsequent development.[47]

But glimpses of American innovations were made available by a number of visiting musicians who were moving towards a new, free aesthetic. First among these was John Coltrane, who played at the Olympia with Miles Davis's quintet in 1960 and returned almost annually until 1965. Over that time, Coltrane's much-discussed group moved through and radicalized a modally based repertoire, this all but free by the time of the group's 1965 Antibes performance. Ornette Coleman's first appearance in the country came in November of that year, when he appeared on the same bill as Sonny Rollins (he returned in March 1966). Rollins, though, had long been absorbing the possibilities afforded by the Texan saxophonist's music, and his 1963 visit to France—in a quartet alongside Coleman's associates Don Cherry and Billy Higgins, and bassist Henry Grimes—had given Paris audiences a close-up view of the new music before Coleman could.[48]

The biggest names visited only briefly, but at least as significant were those players whose club residencies allowed them to meet and work with local musicians. Eric Dolphy, first heard in France with Charles Mingus in 1960, returned in 1964—having just made his important experimental album, *Out to Lunch*—to play at Le Chat qui Pêche, being joined by French players like tenorist Jean-Louis Chautemps and the drummers Daniel Humair and Jacques Thollot, being studied by an audience of many others (Michel Portal reported the great effect Dolphy's stay had on his own playing).[49] Steve Lacy spent several weeks in Paris during 1965, later returning to live in the city. But by some distance the most important visiting American musician was Don Cherry, whose collaborative attitude and several stays between 1964 and 1967 helped galvanize a core of French free jazz musicians.

Jedediah Sklower has skillfully reconstructed the networks and alliances of French (or France-based) players developing a free jazz practice that, finally, cohered around Cherry. The altoist Jackie McLean, himself increasingly under the influence of Ornette Coleman, had heard drummer Aldo Romano and bassist Jean-François Jenny-Clark jamming in Paris, the two joining the American for his 1961 Paris residency. Soon becoming known as an exceptional rhythm section partnership, Romano and Jenny-Clark joined tenor saxophonist François Jeanneau's quartet, touring Europe in 1963 and in the process encountering Cherry in Denmark. Meanwhile, François Tusques and bassist Beb Guérin were playing together in Nantes, visiting Paris often and playing at the Vieille Grille, where—generally free from the scrutiny of paying customers, though paying customers were notionally welcome—they jammed with Romano, Jenny-Clark, Thollot, Jeanneau, trumpeter Bernard Vitet, bassist Henri Texier and others. Don Cherry's eventual encounter with the Vielle Grille colleagues was, Texier recalled, "a turning point."[50] The group that Cherry fronted in summer 1965 at Le Chat qui Pêche was a Parisian phenomenon: the Argentinean tenor Gato Barbieri, whom Cherry had met in the city, was joined by Romano, Jenny-Clark and Karl Berger, the German vibraphonist who had moved to Paris a year earlier. The music this group developed would be documented on *Togetherness* (1965) and in a series of 1966 radio broadcasts made from the Café Montmartre in Copenhagen; Barbieri, Jenny-Clark and Berger would variously feature on the trumpeter's Blue Note albums *Complete Communion* and *Symphony for Improvisers* (both released in 1966), important records that, by virtue of their leader's nationality and American recording location, have become identified as documents of American free jazz's history rather than of the international links that helped bring them into being.

Four months after Cherry's stay at Le Chat qui Pêche, François Tusques led a group into the studio—Vitet, Jeanneau, Portal, Beb Guérin and drummer Charles Saudrais—to record *Free jazz*, an album that, although sharing the name of Coleman's double quartet record of 1960, must be seen as an early marker of a particularly European tradition of free jazz and improvised music. In a two-page *Jazz hot* feature coinciding with the record's release, Tusques explained his methods to the writer Yves Buin, and to a readership that was still not assumed to understand the new style's conceptual points of departure. The spontaneity of the music is played up: "before each piece we didn't know what was going to happen," Tusques said. "That's really fascinating. To that extent I realize what we owe to our Parisian experiences with Don Cherry."[51] If each performance's final form was unknowable, then much preparatory work had already been put in to the music's compositional materials (this a hallmark of Cherry's work and what he called his "cocktail compositions"); "Souvenir de l'oiseau," a piece written in memory of Charlie Parker, resembles Cherry's music of the time in method though not sound, unison bebop ensemble lines curling unexpectedly out of a lively swarm of freer ensemble improvisation.[52]

Other passages briefly reference the Coltrane quartet. Besides bebop, though, Tusques's music betrays another compositional heritage. As the pianist later explained to Vincent Cotro, the Bird-like theme fragments form part of a faux-dodecaphonic passage, any notes of the chromatic scale missing from these fragments made up by the stiffly enunciated unisons that break up the bebop (four different "series" resulting).[53] This is a much more local organization than orthodox twelve-tone technique would demand; the thematic material is open, in the midst of performance, to improvised arrival, statement and departure, and as such serves none of the long-range organizational purposes for which twelve-tone and serial harmonic methods were designed. But Tusques's homemade, truncated use of the technique manages to decenter the piece's tonality, imbuing the music with the sound of Charlie Parker—one of tonal harmony's great masters—while rendering it diffuse, the harmonic and formal gauziness that results appropriate to the idea of the "souvenir," of memory (whether of Parker, or those old and now impossible tonal methods).

Buin's *Jazz hot* feature on the record was headed with a rhetorical question: "In France, aren't there only jazz musicians, and no jazz?" Implicit in that largely unanswered enquiry was that Tusques's record was somehow more authentically European than extant forms of (free) jazz. And while ensemble writing that evokes Charles Mingus, Eric Dolphy, Booker Little or George Russell emerges to claim a relationship of some kind to recent American practice, the music does seem to be looking at that music from afar; *Free jazz* also differs significantly from its American namesake and other music in that named style. Ekkehard Jost has written that the sense of ensemble collectivity present here goes farther than had been the case in American free jazz until that point, and it's true that the music of Coleman, Ayler, Cherry and Coltrane made much more room for soloists than do these pieces, where—in anticipation of what would become the norm in the European free improvisation of the 1970s and onwards—individual voices appear and resubmerge very quickly.[54] The great amount of dynamic contrast, and the timbral light and shade that the players are clearly, consciously attentive to, are also worlds apart from American fire music; the good diction of Jeanneau's saxophones and Portal's bass clarinet owes much to the conservatoire aesthetic into which both men had been inculcated. And while the chordal events that the autodidact Tusques introduces near the end of "Description . . . 2" (12:00) emanate from a much less polished and tutored place—even more than Monk's chords, these are blocks of pure sound rather than convergences of voices—there is here (as elsewhere in Tusques's work) more than a touch of Bartók's harmonic sensibility. Though little known outside France, or even inside, Tusques's *Free jazz* deserves to be hardly less central to the history of jazz in the 1960s than Ornette Coleman's comparatively conflicted album, recording as it does a collaborative and astonishingly complete proposition as to what a European improvised music might sound like. It was not surprising that Barney Wilen, still in search of something similar, would fall in with this new cadre of free players on his return to the Paris jazz scene.

Wilen's Return

It was as part of a decidedly Coleman-like trio that Wilen took up residency at the Requin Chagrin in October 1965. The tenor player was joined by Jacques Thollot and a number of different bassists, including old hand Lloyd Thompson and young French players Henri Texier, Beb Guérin and Jean-François Jenny-Clark.[55] In a *Jazz hot* report on the gig, Michel Delorme applauded Wilen's bravery in spurning a successful bebop practice, and indeed the saxophonist who in January 1966 recorded *Zodiac* with Berger, Jenny-Clark and Thollot was a musician seemingly radically transformed in the four years since his last recording.[56] Still, *Zodiac* does show continuities with late-stage bop: though a second generation of free musicians headed by Albert Ayler had already rejected swing time along with chord progressions, the recent music of older innovators like Ornette Coleman and John Coltrane had largely remained wedded to that regular pulse, even if bebop harmonic structures had been rejected (this approach becoming known in Anglophone countries as "time-no-changes"). Wilen makes use of that technique here in music that sometimes closely resembles that of both Coleman and Coltrane's ensembles.[57]

But much of the music is unmetered, floating free of pulse (and these performances, each named after a sign of the zodiac, are kept to a couple of minutes each, the group apparently mindful of the music's difficulty). Vincent Cotro notes that the record has a glinting, metallic texture, a description befitting Berger's showering vibes and Thollot's drumming, cymbal-heavy though propulsive before trickily polyrhythmic. To the hindsight-equipped, both the sound world and patterns of group interaction recall then-recent Blue Note albums like Eric Dolphy's *Out to Lunch* (1964) and Grachan Moncur III's *Some Other Stuff* (1965). But while *Zodiac* is perhaps metrically and harmonically "freer" than the freest music on those records, it is much more fragile in texture; though it contains much less composed thematic material than them, it is much more continually infused by consciously melodic statement and by a sense of tonality in which tonal centers are rarely settled upon but which, continually changing, are continually implied. The skill and evolved individualism of Wilen's partners are all the more remarkable given that Thollot was just nineteen, and Jenny-Clark, twenty-one.

The most striking change to Wilen's own playing lies in the arrival of a great many Coltranisms—in lines that are littered with multiphonics, which break into a bark at the bottom, or which worry over multiple permutations of a single scale. In a much-discussed 1960 *Down Beat* article, Coltrane had given a hypothetical example of the technique of chord superimposition he had been using during his second tenure with Miles Davis: "I could stack up chords—say, on a C7, I sometimes superimposed an E♭7, up to an F♯7, down to an F. That way I could play three chords on one."[58] Coltrane's example involved juxtaposing chords moving in thirds, and he would develop this idea over the next few years: the harmonic basis of "Giant Steps" (1959)—in which larger tonal centers a major third apart from one another are established by local chord progressions in which chords often move by minor thirds—spawned extended compositional and improvisational investigations of the augmented scale (built from interlocking minor and major thirds), and of the free juxtaposition of arpeggios or tonal areas moving in a similar manner (as in the celebrated cadenza on "I Want To Talk About You," recorded at Birdland in 1963).[59] On *Zodiac*, free of any underlying chord progression (but closely shadowed by the exceptionally agile Jenny-Clark), Wilen seems to be rotating arpeggios in a similar way:

Poissons, 1:23

Elsewhere, there are brief hints of what sounds like the Coltranian augmented scale.[60] Assigning analytical descriptions to improvised strategies after the fact is fraught with risk, and whether Wilen conceived of these harmonic materials in such a way is moot; what's clear is that, systematized after Coltrane or seeking after some of his sound in a more intuitive manner, Wilen's playing was now deeply marked by the American's. Still, while the playing on *Zodiac* is much more interested and committed than that shown on his last bebop recordings—and while it incorporates some of Coltrane's timbral extremes—Wilen had somehow maintained his sense of reserve and interiority. Like François Tusques, Wilen was developing a free music that was related to but distinct from an American practice often described as cathartic, coruscating.

Yet the relationship towards "jazz" described by Tusques's first record was subject to renegotiation on the pianist's follow-up release, *Le Nouveau jazz*, recorded in February 1967 with Beb Guérin, Jenny-Clark, Romano and Wilen, the saxophonist by now a regular associate of the Parisian free players. Here, the sheer energy of American free jazz is to the fore, many more of that style's recordings and musicians having arrived in Paris since Tusques' first recording. On "Dialogue 1," Romano sounds somewhat like Sunny Murray, Tusques somewhat like Cecil Taylor (and on "Les Sorcières," the pianist quotes Archie Shepp's piece "Hambone");[61] on "Cantique du diable" this approach is framed with and identified by the kind of cell-like anti-themes heard in Coltrane's recently released *Meditations* (1966).[62]

If the album bears much closer resemblance to American free jazz, it's largely owed to the absence of the almost orchestral interplay of Tusques's *Free jazz* and to the presence of a single, dominant horn player—Wilen, a saxophonist still assessing the possibilities suggested by the big names of the free style, this recording suggesting an increased attention to the sonic flare-ups of an Albert Ayler or a John Gilmore. Shrieking passages are intercut with declamatory, Coltrane-like statements—again, Wilen seems to form these from tonal areas moving by thirds—and synthetic scale materials native to Tusques' compositions, these articulated in breakneck Coltrane style.[63]

It's powerful, masculine stuff. Yet Wilen seems sometimes to want

to renounce this by now standard free jazz approach, moving between these and much quieter and more texturally detailed passages, often too quickly for the rhythm section to follow.

That push-and-pull was only partly a quandary of technique or performance. The earliest recordings of French free jazz show a music shaped by half-heard American developments, but also by a surprisingly compatible and much more familiar native contemporary music aesthetic, and on *Free jazz* and *Zodiac* that marriage had enabled local experiments that would do more than just imitate American models. In Wilen's case, this new development was, as we will continue to see, momentarily linked to his search for forms of economic support other than the popular. But the cultivation of an aesthetic and institutional gameness that would ally free jazz with an existing European high-cultural world was by no means complete, nor necessarily shared by Wilen's colleagues; the arrival after 1965 of a free jazz that bore newly radical political meanings and aspirations—such music as had already shaped *Le Nouveau jazz*—would complicate that project further, giving both opportunities and pause to French musicians working in the tumultuous final years of the 1960s.

The Politics of Free Jazz

As in the United States, a broadening youth interest in non-Western and (black) popular music—and a corresponding loss of faith in the saleability of jazz stars—was articulated by jazz magazine covers: in consecutive months during 1966 *Jazz hot* was heralded by James Brown and then Ravi Shankar (this presaging the launch of a sister magazine, *Rock & Folk*). But the most frequently featured musicians in the second half of the decade would be the American stars of free jazz's second wave: Archie Shepp, Don Cherry, Albert Ayler, Cecil Taylor. This editorial policy was not the result of a commercial decision—quite the opposite, it resulted instead from the forceful campaigning of a group of young critics who, coming to prominence at the major jazz publications around 1965, defined themselves by their commitment to the new music. Jean-Louis Comolli and his boyhood friend Philippe Carles installed themselves at *Jazz magazine*, and Guy Kopelowicz, Yves Buin, Philippe Constantin, Bruno Vincent and Michel Le Bris at *Jazz hot*; Carles would eventually edit the former title and Le Bris the latter. Free jazz wasn't only covered by the two big specialist jazz publications. Through the latter 1960s and early 1970s, literary magazines like *Les Lettres françaises* and *Les Nouvelles littéraires*, countercultural publications like *Hara-kiri hebdo* and, when that was banned, its successor *Charlie hebdo*, even rightist journals *Le Point* and *Minute* debated the music to one extent or another; continuing (if brief and irregular) jazz coverage in *Le Monde*, *Figaro*, *L'Humanité*, *Le Nouvel observateur* and *Combat* also broached the style.[64] Nevertheless it was in *Jazz hot* and *Jazz magazine* that free jazz's critical devotees did their most significant work, and while these writers were often concerned to establish a new form of jazz criticism, they also sometimes participated in replays of earlier scenes from the history of jazz's French reception.

These scenes began, as they had done since Hugues Panassié's time, with a return to the source: that central genre in the canon of French jazz criticism, the long report from the Frenchman in New York, was revisited with the emerging free jazz now the topic of interest. This was best illustrated by Guy Kopelowicz's three-part series "Autumn in New York," appearing in *Jazz hot* in late 1965 and early 1966, the writer richly describing musical and social encounters with the Ayler brothers, Cecil Taylor, Sunny Murray, Burton Greene and the demimonde of the Lower East Side.[65] And just as the critics of the 1950s and early '60s had revivified the French discourse around jazz with reference to new (or newly fashionable) philosophical writing, so the new writers were atuned to French intellectual trends. Michel Le Bris and Bruno Vincent's 1967 three-part series, "La Tête, le cœur et le pied," attempted a Roland Barthes–like reading of jazz "mythology," describing common images of the jazz body and their relation to "ideology"—this the beginnings of a scholarly project that was only picked up again by writers on jazz a quarter of a century later. Elsewhere, Michel Foucault and Pierre Bourdieu were invoked.[66] Finally, just as the modernist critics had clashed with Panassié and his allies—in principle and in method, in print and at length—likewise the pages of *Jazz magazine* and *Jazz hot* soon came to host intergenerational diatribes.

Though they would often differ in their interpretations of the meaning and import of the new jazz, the young jazz critics nevertheless shared a "political" predisposition in tune with those who would soon coordinate the actions of May 1968. This manifested itself above all else as an interest in the affairs of a people only recently self-entitled Afro-American, and especially—indeed, almost exclusively—the incoming politics of black power. The playwright and jazz critic LeRoi Jones, by now one of those radicals as well as the author of *Blues People*, was a constant touchstone. But the Marxian tenor of much of the Europeans' work meant that those interests soon broadened. Such was apparent in the first developed articulation of the new criticism, "Voyage au bout de la New Thing," Jean-Louis Comolli's landmark *Jazz magazine* essay of April 1966. There, Comolli argued that as the conditions of what was beginning to be called Afro-American society changed, so, being an expression of that society, did its music; free jazz's rejection of a conventional ("Western") aesthetics of beauty was symptomatic of a wider black rejection of Western values and the first statement of a properly Afro-American ethic. Comolli's article sparked what was to become a long-running debate among jazz writers about the nature of the relationship between music and society, a number of critics—of both the old guard and the new—objecting to what they saw as Comolli's simplistic sociomusical homology.[67]

If that relationship was starkly drawn in Comolli's piece, then so it had been in arguments made by LeRoi Jones and the other American theorists of what would shortly emerge as the Black Arts Movement. But Comolli, writing from Europe, did not limit his analysis to the nature of local black-white relations as those writers sometimes (but by no means always) did, instead portraying this Afro-American "rejection" of Euro-American values as a local instance in a global trend of decolonization, both territorial and mental. Writers like Yves Buin, Philippe Carles, Bruno Vincent and Michel Le Bris would soon take up this idea; in its postcolonial internationalism, Eric Drott has argued, the new jazz criticism was informed by what was becoming a powerful strand of leftist French thinking, *tiers-mondisme*, or third worldism.[68] To an extent—within limits that would turn out to be prematurely defined—debates around the new radicality of jazz gave young French critics, fans and musicians a vocabulary with which to articulate questions about France's place in the world. That had been true before, of course. But whereas the music's early arrival had prompted flag-waving arguments about the rise of America, now it allowed reflection on the recent fall of France's empire.

At its height, the French empire's reach was bested only by the British, and in the early decades of the 20th century its possessions were at least as secure. Anti-colonialist sentiment and action appeared in fits and starts—nationalist movements were established in north Africa and Vietnam in the 1920s, Paris's colonial exhibition of 1931 attracted opposition from personalities as varied as André Breton and Léon Blum; a small number of journalists and intellectuals wrote exposés or fiction concerned with the plight of the colonized, but these were isolated efforts.[69] The first secessions would begin during the war to come, though, and at its end, with decolonization already in process and the enfeebled mother country vulnerable to further demands, sustained anti-colonial action and discourses emerged in the colonies and in France. Late 1940s uprisings in Algeria, Morocco, Madagascar and Vietnam led to appalling repression and, in Vietnam, the start of a war that would last beyond France's defeat there in 1954; these drawn-out, violent conflicts emboldened colonial subjects and dented popular French confidence in the sustainability of the empire. The loss of Vietnam spurred the start of a campaign by the Front de Libération Nationale (FLN) in Algeria. This war, by far the bloodiest of France's terminal colonial decline, would last eight years and claim many hundreds of thousands of lives.[70] By 1962 and the granting of Algeria's independence, the empire, apart from a few tiny possessions—and the much more important and enduring economic and cultural links between France and many Francophone ex-colonies—had vanished.[71]

Foreign struggles and victories over imperialist rule once again emboldened a French left that, in the 1950s, had been fatigued by the dogged loyalty shown by the Parti Communiste Français (PCF) towards Moscow—even in the face of the gulag, and the crushing of the Hungarian uprising of 1956—and by perceived inactivity and compromise at home. Kristin Ross has argued that, for a growing number of French intellectuals, the revolutionary subject was no longer best represented by the auto worker at the Renault factory in Billancourt, long a site for leftist organization for a socialist revolution that had never materialized, but by those victorious postcolonial freedom fighters in Africa, Asia and South America and, especially, the Vietnamese fighters now engaged in a war against American imperialism.[72] Likewise, revolutionary intellectual writing from the scenes of those struggles was now to inform thought and praxis in the West. The leftists' developing image of the colonial revolutionary was commonly elaborated by readings of Mao and Guevara, as well as Francophone figures like the Senegalese Léopold Senghor, the Tunisian Albert Memmi and the Martiniquais Frantz Fanon, and these names joined those of more local Marxist and Marxisant thinkers in the declamations of the French left as a whole.[73]

Often swimming in the same, rising tide, the new jazz critics also added to their French intellectual references ideas arriving from elsewhere. From 1967 to 1969, and in *Jazz hot* especially, a number of long articles appeared in which writers, confident enough to discuss music only secondarily, outlined recent Afro-American political activity and thinking. Guy Kopelowicz's 1967 *Jazz hot* piece "Le Nouveau jazz et la réalité américaine" comprised a detailed history of the civil rights movement, reading both the Watts riots of 1965 and free jazz aesthetics through Fanon's *Les Damnés de la terre*.[74] Annette Lena's 1969 article for the same magazine, "Révolution culturelle à Harlem," described over four pages the project of black cultural nationalism led by Ron Karenga, acknowledging if not resolving the difficulty presented by such to "a European used to reasoning according to an ideology based on the class struggle." Eric Plaisance's *Cahiers du jazz* piece "Jazz, racisme et sexualité" read jazz through the lens of Calvin C. Hernton's important 1965 study, *Sex and Racism in America*.[75]

This sociopolitical focus, radically different from the connoisseurism of earlier (and later) jazz writing, sparked a contest of legitimacy between the young critics and their elders (one that, as we will see, mirrored that then being played out by Parisian university students and administrators). The battle was fought no more vigorously than in a 1969 exchange between Michel Le Bris, by then editor of *Jazz hot*, and the veteran jazz writer Jacques B. Hess. Hess had written a *Jazz magazine* column against the new criticism; in an editorial for *Jazz hot*, Le Bris responded by targeting and rejecting the tenets of the modernist critical method.

> To a Marxist discourse is opposed one which is vaguely religious, vaguely humanist, vaguely phenomenological. What's at stake: the expulsion or reduction/banalization of the political dimension, the refusal of the idea that art, in its modes of consumption, is a part of ideology, and that it can therefore become a weapon in the ideological struggle.[76]

Le Bris condemned Hess, a survivor of Buchenwald, for his insufficiently politicized approach, and for apparently suggesting that jazz criticism return to "the little games of years gone by, to establish comparisons between musicians, hierarchies, based on what one isn't sure": the function of the new writing, Le Bris argued, was not to determine the respective value of musicians,

> but, as a matter of priority, to learn how to listen to the New Thing, to distinguish the values confronted within and which constitute the music as such, to distinguish the place where the principal contradiction is situated, and the principal aspect of that contradiction (that's a bit of Maoist doctrine, of course). Only then will it become possible, if one wants, to determine which are the most important musicians.[77]

That project was Le Bris's own, to be sure. But related kinds of "structural" criticism were advanced more widely, and these were no more fully realized than in Philippe Carles and Jean-Louis Comolli's 1971 book *Free Jazz / Black Power*. The book has sometimes been unkindly assessed as a French equivalent of the American writer Frank Kofsky's contemporary, and highly problematic, attempts to transform jazz musicians into both the hopeless marks of capitalism and the commanding voices of black revolution. Some of Kofsky's work is indeed cited (as is the writing of A. B. Spellman and, especially, LeRoi Jones). But Carles and Comolli's book is much more nuanced and much more scholarly than that characterization suggests: *Free Jazz / Black Power* is an *Hommes et problèmes du jazz* for the free jazz era, Hodeir's formalism replaced by a materialist method that explicitly, and at every turn, seeks to account for and interpret jazz creativity by way of social and political movements. Free jazz was its selling point, but the book offers a complete retelling of the history of jazz in this Marxian light, and events in black American history, particularly relating to (musical) labor and its organization, are presented *en bloc* in an analysis that aims to confront the reader like a *Blues People* with an academic footnote habit.[78]

Despite Carles and Comolli's close familiarity with French (free) jazz musicians, *Free Jazz / Black Power* does not consider local players' work beyond a few biographies in an appendix of 100 free musicians; despite the presentation of free jazz as a postcolonial phenomenon, almost no questions are raised in relation to France's own, ongoing imperial hangover (even though the authors had both grown up in Algeria). The tendency to opine upon distant race politics to the exclusion of those at home is one which, as we've seen, can be found in the jazz writing of the Panassié period. And however admirable the writerly commitment of the young critics at *Jazz hot* and *Jazz magazine*, there is a lingering suspicion that the noisy debates on fire music's political significance, made from a position of relatively safe remove, were shot through with frissons of exotica as that old discourse had been.

The rub between radical black image and French reality came when, in 1968–69, many of the central figures of a second generation of American free jazz musicians visited, stayed in or relocated to Paris, tempted by working opportunities above all else.[79] Stephen Lehman has shown how, at the turn of the decade, the French reception of musicians like Anthony Braxton, Leo Smith, George Lewis and even Ornette Coleman was—much like that of their forebears—often shaped by circumscribed ideas of what was fit and proper activity for black American musicians. Most mistrusted were techniques of composition that, a number of critics seemed to believe, were a sign of interior colonization by the forces of bourgeois white culture, a renunciation of black musical tradition; the uninterrupted tirade that constitutes Anthony Braxton's 1972 *Jazz magazine* interview "Le Jazz est une musique dangereuse," records many of these slights firsthand.[80]

Its shortcomings were real, but the new free jazz writing made a sincere attempt to locate the new music's global, political import, and—if only abortively—to design a method for doing so. Eric Drott's reading of French free jazz criticism as a musical articulation of leftist *tiers-mondisme* seems compelling, then; this jazz discourse was in large measure given its vocabulary by anti-imperialist works.

But it is difficult to see that intellectual movement as the sole nourishing source for the young writers' internationalist outlook. No matter how they would address their elders once publishing themselves, these were people formed in the 1950s by an avowedly anti-racist, intellectualist jazz critical discourse; before the arrival of 1960s *tiers-mondisme*, they were people whose lives had been shaped by a devotion to, and an imaginary version of, an oppressed and yet all-powerful other—the black American musician.[81] Indeed, African American musicians had themselves long since been constructing (imaginary) alliances beyond the first world. It is not fantastical to see the Afro-Cuban music first presented to Paris by Dizzy Gillespie in 1948 as a knowing, sonic demonstration of diaspora, one also long reflected in both France and Britain by Caribbean musicians' adaptations of American jazz; it's not hard to hear John Coltrane's early 1960s allusions to North African and Indian music as a demonstration of the commonality of improvisation outside the West. Those brought up in the unusually intellectually engaged French jazz critical culture of the postwar period had been given a glimpse of the world beyond the nation's borders as adolescents, and the radical leftist thought of the latter 1960s refocused this outlook rather than suggested it for the first time. Yet this focus would pose difficulties for white French players looking to involve themselves in the new music.

Art, Rock and the Problem of Blackness

However keen many French jazz musicians were to move away from the rigmarole of bebop, the widespread identification of free jazz and black American politics came to render any simple assimilation of the new style highly problematic. Of course jazz had always been identified in France with black Americans, and, whether implicitly or explicitly, with the particular travails of that people. But now the music's formalist concerns had been drastically revisioned in the name of an essential, and black, cry of anguish. Various problems of technique had, during the bebop era especially, acted as a kind of cordon-sanitaire between a singular American political reality and recontextualized musical study and execution: it was fascinating to learn how to negotiate Dizzy Gillespie's harmonic traps, endlessly engaging to master the alto as had Charlie Parker. But these were now rendered secondary to the question of whether such a supposedly artless and charged style as free could be adopted at all by white musicians (if not by those French players of Caribbean origin, like Jacques Coursil and Eddy Gaumont). Yves Buin suggested that if French musicians were to harness the style's power they must harness some local variant of its political rage;[82] the multi-instrumentalist Michel Portal complained that, "for us,"

> the trouble is that we're playing a stolen music . . . *Le noir* has something that condenses everything against which he can revolt: the white American and his culture. What is it that we fight against?[83]

The free jazz critics' attempt to show the profound interdependence of musical and social realities also necessitated the constant refusal of the "art" status that a previous generation of jazz musicians and critics had craved. This was not to realign the music with the world of entertainment: the bourgeois Western aesthetics by which those progressive critics judged jazz were part of the same capitalist ideology that spawned the entertainment industry in all its forms. Both 1950s modernists and prewar traditionalists were on the same side, Carles and Comolli wrote, and "the crowning of jazz as art, considered everywhere as a victory of the 'progressivists' over the conservatives, completed the colonization begun by commerce."[84] French players, then, risked being seen to act in aestheticizing, bourgeois bad faith if they adopted merely the form, the "art," of the new jazz.

In the face of these problems, a number of musicians experimenting with the style made explicit attempts to explain its tenor by reference to the social. "A musician doesn't only make beautiful stuff," Jacques Thollot said in 1970. "Who could say that what's going on around us in the world inspires beauty? If he's sincere, a musician can't confine his talent to beauty . . . Sometimes it's interesting to yell, and that can be beautiful as well." Others concurred, these comments echoing those habitually made on the other side of the Atlantic.[85] Some French players went further and performed at political rallies, though concerts organized in 1966 and 1967 in opposition to American racial oppression and the Vietnam War—but which featured no American musicians, their visas at risk—attracted criticism, action once again seemingly parasitical upon a distant problem.[86]

Though in many ways a political person, playing at those anti-Vietnam concerts, shortly to engage in local organization in a much more direct manner, Barney Wilen did not make that his musical raison d'être; though a musician much given to claiming trust in chance and the unformalized self, the always reserved saxophonist would not have considered the self-revelation supposedly enabled by a reductive free jazz to be of interest. Wilen was formed amid a social setting in which the works and practitioners of bourgeois high culture were utterly familiar, and he was unmoved by the revolutionary imperatives of a number of his critic and musician contemporaries. And so, almost uniquely among his generation, the saxophonist argued that the successful French adoption of free jazz would depend not on its finding a local political struggle to match that of the black liberationists, but, on the contrary, on an aestheticization that removed it from political specificities altogether.[87] This was why, he said to *Arts* in early 1967, "I insist on the terminology *nouveau jazz* . . . nothing to do with protest, nothing political, nothing social. Nothing but an aesthetic renewal."[88]

Renewal was difficult, though. Wilen still felt tied to the late bebop period and to the examples of its masters. "I have a passion for Coltrane," he said in 1967, mindful no doubt of the ways that the American had come to shape his playing. "But recently I've listened to him less and less because I don't want to just give in to his influence. It's always seemed to me that to imitate Coltrane is a small crime of *lèse-majesté*. When Charles Lloyd does it I find it detestable, indecent even."[89] Here, in Wilen's estimation, was the real problem: not the nontransferability of free jazz's social meaning, but of the reliance on past, and foreign, musical example. Yet it was a foreign example that also suggested the solution. In the same interview, Wilen expressed admiration for Albert Ayler precisely because of what the Frenchman called the "supreme detachment" that Ayler showed towards the jazz that preceded his own.[90] Wilen had already asserted his support for the new, however far-reaching and beyond his initial formation it may have been. Now he would do the same again, even if that would sometimes mean removing himself from what was accepted as "jazz" almost altogether.

A flurry of attempted self-redefinitions was hosted by the German label MPS, with which Wilen was associated in 1967–68. The first of these was no more than a walk-on part in someone else's musical utopia, this another reflection of the internationalist times: as part of his Jazz Meets the World series for the label, in October 1967 the German critic-producer Joachim-Ernst Berendt organized two concerts and a recording that united Wilen, the German trumpeter Manfred Schoof and the trio of Swiss pianist Irène Schweizer with three Indian classical musicians led by Dewan Motihar, the latter's sitar and vocals joined by tabla and tamboura. "The recording was done just like that," Wilen said later, "with no preparation at all. It's good that way: it's like having confidence in the unforeseen."[91] On the album, Schweizer and her trio provide both a more restrained and rhapsodic version of McCoy Tyner and Elvin Jones's rolling method and newer, freer, clustered attacks, all the while underpinned by tamboura drone and overlaid with sitar shimmer. Schoof and Wilen (on tenor) engage in capable but rather perfunctory free jazz interplay on two long tracks; much more successful are the passages in which Wilen's soprano, its softly broadcast melodies signal-jammed with multiphonics, summons a much keener collective concentration.

This was Wilen as saxophone-for-hire, but the player's new commitment to develop his work as an "artist"—by no means an attitude held by all jazz players of the time—meant that he was at that time in the midst of another, less ephemeral project. This work would mark the beginning of a documentary approach that would take him deeper into the "social" than any purely instrumental style could. In 1964, Wilen, a motor sports enthusiast of long standing, had made a rough recording of the Monaco Grand Prix, eventually using it in a radio broadcast during which he played along to the engine noise.[92] In May 1967, better equipped technically—he had come by three Nagra recorders and two willing assistants—he returned to the Monaco race to record it in its entirety, there stumbling upon François de Ménil, a director who was filming the event with the intention of making a Grand Prix documentary. During the race, the champion Italian driver Lorenzo Bandini crashed and died; when Ménil's project fell through, Wilen aquired the images, and in the following months he shaped the sound and film recordings into what would now be thought of as a multimedia work, *The Tragic Destiny of Lorenzo Bandini*.[93] The saxophonist presented the project internationally, and, significantly, at museums and exhibitions: at Paris's Musée d'Art Moderne in October 1967, as part of a New York University show called "Man and Machine" soon after, and, over the course of 1968, at the new Rennes Maison de la Culture and Berlin Jazz Days, among other locations.[94] In these performances, which featured different musicians and were set up in slightly different ways each time, film of the race was projected, found sounds and free improvisation were interspersed, and the whole was splattered by a light show such as was obligatory at the time. Yet the impulse to stage a performance in which musicians interacted with moving images surely lay in an earlier experience: Wilen's recording for *Ascenseur pour l'échafaud* with Miles Davis. That piece of experimental "art" was made in a popular arena rather less accessible to jazz by this time; instead, by allying his music with visuals and presenting it as part of a conceptually driven artwork, Wilen had forced an entry into high culture venues that would otherwise have little use for his music, distancing himself from the political preoccupations of free jazz as he did so.

Bandini was evidently powerful in live performance, sometimes too powerful. In *Jazz hot*, J.-P. Binchet reported of the Paris show that the drummers

> Jacques Thollot and Eddy Gaumont hammered at their instruments, their arms so many crazed spindles, raging pistons. Their bodies, their fracas, their sonic and rhythmic delirium (the counterpoint to the mechanical orgy that rolled above their heads): if it didn't obscure the motors' song, it had the tendency to stifle Barney's.[95]

Even if stripped of the visual and spatial element, The February 1968 MPS recording of *Bandini*—the title now prefixed *Auto Jazz*—retains an oppressiveness at first sonic and then, as the narrative unfolds, emotional. Indeed one of Wilen's achievements here lies in his crafting of a plot from a momentary event. The album opens with racetrack noise and an exchange between crowd members:

Ô putain! [Fuck!]
–Qui c'est? [Who is it?]
Bandini!
–Bandini!

On record blind, the meaning of this exchange isn't clear: it sounds as much like a fan ovation for a masterful move as anything else, and the roars continue. François Tusques's piano, with its odd mixing of Monk, Taylor and Darmstadt serialism, together with Eddy Gaumont's anxiously fleet free drumming, support a Wilen whose strained lyricism and polytonal switchbacks mark the high point of his investment in the Coltrane style—even if, unlike so many of Coltrane's imitators then and since, the Frenchman never attempts to match his model's tonal intensity. On their own, the group play tight and highly responsive energy jazz, but they are not long left uninterrupted by the audio recording of that day in Monaco. Announcers and commentators declaim excitedly, and a military march plays through a PA system, the resultant chaos inevitably Ivesian; what sounds like workshop hammering and tuning is punningly accompanied by a Gaumont drum solo; engine noises periodically swoop in amid high drama only to vanish leaving quiet crowd chatter in their wake (the piece includes a number of these moments of calm in which little happens, the action elsewhere). Over rushes of mechanical sound and Gaumont's whiplash cymbal catches, Wilen flutters between euphoric hollers and a hymn figure which, as Vincent Cotro has pointed out, recalls Coltrane's *A Love Supreme* among other hymnic works of the American saxophonist's.[96] But the work's narrative motor is primal, and terrible—knowing the piece's premise we await the crash, preemptive rubberneckers—and Wilen expertly manipulates both the drama and its listeners. As the end approaches the band withdraws, and car noise continues while a series of otherworldly, chromatic organ chords pull a veil over whatever is happening (on record, only imagined, the scene acquires the confusion of a spectator's obscured view). There is no finality or definitive sonic event here; but it is at this point that the opening taped conversation returns, the exchange now revealed as a response to a rising plume of smoke in the distance. *Ô putain! Qui c'est? Bandini!* Lorenzo Bandini's tragic destiny is not only to die but to die a spectacle, on loop forever. Wilen's tenor contributes a brief comment, and the piece closes.

Bandini is Wilen's most fully realized music; in its recorded realization the playing of all involved is dramatically committed.[97] But more significantly than that, the work's documentary style—its taking and use of recorded sound in a manner akin to Louis Malle's contemporary *cinéma direct*—was singular. The title was even chosen for its tabloid qualities: "you can see it as a headline in *France Dimanche*," Wilen said.[98] To put black American free jazz in the service of reportage on the favorite pastime of the reckless rich was an unlikely decision, and a bold one, given the forcefully articulated political engagement of a number of his contemporaries. Yet Wilen's frame of reference had expanded beyond that of American jazz, and this was the beginning of what he would later describe as a collage technique in the style of Max Ernst.[99] That visual artist's work was not an uncommon reference in late 1960s musical circles: the joyful disregard for generic boundaries was one of the period's most productive attitudes, and Ernst's juxtaposition and deformation of found images was cited by others interested by both high art and low popular culture.

These kinds of collage aside, a number of French art music composers and jazz improvisers were collaborating, or appropriating each other's methods, in order to produce hybrid works that reflected similar formal or institutional ambitions as *Bandini* and in which the socioaesthetic codings of black American free jazz were similarly scrambled. In 1966, Bernard Parmegiani had taken sound sources from Bernard Vitet, Bibi Rovère, Jean-Louis Chautemps and Charles Saudrais for his tape piece *Jazzex*.[100] Vitet's own work *La Guepe* (1972) seized the historically storied, institutionally prestigious (but, by the early 1970s, stone dead) twelve-tone gestural vocabulary to set a long poem by Francis Ponge. Several of the musicians who had made their names playing free jazz—Jenny-Clark, Chautemps and, especially, Michel Portal—performed with both jazz and contemporary music ensembles as a matter of course, while some jazzworld animateurs, like Daniel Caux, were involved in contemporary art music as much as jazz; the Shandar label, with which Caux was associated, released early recordings by the American minimalist composers Terry Riley and La Monte Young as well as free jazz musicians. Eric Drott notes that these composers and others of their ilk were even for a time covered in magazines like *Rock & Folk*, and that such cultural presence meant that new music festivals at the end of the decade could draw many thousands of attendees.[101] But this was a brief flourish: Drott also records a steep decline in the number of composed works registered with the Société des Auteurs, Compositeurs et Editeurs de Musique (SACEM) in the first half of the 1970s, this more than matched by a large increase in the total number of copyright registrations and suggesting a dramatic rise in popular song production during the same period.[102] In the 1970s, most of jazz's experiments with style would take place in the laboratory of popular rather than art music.

The days when European concerts by groups like Art Blakey's or Sidney Bechet's could attract thousands of adolescents and young adults were gone by the mid-1960s; in a 1964 issue of *Jazz hip*—one of the Marseille magazine's last—Roger Luccioni had written of the public's "progressive, inexorable disaffection" with jazz, speculating from his experiences as an organizer that from a peak around 1960 concert attendance had declined some 30 percent, and noting that one of his city's major record shops was selling a tenth of the jazz discs that it once had.[103] Just as in the United States, a more "sophisticated" brand of rock—not only The Beatles, Beach Boys and Bob Dylan, but also their French copyists and equivalents—had cost jazz much of its mass and youth audience support. And by the latter part of the decade some rock presented a rival claim to the radicality that the French free jazz coterie were so keen to promote. While leftists of a traditional bent were suspicious of rock's cultural-industrial provenance and the decadent countercultural distraction it afforded, others—like those former *gauchistes* who took over at the magazine *Actuel* in 1970—saw the music as offering a route into a "revolution for pleasure" which, as Drott writes, would "put an end to the self-abnegating rhetoric of the extreme left" and lead to the overthrow of stultifying social practices and a utopian transformation of everyday life.[104] Shared sympathies of politics and aesthetics meant that, for now, (free) jazz was a feature in rock's countercultural rock landscape, both musics being programmed at important events like the Amougies festival in 1969, and on José Artur's France Inter radio show Pop-Club, a daily rallying point for French counterculturalists.[105]

Still, early jazz attempts to tap rock's currency—in both senses of the word—often met with hostility, as Wilen, beginning his own rock experiment, would shortly see. Alongside *Bandini*, and like *Bandini* somewhat by accident, in 1967 Wilen had begun to develop a project focused on the popular rather than the institutional (all bases were to be covered). The saxophonist had been booked to play in Zurich but, upon arrival, had found that the promoter had left town with no gigs arranged. Needing money to get back to France, he recruited Irène Schweizer's trio to form the first version of Barney Wilen and his Amazing Free Rock Group—"I needed something punchy"—and the band gave a series of hastily arranged concerts around Switzerland.[106]

A different lineup recorded *Dear Prof. Leary* for MPS in June 1968.

Wilen's remarks to the press about his rock group speak of the contemporary mistrust of cultural hierarchy: "there is an audience that is passionate about cinema and modern literature and listens to free jazz, rock, avant garde pop and contemporary music in the same way," he said in December that year. "It's that audience that interests me." This free spiritedness inevitably translated into a critique of both genre and traditional technique.

> It's incontestable that there's a convergence between different forms of music. Where jazz stops and pop music begins is difficult to say, and these categories aren't of much interest. Jimi Hendrix is a fantastic musician, where do you put him? I've had enough of this stupid sectarianism . . . The problem of what one calls the "quality" of music is immaterial to me, what counts is the pleasure of playing. [Actor and musician] Jean-Pierre Kalfon doesn't have a towering technique on the electric guitar, but he's passionate about music, and for me that hunger—which doesn't respect genre—is important.[107]

The "revolution for pleasure" was signaled by *Dear Prof. Leary*'s winking title, stylistic openness by the inclusion of both Beatles and Ornette Coleman pieces, attitudinal radicality by free jazz improvisation. The album's genre mix was hailed as a landmark moment by at least one member of the French jazz press. Philippe Constantin wrote two reviews of the record, one for *Jazz hot*, in which it was taken as a merging of two styles that tended to regress towards the "primal," and the other in *Jeune Afrique*, in which—"primality" here presumably not thought a suitable line of argument—the combination of (white) rock and (black) free jazz foretold a grand social union.[108] Yet if Constantin (and much later, Eric Drott) took the record rather seriously, it's not clear that Wilen himself did: there is something tongue in cheek about the production as a whole. The saxophonist's expressions of stylistic ecumenicalism, for instance, were somewhat undone by his frank admission in the album's liner notes that he had "no particular interest in today's pop music. What I listen to is jazz." That phrase was picked up on in *Down Beat*'s brutal review, which upbraided Wilen for his "disrespectful" attitude towards rock and called the record "a shuck and an insult."[109]

On the recording, Wilen is joined by Joachim Kühn—the Paris-based, East German keyboardist whose own records, like 1969's *Sound of Feelings*, would similarly meld free jazz and pop-rock—and by Aldo Romano and Wolfgang Paap on drums, Mimi Lorenzini on guitar and Günter Lenz on electric bass. The opening track, The Beatles's "Fool on the

Hill," is the most faithfully treated cover (though it is woefully handled, Wilen's closing, straining soprano melody truly painful); other pop hits ("Ode to Billie Joe," "You Keep Me Hanging On," "Respect") are mined for single riffs or elements of their chord progressions, the rest junked in favor of blowing—blowing which, on Wilen's part at least, is boringly facile. The saxophonist reels out blues licks, occasional free flurries thrown in for what seems like the sake of contemporaneity. The most developed piece, and the most successful, is the title track, the form and content of which strongly recall some of the experiments of Frank Zappa's *Freak Out!* (1966): here, a backbeat, and Kühn's stop-go organ solo, cede to a hefty blues rock riff and then a spliced-in breakdown, during which the band members vocalize animal noises and practice their English in what seems like a bad-trip soundtrack.

Whatever charm the album has is due to its spontaneity and splashy energy, this largely owed to the efforts of Kühn and the two drummers. But the record also features some interesting overdubbing and spatial effects of the kind that Wilen would put to more profound use later. Ornette Coleman's "Lonely Woman"—a track singled out by the disgusted *Down Beat* reviewer—has Wilen enunciating an atmospheric if not pitch-perfect melody as an overdubbed backbeat floats in and out, completely disconnected in meter and room space from the rest of the performance; this early example of jazz studio play is oddly affecting. Wilen would return to and develop those techniques for his next project, a work that would also be informed by the ideas that were charging through France at the moment *Prof. Leary* was being recorded.

May 1968

The *événements* that began in May 1968—when demonstrations engulfed the Sorbonne, then the streets of the Latin Quarter, then Paris, then much of France, when millions of people across France stopped working and the government looked to be on the brink of collapse—have become central to a French memory of the latter 20th century. Yet the often ambiguous nature of the protesters' demands, memorialized in once-gnomic but now-hackneyed slogans ("beneath the paving stones, the beach") were matched by ambiguous outcomes, and rival interpretations of the moment's heritage have done ritualized battle across printed pages and talk-show studios since the mid-1970s. The subversive wit of the posters and graffiti that flourished throughout the early summer are some of the events' most defining features, and their continual recirculation has abetted the historical construction of May as a countercultural festival, an indulgently violent one at that; commentators of both the right and the traditional left have depicted the uprisings as a foretaste of the hedonistic individualism that would soon flourish in the shape of an untrammeled and uncontested consumer culture.[110] Meanwhile, others have portrayed a potentially revolutionary moment forestalled, a visionary reformulation of the relationship between the worker and work, politics and society, abandoned incomplete.[111] Still others have questioned the centrality of 1968 as a breach of any kind, emphasizing the continuity in periods before and after the actions, or else nullifying their import: "nothing happened."[112]

It's a high-handed way to describe an explosive moment. Student unrest had been brewing at the suburban Nanterre campus of the University of Paris throughout 1967, the university administration in constant conflict with students over issues concerning teaching and curriculum, but also free movement between male and female dormitories.[113] But this student body, only slightly younger than the free jazz activists, was lodged at an intersection of age, class and location that engendered an unusually acute political awareness, having grown up in the shadow of the wars of decolonization that touched a great many French families in some way; that global theoretical perspective—informed by the numerous brands of Marxian and anti-imperialist thinking then flourishing—meant that student demands, though including reform of the university system, were never limited to or even focused upon the students' immediate context.[114] Anti–Vietnam War sentiment was bitter and widespread, and when, on March 20, a student was arrested for breaking a window of Paris's American Express building, demonstrations were organized to protest this and other arrests. Two days later, students, led by Daniel Cohn-Bendit and others, occupied Nanterre University.[115] Disruption continuing, the Nanterre campus was finally closed on May 2. A meeting at the Sorbonne, called the following day to protest the closure, turned into a violent demonstration, which led to the police being ordered in to the university for the first time in its history. The closure of the Sorbonne left hordes of outraged, politicized students with nothing to do except demonstrate against the police occupation, and events took on a new momentum.

Student demonstrations—often similarly protesting authoritarian government at home and imperialist adventure abroad—were taking or would soon take place in Italy, Japan, Mexico, Germany and the United States. And in France as elsewhere, the student movement attempted to forge alliances with a wider, working population. Despite the contention of the student intellectual hero Louis Althusser that intellectual activity was a form of praxis—and perhaps because a similarly favored Maoist thinking stressed the need to unite divided groups sharing revolutionary intent—*gauchiste* students were aware that alone they could not form a revolutionary class; immediately following the first events at the Sorbonne overtures were made towards industrial workers, who, responding to a call by the Confédération Générale du Travail (CGT) and other unions, struck on May 13 and thereafter occupied factories in increasing numbers. Workers' desires for change—higher pay, a shorter week, better working conditions—were strong enough for 9 million of them to have begun striking within days of the students' first actions. Even if the internationalism and the carnival of the student protests were often scorned by industrial workers, large swathes of them, like the public and press in general, at first held no little sympathy for those youths who, especially on the "Night of the Barricades" of May 10–11, had been the victims of brutal police treatment.[116]

Recalling the small-scale committees formed during the Popular Front period, during May and its immediate aftermath hundreds of *comités d'action* were established by groups of work colleagues, neighbors, fellow students or political associates in order to pursue highly localized goals—whether that meant pressing an employer for reform, organizing a community's striking arrangements or producing posters and literature.[117] Musicians, too, banded together during this time. The most visible was the Comité Action Musique (CAM), which had been active in organizing anti-Vietnam concerts over the previous two years. CAM comprised free jazz musicians Jean Frénay, Jean Vern, Daniel Laloux, Portal, Vitet, Tusques, Beb Guérin, Jenny-Clark, Romano, Thollot and Gaumont, and during May the group engaged in a flurry of activity: the highly sympathetic editorial team of *Jazz hot* granted the committee two dense pages of the August–September issue to present the reasons it had struck during the protests.[118] Like other *gauchiste* "groupuscules," CAM positioned itself against what it saw as the nearly "apolitical" stance of the main trade union; radical musicians were furious that, after a general meeting and an agreement to strike (visiting and performing in factories and universities having been ruled out), musicians' union leaders had immediately begun negotiating a return to work. The leftist demand for societal restructuring—CAM pressed for a new "analysis" of the role of the musician in society as well as the rejection of various aspects of union bureaucracy—and corresponding, much milder union demands for employment amelioration and reform of various kinds, met in deadlock in the muscial sphere as they did across French industry.[119]

In his study of music during May 1968, Eric Drott records the activities of other *gauchiste* committees that, formed or active during the événements, shared CAM's concerns. While the Comité Révolutionnaire d'Agitation Culturelle (CRAC) worried over the relationship between performing arts and artists and their audiences, the more radical Comité d'Action Révolutionnaire (CAR)—in keeping with contemporary thought from Lefebvre to Debord to Mao—rejected the very structure of that relationship, demanding that cultural forms and institutions not be "democratized" but incorporated into everyday life.[120] While spontaneous music and performance played a role in the student demonstrations, some felt that these carnivalistic elements detracted from the seriousness of the endeavor. These included both *gauchistes* and those ranged against them, including the Parti Communiste, which saw the students as bourgeois adventurists who would only harm the workers' movement. In June, Georges Marchais, a future PCF head, contributed an article to *L'Humanité* that forcefully criticized the students' ringleaders.

> A group of anarchists and Situationists have dirtied the walls of the university with the giant letters of their slogan, "NEVER WORK." For these forty or so students, action means disrupting lectures . . . jazz shows, theatrical events, occupying buildings, and covering walls with graffiti.[121]

Marchais was a jazz lover who would eventually be buried to the accompaniment of a Miles Davis record: the students' attempts at defining a celebratory, communalist politics fell on deaf ears across the spectrum of both organized politics and taste.[122]

As the strikes and demonstrations dragged on, worker and wider opinion began to turn against what was increasingly felt, by nonradicals at least, to be an overdose of civic violence and the obstruction of work.[123] On May 27 the Grenelle Accords, negotiated between the government and trade unions, announced a 35 percent increase in the minimum wage, among other improvements. The agreements were rejected by workers, but on May 30 over 300,000 demonstrators marched down the Champs-Elysées in support of de Gaulle and a return to order. Here, intellectuals and cabinet ministers were joined by celebrities (including Josephine Baker), members of the public, and the rightist mobs that had, throughout May, launched street attacks on strikers and students.[124] The strength of this counterdemonstration, and the fear inspired among militants by reports of troops encircling Paris, led to the beginnings of worker compromise and a return to the factories, while students began to trickle out of Paris for the summer break.[125]

However committed to anti-authoritarian action they were, those students who demonstrated in May and June belonged to a larger body that was poised to enter the world of middle-class work. Similarly, while industrial workers' support for their union and party political representatives was far from uncritical, the CGT and PCF nevertheless finally inspired much more loyalty and confidence than did the militant and often Maoist groups that were May's most dynamic agitators. By the late 1960s, Michael Seidman argues, the French working classes were too thoroughly invested in bourgeois democracy and consumer culture to disavow it, much keener to climb the social ladder than to kick it away, and the same could surely be said for the overwhelming majority of French students at the time.[126]

And of jazz fans. *Jazz hot*'s editorial agenda had led to an increasingly politicized letters page, readers writing in to support the new free jazz criticism but also to attack it; nearing the end of the decade it became clear that, whatever the mood had been in the Paris streets of May 1968, the politically preoccupied jazz press was out of step with most of its readers.[127] Though leftists retained editorial control of *Jazz hot*, the ultimate head of the magazine was still the veteran Charles Delaunay, and he watched from the sidelines as sales of his publication tumbled.[128] Delaunay's long struggle to regain control of the magazine, which lasted from summer 1968 to winter of the following year, can be tracked through editorial announcements and content confusion: following the elder's first intervention, Claude Bolling and other mainstream stars of decades past suddenly found a new place in *Jazz hot*'s pages—those, that is, which weren't still covered in polemic and rendered in the faux-zamizdat typeface that the *gauchistes* had instituted. Delaunay and his allies finally rid themselves of the faction led by Michel Le Bris late in 1969. In December, an editorial stressed that the new production team was charged with enthusiasm for music rather than politics or ideology. Apologies were offered for the "errors" of the previous year, and a promise made that a new stylistic inclusiveness would be instituted to put the magazine back on a healthy economic footing.[129]

Yet the moment of radicalism wasn't over, and some of the ideas and modes of organization that emerged during May would have long-term implications for French culture and music. The references to Maoism that litter French intellectual and popular culture from the mid-1960s onwards—the films of Godard, the pages of *Jazz hot*, some of the music of François Tusques, the satire of Nino Ferrer's well-known 1967 song "Mao et moa"—reflected the left's attempt to find a new kind of activist politics that could evade party machinery. As Kristin Ross notes, the intellectuals' "China" was an imagined place, one filled with traditionally French utopian visions and constructed in ignorance or disregard not just of Chinese tensions with Vietnam, but also of the limitless humanitarian disaster Mao had already engendered. It was, nevertheless, an imaginary that facilitated a new kind of activity at home (just as its African American counterpart had done).[130] This activity would be centered on the creation of links across compartmentalized but potentially sympathetic "classes" or groups—most immediately students and workers—to create broader anti-capitalist and anti-imperialist alliances. And if bourgeois domination was founded upon the maintenance of the divisions between bodies, then these divisions were enacted by the powerful and supposedly knowledgeable against the weak and supposedly idea-less.[131] Another powerful new current, then—one echoed in many other late 1960s politics and practices in the West—ran against "expertise" and virtuosity of all kinds. An interpretation of that idea would lead to murder beyond belief in southeast Asia during the 1970s; in light of this it is rather bathetic to note that in France, such thinking, reinforced by a Situationist-derived reframing of the artistic "spectacle," would foster a musical turn towards collaboration and community. But these ideas circulated in multiple forms, and it wasn't only activists and ideologues that put them into practice: Barney Wilen—who was neither of those things, but for whom the rejection of virtuosity was becoming a favorite figure— would enact some of them in his new, and literal, departure.

Moshi

Wilen's Amazing Free Rock Group was still finding only limited critical favor. Reviewing a spring 1969 Paris concert by the band—which now included a vocalist who recited passages from Mao's *Little Red Book*— *Jazz hot*'s Denis Constant poured scorn on the bad faith of it all. "To have a charming young thing [*minette*] declaim a Chinese text over a background of bad rock helps nothing," he wrote, "not music, and not the struggles currently seen in France."[132] The "charming" vocalist was Caroline de Bendern, Wilen's new partner. The twenty-four-year-old came from an aristocratic family and had moved in society and bohemian circles in Britain, Austria and the United States. But she had been disinherited when she was photographed at a May 1968 demonstration, perched on the shoulders of the artist and activist Jean-Jacques Lebel while bearing a Vietnamese flag, Marianne-like; the photo was printed in *Life* magazine and soon achieved iconic status in France.[133]

The partnership with Bendern would motivate Wilen to escape again from an unsatisfactory Parisian musical life. On a number of occasions the saxophonist had told journalists that *le free* was jazz's future. And yet in 1965, at the very beginning of his experiments with free playing, Wilen had told Michel Delorme that he could already see a time when he would leave the method behind. "He is looking to create a process of spontaneous elaboration," Delorme reported from the Requin Chagrin, "one that would depend on himself, his accompanists and his audience, a process that he will abandon 'when it becomes procedure.'"[134] Wilen's interviews suggest that his intellectual commitment to both free jazz and rock surpassed what turned out to be the length and level of his musical commitment. But now the possibility of a journey to Africa beckoned, and with it a plan that undoubtedly—and in the wake of 1968, especially—led out of the ideas of collaborative, nonspecialist and documentary creativity that had informed Wilen's work over the previous few years.

As had been the case with *Bandini*, a seemingly chance convergence of interests and enablers led to Wilen's leaving Paris. The saxophonist had heard and been fascinated by a recording of Congolese pygmy music at Paris's Musée de l'homme. Meanwhile, Bandern was associated with several young blades who, *gauchistes* of the well-connected tendency, had formed a film production company that aimed to make artistically revolutionary films. (The company's name, Zanzibar, was chosen in honor of the African state, then Beijing-aligned.) The group, largely comprising actors and painters, was underwritten by the aesthetically and politically sympathetic heiress Sylvina Boissonnas. Its few, now obscure films were characterized by a rejection of auteurism (the films decidedly collective in their construction), their minimal dialogue and their drug-influenced noncontinuities (film sets were heavily narcoticized).[135] Boissonnas funded anyone with an idea; Wilen's ethnographic interests and artistic wanderlust began to cohere into a project.

The plan was to set off from Paris in late March 1969 and to travel—via Spain, Tangiers, Mali, the Congo and mainland Tanzania—to Zanzibar itself, in the process making a film for which Wilen, like the cameramen recording the locals as they went, would provide the soundtrack. Three Land Rovers and a team of a dozen partipants were assembled. Among these were the actors Didier Léon and Daniel Pommereulle, the saxophonist-pharmacist Jacques Pelzer, and the director Serge Bard, who in 1968 had made the first Zanzibar film, *Détruisez-vous* (featuring Bendern), as well as *Fun and Games for Everyone* (in which Wilen appeared alongside Sunny Murray).[136] Its writer a victim either of leg-pulling or bad hearing, a *Jazz hot* news item reported that the English guitarist "Jimmy McLaughlin" was also to have joined the group but had been called to the United States (where, indeed, John McLaughlin had begun working with Miles Davis).[137] "For Barney," the story continued, "by far the most serious of the group,"

> it's a question of going back to music's source, that of the pygmis of the Congo, who have perpetuated in quasi-purity their ancestral musical traditions. He envisages playing in villages with his companions— who aren't musicians but "who will become so" in the course of the journey—to provoke reactions on the part of the locals. If everything goes well, he is sure he will begin to play differently in this newly created situation, and even bring back local musicians to play with them in Paris a music truly unheard of: primitive free rock.[138]

So the ghost of an old jazz primitivism haunted the mission, as a rather ironic Wilen acknowledged after the group had returned to Paris: planning the journey, the saxophonist said, "we had crazy visions of the jungle, the deserts and the bush, lions, snakes, crocodiles, and"—he added in English—"*beautiful black people swingin' and singin'*."[139] In their experienced ruefulness, Wilen's words revoiced those of an earlier product of jazz- and primitivism-infused French ethnography: Michel Leiris's 1934 book, *L'Afrique fantôme*. As noted earlier, Leiris had written important early pieces on jazz in the surrealist magazine *Documents*, and the interest in blackness that the music inspired led him to join Marcel Griaule's 1930 Dakar-Djibouti ethnographic mission. Leiris's book documented the writer's experiences during the trip, which were characterized by disappointment, disgust and existential doubt, the text's subject the travelers themselves as much as that they were supposed to be studying. Leiris's work had long been regarded as a classic in France—its title was taken by an article appearing in the same issue of *Jazz magazine* as the returning Wilen's account of his journey—and the air of failure that hangs over Leiris's narrative clouded Wilen's trip, too. Wilen and Bendern had soon become contemptuous of the filmmakers, who hadn't approached the project "in the same spirit" as the saxophonist and his partner: Wilen recounted a comic image of the French in the bush, the technicians heating up canned choucroute on an electric plate as he and

Bendern tried to adapt by building a fire and roasting antelope.[140] After six months, the team hadn't got beyond the oasis city of Tamanrasset in the Algerian Sahara. Serge Bard, who had yet to commence filming, nevertheless returned to Paris claiming to need more materials. Those remaining members of the party eventually left for Agadez in Niger; when Bard rejoined the group there six months later, it was with the news that he had converted to Islam, and was no longer able to represent the human image on film. The group fought, Bard left, and the last remaining voyagers—Wilen, Bendern and Léon—soon returned to Paris.[141]

In Africa, Wilen and his group had inevitably been regarded with suspicion by those they encountered, and were aware of being "under observation" for months before being accepted. The saxophonist was keen to avoid that anthropological intrusiveness which spoke of old colonial power relationships: "we didn't arrive in a village with our tape recorders and say to the people, 'sit there and sing, or play,'" he said.[142] The negotiation of these intercultural problems, compounded by practical issues—"when you've just done a 500km journey you don't really feel like getting the amplifiers, guitars and sax out for a jam"—meant that the music-making that had been the object of the journey would materialize only intermittently.

> The music came to us. Certain full-moon evenings they had a celebration, or a Bororogi came to the house alone, and started to sing . . . traditional epic poems that recounted the lives of great men of the tribe, that spoke of ancestors.[143]

However sensitive the group's attitude towards those they encountered, by its very nature the project replayed old practices, and Wilen was obliged to answer *Jazz magazine*'s questions as to whether there was not a kind of neo-colonialism inherent in his attempt to document and preserve African music.[144] The weakness of Wilen's universalist verbal response—"all musics belong to everybody"—is countered by the comparative sonic interest of *Moshi*, the album that Wilen and his band assembled on their return to Paris in 1971.

The album's long title track opens with a fade up into a taped African soundscape, a dog barking, insects chirping, and a man in what sounds like a trance of some kind. *Moshi!*, he shouts, and a jump cut takes us to another location, this one the scene of a group chant—some men hold what Western musicians would identify as a pedal note, while others provide slow descending lines down a minor pentatonic scale. It's significant that of all the African music recorded this is offered up first, since it is

this minor pentatonic scale—and its indistinct slide between fifth and fourth degrees—that underpinned much blues, contemporary rock and jazz: "the blues, it's the only thing you hear in West Africa," Wilen said on his return. "It isn't the codified blues that jazz fans know of course, but in terms of the roots, it's the blues."[145] Here is the first of the record's aims: to create and demonstrate a diasporic, multi-stylistic relationship between African and Afro-Western forms and people.

The field recording of the chant continues, its descending lines now faster and overlapping, the recording placed centrally in the mix, slightly gray because of its handheld, happenstance provenance. Panned left and right, Michel Graillier's electric piano, Micheline Pelzer's drums and Pierre Chaze's guitar provide a rippling, out-of-tempo accompaniment, joined eventually by Wilen's tenor, recorded so as to sound as throaty as a bass clarinet. They add little to the music as such, which at this point is unfolding at the site of the taped event: the chant grows, more and more voices joining in, occasional triple-time clapping punctuating the increasingly overlapping waves of that falling pentatonic line. But the Westerners, clearly in a different, brighter and more highly defined sonic space, here frame the tape, providing the African performance with a stage. They drop out when the taped group develops out of the long preparatory line a truncated, metered melody, and accompanying clapping patterns that Western ears are likely to hear as resembling a blues shuffle; six-and-a-half minutes into the track, this performance is replaced by the band in Paris, which takes over with a blues rock groove on one chord, Wilen soloing on the same pentatonic scale (and "blues" inflections) just heard on the African recording.

The Afro-diasporic call-and-response this creates is all the more intriguing for its being made by white Europeans, an irony noted by *Jazz magazine* and responded to by a laconic Wilen: "I'm not as white as all that."[146] But the travelers were as caught up as any in the colonial history of those places, often Francophone, that their Land Rovers visited—especially since the eponymous "Moshi" was a ritual developed in response to that relationship, as Wilen explained.

> It's a recent phenomenon among the Peul people of Niger. A certain number of them went to sing and dance at the Théâtre des Nations. On their return, they had the *moshi*, a sort of trance induced by the memories, horrible and magnificent, of their time in France. In *moshi*, you find the basic sonorities of African languages. When you listen to a certain passage on the record, it seems like a corruption of

"Monsieur." It's only a hypothesis. What I do know is that the ancients of the tribe disapprove of *moshi*. *Moshi* is outside of the tradition.[147]

Wilen's evocation of *moshi* recalls the films—much lauded by the new wave critic-directors—that the French ethnographer Jean Rouch made in the 1950s and '60s, especially the famous *Les Maîtres fous* (1955): here, Rouch filmed a secret ritual in which a group of men would go into a trance and then take on the roles, and claim the powers, of local British colonial dignitaries.[148] At their best, and despite the history of one-sided anthropology in which they participate, the content and viewpoint of Rouch's films manage to temporarily render Westerners, and the Western gaze—the director's and the viewers'—as the Other, as subject rather than object.

If *Moshi* doesn't quite go that far, Wilen's music certainly enters into virtualized dialogue with that which he found in Africa, as well as suggesting dialogues between African and African American practices. "Griots sing the blues," Wilen recalled on his return. "When a guy hasn't got the 25 francs he needs to eat, he sings the blues in the street, but on one chord."[149] "Guide's Song to Binkirri" is an untreated field recording of just that: for three minutes a man sings a melody over and again, the repetition inviting concentration first on the melodic material (again, the minor pentatonic scale) and then on the developing timbre of the signer's voice, which, decorated at first with a rasp common to the blues, eventually incorporates a full-blown multiphonic of the kind that Wilen, following Ayler, Coltrane and other free saxophonists, had recently integrated into his playing. If the trip began under the sign of a naive primitivism, it ended with a record that posits an African musical contemporaneity; by positioning the *moshi* chant and other African musical materials centrally and then responding to them with other sounding evidence of colonial history (the French jazz musicians bearing witness to a musical heritage that had by now crossed the Atlantic twice), they also complicate a number of extant European "privileges"—namely, cultural centrality, and the power to observe and record. For all their informed politics of race and blackness, even the radical free jazz critics sometimes seemed uninterested in the fact that France, too, was implicated in the colonial project that they vilified in its American form. Without making grand claims for a record that hardly makes any for itself, Wilen's music can be seen as drawing a map of colonial and postcolonial cultural flows, making points in sound that had too rarely been made in words.

Wilen saw the use of documentary recording as "a means of progressing" and, in the case of Moshi, a way of raising popular (rather than scholarly) awareness of "so-called ethnological" music: "if Moshi brings people to African music," he said, "that would be an appreciable result." But he was aware that the assimilation was imperfect, ackowledging that the record had been made too soon—a 2013 release culled by Patrick Wilen from his father's field recordings, *Moshi Too* (Sonorama), begins to suggest the true richness of the source material and musical experiments left unexplored—and indeed the original project's conceptual sophistication is often undermined by a loss of performance nerve.[150] Still, it's arguable that a total synthesis of Wilen's jazz with African music would have been undesirable, lapsing into the pastiche that Wilen explicitly stated he wanted to avoid;[151] aside from its historical prescience—it looks forward to "ethnographic" works by later artists, from David Byrne and Brian Eno to Damon Albarn—the interest of the album lies precisely in its collision of different worlds, and its suggestions of their similarities.

Wilen and band performed music from *Moshi* live to apparent good effect. By 1972, the saxophonist felt that the group's current work and use of the taped material were more sophisticated than the record had shown, and a *Jazz hot* concert review by Philippe Carles praised the balance and thoughtfulness of what the writer recognized as a "rereading . . . of the history of jazz," jazz "interrogated" via an interposed Africa.[152] But as *Moshi* evolved in France, other concerns emerged: in 1974 Niger had been ravaged by drought and then a coup d'état, and the saxophonist and his partner set about raising money to take medicine to the friends they had made in the country. Bendern's father ponied up; family connections meant that Princess Grace of Monaco contributed too. Once in Niger, bureaucratic problems with the Red Cross and local administration forced the pair to move around and distribute their drugs clandestinely. Though Wilen and Bendern's project in Africa had begun as a creative one, rooted in ideas of everyday, nonspecialist music-making—and though an ill and immobile Bendern shot a film of passing street life on this trip, *Caminando*—an interest in human welfare had come to dwarf that of artistic inspiration or rejuvenation.[153]

Wilen's readiness to vanish from the jazz scene was, by now, well established. But unlike the disappearances of many other members of the French bebop generation, the saxophonist's vanishings were as much methodological as enforced. Whereas a highly accomplished bebop player like René Urtreger had for want of work taken a long running gig with the pop singer Claude François, Wilen was a strong enough personality simply to renounce music when necessary, the tremendous changes in both jazz and French society seen during the first half of his career imposing these pauses with disorientating regularity. Those disruptions had during the 1960s rendered bebop no longer plausible, had inspired the beginnings of a European free improvised music, and had opened jazz up to musics from around the world; Wilen had found himself, had positioned himself, at the musical center of what were culture-wide transformations.

The next chapter explores how new interests in local and regional musics were further expressed in the French jazz of the 1970s, America—and imagined black Americans—no longer the primary point of reference following the cataclysms of *le free* and 1968. Memories of a bebop past would return, though; Barney Wilen, still playing with images, once again the quintessential jazzman *à l'Américaine*, would in the 1980s wander back into French jazz as it took a postmodern turn.

SIX

Looking for Something
We Don't Yet Know

Towards a French Jazz

For as long as the music had been played and talked about in France, musicians and critics had debated the possibility, and the desirability, of a properly local jazz style. From the symphonic jazz and Quintette du Hot-club successes of the 1930s, past the claims both mendacious and strategic made for jazz's essential Frenchness in the 1940s, the search for and identification of specifically French jazz continued sporadically throughout the 1950s and '60s. But this effort grew stronger thereafter: it was only in the 1970s that a significant number of French players and activists began to develop truly idiosyncratic creative practices, only then that these local endeavors were met with a fully confident critical uptake. So, beginning postwar but focusing on that latter period, this chapter asks what claims to the existence of a "French" jazz were made— and when, why, by whom. Weighing up those arguments also means asking whether local activities were bound together by a singular aesthetic, or else defined as French simply by dint of their coming into being in France; trying to separate the national from the international in turn means questioning whether this elaboration of new jazz practices was singular, or else witnessed too in other (European) countries.

It's a problem as thick as one of André Hodeir's chord voicings, and one only complexified by the fact that, while the conversation on French musicians' ability to play their own jazz was long-running, its terms varied from moment to moment. In the 1930s the music's reception had been bound up with a notion of black exceptionalism, and so, until mid-century, when commentators entertained the possibility of a successful French jazz they had first to entertain that of a successful white jazz. As shown earlier, prewar worries over white jazz deficiency would return in the 1960s alongside a racially charged free style. But this anxiety temporarily subsided for the 1950s: in a 1949 article published in *Jazz hot*, Lucien Malson drew on then-prominent anthropologists Ruth Benedict and Margaret Mead to argue for cultural rather than biological conceptions of race ability, and, as Ludovic Tournès has noted, this piece confirmed the modernist critics' disavowal of the old, racialist jazz writing and helped clear the way for an unambiguous critical acceptance of non-black musicians.[1]

So much for whiteness. But, as was argued in chapter 3, the modernists of the 1950s espoused a jazz "universalism" that chimed with old and specifically European projects and worries, these centering on the separation of the popular (or the passing) and the classical (and the timeless). During this period, then, when exceptional local musicians or practices were identified they were congratulated, as often as not, for heralding the arrival of a "European" rather than French jazz; Lucien Malson's appraisals of André Hodeir were usually made in these terms. Black/white, American/European, these monolithic oppositions had to be broken down by years of musical and critical experience before the more specific question of Frenchness could fully be broached. Even then, the terms "French," "European" and "white" would often remain interchangeable in discussions of French jazz aptitude.

Nevertheless, there were sporadic efforts to locate and promote a national jazz. In 1955, a number of leading critics established the Académie du Jazz to this end. Local confidence growing throughout the decade, in 1957 André Hodeir, a founder member of the Académie, told the American journal *Jazz Today* that

> Paris has become the real jazz center in Europe now. The musicians have left such places as Brussels, just to come to Paris to play with Kenny Clarke and Billy Byers. So there are about ten jazz nightclubs in Paris. You know, the general level of musicianship has gone way up. Five years ago, we were conscious of our faults; now you will be surprised.[2]

As much as it reflected a new, collective confidence, the critical sponsorship of French jazz was owed to a few motivated and well-placed individuals. Chief among these was Lucien Malson. Becoming *Arts'* jazz correspondent in 1957, Malson made a valiant and extended attempt to feature local musicians in his record reviews and interviews, by 1960 routinely featuring players like René Urtreger, François Jeanneau and Michel de Villers.[3] Malson's work seemed to be in tune with his readers' enthusiasms: polls—one attracted 5,000 respondents—routinely asked whether French musicians were as good as American, and they received increasingly positive answers.[4] In describing the growing embrace of local players, Tournès calculates that in 1961 a previously unlikely 30 percent of *Jazz magazine*'s features were given to French players, and the direction of Malson's work in *Arts* seems to suggest the same trend.[5]

But Tournès' method is too focused on such moments of arrival, and coverage of French players would greatly fluctuate in the specialist jazz magazines of the 1960s.[6] It was only the semi-commercial, volunteer-run *Jazz / Jazz hip* that dared publish full issues devoted to French players.[7] And Malson's effort in *Arts* seems not to have pleased enough among the journal's readership and editorial board: from late in 1960 his column was split with Leonard Feather's news roundup from the United States, and by 1961 local players were almost nowhere to be found. Whatever the popularity of French players reported by those surveys, such didn't translate economically, and in the early 1960s most French musicians inspired neither ticket nor record sales to any great extent.

Even their own colleagues were cool. In a 1960 roundtable in *Arts*— entitled "A white is as good as a black" but with the subheading "A French musician can't earn a good living"—Villers admitted that he rarely listened to his fellow French players in performance (Malson, the discussion's convenor, asked how this squared with the common conception among French players that critics ignored them). "We are victims of a false shame," Villers said of the local musicians, "a crippling modesty."[8] In 1963 Martial Solal complained about a critical "pro-American complex" but acknowledged that "7, 8 or 9 times out of 10" writers were correct to value American over French musicians.[9]

However good the players, however variable the critical profile of French jazz, those concerned labored under practical conditions that were unchangingly difficult. In a 1958 *Jazz hot* article, Villers and Barney Wilen angrily responded to a German promoter's suggestion that French musicians, compared with their better-value and better-known American counterparts, charged too much and drew too few. From the 1940s onwards, sporadic (and, until the 1970s, ineffectual) attempts were made by a few jazz musicians to organize, campaigning against what they saw as neglect on the part of potential employers who were ever keener

to hire foreign visitors.[10] The several "Spécial France" editions of *Jazz /
Jazz hip* made for gloomy reading. Editor (and bassist) Roger Luccioni
lamented that jazz's boom in popularity had helped French musicians
hardly at all and, with even the best-known French musicians' records
selling so poorly, labels were inevitably more interested in forgoing recording costs and instead licensing masters from American companies.[11]

In fact, the French jazz life could be as tough for expat Americans as
it was the locals, but the latters' efforts were still largely devoted to becoming better imitators of the American model rather than developing
a form more redolent of truly popular French styles.[12] It hadn't always
been like that, Jef Gilson argued in a 1961 issue of *Jazz hot*, and before
World War II a number of French players had found it easier to put their
own European stamp on what remained jazz—but a kind of inverted
"snobbism," apparently engendered by Marshall Plan–era Ameriphilia,
now discouraged anything different from the transatlantic original.[13] In
the same article, Malson argued that the only way for French jazz to suc-
ceed would be for it to carve out its own niche.

> Why read the tragedies of Voltaire when one could read Racine's?
> French musicians are secretly of the same opinion: their record li-
> braries are essentially American. To get out of that one must smash
> the stereotypes. It's a difficult issue, but it's the only one.[14]

Of course, the name always invoked in these kinds of discussions—
and Gilson invoked it in that piece—was that of Django Reinhardt, still
the only French musician who had definitively shaped international jazz
practice. It was not accidental that, upon its establishment, the Académie
du Jazz had inagurated the annual Prix Django Reinhardt for best French
jazz musician, this award subsequently heralded with as much pomp and
controversy as the critical establishment could muster: Reinhardt had
long since become a patron saint of French jazz, his name used to brow-
beat insufficiently distinctive local musicians, or else to honor those few
deemed worthy of the great man's company.[15]

During the 1950s André Hodeir and Barney Wilen had sometimes
been mentioned in these terms. But the player most routinely accorded
the Reinhardt imprimatur, then and thereafter, was the pianist Martial
Solal.[16] Solal recorded alongside Reinhardt in 1953, and this encounter
was ascribed a mystical importance in retrospect: Solal's first day in the
studio was also Reinhardt's last, and "in the meeting of these two talents,"
as the jazz historian Denis-Constant Martin wrote at the turn of the 21st
century, "the evolution of French jazz symbolically resumed."[17] It's the

thinnest of arguments—a national music tradition pinned on two men—but it's illuminating to dally with it for a moment, not so much because of Solal's critical stature as despite it; whatever his extraordinary abilities, whatever the critics' efforts, the pianist has not often found a place in the imaginary museum of jazz icons that Reinhardt occupies, and his music, made to stand for a French jazz much greater than itself, tests the limited power of such critical sponsorship and narrative construction.

The Extraordinary Individual

Solal was born in Algiers in 1927. He learned his craft touring the towns of French North Africa with a succession of music-hall acts before turning professional in his late teens and moving to Paris in 1950. There, he played in popular bands like Aimé Barelli's before making his first trio recordings for Vogue.[18] This was, and would remain, Solal's preferred recording context; these records announce the pianist as a special attraction, and a succession of rhythm section partners—variously including drummers Roy Haynes, Jean-Louis Viale and Christian Garros—are invited only to keep up. The first, 1953 recordings show how much Solal owed to pre-bebop players: jumpy stride figures recall Art Tatum and Fats Waller, trails of notes aristocratically waved away suggest Teddy Wilson, even if the fluidity of line, and the trio's performance framing, accords with bebop norms. Solal wasn't the only French pianist to be working across what, in retrospect, is often made to seem like a stylistic canyon between swing and bebop, and players like Bernard Peiffer were also formed before Bud Powell's innovations began to come as standard with the instrument. In Solal's case, though, those older Americans' examples—while never entirely abandoned—soon gave way to an approach more definitively "modern"; the Frenchman's version of "All God's Chillun Got Rhythm," captured during one of his 1956 solo sessions for Vogue, is a nod to Powell's own version, and references to Monk are dotted around other recordings of the time.

Solal's virtuosity and conviction were unrivaled by any French player (apart, of course, from Reinhardt), and these characteristics only grew more pronounced through the 1950s and '60s: almost every recorded performance is stuffed full of fast flights of notes each one struck perfectly dead-center, masses of intersecting lines, ceaseless harmonic invention. When Solal allows the torrential pace and gesture to subside, there is a complex yet utterly transparent logic to his direction and redirection of a phrase and to the interaction of upper and lower parts (see "Love

Walked In," January 1956). The super competence and sheer abundance of the pianist's music accounted for his early critical celebration; to French listeners and writers of the 1950s and '60s otherwise accustomed to the wallflower timidity of an Henri Renaud, or even the enjoyable predictability of a René Urtreger, Solal's power was spectacular.

That spectacle, though, could become problematic. For the younger Solal, dialogue was not something that occurred between musicians, but between his left and right hands. With individual invention and force of technique the overwhelming concern, the pianist's music before the 1970s is very rarely open, spacious, pensive, reflective. And like many personalities apparently not given to self-revelation, the pianist's musical self is hidden behind humor. For Ludovic Tournès, heralding in Solal a new French command over jazz, the sudden jolt into double-time in the pianist's 1955 arrangement of the ballad "My Funny Valentine" is a sign of the pianist's "personal interpretation" of the style. It's the kind of platitude that undermines many attempted lionizations of a player who, an exceptional executant more than a conceptual innovator, resists anything more substantive. For other listeners, though, rather than interpretive boons, those humorous devices—they litter the pianist's output—signal a certain bad faith. The smirking insincerity of Solal's *Blue Danube* derivation "Le Beau Danube bleu," the version of the West Coast jazz standard "Four Brothers" recorded on harpsichord, the hoax free jazz of the punningly titled piece "Jazz frit"—"free/fried jazz," in which a rhapsodic melody delighting in its own loveliness is broken up by parodic free playing as if to ask, topically, which the listener prefers—whatever attitude these tactics betray, it is not one designed to meet either material or audience face on, as equals.[19]

Perhaps he felt that mere improvisation was beneath him. Solal thought of himself not just as a performer, but as a pianist-composer (and had done, he later explained, since realizing that this was a better way of introducing himself to his prospective father-in-law).[20] A number of big-band charts recorded for Vogue in 1956–57 are overwritten, but Solal's late 1950s and early '60s soundtrack work is more convincing, his large-group writing taking on a new kind of detail in the new decade; the musician professed his allegiance to the simulated improvisation of his colleague André Hodeir, and that technique is skillfully employed in the scoring of some large-group pieces from this period.[21]

More than any other piece, though, it is the grandly titled Suite en ré bémol pour quartette de jazz (1959) that has accompanied discussions of Solal's work and importance. Writing in 1963, Claude Lenissois and Jef

Gilson cited the Suite as the moment of Solal's final maturation, claiming the piece was "as important in the history of jazz as 'Concerto for Cootie'"—that judgment surely as reflective of local pride, and of André Hodeir's earlier canonizing analysis of Ellington's piece, as it was of realistic critical stock-taking.[22] Thirty-five years later, Ludovic Tournès would similarly praise the Suite for its innovative borrowing from "classical music." But it would be better to say classical or light music history: in its recorded form Solal's work comprises a sixteen-minute stringing together of scored fragments and improvisation, and though a kind of unity is suggested by the reoccurrence of a limited number of compositional motifs, the piece's relationship to any developed art music practice (and what Lenissois and Gilson identified as art music's "internal rigor") was somewhat dubious. In trying to claim for Solal's music a significance its dazzle seems to demand, these and other writers identified the Suite— accompanied as it was by a suggestion of the methods and titular markers of the "classical"—as a moment of European arrival, the sign, as Tournès would put it, of "an innovator pulling his weight in the evolution of jazz." But it's hard to reconcile this isolated and soon obscure individual act with the image of a man bestriding a tradition.[23]

The brilliance, as was sometimes said at the time, could seem to cover a lack of deeper musical significance.[24] Though Solal habitually appeared at or near the top of early 1960s French audience polls, throughout his career critics would frame the pianist as a figure finally "spurned by wide popularity," as Jacques B. Hess wrote in 1975, "accorded an admiration often more respectful than enthusiastic."[25] No matter how much French critics (and later historians) have willed their local hero on to a place in an international jazz tradition, the pianist's work—unlike Django Reinhardt's—had little influence on his fellow instrumentalists' methods or on jazz in general.[26] That's no criticism, since the same could be said for all but a handful of American players: less than Solal's own shortcomings, these unsuccessful critical efforts expose the flaws of an interpretive project that cannot allow musicians or recordings merely to be excellent local exemplars of a practice, but must instead boost the excellent to the historic, an amplification that rings hollow. The same phenomenon could long be observed in writing on other non-American jazz musicians and national scenes.[27]

Solal continued to excel according to his entirely personal standards throughout the 1960s, his unchanging status as one of France's best-known and most highly regarded modern jazz musicians assured not just by his skill, but also by the music's failing popularity. Yet at the start of the

1970s, the striving for personal, executive brilliance on which jazz's development had long been carried began to weaken; like their colleagues elsewhere, French musicians would begin to turn away the figure of the exceptional jazz performer, many finding a rich, and increasingly original, jazz creativity as a result. But before a more "French" jazz could be celebrated, the natures of both music and country would be subject to scrutiny.

Collectivism (rethinking "jazz")

By the end of the 1960s, many of the French musicians previously invested in free jazz were voicing their frustrations with the style and proposing new ways forward. Since *le free* had stressed the improvised—and stressed it to breaking—attempts to innovate would not now necessarily be focused, as they so often had been, on the creation of new improvisational materials; for many French players, the impasse brought about by free was not to be overcome by the development of new, personalized harmonic and rhythmic "vocabularies" alone. Instead, and in the wake of a cultural-political moment in which ideas of the social had been so hotly contested, a number of musicians banded together in the search for original but collaborative methods—concerning composition, structuration, performance and even pedagogy—that would be unique to the group concerned rather than to the extraordinary jazz individual.

This was an important change of priority. Certainly cooperative jazz groups had existed before, in France and abroad—with the Jazz Messengers, at first co-led by Horace Silver and Art Blakey, or the trio HUM, which comprised Daniel Humair, René Urtreger and Pierre Michelot—and certainly they had their own repertoires and conventions. But such units, and their music, nevertheless adhered to a jazz "common practice," both musicians and music easily transferable from one organization to another. And while the stability of these groups had been dependent on the regularity of work, by the 1970s the venues that had once played host to them were going out of business or changing their music policies, in France as elsewhere. Jazz clubs booked groups for fewer and fewer long stints; club residencies of one or two nights, and one-off concert or festival performances, were becoming the norm in a market that was anyway increasingly precarious.[28] Developing new, collaborative music would also mean developing new places to play, even new ways of living.

Axiomatic were the aims, experiences and words of the members of the ensemble Cohelmec, which, at first comprising a traditional three-piece rhythm section and saxophonist, was established in 1968 and continued for a decade with intermittent personnel changes.[29] In a 1971 interview, saxophonist Jean Cohen cited John Coltrane, Albert Ayler and Archie Shepp as his formative influences, but nevertheless claimed that

> the music I want to play actually has little to do with jazz . . . At most I'd like to use the new conception of the instrument developed by those players to create a music less "free," more structured, in a spirit close to that which seems to have animated giants like Varèse or Stockhausen.[30]

The appeal to European, non-jazz sources was made by other musicians, too.[31] Cohen and his bandmates suggested that, in seeking a more structured way of working, they had evolved idiosyncratic notational practices that, designed to record their ideas of the moment, were "cabalistic" enough to be indecipherable even to them at a distance of a few months. What was important, the musicians asserted, was that the group avoid "this 'free' style that's characterized by a hard-hitting drummer and a saxophonist delirious in the upper register."[32] This ambivalence towards American models was common across the emerging field of collectives. Gérard Marais of Le Dharma, a small group of changing lineup that emerged proper around 1970, would later cite a similar formative urge to get away from a free music so identified with a particular American blackness.[33]

Whatever rhetorical efforts these groups made at the time to distinguish themselves from their jazz beginnings, when Vincent Cotro interviewed their members thirty years later it was the AACM and Art Ensemble of Chicago that were most often cited as having been the models for collective activity.[34] Still, this new work emerged alongside rather than trailed American example. Several of the French collectives that would come to prominence in the 1970s had already been formed by the time the Art Ensemble arrived in Paris in June 1969: the Free Jazz Workshop de Lyon began in 1967, Cohelmec in 1968, New Phonic Art the following spring. And collaborative activity wasn't the province of jazz players alone. Cohelmec's drummer Jean-Louis Méchali remembered that, as white Europeans, the group had been attracted by the example of rock groups like The Beatles and Pink Floyd.[35]

Verbally stated aims aside, many of Cohelmec's early musical cues still came from late period John Coltrane, and the concentrated but still rhapsodic free jazz the saxophonist recorded with his pianist wife, Alice, near the end of his life.[36] Other ensembles paid more attention to Miles

Davis's most recent music. The keyboards of the Dharma Trio's Patricio Villarroel often recalled the romanticism of mid-1960s Herbie Hancock, while some of the compositions on the group's *Snoopy's Time* (1970) pastiched then-current Davis records like *In a Silent Way* and *Bitches Brew*. In music made by the larger ensembles that Villarroel established under the name Machi Oul with his brother Manuel, "free jazz" often functioned as a coloristic interlude rather than as the practice's basis (though the few tracks on 1971's *Terremoto* that don't take off McCoy Tyner or Pharoah Sanders's contemporary styles are impressively raucous in the Ornette Coleman or Don Cherry vein).[37]

Quicker to mature was the music of Perception. On that band's self-titled debut, which appeared on Futura in 1971, Jean My Truong's drumming darts from loping to limber, groove to free, the German pianist Siegfried Kessler and bassist Didier Levallet following suit; the Paris-based Hungarian saxophonist and bass clarinetist Yotchk'o (Jeff) Seffer contributes an improvisation style based on polished-up Coltrane and Ayler, and compositional materials that recall eastern European folk modality by way of Bartók. But that "European" element does not obscure the presence of informing Coltranian free jazz and Davisian jazz rock that other French collectives also concerned themselves with, albeit less successfully.

Whatever the qualities of these groups, their early recordings—Perception apart, perhaps—betrayed a largely familiar approach to jazz making, one that had not kept pace with interview appeals to European art music idols and innovative intent. Efforts to develop a truly distinct ensemble music lagged behind similar projects being conducted in London, Amsterdam and Berlin, and by musicians involved with AMM, the Instant Composers Pool and the Globe Unity Orchestra. On record at least, the stylistic braveness of those jazz-born collectives was beginning to be matched in France only several years later. By the time of *Mestari*, recorded late in 1973, Perception had arrived at a method that, refusing free jazz gesture and continual (if multiple) pulsation, was now atomized and spacious. The Cohelmec Ensemble's *5 Octobre Live* (Chevance), recorded in 1974, demonstrated the same, making even more (or rather, less) of the quiet and the texturally reduced. While Jean-Marc Boutin's virtuosic, Cecil Taylor-like pianism was at the center of the X-tet's music, the group—which performed widely but recorded hardly at all—was by this time exploring other compositional and improvisational tactics too, a December 1974 France Musique broadcast showing the ensemble moving through a long, often spare, open-form composition.[38] Limiting a soloistic free jazz vocabulary to its formative elements and dispersing these in wider space, emphasizing collective creation rather than individual statement, all of this was playing a part in the emergence of a "European" improvised music increasingly thought distinct from free jazz, and discussed in more detail later.

The difficult attempt to realize new ways of working led French players to create new spaces of musical development and performance. The members of Le Dharma lived together in Nanterre before installing themselves in a chalet near Annecy, a provincial town of 50,000 near the Swiss border. This, the group members told *Jazz magazine* in 1972, enabled them to concentrate on their music, but it was also an attempt to find a more tranquil space removed from Paris and what they called the "intrigues" that existed between musicians there. The indeterminately sized X-tet, also living together outside Annecy (and making their musical base an old abbey), expressed identical sentiments; elsewhere, others were also experimenting with rural, communal living and working arrangements.[39] This provincialization removed groups from traditional performance routines, and, many argued, for the better. Just as Cohelmec made much of their tendency to stage impromptu performances in the squares and streets of Paris, so Le Dharma's members articulated a desire to get away from sclerotic concert presentation and to "create a new form of spectacle," one that would escape the stage to create a new musical communality.[40]

It was no accident that so many underground jazz musicians had been drawn to Annecy—among others, the American free jazz pianist Burton Greene eventually arrived—since the town played host to a group of jazz lovers who, driven by the contemporary spirit, invested themselves in the creation, promotion, education and dissemination of jazz and improvisation under the banner Annecy Jazz Action (AJA). The AJA was one of the first, and most influential, of many such organizations to be established in France before the mid-1970s. In a collectively authored 1973 *Jazz hot* article discussing their project, the AJA's "Comice Khulturel" decried the "suicidal Parisianization of Khulture," which was a result of both commercial and governmental practice. The concentration of jazz activity in a "ghetto" of Parisian venues, and the lack of real penetration that jazz had achieved outside those venues, had been ignored by a complacent metropolitan jazz press—"isn't there a great void," the writers asked, "between the Chat qui Pêche and the pumpkin farmers' annual dance?"—and the parlous nature of French jazz had been "papered over" by a discourse concerned first and foremost with the meaning of the new jazz and black music. Neither a plaything for the Parisian in-crowd, nor the token of an exotic black culture, the AJA demanded the creation of a jazz reality in which jazz was "first and foremost . . . something to live."[41] The earliest French writers on jazz had celebrated the ways that the music seemed to dance over what in Europe had been a fissure between "art" and "life"; despite being formed in a radically different cultural moment, the post-1968 generation of musicians would begin to plug that gap.

The AJA had begun by running a club, and by putting on weekly concerts by the likes of Sunny Murray, John Tchicai and Champion Jack Dupree.[42] But this was not enough. Instead, the group aimed to organize public performances involving all kinds of musics (they named jazz, pop, blues, folk, Indian and Arab styles) and involving all kinds of activities (a journal, a library, cinema screenings, poster-making), this activity to be as spontaneous and mobile as possible. Beyond the simple promotion of jazz as a bounded genre or professional proposition, the AJA, proclaimed the committee, found in the style "the point of departure for popular cultural action, the language of which is music."[43]

As the committee acknowledged, the AJA's activity was only one articulation of what was widely felt as a "need to organize . . . from the basis of a free and authentic form of expression, and independently."[44] Other groups, like Rouen Jazz Action, would explicitly position their work as an outgrowth of post-1968 organization.[45] From the turn of the decade, collectives of similarly minded jazz activists had emerged in Bordeaux (Le Béret Cosmique), Lyon (Musique Actuelle), Marseille (Musique 70), Lille (Après la Pluie le Beau Temps), Compiègne (Jazz Pop Action), Paris (Le Souterrain), Poitiers (Varlope), and in Montpellier, Aix-en-Provence, Roanne. After a September 1972 congress, these groups developed a network, Rezo Zero, to facilitate tours while bypassing the commercial sector and its impresarios. In the following year, more groups joined: Lille Jazz Action, Le Groupe d'Action Musicale de Rennes, Jazz Action Marseille, Brest Jazz Action, as well as organizations in Avignon, Metz and elsewhere.[46] Lyon's Association à la Recherche d'un Folklore Imaginaire (ARFI) was formed in 1977 and would prove the most durable of the collectives, continuing along with the Rouen group into the 21st century.[47]

The nature, extent and duration of these organizations' activities varied greatly, but one widely held aim was to engage in a kind of pedagogy absolutely contrary to state cultural policy of the previous decades.[48] Then, the key policy tenet had been that of the "right to culture," the belief that every citizen should have access to a traditionally defined (and often French) high culture. In the hands of André Malraux, de Gaulle's minister of culture from the post's 1959 creation onwards, that meant the institution of a number of regional arts centers, the Maisons de la Culture. As Brian Rigby has written, Malraux insisted that "only culture of the most distinguished and most demanding kind should be offered" at the Maisons, and that "there would be no suggestion of amateurism, nor any hint that culture was being watered down at the provincial level."[49] Such watering down included didactic or explanatory work: these centers were to be modern cathedrals at which people would have epiphanic experiences in front of art, not night schools hosting effortful, petit-bourgeois attempts at self-improvement. This cultural policy, of course, had no room for popular music or art of any kind.

In contrast, and like other post-1968 groups in all areas of the arts, the jazz actions practiced what was increasingly referred to as *animation*. In line with the new thinking, animation often sought to erase the boundaries between professional activity and pedagogy, between performers and public. While this activity was often conceived as educational— though even that was questioned, some artists beginning to create work only with the involvement of those they were engaged to engage—in emphasizing creative participation rather than hands-off appreciation, animation circumvented what was often considered a stultifying canon of high art in order to embrace *différence*.[50] In their interviews, members of Le Dharma, X-tet and the Workshop de Lyon enthused about their animation activities with the disabled, or with school children, especially those who were poor or troubled; though spreading awareness and understanding of jazz and improvisation was a factor, that was sometimes presented as secondary to the exploration of creativity untrammeled by more traditional concerns of genre or craft.[51]

But, away from the workshop or hospital ward, cultural activity was to be conceived as a political battleground. So the jazz actions often presented themselves with aggressive oppositionalism, rarely missing an opportunity to provide their own public critique of those commercial or state-funded organizations with which they sometimes found themselves associated. When granted access to the mainstream jazz press, the actions' jointly authored accounts of group activity were routinely colored by provocation and a dwelling on difficulty, failure and public ambivalence. Along with several musicians, the Annecy Jazz Action sent a number of vehicles to the 1978 Nancy jazz festival, these fitted out with printing equipment so that the AJA could publish a daily bulletin complementing "or contradicting" official festival public relations material.[52] In 1978 *Jazz magazine* invited Rouen Jazz Action to provide a report on a concert the group had arranged with Peter Brötzmann, Han Bennink and Joe McPhee. But the jazz activists submitted instead a Godardian exposure of the concert's production, providing a balance sheet for the enterprise (showing a loss of 850 francs), underplaying the music made in favor of blunt critiques of the pre- and postconcert behavior of the European *vedettes*, "stars."[53] If the artists were criticized, it was because the jazz actions, valuing the local and organic above all, were distrustful of a traveling "vedettariat"; if *Jazz magazine*'s article request was unceremoniously flouted it was because the invitation to assimilate jazz action activities into a Parisian commercial operation was not an altogether agreeable one. Indeed, group members gibed at the Parisian jazz world whenever presented with an opportunity. In 1976 Lille Jazz Action's Gaby Bizien, a drummer, told *Jazz magazine* that he would be happy to accept a gig in the capital—but no more than he would one in the (pointedly unglamorous) towns of Metz or Dunkirk.[54]

Not every jazz organization cast itself so contrarily. Having returned from Africa, Barney Wilen and Caroline de Bendern had installed themselves in Monaco, and from 1976 they set about constructing and participating in local jazz projects. Chief among these was a scheme along the lines of New York's Jazzmobile, in which musicians gave free, peripatetic concerts from the back of a truck. In late 1977 Wilen's project, eventually named Burodujazz, was given a grant by the city's Action Culturelle Municipale—Wilen had enlisted the support of a family friend, the controversial mayor Jacques Médecin—and just as the saxophonist was keener than the younger action members to seek institutional cooperation, so he framed his brand of animation in an old-fashioned, somewhat patrician manner: this was, Wilen said, "a civic act. I think that we don't teach enough of that in France, Civic Education." The saxophonist's personal relationship with Médecin could not protect his project from the massive corruption of the mayor's administration, and Burodujazz came to an end in 1979 after its funds were allegedly embezzled.[55]

Regionalism (rethinking "France")

The jazz action activities—and the potshots at Paris—were part of a much broader renewal of interest and faith in the country's provincial cultures. The history of France after 1800 is in no small part defined by the centralizing state's conflicted attitude towards regional identities, these sometimes venerated, sometimes suppressed. On the one hand, the comestible produce of the *terroirs* was legally defined and protected by increasingly fastidious *appellations d'origine*. But the bureaucratic strands that had run through the texture of everyday French life from Napoleon's time, thickening markedly during the Third Republic, acted to choke local difference when it threatened centralized political power—the latter under threat during a 19th century strewn with regional resistance and provincially plotted counterrevolutions. The Third Republic's secularization and formalization of now-compulsory primary schooling was the first step towards a unified, Republican national identity, and by the turn of the 20th century teachers were forced to teach and children were forced to learn French—a language that in many regions had been spoken only among high society—as well as the values and ideals of the nation that, pupils were now instructed, had replaced their *pays* as the fatherland.[56]

Since the Republic proclaimed its universalist egalitarianism, from the late 19th century until the 1950s a competing regionalism—at its strongest in Brittany, Flanders, Corsica, Alsace and Lorraine—was often identified with the rightist and reactionary. During World War II, a number of regionalist leaders had attempted to align themselves with Vichy's folk-nationalist rhetoric to their own ends, this leaving their movements discredited after liberation. But postwar critiques of colonialism, later combined with notions of *autogestion*—a key tenet of 1968, standing for ground-up "self-determination" rather than top-down political organization—had enabled the development of a new, leftist regionalism. Now, the regions, especially in the poorer south and west of the country, were conceived as "internal colonies" whose people and produce were sucked into and exploited by the center, Paris, and which had been left economically, culturally and demographically impoverished as a result. The 1970s career of *Jazz hot*'s former editor Michel Le Bris describes the changing tenor of the times. After serving a prison sentence for his editing of the banned Maoist journal *La Cause du peuple*, he turned his attention to the regionalist movements of Occitania (Languedoc and Provence) and his native Brittany. In the fiction and nonfiction he wrote at his new Breton base, Le Bris portrayed a region full of alienated peasants, their smallholdings occupied by capitalists, their traditions and beliefs pulverized by Paris-imposed agricultural science and industry.[57] Terrorist campaigns carried out on behalf of Breton, Basque and Corsican separatists announced that it was in the regions that radicalism now lay; the regionalist cause was taken up in mass circulation left wing newspapers and journals like *Libération* and *Les Temps modernes*.

This politics was articulated in music, too. Forms such as the *nòva cançon occitana*, the new Occitan song, would become important media through which a new and oppositionalist regional history and identity could be forged. As the historian Robert Gildea suggests, such creative activity was necessary, this Occitania as much an imaginative local response to a contemporary political situation as it was a historical entity to be protected.[58]

Though the methods were different, a similarly synthetic project could be seen in the 1970s work of François Tusques, whose ideological trajectory resembled that of his friend Le Bris. The pianist-composer began the decade as a Maoist, the two volumes of piano solos he recorded for Futura in 1970 and 1971 entitled *Piano dazibao* after the wall-painted propaganda slogans of the Chinese cultural revolution. The music squeezes free jazz, ragtime, blues, R&B, Monk, Bartók and French impressionism into an out-of-tune piano before exploding with ideas and vitality that seem absent from the musician's rote interviews of the period: there, Maoist doctrine is faithfully mouthed as Tusques summons visions of idealized Chinese artists, preparing for performances by going into the factories to learn from the workers.[59] However romantic that notion, Tusques would prove willing to abandon his complex, improvisation-based method for the sake of the People. In 1972 he told *Jazz magazine* of a regional gig during which he had watched a pop group establish a rapport with the audience that his free music would never attain; henceforth basing his music on popular forms, Tusques formed the Intercommunal Free Dance Music Orchestra, the stable lineup of which featured Paris-based musicians from determinedly diverse regions and communities—notably the Guinean saxophonist Jo Maka, Togan trombonist Adolf Winkler (aka Ramadolf) and Catalan vocalist Carlos Andreu.[60] This group was to "return to popular roots" and to represent those "communities that live and work in Paris," the provincial, the immigrant, the marginal.[61] As such, over the next decade it usually played away from the jazz and concert circuit, its recorded repertoire combining African, Iberian, Breton and many other styles, with Tusques's piano a Monkish constant. The musician's 1979 Chant du Monde album *Après la marée noire* expresses a commitment to an internally colonized Brittany, Carlos Andreu's texts plain on the matter. Breton bombards— double-reed instruments with the power of a trumpet—shout across an Afro dance groove; the biniou koz, a kind of bagpipes, spells out a melody while Tusques provides heavy jazz accompaniment.[62]

By dint of their transatlantic formation, even lapsed jazz musicians could never make music that satisfied an uncomplicated idea of regional identity. Whatever Tusques's commitment to the regional cause, folk traditionalists were not kind towards his efforts, since in both content and framing—the album was subtitled *Vers une musique bretonne nouvelle*, towards a new Breton music—the work advocated engaged cultural-political syncretism as much as it did singular, traditionary engagement.[63] To that extent, Tusques's project was of a piece with other 1970s French jazz incorporations of regional styles, even if most of that other work was much less strongly identified with radical regional politics. Most notable were the productions of Lyon's ARFI, the organization that first espoused *un folklore imaginaire* and which would, into the 21st century, host a number of ensembles continuing that line of exploration.[64]

The musical collage (and cultural fabulism) espoused by these groups was important, allowing as it did a mobilization of regional traditions and practices that did not simultaneously summon the ghost of ethnic purity, one that could still otherwise linger around claims to local exceptionalism.[65] Nevertheless, a feeling that the provincial *terroirs* could retain and inspire an organic link between musicians and public endured. In 1975, the virtuoso multi-instrumentalist Bernard Lubat recalled the conservatoire training he had received a decade earlier as his moment of awakening, the point at which he appreciated for the first time how musical practices could inscribe divisions in social class. In Lubat's reminiscence, the *bals* and communal music-making of his southwestern youth had evaded the institutional hierarchy and stylistic ossification he subsequently experienced.

> In France we are trying to recover an identity; the music has distanced itself from folklore, it's become a music of an elite that's passed on from one initiate to another, it's lost contact with the street. Music still keeps its roots in underdeveloped countries. Here it belongs to the classes who have the possibility of knowing that it exists. There's a job to do, and it's to relocate music at a quotidian level.[66]

Lubat was hardly a political reactionary. But his professed anti-institutionalism and localism chimed with those of another southwesterner, Hugues Panassié; that the pair shared ideas and vocabularies across the decades shows how the issue of organic regional culture could traverse the political spectrum, the constant enemy being the centralizing state and metropolitan elite.

Lubat's thinking inspired him to establish his own provincial festival, at his native Uzeste, in 1977. Events like this provided the most high-profile opportunities for post–free French jazz musicians throughout the 1970s: the Festival de Châtellerault had been established in 1970; Jazz à Châteauvallon in 1971; the Festivals of Nîmes, Le Castelet and Saint-Rémy-de-Provence in 1976; Marciac in 1977.[67] Catering to what were understood to be audiences with overlapping tastes, these festivals often offered a broad mix of contemporary music: the 1969 Saint-Paul-de-Vence festival featured avant-garde jazz and improvisation from Cecil Taylor and contemporary art music from Stockhausen, and such a stylistic mixture was not uncommon.[68] The festivals of the 1970s contributed to the breaking down of boundaries between formerly elite and formerly popular styles, as well as to an ongoing de-urbanization of musics that had formerly been identified with cosmopolitan city life.

Perhaps the most important of these eclectic, provincial festivals was that held at Châteauvallon, Provence. The event's 1971 launch had featured Dizzy Gillespie, Memphis Slim and Gerry Mulligan, but the subsequent couple of years saw more adventurous programming, with Don Cherry, Marion Brown and others invited. After a break in 1974 and 1975, the festival returned, the word "jazz" missing from its title: now, and significantly, it was dubbed Musique ouverte à Châteauvallon, this gesture towards a more broadly defined "open music"—embracing jazz, art and non-European traditional work—made partly to secure municipal funding from nearby Toulon, but also in deference to the wider stylistic interests prevalent among jazz-formed musicians and audiences by mid-decade.[69] Indeed, the "openness" heralded at Châteauvallon well represented emergent trends that would later be taken as characterizing a newly "French" jazz creativity; some of the most durable efforts in this direction would be made by the subject of this chapter's next section, Michel Portal, and made at the festival itself.

Polyvalent Portal

Portal was born in Bayonne, in France's Basque southwestern corner, in 1935. Following conservatoire clarinet study in Paris and then a two-and-a-half-year spell of national service in Algeria, he embarked on a freelance career, the variety, or, as it was often described, the "polyvalence" of which defined Portal's early image. Versatility was the focal point of the player's every magazine feature: he was as comfortable sitting in the pit bands of chanson stars like Edith Piaf, Charles Trenet, Tino Rossi or Claude Nougaro as he was as a soloist playing the classical clarinet repertoire.[70] Despite his ubiquity, Portal rarely recorded as a jazz soloist before the end of the 1960s, but when he did, it was often similarly to order: the accompaniment that he lent the chanteuse Barbara on her dulcet 1964 hit "Pierre" was delivered with West Coast tenderness, yet cut with something more acid; the latter was brought out on Serge Gainsbourg's psychopath fantasy "Quand mon 6.35," recorded in the same year, on which the saxophonist fulfilled with uncanny accuracy the jazz-loving songwriter's request for a Jackie McLean imitation. Apart from Tusques' *Free jazz*—and brief appearances on Jef Gilson's *Enfin !* (1963), Jean-Luc Ponty's debut *Jazz Long Playing* (1964) and *Jef Gilson à Gaveau* (1965)— that was about it.[71] But an early picture of Portal as Portal emerges from Pierre Michelot's 1963 Mercury album *Round About a Bass*. Both Michelot's arrangements and their execution by the cream of Paris's jazz studio circuit—the album showcases skillful but otherwise underfeatured improvisers like Roger Guérin (trumpet), Georges Grenu (soprano) and Pierre Gossez (tenor and baritone)—are immaculate, a world away from the French big-band recordings of the 1950s (even though featuring some of the same key players). Plenty of the ensemble polish emanates from Portal's alto, but his solos are more conflicted. On "Elephant Green" and "Bye, Bye, Blackbird," the saxophonist is expressive, always playing out, and yet there is a tight-chested quality to his sound, his lines often fraying into loose ends; the latter, at least, seems owed to a lack of saturation in the bebop vocabulary. Certainly Charlie Parker's by-now venerable formulae receive due citation ("Bye, Bye, Blackbird," 1:59), but those licks constitute much less of the saxophonist's melodically conceived phraseology than they had done for a player like Barney Wilen.

Portal had, he said in 1967, studied Parker's solos note for note, but he had resisted the temptation to form himself in the "Parkerian" style: "I know perfectly well how to blow a saxophone, but that style, I don't want. It's not me, I don't live solely in that universe."[72] The musician thought it vital not to sign one's creativity over to this or that school. When Dizzy Gillespie arrived in France after the war, Portal said in 1973, "it was fantastic."

> People needed it, like they did chewing gum. There were plenty of guys who got caught up in that but don't play anymore. They realized that no development is possible with a music you take up one day, just like that. I don't want to fall into that trap, I don't want to defend a music that I'm entombed in. I want to escape.[73]

In the short term, the evasion of bebop technicality would cause Portal's jazz solos problems, but demands for that kind of playing were already receding when the saxophonist began making professional headway; in the longer term it was this stylistic nonalignment that would account for the success and originality of the musician's output.

As the previous chapter showed, Portal was an important figure in the French free jazz movement of the late 1960s. But he was also one of the players to articulate a widespread uneasiness around the white, European assimilation of a music so strongly identified with African American politics and culture.[74] The radicality of that politics had been matched by a radically confrontational sound world, and even if he played his part in such energy jazz performances—as he did on Sunny Murray's self-titled 1968 Shandar album—the musician continually expressed his ambivalence towards the free aesthetic: "there's a kind of energy that I don't get," he said in 1967. "I don't understand why there is so little repose in this music."[75] In keeping with the thinking of those musicians cited earlier, by the early 1970s this professed bafflement had matured into something more decided and dismissive both of free jazz's technique and its ethics, the music "perhaps a bit decadent."

> Always the wailing lament, always the people's alienation, demonstrated on stage by us . . . It's maybe not too strong as an idea. Maybe we need to go elsewhere.[76]

The music Portal had by then recorded under his own name featured no little wailing, but even his 1969 debut album, *Our Meanings and Our Feelings* (Pathé), betrayed polystylistic concerns. Portal's tenor and assorted reed instruments are deeply marked by *Ascension*-era John Coltrane, both in sound and phrase shape—though his lines, distilling if not diverging from Coltrane's methods, are more discontinuous, repetitious. Behind him, Joachim Kühn draws curtains of piano notes. But these standard features of free are placed in relation to materials that—even if their presence recalls the stylistic development of Albert Ayler's music—bear unusually strong non-jazz generic identities. The energy blowing of "For My Mother" climaxes with a melody half-churchly, half-tin pan alley; "Walking Through the Land" is an imaginary North African landscape, Kühn using the zoukra, a reed flute, to announce a circling, microtonal chant figure over a steady ritual rhythm; "A Train in a Very Small Town" scatters deconstructed R&B over an unreconstructed backbeat. Similar stylistic extravagances are shown on the 1970 Futura album Portal recorded with John Surman and the Englishman's group, *Alors !!!* , but so, too, on the latter is what would become identified as a rather "European" formal sensibility. On these pieces, composed by Surman, bassist

Barre Phillips and drummer Stu Martin, free improvisation—often detailed, quiet, in literally stark contrast to free jazz norms—envelops what are often extended if loose song forms.

That method of improvisation Portal was exploring more fully elsewhere. In 1969 he had helped form New Phonic Art, an improvising ensemble featuring three players who were active in art music composition as well as a new spontaneous art music practice: Carlos Roqué Alsina (mostly playing keyboards), Jean-Pierre Drouet (percussion) and Vinko Globokar (trombone). The sonic, spatial and gestural vocabularies of the group's work owed less to African American free jazz than to the planar, post-Cagean improvisation of Europe-based improvisation groups like AMM and MEV, or the post-serial work of composers such as Stockhausen; like the group's name itself, New Phonic Art's 1971 Wergo album articulated the desire for a culturally realigned improvisation, and a three-LP set released on the blue-chip classical label Deutsche Grammophon in 1973—entitled *Free Improvisation*, and in addition to Portal's group including the British improvisers Derek Bailey and Paul Rutherford, among others—also helped shape a sense of an emergent European "art music" improvisation distinct from jazz.

In the same period Portal performed and recorded, as a member of the chamber ensemble Musique Vivante or a soloist, with Stockhausen (*Aus Den Sieben Tagen*) and Luciano Berio (*Laborintus II*, both albums Harmonia Mundi, 1969), Pierre Boulez (*Domaines*, Harmonia Mundi, 1971) and Mauricio Kagel (*Exotica/Taktil*, Deutsche Grammophon, 1972). Where these composers called upon Portal to generate their own musical material—as in those text scores of Stockhausen's recorded in 1969—and where Portal played with the New Phonic Art, his playing was stripped of jazz identity, furnishing instead gestural and textural devices in the service of a carefully collaborative, depersonalized architecture. Though the terms suggest a dubious essentialism, and though the division of practices and traditions was less clear than it might have seemed, there is nevertheless some truth in George Lewis's later contrasting of this new, corporate "Eurological" improvisation with an older, individualist "Afrological" method.[77] Indeed, Portal saw his conservatoire training as an instrumentalist, an interpreter, and an ensemble player as having instilled a "fluidity" that now allowed him to move between musical situations with ease; although his playing was not stamped with the strongest marks of individuality, the musician did not consider this a drawback.[78] Portal would shortly emerge as one of those comparatively rare players whose work, despite having emerged from somewhere in the jazz tradition, was defined not just by its singular instrumental or compositional personality, but also by its marshaling of disparate talents and stylistic impulses, these set in an original conceptual context.

"We'd like to play our own music," Portal had said of the French free jazz players as early as 1967. But, he added, no one knew what that was. Even then, the instrumentalist had sensed that what was lacking was *une écriture*,

> a kind of writing and firmer structure, but that, I'm not ready to do. Basically we need a contemporary music that is neither classical nor jazz. We're looking for something we don't yet know.[79]

New Phonic Art showed that, in the first years of the 1970s, one version of that something was coming into focus, even if "writing" was still nowhere to be seen. But while it entertained similar concerns, the music Portal was then beginning to make under his own name—and in which composition did play a part—cleaved much closer to the jazz tradition; even if this music was "collective, not based solely on me, on my pleasure," as he said in 1973, it was to "apply the jazz attitude in situations that are specifically European."[80] While free improvisation would develop as an increasingly separate practice, Portal was among those marking out another conceptual space, one that—despite, or perhaps because of its more direct acknowledgment of jazz precedent—would contribute to a notionally "French" jazz that attempted to sound like nothing but itself.

Our Meanings and our Feelings had been made alongside Joachim Kühn's group, *Alors !!!* alongside John Surman's, and Portal was only one of the composers responsible for those albums. The beginning of Portal's oeuvre proper came with the 1971 recording of *Splendid Yzlment* (CBS). The music, mostly composed by Portal for an international septet in which almost all the musicians play multiple instruments, is a rather strange mixture of free jazz dramatics, folk-music allusion and the most elemental of horn arrangements: as would continue to be the case, Portal's composed statements are often simply minimalist, calculatedly inelegant gestural groupings or collections of pitches, these much less melody and phrase than structural markers. With a wide range of sources cited in such reduced form—a grammarless, guidebook language blunt but facilitating a remarkable tour of world musical style—the music is truly cosmopolitan. The album's title track, for instance, leads off from a much repeated brass section ostinato, the pitch content of which could come from contemporary funk, the rhythmic articulation of which is anything but, Howard Johnson's amusingly aimless tuba bassnotes giving the music the grimmest plod. Over this ostinato emerges Portal's bandoneon and an Astor Piazzolla–type tango; later in the piece, Johnson and the brilliant Swiss percussionist Pierre Favre summon a powerful gust of free improvisation, but the overriding identity of the piece rests in its steadily pulsed, stylistic suggestions.

Portal's addition of the bandoneon to his instrumental array marked a departure from free jazz norms and the beginning of an embrace of regional, folk forms—one that marked a public recognition of his own heritage, since he had been playing the instrument (much used in the French southwest and throughout the Basque diaspora) since childhood. The musician would soon express an unease about its employment, remarking that audiences often thought his interpolation of tango was parodic, a comment on the death of that form in keeping with what was then a satiric use of stylistic quotation on the part of contemporary art music composers like Kagel. It wasn't the case, Portal protested, and indeed, here and elsewhere, the Frenchman's use of generic musics and signifiers rarely betrays the kind of irony or nostalgia that would become even more commonplace in the 1980s.[81] Instead, the reduction of these stylistic elements to their bare outlines, and their placement in a musical space that is at once all-embracing and methodically, attitudinally consistent and coherent, meant that Portal's music, despite its wit, did not trade on the frisson of the incongruous.

Portal's stature as a leader continued to grow after the foundation of the Michel Portal Unit, comprising Portal, Bernard Vitet on trumpet and other brass instruments, Beb Guérin and Léon Francioli on basses, and drummer Pierre Favre.[82] The group would only release one record under this name, but it toured widely throughout the first half of the 1970s, and anyway, recording was not a priority during this period: "the question wasn't of leaving a mark," Portal said later, "only the concert counted, what was *live*, and the conviction that spontaneity was the condition of invention." Recordings were "dead music, canned music" that "couldn't help but misrepresent what we wanted to do."[83] (Portal's fellow saxophonist Jean-Louis Chautemps expressed the same sentiment, his feeling that a recording artist was a kind of "grocer" selling canned goods stretching back to the late 1950s and accounting for his relatively limited discography.)[84] This was an expression of contemporary, anticonsumerist sentiment. Nevertheless, it was a release of the Unit's August 1972 appearance at the Châteauvallon festival, titled *No, no but it may be*, that finally reframed Portal's public and press reception. No longer merely "polyvalent," he was now leading the creation of a European jazz production.[85]

Again, the music is divided up by "themes," these now even simpler, like the unison stabs for Portal and trumpeter Bernard Vitet that open the piece; again, Portal's improvisations proceed motivically, organically, providing an obvious line of development, seamlessly incorporating composed elements (6:00–9:19). The musical space is wide, the detail within these simplified compositional and improvisational events standing out against a backdrop of such reduced activity and texture. The openness of form is apparent from the great differences between the record's side 1 and side 2—notionally two performances of the "same" piece, only the most scant of thematic echoes suggesting any commonality—and from Portal's onstage verbal directions that, from time to time, the microphones pick up (later, Portal would say that he liked "to give out roles before a concert, like you give out shirts to a rugby team").[86]

The assimilation of free jazz into a rationalized and somewhat "arranged" musical project might have struck some as a dilution of the music's earlier intent. Still, aside from enabling the realization of long-held musical ambitions, the method also called after those audiences trickling away from jazz after free. For Portal, the relationship between his group and its listeners was vital, and in a 1973 interview he ruminated at length on a recent, "disastrous" gig in Bordeaux at which an unsympathetic crowd had inspired unsuccessful music. In contrast was one of Portal's most celebrated recordings, made with a slightly different lineup at the Châteauvallon festival in 1976, four years to the day after the Unit's first recording there.[87] Though the textural predetermination and motivic logic of earlier performances are on show in the long opening piece, "Soufrière"—which, bearing the name of a volcano then erupting in Guadeloupe, puts a brooding two-bass rumble under Portal's tenor working and reworking of a rapidly descending chromatic sequence—this quickly subsides in favor of an onstage comedy, which, unintelligible on record, was evidently successful at the time. Audience laughter litters the set, which includes instrumentalized dog barking and a schmaltzy version of Albert Ayler's "Angels" backed by Bernard Lubat's gurgling industrial synthesizer and live firecrackers.

You had to be there, but that was the point. A recording of a broadcast made just over a week later from the Willisau festival in Switzerland shows the Unit recombining the same compositional materials in much the same order, though they are treated differently here: the low, two-bass texture is more mobile, the chromatic motif that Portal sets over it is dispatched once rather than continually revisited, the 12/8 bass line that marked the first appearance of the comedy at Willisau briefly appears in 6/4 form before making a full appearance much later, and space is opened up throughout for guest trombonist Albert Mangelsdorff. Much of the humor is removed from the Swiss performance, and there is more focus instead on powerful, glinting grooves, these driven by the bassists' now-charged playing and—especially—by Pierre Favre's tremendously inventive melding of both Afro-Caribbean and contemporary European art music gestural traditions, this articulated by stick rattle, cymbal and bell metals bright and dark, the taut thunk of skin.

Inevitably, Portal's music became enclosed in the Reinhardtian narrative, from his 1968 winning of the prize bearing the guitarist's name to the 2003 CD rerelease of the first Châteauvallon recording, the cover of which bore a sticker proclaiming the music as "without doubt the most beautiful and strongest declaration of independence since Django Reinhardt." Was this then a new, "French" or "European" jazz? Certainly some of Portal's comments helped build his music into what one jazz action activist had called "the exploding contemporary movement that no longer tries to take its lessons from the black American school, but writes itself into specifically European traditions"; the musician's active presence in both art music and jazz worlds primed critics and listeners to seek accordances between the two in the musician's own work.[88] This has continued in French historical evaluations, Ludovic Tournès citing Portal as the first among a cadre of French musicians to pass through the newly "permeable" barriers between art music and jazz and able to arrive at a music liberated from its "American masters," Jedediah Sklower noting that the spaciousness and clarity of texture in Portal's 1970s music were informed by contemporary European art music methods.[89]

Neither claim is wrong. But at least as much as it describes a musical reality, the mobilization of a notional "European" art music in these arguments acts to define what might be an imaginary difference. Because in truth, that art music, in any of its varieties, differed dramatically from Portal's work—even the "art music" improvisation in which Portal took part as a member of New Phonic Art was far removed from the musician's personal project—and the Frenchman's own work was at least as indebted to innovative African American musicians of the period as it was any European school.[90] It may be by chance that the stabs-in-space theme and blistering crotales passage found in Anthony Braxton's "Composition No. 1," recorded in Paris in 1969 as part of This Time (BYG), resembled the same devices as heard on Portal's 1972 Châteauvallon recording. It may be accidental that the nonironic invocation of highly generic material, together with an extreme thematic economy and compensatory construction of shifting "orchestral" texture—of which an extended percussion palette is an important part—is found in both Portal's work and the French recordings of the Art Ensemble of Chicago (see *People in Sorrow*, and *A Jackson in Your House*, both BYG 1969). Perhaps it is fortuitous that the Unit recordings, which show one player introducing a new musical area by way of a thematic signal, responded to by his bandmates, recall Don Cherry's earlier music using the same technique.[91] None of that matters as such, and it's not necessary to construct a simple antecedent-consequent relationship between these highly individuated approaches and Portal's own. But what is important is that the binary "improvisation," once again standing for African American, and "composition," once again standing for (white) French and European, is and was artificial: a division that has shored up received notions of cultural identity and tradition, perhaps, but not one that has been much respected by musicians of either cultural background or musical inclination.

Portal's 1970s music was a transcultural construction. Yet it's true that his work did also participate in a growing movement towards jazz regionalism particularly marked in France (though this was a global phenomenon, and the first extended efforts to meld jazz and European folk forms had been made by the Swedish pianist Jan Johansson in the early 1960s).[92] Portal's native Basque region was one in which a sense of local identity, and the practice of folk traditions, had remained strong; the musician's grandfather was the head of a Bayonne fanfare, and in the 1970s Portal recalled the tambours and bandoneons that surrounded him from his youth.[93] Aspects of southern European folk musics had been apparent in Portal's recorded music from early in that decade, and "Eastern European" folk meters and vamps were important elements of some Unit performances in the mid-1970s. The most explicit address of regional and folk interests, however, came in the musician's 1979 solo album, *¡Dejarme solo!* ("leave me alone," in Basque dialect). The use of bandoneon, *tarogato* (a clarinet used in southeastern Europe) and *tenora* (a Catalan shawm), the microtonal folk melodies and vamps: all these elements build a composite image of southern folk music. Yet once again, Portal's appeal was not to an authentic, but an "imaginary" folklore, one in which the instrumental, modal, melodic and rhythmic resources of not only European, but also African traditional musics were resituated in a post–free jazz sound world. The voices of Albert Ayler and John

Coltrane are never far away from these soundscapes, pictured, as Portal attested, from fragments and memories of Creole, Bulgarian, Basque and Mozambican styles.[94] Portal had acknowledged a love for folk music timbres while expressing reservations about the propriety of making use of folk music as such; the synthetic "meta-folk" that he and other French musicians were arriving at sidestepped that problem.[95]

This wasn't simply a world musical pick-and-mix. Portal's internationalist folk belonged largely to the crescent of southern Europe and northern Africa, and these were much-communicating territories and styles to which he was culturally and geographically connected by birth. (The "American" jazz and "European" art music techniques through which he articulated his ideas were equally embedded in his early musical life.) And while this was a landscape broader than the national, it was nevertheless a constructed, imagined musical "space" of the kind that was, during the 1970s, giving French jazz a new kind of identity. The emergence of so many provincial festivals, and regionally based bands, forged a new association between jazz creativity and (previously unlikely) regional sites. The long festival reports and photo features that dominated the summer editions of the jazz magazines during this period pictured musicians playing in pastoral French settings, centuries-old churches, scorched Provençal hillsides; the "open music" celebrated at Châteauvallon was created in an open-air amphitheater, and this space, sounding so different from New York's nightclubs or Paris's *caves*, was audible on the important recordings made there by Portal's group. Without necessarily being articulated as such, nor contained by the country's limits, an idea of France as a territory infused with jazz creativity—this idea realized in pictures, heard in sonic spaces and described in words—enveloped the creation of a new jazz that, reversing those jazz-age commentaries on France's American future, now celebrated the regional, the folk, the nonmetropolitan. And this was a time of significantly increased critical confidence in and audience uptake of jazz in France: the front page of a 1977 special edition of the high-culture journal *Les Nouvelles littéraires* announced a "Return to Jazz"—though excited readers might have been disappointed to read Alain Gerber's opening comment that, while the jazz scene had a new and chaotic energy, it was ever harder for musicians, "particularly in Europe," to make a living.[96]

Improvised Music and Fusions

Following the explosion and dissipation of *le free*, the local jazz press had begun the 1970s in ecumenical mode, free players mixing with New Orleans, post bop and fusion, though the major magazines remained overwhelmingly devoted to American artists. Approaching the middle of the decade, however, both titles carried increasing coverage of European and Europe-based musicians, labels and scenes.[97] Certainly locals figured highly in this new trend, both mainstream players like the guitarist Christian Escoudé and more left-field figures like Bernard Lubat, but it was an internationalist moment—and, alongside the radicalized jazz of players like Portal or those exiled South African musicians associated with the London-based Brotherhood of Breath—it was one in large part defined by the practice then becoming known as *la musique improvisée européenne*, European improvised music.[98] This practice, often (as previously suggested) envisaged as a synthesis of free jazz and post-Cagean art music approaches, was championed in *Jazz magazine* by its editor, Philippe Carles, and, especially, the writer Gérard Rouy; *Jazz hot*, under Laurent Goddet and with Denis Constant as the most dedicated correspondent, followed suit. Similar changes were being made at the German magazine *Jazz Podium*, and European editors and reporters had evidently begun to see it as their duty to record—and in so doing, help contribute to—musical activity that was seen as enacting what Rouy would later call "an important and definitive break" from earlier, and American, jazz tradition.[99]

The most important sites for this developing music were proving to be in Germany, the Netherlands and Britain. The French jazz journals paid these scenes and organizations regular attention. Locally, too, a number of musicians who had begun playing free jazz were by mid-decade operating in this area, their work documented on enthusiast-run labels like Futura, Saravah, PALM and Sun. Free jazz's high countercultural profile was by now a thing of the past, and audiences for this music were, and were to remain, small.[100] But the new improvisation's commercial marginality would be forever at odds with the commitment of its musicians, promoters and listeners; many of those involved in the early 1970s, whether in France or elsewhere, would remain so long into the 21st century.

Improvisers were not excluded from venues of "standing," and though these opportunities did not provide a day-to-day income, players performed at Parisian concert spaces like the Théâtre Mouffetard, the Maisons de la Culture, the numerous festivals emerging through the 1970s and '80s and on André Francis's Radio France broadcasts.[101] Yet, the practice's economic precarity notwithstanding, many musicians sought to remain outside such professionalized structures. A 1975 *Jazz magazine* panel that brought together a number of the music's French players and organizers highlighted the problem. Along with François Tusques, the Free Jazz Workshop de Lyon trumpeter Jean Mereu insisted that the music should form part of the struggle against capitalist power; the percussionist Bertrand Gauthier's suggestion that musicians seek governmental support was waved away by others who argued that such support always led to interference. Gérard Terronès, owner of Futura and an important figure in the promotion and documentation of French free jazz and improvisation, called instead for "parallel circuits" of associations and cooperatives, and indeed, alongside the collectives described earlier, the bassist Didier Levallet had in the early 1970s established l'ADMI, the Association pour le Développement de la Musique Improvisée.[102] But this promotional network and record label was quickly aborted, and French improvisers would sometimes cast forlorn glances towards those foreign scenes that they felt had more organizational spirit, and more cohesive musical identities, than did their own.[103] Free improvisation collectives that would elsewhere continue into the next century included the Instant Composers Pool in the Netherlands (established in 1967), Free Music Produktion in Berlin (1969) and the London Musicians' Collective in Britain (1975). With the notable exception of Lyon's ARFI, established in 1977, French improvisers would either miss or evade the formation of local "schools" (though underground venues, chief among them Paris's 28 rue Dunois, would spring up to act as performance hubs).[104]

Perhaps the most celebrated of the free improvisers active in France at this time was the American Steve Lacy, a Paris resident from 1970 until 2002 (he died in 2004). But towards the end of the 1970s, a number of younger French players began to emerge; interested in but not formed alongside 1960s free jazz, these players and their successors would find it easier to move in and out of the jazz tradition than had players of Portal's generation. While figures like the ARFI mainstay Louis Sclavis and Jacques (later Jac) Berrocal could readily identify with the term "European improvised music"—it "marked the distance" between the new approach and its black American sources, Berrocal said in 1977—those jazz influences were not often denied; still, it was significant that the Free Jazz Workshop de Lyon had in 1976 dropped "Free Jazz" from its name, Sclavis suggesting that this represented not a disavowal, instead a move beyond that singular, and now somewhat passé, idiom.[105]

They were very different from each other, but the works of Sclavis and Berrocal represented both a decisively new "European" approach and what was a wider resistance to stylistic or Euro-nationalist chauvinism. The Workshop de Lyon's confident (and sometimes comic) *Tiens ! Les*

Bourgeois éclatent . . . , recorded for L'Oiseau Musicien in 1977, has the rambunctious polystylism of an Art Ensemble of Chicago album—and, with Mingus, Dolphy, Bessie Smith and old-time marching bands variously alluded to, some of the same informing sources—but the brittle duets that are pieced together by Sclavis and fellow reeds player Maurice Merle seem more reflective of recent continental approaches than anything else. Berrocal's 1976 breakthrough *Parallèles* (d'Avantage) is similarly catholic. An opening duet for Berrocal and Roger Ferlet's trombones is all space and barely pitched plumbing noise; one improvisation, overlaid by the reading of a decidedly odd postcard message found in a bin, is recorded in a pig shed and so backed by industrial clanking and porcine squealing; the subsequently celebrated "Rock and Roll Station" has the tragic early rocker Vince Taylor intone a circular text over the steady accompaniment of a double bass riff and the ting-ting of Berrocal's bicycle. The record's side 2 is taken up by a twenty-four-minute tribute to the Futurist artist and noise-music precursor Luigi Russolo, in which objects and instruments are variously and energetically roughed up. Berrocal's early work, and his DIY trumpet playing, coincided with surrealist tradition and punk anti-tradition as much as the jazz and art music reference points he also cited. Later recordings like *Hotel Hotel* (Nato, 1986) added to the mix persona play, Japanese and Arab exotica, weird pop and chanson, this work a French counterpart to contemporary American efforts by John Zorn, John Lurie and Jon Hassell.

One of Berrocal's occasional partners was the alto saxophonist Daunik Lazro. As a youth Lazro had quickly progressed from an admiration of Sidney Bechet to John Coltrane and Albert Ayler, purposefully avoiding learning bebop in between.[106] The saxophonist's significant early works were live recordings—of a long solo and a duo performance with bassist Jean-Jacques Avenel on *The Entrance Gates Of Tshee Park* (Hat Hut, 1980), of various ensembles on *Sweet Zee* (Hat ART, 1985)—and these capture the exceptional density and projecting power of Lazro's tone. So much was obviously owed to the free jazz and African American traditions, to Ayler, Ornette Coleman and the rock and roll saxophone that they had sometimes played. But Lazro was not simply a free jazz player in a new, supposedly more "European" context: this thick jazz tonality was not rolled out into jazz lines, instead enclosing static sonic objects, a note, multiphonic or truncated motif hoisted up and examined over and again for timbral detail.

Still, the jazz heritage was not much disguised, and in uniting for the 1993 album *Outlaws in Jazz* (Bleu Regard) Lazro and Berrocal would pay tribute to Ayler, Coleman and others. But the two Frenchmen might be seen as wandering along an artificial border separating jazz and European improvised music in their supposedly purer states—states in which traffic between the two neighbors was sometimes suppressed rather than encouraged. Indeed, it was because stylistic repertoires and generic devices of all kinds could seem more welcome in French improvisation than they had at first in Berlin or London that a French "approach" remained difficult to describe into the 1980s.[107] If Joëlle Léandre's bass playing bore the traces of her contemporary art music formation and early collaborations with Boulez and Cage, then Raymond Boni's guitar playing advertised its allegiances to rock and flamenco; the group Axolotl took their methods from British free players, but also from *musique concrète*, synthpop and garage rock. Even the imaginary folk landscapes of jazz players like Tusques and Portal could crop up in French free improvisation: on soprano saxophonist Michel Doneda's 1985 debut album *Terra* (Nato), southern European folksong and clouds of East Asian tuned gongs and bowls are surrounded by skirling saxophone figures, these recalling Indian and North African traditions at least as much as they do John Coltrane or Evan Parker.

Free improvisation accounted for only one of the approaches developed by French jazz players in the 1970s; as we've seen, it was apt for Philippe Carles to describe French jazz circa 1975 as being defined by its "syncretism, ecumenicalism, eclecticism and internationalism."[108] French historians of the music have quite rightly followed this contemporary evaluation, and indeed a related narrative—in which a single flow of developing jazz tradition disperses, during the 1970s, into what is often described as something like a "delta of many streams"—has commonly been made to account for jazz in the United States as well as in its globally developing variants.[109] This kind of progressivist tale writes out the multiplicity and simultaneity of local, stylistic and historical jazz practices that had always existed. But it is accurate in that, more than a mere description of aggregated jazz activity, such multiplicity was now embraced as a method itself.

This was no less true in France than it was elsewhere. But while after 1970 fewer and fewer French players would model their work on recent American developments—and while local folk styles and materials now occupied many of those players as never before—this was not at the time accompanied by any widespread celebration of a newly autonomous "French jazz": not only was the internationalist eclecticism that

Carles celebrated antithetical to such a project, but so too was "France" a rather thin signifier, one suggesting bureaucratic statehood rather than cultural wealth, one endowed with neither the traditional vivacity nor the canonic implications of those musical and rhetorical appeals that *were* often made to the "regional" and the "European." Instead, it was in their many new stylistic fusions that French jazz musicians attempted to develop both new musical practices and, the jazz audience shrinking all the time, new markets for their work.

Some of these projects were pitched between jazz and art music. Jacques Thollot's 1971 *Quand le son devient aigu, jeter la girafe à la mer* (Futura) layers looping percussion, minimalist melodic shapes and studio-treated atmospheres, the work sometimes anticipating the ambient music of Brian Eno (Thollot's subsequent albums explored jazz rock and Elizabethan music). In the mid-1970s, Yotchk'o Seffer's group Neffesh Music recorded three albums for Moshé-Naïm, these uneasy conjunctions of a jazz rock rhythm section, Seffer's reeds, keyboards and vocals, and—dominating the whole—a classical string quartet; the group's bizarre repertoire combined Hungarian folk materials (some of which had already been used by Bartók), static soundscapes and Seffer's microtonally inflected reeds.

But most jazz fusions looked towards popular forms. In 1970, Henri Texier and Aldo Romano had founded the jazz rock group Total Issue, which set one-chord vamps, wordless vocal lines and improvised modal ponderings in a Hendrixian soundworld. "For some time," Texier said in 1971, "jazz hasn't been enough for us. We're trying to find in our music the depth of ancient, folkloric musics." For Romano, now naming Ringo Starr as his favorite drummer, the turn towards rock was an attempt to recover some of the anti-establishment energy he saw seeping away from a newly respectable jazz. "Jazz is completely sclerotic," he said, "a museum."[110] Similarly attempting to find a new direction (and to go on making a musical living), saxophonist François Jeanneau had also helped form a rock group, Triangle, for which he provided backing lines, horn solos and synthesizer textures while the group's vocalist strong-armed French lyrics into the melodic rhythms of Anglo-American rock. The less-than-stellar success of Total Issue's self-titled 1971 United Artists album release was hardly bettered by that of Triangle's three LPs, and both groups disbanded within a few years.

If not art music, or rock, then folk. Following the Total Issue experiment, in 1976 Texier released *Amir* (Eurodisc), the first of a series of solo albums on which the player overdubbed various bass, string and occasionally percussion instruments to create what he saw as a hybrid form: part jazz, this owed to the "dynamic of improvisation" that ran across the album's tracks, the music was also part folk, since, the bassist said, its rhythmic, melodic and harmonic characteristics owed more to North African, Indian and "Celtic" musics than they did the American idiom as such (this exploration of global styles Texier would continue into the 21st century).[111] So on *Amir* as on 1977's *Varech*—named after a kind of algae found on the beaches of Brittany—and 1979's *A Cordes et à cris* (both JMS), Texier constructs plaintive folkish melodies over bass pedals and drones, these soundscapes woody and dark but glossily produced. Apart from shakers and the occasional tambour, percussion is kept to a bare minimum, and with it the suggestion of jazz and African America; the melodies are delivered by strings, pipes and penny whistles, but also Texier's voice, which—double-tracked and swathed in reverb, delivering wordless, syllable-based lines—removes itself from the notion of a performed, "authentic" human expression, instead becoming multiple, collective, the attempt seemingly to evoke geographies and cultures before a singular author or personality.

Texier's wordless vocals also neatly sidestepped the problem of international comprehension faced by non-Anglophone groups (as was common, Triangle had released some of their music with lyrics rerecorded in Spanish). Going far beyond that solution, and enjoying much more enduring success, was Magma, the progressive rock group formed by the drummer Christian Vander—son of the Belgian jazz pianist Maurice—and at various times including jazz musicians like the pianist Michel Graillier, violinist Didier Lockwood and Yotchk'o Seffer. Magma's cultic iconography extended from its cover imagery to the Tolkienesque "language," Kobaïa, that was created to convey the song lyrics, this only one element of a more-or-less preposterous whole that rested on Vander's forceful funk-rock grooves. Along the same lines, but more strongly infused with jazz improvisation and harmonic sensibility, was the music of a spin-off group, Zao, that included Lockwood, Seffer, and Seffer's drummer partner from Perception, Jean-My Truong.

The shiny jazz fusion of American groups like Weather Report did not blaze a trail through French jazz, though international record company promotional efforts ensured that the style established something of a toehold in *Jazz hot* in particular as the 1970s wore on.[112] Nevertheless, in the United States the violinist Jean-Luc Ponty, who had traveled to that country from France in the late 1960s to work with Frank Zappa, emerged as one of jazz fusion's leading names, playing with John McLaughlin's

Mahavishnu Orchestra and recording a series of high-selling albums for Atlantic; the titles of these—*Imaginary Voyage, Cosmic Messenger, Enigmatic Ocean*—describe something of the music's general vapidity if not the more tough-minded Coltranisms of the violinist's own improvisation. At home in France, Didier Lockwood would pursue a similar direction in the early 1980s, albums like *Fasten Seat Belts* (JMS, 1982) pastiching Weather Report, Steely Dan, the Coltrane quartet and various world musics in a sleekly crafted pitch for radio play and audience triangulation.

Such was the state of French jazz, at its most broadly defined, as the 1980s began. But things were about to change. With the arrival of a new, leftist government, state spending on the music would increase dramatically, and previously marginal practices allowed to flourish—if only for a moment.

Jazz in the Mitterrand Era

François Mitterrand's Parti Socialiste (PS), formed in 1969, had spent the 1970s out of government and attempting to define a modern socialism that would not be tarred by the failures of a Soviet communism still notionally recognized by the Parti Communiste. Towards the end of the decade, amid slowing economic growth and spiraling unemployment, the PS began to develop a wider appeal, and Mitterrand won the presidential elections of May 1981. Upon taking power, the new government instituted a program of banking and utility nationalization, administrative decentralization, and public spending on a grand scale; in addition to a shorter working week, a lowered retirement age, and increases in state benefits, pensions and the minimum wage—these to be paid for by a rise in high-earner taxation—the government now released unprecedented funds for cultural activity. Indeed, the Ministry of Culture, directed by the young, charismatic minister Jack Lang, saw its budget triple between 1981 and 1985, this the largest increase enjoyed by any governmental department.[113]

Like a number of his colleagues, Lang was a product of 1968, a moment, he claimed, which "prefigured the changes that we in the government are currently entrusted with inscribing in everyday life." Even if paradoxically enacted by government, the anti-patrician priority was to bolster cultural activity across the country—Paris's share of the cultural budget declined from 60 to 45 percent in the four years following Mitterrand's election—and to render that activity more broadly defined and broadly participatory.[114] Additionally, whereas "mass culture" had once signified those industrialized entertainments disdained by French government policy and intellectuals of the left and right alike, by the end of the 1970s both politicians and thinkers had begun to accept that many people were daily afforded "authentic" cultural experiences by those forms.[115] In tandem with a hardly less significant governmental acknowledgment of the French culture industries' economic potential, these ideas gave rise to a nonprescriptive cultural policy that championed the "popular" and the "high" in all their diverse forms, any suggestion of a capitulation to globally dominant cultural industries and tastes offset by Lang's habitual public anti-Americanism.[116]

Newly nourished by state support, the sector now often referred to as "jazz and improvised music" would enjoy a brief but variegated flourish. Jazz's "cultural rehabilitation" was one named priority of the 1981 culture ministry budget, this to comprise a new presence in the conservatoires, support of creative work, and funding for venues and other agents of the music's "diffusion."[117] By 1982, both a jazz and popular music subsection, and a *commission consultative* on jazz and improvised music, had been established within the Ministry of Culture, and following this new regional projects and venues offered new performance opportunities and funds to jazz musicians. (Jazz was something of a privileged subject, and would often receive more than its fair share of the ministry budget allocated to jazz and popular forms like chanson and rock collectively; those other, more commercially lucrative styles were the victims of what the sociologist Philippe Coulangeon identified as a "redistributive intent.")[118] Aside from an annual national celebration of music, launched by Lang and arts administrator Maurice Fleuret in 1982 and becoming known as La Fête de la Musique, numerous festivals featuring jazz emerged during this period, whether in large regional cities like Montauban or tiny towns like Coutances. Ongoing jazz action projects received support, as did a large number of new, experimental endeavors like the radio-art music magazine *Planeta*, a centrally produced and regionally syndicated program that collaged jazz, free improvisation and musician interviews between 1984 and 1986.[119]

This kind of support was welcomed by those devoted to a music that, as well as more stylistically fragmented than ever, was long past its peak of popularity and commercial viability (major jazz festivals like Nice, Antibes and, in Switzerland, Montreux had already broadened their repertoire to include pop and soul stars, a trend that would only gather pace). In light of this decline, and in France as elsewhere, jazz musicians had increasingly attempted to make inroads into education, teaching jobs guaranteeing both income and some kind of cultural continuation for the music; these efforts saw widespread success in the United States from the mid-1970s. Several jazz players had been trained at the conservatoires during the 1940s and '50s, but what they had studied had almost never been jazz.[120] And while Guy Longnon had offered a jazz course at the Marseille conservatoire since 1964, and Kenny Clarke had set up his Paris drum school three years later, those projects—much less radical in attitude and experimental in method than the jazz action pedagogy of the next decade—had remained somewhat isolated until the formation of several private jazz schools in the latter 1970s. Among these were the L'Institut Art Culture Perception and Le Centre d'Informations Musicales (CIM), established in Paris during 1976 by Alan Silva and Alain Guérrini, respectively; regional projects included Bordeaux's Sigma Jazz Focus, initiated in 1978.[121] Declining performance opportunities meant that centers like Guérrini's CIM could become focal points for the Parisian scene. Not only was the school's staff formed by musicians of the caliber of Pierre Michelot, François Jeanneau and Henri Texier, but so too were the concert activities developed by Guérrini, his staff and students more committed and energetic than many of their commercial counterparts.[122]

Such projects now benefitted from ministerial patronage. But it was under Lang that jazz found a place in state educational and performance institutions. In 1981, only eight conservatoires offered jazz courses. By 1984, the year of a major French conference on jazz pedagogy, jazz instruction was offered in twenty-eight public institutions. A jazz class was offered at the Conservatoire National in 1985—in 1992 a dedicated jazz department would be established under the directorship of François Jeanneau—and a qualificatory certificate for jazz teaching was introduced in 1987. By 1990 some form of jazz study was offered in 329 public education institutions. But the success of the new jazz pedagogy would eventually breed new problems. The dramatically increased numbers of professionally accredited jazz musicians, or what Philippe Coulangeon described as the "banalization of competence," was not matched by an equivalent rise in jazz audiences; by the last decade of the 20th century, the new glut of jazz musicians in France was making regular public performance difficult and forcing down fees across the field.[123]

French jazz's Langian golden age would not last. Hampered by problems of inflation and the balance of trade, the Mitterrand government soon reined in public spending. Still, even by 1985—with a downscaling of governmental ambitions and an austerity drive well under way—the culture ministry was bold enough to allocate an extra 4 million francs to the jazz budget towards the establishment of the Orchestre National de Jazz (ONJ). Giving its first concert in February 1986, musicians decked out in Stéphane Plassier's polka-dot couture, the ONJ was one of the very first state-funded jazz ensembles to exist on a similar footing to the many art music orchestras and ensembles routinely supported by governments in Europe and elsewhere outside the United States. The establishment of the orchestra has been read as the moment of art-institutional arrival campaigned for by figures like André Hodeir since the 1950s, but, as the polka dots suggested, there were strings attached; with only 55 percent of its 8 million franc budget being provided by the state, the group was expected to make its way as a commercial proposition to an extent not expected of symphony orchestras, this perhaps accounting for the cold pop-fusion glitz of the first ONJ albums.[124]

But that was surely a reflection of other intentions, too. Maurice Fleuret had sought a way to provide support for jazz without engendering what he called its "museumification," and in contrast to other institutional jazz projects of the 1980s—most obviously that of the Lincoln Center in New York—the new government policies led to a flourishing of original creative work rather than classicizing repertory.[125] Yet this was achieved at a price, during and beyond the Mitterrand years. Musicians working according to the standards and styles of earlier eras, whether New Orleans or textbook bebop, were not smiled upon by culture ministry administrators whose stated priority was to support music that claimed for itself some kind of creative singularity. So, beginning in the 1980s and gathering pace during the 1990s, the tendency would be towards the staging not of groups but of "projects," works strongly characterized, if not by their composition, then by their conceptual framing. In presentations like Louis Sclavis's Ellington reworking *Ellington on the Air*, which the reeds player gave at festivals in 1990 and later recorded for IDA—this one of the works that would make Sclavis one of the most celebrated French players of the period immediately following the present study's own—musicians would seek not only inspiration, but also the tangible claims to originality recognized by commissioners, label executives and audiences alike.[126] Here was an important change in jazz's ontological makeup: a "dilution" of the music's earlier emphasis on internalized repertoires and embodied skills, and a concomitant strengthening, and advertisement, of composition and devising.

Although it appealed to record labels too, this strategy—an international phenomenon—made its primary play for the festival and concert hall circuit. Even before the trend towards the "project" took shape, similarly motivated formations like the long-running duo of pianist François Couturier and bassist Jean-Paul Celea—whose first, self-titled album was released on JMS in 1980—had developed approaches that hovered between jazz (featuring neatly turned improvisations and arrangements) and a comfortably familiar art music soundworld (the French impressionists evoked in particular). Jazz's long pursuit of art music's institutional status, then, went hand in hand with a gradual acquisition of some of the latter music's characteristics and performance polish, and by the early 1990s, in France as elsewhere, this had inevitably led to a correlation between institutions and venues hosting jazz and those hosting art music.[127] For Coulangeon and some of the French musicians the sociologist interviewed in the mid-1990s, in emphasizing singularity of material and thereby gaining access to prestigious funding and concert stages, jazz had also atomized itself, evaporating any notion of a common repertoire. Perhaps not coincidentally, this had been matched by an atomization of the jazz audience, the spending power of which remained directed more towards reissues of American jazz from decades past than towards local, contemporary musical production.[128]

That schism, and those reissued remnants of jazz history, we return to in the coda. But what about those ideas set out in the book's introduction, of "acceptance" and "acculturation," the notion that after its dramatic arrival in France, jazz was slowly comprehended and adapted by local musicians, critics and listeners, until—by the 1980s—a properly "French jazz" had been arrived at?

A Conclusion

That's the dominant narrative in French-written histories. For Ludovic Tournès, the moment of jazz's French arrival coincides with its absorption into state-supported institutional structures; writing their own, very different books on the music in France at the turn of the 21st century, both Jean-Dominique Brierre and Philippe Coulangeon asserted that French jazz had undergone what one termed a "progressive emancipation" from American models, the local music liberated entirely in the final decades of the old millennium.[129] Perhaps these propositions—in which the state is identified with the proper, and American cultural influence is only uneasily welcomed—betray particularly French attitudes. But their argument is hardly fanciful, and as we've seen, by the 1970s many French jazz musicians—indeed, jazz musicians across the world—were confident enough to cultivate a distance between their work and American precedents, often by invoking local non-jazz styles of various kinds.

Still, while that progressivist narrative seems reasonable enough seen from either end—a fascinated first encounter with an American import on the one hand, a more autonomous French jazz creativity on the other—the story is more conflicted than that. Rather than a singular, gradual process, the French "acceptance" or "acculturation" of jazz was more like a switch, one repeatedly flipped as new generations encountered and responded to new musical and cultural-political phenomena. As we have seen in each chapter, musicians, listeners and critics who had developed a profound familiarity with particular jazz forms were constantly being overtaken by stylistic developments, innovations that, until the 1970s, almost always emerged from the United States. Histories that identify jazz as ensconced when its mainstream newsworthiness subsides ignore the bitter battles that these changes were causing elsewhere, and it's hardly possible to divide France into those that had or hadn't "accepted" jazz after a certain point, since so many people occupied both positions at the same time: from the 1940s into the 21st century, the loudest objections to one jazz style came from partisans of another. Such progressivism also fails to take account of the circling and revisiting that marked both critical and musical activity during the period. Arguments about blackness thought done in the late 1940s flared up again twenty years later (this time wearing different clothes); as will be addressed shortly, musicians of the 1980s returned to the styles of earlier decades in a postmodern spirit.

So one of the central problems of the acculturation narrative is in its assumption that jazz was ever a stable, bounded entity, that the music arriving during the interwar years was already fully formed and complete—as if Lester Bowie didn't just admire Louis Armstrong but was simply equivalent to him. "France" was similarly changing. It makes less sense to think about the music mapped onto the country as a whole than it does to see it circulating amid numerous communities, these often constructed around the music rather than vice versa, their demographic, geographic and political natures sharply differentiated. Think of those young teenagers and music-hall habitués who thronged to see Sidney Bechet, and those who, sometimes more educated, often older but almost always more self-consciously sophisticated, preferred Solal or the MJQ; the New Orleansians affiliated with the political right, and the *new thingers* affiliated with the left; those from the provinces who tried to cultivate an organic jazz activity different from metropolitan forms, and those businessmen whose entrée to a lucrative entertainment industry was made via the music; those players and organizers for whom jazz was to resist bourgeois power, and those civil servants who shuffled papers and stamped budget plans on the music's behalf. The term "jazz" covered a huge variety of musical practices, and the same was true of "France" and its social practices. Even if the lines of demarcation were temporary and permeable, the way jazz was made, appreciated and used by each of these groups helped affirm their often fractious differences as much as overcome them.

Despite all that, it's fair to say that while French players from an earlier period aspired to emulate and were congratulated for their successful imitation of American idols, later players, not so motivated or greeted, searched instead for a local originality. Fair, but not especially telling: that account's implicit relative valuation of the imitative and the original doesn't reflect the complexities of identity and identification that jazz helped form at mid-century. This was never just a question of musical propriety, but also one of how players, listeners and critics were to react and relate to a cultural Other and to American superpower. As we saw in this book's introduction, jazz historians have long identified this dynamic in its 1920s and '30s state, but, even if it was less acknowledged and discussed, it continued unabated during and after the Marshall Plan years. It's striking that those jazz musicians most celebrated during the postwar period were those who, to the French, could be "one of us" while harboring something of "one of them": Django Reinhardt, often said to play with the improvisational abandon of *un noir*, the gypsy's liminal position in French society making him the perfect analogue of the African American "primitive" or outcast; Barney Wilen, "*l'Américain,*" his spoken English and his saxophone playing authentically accented thanks to a childhood spent stateside; Martial Solal, his technique simply outstripping everyone else's, whether at home or abroad. Sidney Bechet, too, occupied this in-between position although, American before French, his status was commensurably greater. But all of these players were locals who could speak the language of a desirable Other, go-betweens in a continuing cultural encounter between (black) America and (white) Europe (and that their Rom, Creole, Jewish, American and Algerian backgrounds removed them from an imagined white French norm was likely significant). If "French jazz" had not properly cohered as an imaginary category before the 1970s, it was because few had thought such a thing desirable immediately following the war: it was America that fascinated, not France.

That doesn't explain why French imitations for so long lacked the horsepower and finish of the imported models. It certainly wasn't because the best French players were not good enough that much of the jazz making of the 1950s and '60s was compromised or problematic—more likely, it was because the second-best players so lagged behind. As many studies of American jazz cultures have shown, national and local jazz circuits in the United States had always thrived on (public) competition, on small coteries of instrumentalist colleagues who had spurred each other on, whose work was cooperatively driven even if its success was finally owed to tremendous personal effort.[130] All these phenomena existed in some form in postwar France, but rarely were enough highly skilled players present in the same place at the same time for a critical mass to be reached. Bobby Jaspar had to leave for New York to be tested at all; he left a space filled by Barney Wilen, the younger player doomed to remain unchallenged except by himself. Indeed, this lack of competition, or of a project shared, may have partly explained Wilen's readiness to abandon high-profile musical activity for long stretches of time. André Hodeir, certainly, curtailed what had been promising activity owning to a lack of companionship.

Both men had their reasons, but in purely musical terms these withdrawals were made too soon, and early successes were not capitalized upon. The problem seemed to be recognized by other French players at that time: "we lack the desire for perfection, the desire to progress," complained saxophonist Michel de Villers in a candid moment.[131] The failure to fully invest, seen in these and many other careers, surely bears witness to the precarity of the French jazz economy as well as a less tangible sense of cultural ownership. Yet perhaps—and perhaps in the cases of the highly cultivated Hodeir and Wilen if not others—these retirements were also licensed by a particularly local notion of what it was to be an "artist." Numerous tales of the American modern jazz heroes, authored by observers and by the players themselves, emphasized the endless travails these musicians had undertaken in the pursuit of excellence (I have explored some of these narratives elsewhere).[132] "They say he works on his instrument nearly 15 hours per day," Wilen remarked of John Coltrane in 1961. "Isn't that admirable?"[133] It's difficult to know if the saxophonist inflected the phrase with his characteristic irony, but there is a suggestion that bootstrap pulling, Protestant American cultures of work—in jazz lore absolutely transferable to the realm of creative expression—were at odds with a local, Romantic notion that saw art as the result of indolent reflection, not déclassé beavering. But that meant the Europeans could seem as complacent as they were talented, and before the 1970s—playing the music and thus judged by the standards of their ruthlessly competitive American rivals—too many French musicians sounded like they'd brought a reed knife to a gunfight.

The only thing for it was to change the terms of engagement, and at various times—and increasingly from the late 1960s—this was what a number of musicians did. It's not difficult to identify those verbal or musical rejections of the American style. But it's much harder to describe a putatively "French" jazz method or aesthetic, especially amid the rampant eclecticism that was dominant from the 1970s onwards (unless, of course, that eclecticism *was* the aesthetic). Just as the will to elevate a player like Martial Solal from the ranks of individual excellence to jazz-historical import often founders upon realistic, but necessarily mild claims towards a "personal contribution," so the identification of so many instances of individual originality only multiplies that meekness, translating manifold personal projects into a collective achievement with difficulty. Vincent Cotro identifies the mid-1970s emergence of what he calls an "original sensibility" in post–free French jazz; this, Cotro writes, comprised "sonic clarity," improvisation that was incisive rather than prolix, unusual time signatures, borrowings of all kinds from contemporary music (silence, dynamic range, electroacoustics, musical grammar, writing), and a sense of carnival or festivity. Jean-Dominique Brierre's assessment, less taxonomically minded but similarly reliant on the language of sensibility, is that French jazz had slowly but surely "endowed itself with a particular color and fragrance."[134]

Cotro's description is faithful to the music he addresses, but so it is too to music that emerged in numerous other countries; Brierre's is too nebulous to pin down at all. But if these efforts are suspicious then they are interestingly so, shadowing as they do the national characteristics long allotted French art music by nationalist-minded musicologists, critics and listeners, those for whom Berlioz, Debussy and Ravel had been musicians of "sensibility," given to a sound clearer yet more perfumed and colorful than that of their austere Germanic counterparts. One of the great builders of this tradition was Debussy himself: as a critic he hailed his forebear Rameau for what he called the truly French qualities of musical "clarity," "luminosity," "elegance," and "precise and compact form"; as a musician of synaesthesic, Symbolist inclination he composed pieces with titles as sensuous as "The sounds and fragrances swirl through the evening air" and "Fragrances of the night."[135]

It would be wrong to dismiss any of this tradition-making out of hand for its essentialism or ulterior motives. After all, the music of Hodeir, Solal, the Couturier-Celea duo and many others often does seem to relate closely to a (post-)impressionist sound world. But it's not because sensitivities of timbre are in some way innate to "French" DNA that the country's music has so often displayed those concerns: instead, historically self-conscious musicians and critics have identified that sensibility in the work of the greats, validating these qualities in pedagogical and performance practices, ensuring in so doing that such practices are carried on. Personal taste and a sense of rightness develops in this context, and it doesn't matter if that continuation is the result of traditionary duty or some attitude less intellectualized: either way, sonic clarity and timbral perfume become, in the anthropologist Clifford Geertz's terms, part of "a story" that the French "tell themselves about themselves."[136] If some of the most French music of all has been made by Duke Ellington, Herbie Hancock and Steve Lehman—all Americans and all, in their own ways, inheritors of that tradition of art music "sensibility" that runs from Debussy to Murail—then perhaps, as some wartime writers argued, even American jazz is part French. Or perhaps arguments about national identity only keep from lapsing into absurdity for as long as they are doggedly exclusive.

It's significant that those jazz-nationalist agendas have been pursued by critics and historians more often than by musicians themselves. When, in the 1970s, many French players became interested in ideas of localism, these were expressed in regional and transregional terms, and what was emphasized was not the homogeneity beloved of totalizing states and their national myths, but musical variety, cultural difference, the material abundance required by creative artists.

Indeed it's difficult, finally, to assuage the feeling that such after-the-fact nationalist thinking betrays not so much critical faith and confidence in French jazz as it does anxiety. Nationalist art traditions are only rarely comprehensible in the absence of a dominant Other, a governing tradition that local activity reacts against. From the 1930s through to the 21st century, the periodic celebration of French jazz is never made without reference to a previously triumphant, now supposedly vanquished American jazz hegemony; for their part, a number of American musicians have shown disdain for the idea of a distinct European jazz.[137] It's a replay of that moment when, in the late 19th and early 20th centuries, art music composers heralding from numerous European territories under the rule of one empire or another—these political or merely cultural—attempted to assert a new self-identity through the mobilization of local, folk elements. Writing around 1926, and as usual positioning himself at the center of the dominant Austro-German tradition, Arnold Schoenberg famously dismissed those attempts at a local musical hybridity as a feeble attempt to "achieve a place in the sun," such grafted-on materials and political concerns incompatible with the tradition's technical purity. One wrote music in the Austro-German manner, Schoenberg argued, or one didn't.[138] When writers attempt to identify national jazz styles in the 21st century, they inadvertently accord European jazz activity the status of those proud but benighted provinces, still in unspoken thrall to a condescending and powerful parent tradition. That this isn't a desirable intellectual model is obvious, but neither is it a timely one: the music discussed in this book belongs not to an age characterized by the homogeneous nation state and national tradition, but one dominated by what has, since the 1980s, become known (the planet over) as globalization.

If that term entered common usage at the end of the century, then the world it described—one in which the circulation of people, practices and products was extended and accelerated by new modes of transportation and communication—had been developing for a more than a century.[139] Venturing forth in earnest during the 1920s, jazz, already a product of global movements even while at home in America, was adopted almost immediately in Paris as it was in Shanghai. Spreading that far on record and in person, the music was not reflective of an emergent globalization, it *was* that tendency; jazz snared the world, and the pan-cultural variety of what it trapped defined the music of the latter century in France as it did in many other places. By that time, the concepts of "French," "European" and indeed "American" jazz were not fully meaningful apart from an acknowledgment of this global dimension, even if the United States remained the source of the music's greatest achievements. As it had been all along, this jazz was constructed of countless local musical practices, audiences and communities large and small, all existing as nodes in a musical network that was sometimes practical, sometimes imaginary—but always international.

SEVEN

A Good Jazzman Is a Dead Jazzman

During winter 1985–86, the graphic artist Jacques de Loustal and writer Philippe Paringaux published a comic strip series in the graphic magazine *A Suivre*.[1] The strip, "Barney et la note bleue," told the noirish story of an itinerant jazz saxophonist whose 1950s glory soon ceded to struggle and dissolution, the musician dying of an overdose early in the following decade. Barney Wilen—whose career and person so closely resembled the drawn character's, death apart—was at first amused to discover the strip, though he was less pleased when the fictional character began using heroin. Still, his career in the doldrums, Wilen was canny enough to cultivate a business relationship with the series' authors, and in 1987 he collaborated with them to produce what was promoted as a comeback album, *La Note bleue*.[2] As Paringaux said, this was perhaps "the first soundtrack to a book," since the series was released in hardcover the same year; on the album, fully fledged performances of songs identified with Wilen's 1950s are interspersed with short musical vignettes that accompany episodes in the graphic story. A record to listen to while reading, the project had become another of the experiments joining sound and image that Wilen had been making for decades.

The nostalgia inherent in both the comic's narrative and the accompanying media heralding of the saxophonist—who had returned not just from obscurity, it seemed, but from the past itself—catered to a mid-1980s appetite for images drawn from jazz history. These were being put to use in all kinds of contexts. Even those signs of French jazz-age primitivism that were now widely understood as offensive could be employed, as they were in the videos and album art for Grace Jones's 1985 album

Slave to the Rhythm: working with her (French) partner, the designer and director Jean-Paul Goude, Jones featured in and was surrounded by a symphony of images of the fetishized black body—pickaninnies all skin and teeth, African tribesmen with nose bones, the singer's face as a Picasso-style African mask—and this ensemble was framed by Côte d'Azur beach scenes and Parisian surrealism that acted to confirm the work as a specifically French historical construction. It was far from the only production of the time to cobble together visions of a Frenchified jazz past. The international fashion industries made much of a look that signified cool glamour; one of the most famous of these uses was Yves Saint Laurent's eau de toilette, Jazz, launched in 1986, its high-profile advertising campaign re-creating shots from the 1944 film *Jammin' the Blues* (these striking images soundtracked by a synth-swing version of Yves Montand's old hit, "C'est si bon").[3] Also in 1986 Bertrand Tavernier released his feature film *Autour de minuit*, or *'Round Midnight*, in which Dexter Gordon played a haggard jazzman. The story, which was inspired by graphic designer Francis Paudras's account of his befriending Bud Powell in Paris—but which also included elements of Lester Young's persona and myth—followed Gordon's character as he lived out his last days in Paris's clubs and streets.[4]

Tavernier's film was mentioned more than once in articles on Barney Wilen's graphic alter ego, and the French saxophonist was piqued by what, in the new CD age, was an increasing exploitation of the mythical, doomed and exploitable: "a good jazzman is a dead jazzman," he complained on watching the commemoration industry grind into action after Chet Baker's demise in 1988.[5] But in resolving to prove that he and his musical form were still living, Wilen was not afraid to play along with the persona with which he, like Gordon, had been presented.[6] These still-living embodiments of a sophisticated, historical jazz cool both bore cool's ultimate symbol, a tenor saxophone, and in Wilen's musical and visual representations that horn, again the instrument of popular-song romance, loomed large. Wilen's sonic compression of history was as interesting as Grace Jones's visual effort: the sound that begins the melody of "Bésame Mucho," *La Note bleue*'s opening track, is the same that adorned the song on *Barney* nearly thirty years earlier—even if it is now softer, more diffuse—but Wilen soon climbs into a phrase that recalls those of his early hero Bechet, or even the 1920s society saxophonists with their violin-modeled tone and wide vibrato; the bel canto closing melody statement, like many subsequent performances in the same vein, confirms Wilen as a player molded by the interwar popular song and its singing.[7] If in the mid-1960s Wilen the free jazz adventurer cast only a nervous glance back to what he called his audience-pleasing "Django Reinhardt period," then by the late 1980s that seemed to be the project once again. Stripped of a self-conscious young man's need to progress and to innovate, responding to a new, nostalgic tendency for which those things were not priorities, Wilen was free to become the musician he had been at his naive youngest, a melodist, a recounter of popular airs. The screen that had often seemed to separate the player and his work was at last removed—unless it was precisely a screened version of himself that Loustal and Paringaux had given Wilen, and unless Wilen's final project was to examine from the outside not jazz, not African music, but the person he had once been.

This mid-1980s return to older jazz practices did not mark the first deviation from a modernist rush towards the future, musical or otherwise. For at least a decade, creative forms had been playing host to the reuse and recontextualization of past styles and past subjects—this trend identified by the British historian Raphael Samuel as "retrochic," and by his French counterpart Pascal Ory as *rétrophilie*. In 1983 Ory wrote that, in France, this attention to relatively recent periods, suggested for instance by the resurgent popularity of Art Deco, had also modulated into something darker: observable in the French cinema of the 1970s had been new representations of the German occupation, hitherto scrupulously unexamined. Prominent among such interrogations of French history—which systematically undercut the myth of a country united in resistance against oppressive Nazi and Vichy regimes—was Louis Malle's 1974 film *Lacombe, Lucien*, the story of a countryside brute who collaborates with the Germans, his exploits backed by the music of the Quintette du Hotclub de France.[8]

What became known at the *mode rétro*—and the popularly imagined, jazz-infused history of the earlier 20th century—was not confined to the cinema.[9] In 1975, after years of financial difficulty, Josephine Baker had made her stage comeback in a revue based on her life. At Paris's Bobino theater, Mick Jagger, Sophia Loren, Princess Grace and other stars dotted the worshipful audience on the show's first night. Baker died in her sleep after the second.[10] For many, the American star had been and would remain the preeminent symbol of jazz in France—indeed, dying with little money but as a knight of the Légion d'Honneur, status but not means, her life stood for jazz *tout court*—and with her passing that story was now somehow finished; this rounded-off French jazz history, continually represented in words and images, could contain Baker, Reinhardt and the Left Bank *caves* of the 1950s, but little room was left anything else. Even these elements were chronologically compressed ways that, in other contexts, would be much commented upon by th theorists of an emerging "postmodernity." The Anachronic Jazz Band, founded in 1976 by New Orleans traditionalists Marc Richard (clarinet) and Philippe Baudoin (piano), was a popular and creatively successful attempt to disrupt jazz's stylistic teleology and audience assumptions. Though the band played in the New Orleans style, its repertoire was based on bebop, hard bop and cool jazz standards. That the supposed stylistic disjunction was nowhere to be heard suggested a musical continuum, or at least flexibility, that had been obscured by an earlier generation of partisans both traditionalist and modernist; this, perhaps, was jazz for a newly post-ideological era.[11]

Yet it was ideology that seemed often to drive the efforts of the period's defining jazz figure. In the United States, the emergence around 1980 of Wynton Marsalis—the trumpet prodigy who quickly developed into a ferociously conservative critic of recent jazz styles—cemented what was often called a jazz "resurgence," one perceptible, it's often said, since the expat Dexter Gordon's return to the United States in 1976 (fictional and historical narratives clustered around Gordon and blended into one).[12] Marsalis and his confreres, playing music modeled at first on the post-bop of Miles Davis's mid-1960s group, were the first high-profile jazz musicians for at least a generation. Their music and, perhaps above all, their media images, helped reposition the modern jazz of twenty years earlier as something worth investing in, both musically and economically: before long the trumpeter would be one of several players to appear in advertising campaigns for various luxury goods, and he took on high-profile institutional roles in the latter 1980s and 1990s. The twenty-year-old Marsalis made the cover of *Jazz magazine* in October 1981, and, in France as everywhere else, he was increasingly joined in the pages of the specialist press by his "neo-bop" peers and original players from the modern jazz era. The high intellectualism of the French magazines' 1960s, and the gritty, confrontational localism of their 1970s, were things of the (unrecovered) past.

It wasn't only Americans who were being celebrated for their "straight ahead" modern jazz. Following the disbanding of his rock group Triangle, François Jeanneau had made an early return to post-bop, recording his quartet album *Techniques douces* in 1976 and playing with the trio HJT—alongside Daniel Humair and Henri Texier—from the turn of the 1980s. Musicians like René Urtreger had found it possible to make a return to the style; the pianist's 1978 album, *Récidive*, which revisited the standard and bebop repertoire, marked the start of a new phase of touring and recording in the company of old hands (Aldo Romano, J.-F. Jenny-Clark) and young neo-bop players like the Clifford Brown–styled trumpeter Eric Le Lann (born in 1957, a year after Brown's death). For the first time, young French players in the bebop tradition would cultivate truly international reputations. Most notable among them was the pianist Michel Petrucciani, whose major Parisian debut was made in 1981, his first American appearances following in 1982.[13]

However popular it was proving, the revisiting of older styles did not go uncriticized. A 1984 *Jazz hot* editorial on Marsalis was illustrated by a drawing of an ostrich with its head in a trumpet; a more philosophical rumination on the relationship between music and history was soon offered by Michel-Claude Jalard, who—having left jazz criticism behind not long after writing the article on Thelonious Monk examined in chapter 3—in 1986 published a collection of essays, *Le Jazz est-il encore possible?*, "Is Jazz Still Possible?" Only as a repertory form, was the answer.[14] The canon stood triumphant.

It's useful, finally, to ask how, and in whose interests, this increasingly finalized, mediatized history of jazz in France has functioned. The historian Pierre Nora was, at this time, on his way to becoming one of the most influential French intellectuals of the latter 20th century, largely by dint of the research project that he was leading on cultural memories in and of France—the multivolume product of which would be entitled *Les Lieux de mémoire*, sites of memory. Nora's introductory essay for this work set out what would soon be recognized as an important distinction between history and memory, and described the various "sites," literal or metaphorical, in which each inhered. For Nora, "history" stood for the objectified (though not necessarily objective) archiving and presentation of the past, a form from which lived experience was all but evacuated.

> History is perpetually suspicious of memory, and its true mission is to suppress and destroy it . . . A generalized critical history would no doubt preserve some museums, some medallions and monuments— that is to say, the materials necessary for its work—but it would empty them of what, to us, would make them *lieux de mémoire*.[15]

Monuments and medallions that did function as *lieux de mémoire*, by contrast, were those which acted as focal points for an active memory of the past. It's the difference between "archive memory" and "duty memory," between a line in a deaths register and a bunch of flowers left every year at the scene of an accident: where history is supposedly rationalized and unchanging, memory is fluid and haphazard; where history is supposedly official, memory is unofficial; where history is abstract, memory is rooted in community and place. There's little better example than the Festival Django Reinhardt, held in the guitarist's last hometown of Samois-sur-Seine since 1968, where players in the Reinhardt tradition—celebrities like Boulou Ferré and Biréli Lagrène as much as amateurs of the style—gather every summer to honor their forebear's music.[16]

It's difficult to see how these imaginatively invested jazz memorials might be oppositional, or what all-powerful "history" they might oppose. But if in the 21st century there is an official history of jazz in France, it is probably best represented by the Francophone academic texts referred to throughout this study, some of which began as doctoral dissertations, others of which are by professional university researchers, all of which have in some way been ratified according to the methodologies and value systems of a state higher education system. Certainly, French-authored academic histories (and sociologies) of French jazz—and, this not being seen as being a prestigious subject, there aren't too many—respect disciplinary boundaries that are more heavily policed than in other countries: books are either concerned with musical analysis, or with print-based historical study, but not both. As we've seen, these narratives are prone to weak but significant statist or nationalist tendencies. Exhibitions at large public institutions like the Musée du Quai Branly (*Le Siècle du jazz*, 2009) and the Cité de la musique (*Django Reinhardt, Swing de Paris*, 2012) do similar work, often making much of jazz's links to pre-legitimated local high-art figures like Cocteau and Matisse. In Nora's thinking, this kind of history "suppresses" memory, and what is often excluded here is anecdote, audience testimony, a truly *felt* response to the music; the press, and anyone who worked in published words or images, is correspondingly overprivileged.

An academic history like the present work, which originates outside France and the French system of intellectual production, might evade some of these constraints. But others it won't: it's not their national origin that most defines those "official" French jazz histories, but their subscription to an internationalized academic method, one in which this study surely shares. These are all projects that participate in jazz's transformation, seen over the course of this book, from a popular, commercial pastime to an institutionally supported endeavor (even if all those terms should be read with one eyebrow raised). The unkind might say that the transformation is from something to live into something to be considered, from everyday culture into what the French call *patrimonie*.

In his contribution to Nora's project, André Chastel argues that notions of patrimony, or cultural "inheritance," have rarely concerned those French men and women who, working class or petit bourgeois, were in every way little-bequeathed; even though *patrimonie* in post-revolutionary France has come to stand for the entire nation's cultural heritage—its palaces, its literature—these were often properties seized from or owed to the aristocracy, and subsequently presided over by an educationally privileged class in the name of a people not always interested in what was nominally theirs. "Deep memory is less linked to possession than pleasure," Chastel writes.[17] It's one reason why "officializing" studies aiming for pure historical truth can't have the impact and currency of those creatively collaged images of a jazz past that, satisfying to identify and comprehend in their pop-cultural workings, play on memories of signs (a man with a saxophone), and, whether one was there or not, signs of memory (this in black and white). Such codal competence—the ability to identify, even if vaguely, an element of pastiche and temporal disjunction—is nevertheless a kind of historical literacy; it is only by being versed in the iconographies, looks and textures of different periods that those watching get, and enjoy, what has often been called the postmodern wink.

If the historical wealth that both Chastel and jazz historians describe is destined to be appreciated by the educated minority in whose charge the official past remains, then this other kind of jazz memory circulates at a different level, one sunk in the grubby world of commerce. Here, among culture-industry media rather than governmental and educational networks, are the most commonly recognized fragments of the music's past. Music, and the sites of music-making, have rarely been removed entirely from the market, and that fact demands a complication of Nora's basic model: the interposition—between official history and unofficial, non-textualized memory—of a commercial agent, one that maintains these otherwise unworthy sites out of financial self-interest.

That interest is neither officializing nor charged with the desire to keep lived memory alive, but it nevertheless dallies with both roles. Many of the great New York jazz clubs of the early and mid-century were razed in the course of one redevelopment scheme or another. It might be a generalization too far to suggest that it shows the difference between new- and old-world attitudes toward the past, but in Paris, a number of the venues that played host to important jazz bands and in-crowds from the interwar years onwards remain open in some form: Le Bœuf sur le Toit and Le Caveau de la Huchette form part of Paris's heritage industry, and part of a museumification of the city in process since the 1960s, when culture minister André Malraux hosed down the Haussmannian facades and removed many non-bourgeois communities to the suburbs.[18] Whether solid or virtual, these commercially supported sites of a French jazz past host the elements of an officialized history as well as a still under-construction cultural memory. As Jerome de Groot has written, in the 21st century, histories are ever more coopted and coauthored by these business interests, pastness perhaps "not commodity itself," but very often "part of marketing and commodification." For De Groot, a consumable history ranges "from the branded association of a product with a time period, to the rendering of the past as just one of many tropes used to represent and sell commodities," this inscribing "the status of the past within a set of consumption practices that give it a certain power in the nexus of economic desire."[19]

Looking at the artwork of rapper MC Solaar's 1991 debut album *Qui sème le vent récolte le tempo*, its graphics and image of cool black creativity pastiching the 1950s and '60s album covers of labels like Blue Note and Prestige—or watching a black tap-dancer glide alongside the Seine in the video for Camille's 2002 song "Paris," the clip seemingly playing on jazz band imagery from Jean Vigo's 1934 film *L'Atalante*—it's hard not to wonder how much of this popular jazz history's "power" is owed to the presence in Europe of a blackness still portrayed as exotic.

Jim McGuigan has argued that the long history of racism in America—and, why not, in Europe—"is magically erased in the present" by contemporary consumer-culture associations of blackness with a certain desirable style and attitude.[20] Of course, the nature of what was desirable to the European gaze has changed over time, ideas of blackness emphasizing at first an authenticity of living, then a knowing cool, a radical political righteousness, and finally, more recently, bourgeois buying power; racial fantasies have been hardly less prone to "monetization" than any other aspect of Western social life in the postwar period. But no figure's work better encapsulates this complex of style and consumerist success—and the anachronic crushing together of historical signifiers—than that made by one of this book's most intriguing characters, Miles Davis.[21] The 1957 compilation of the trumpeter's previously marginal 1949 and 1950 nonet recordings as *Birth of the Cool* aimed to enshrine the trumpeter as a progenitor of that by-then popular, cultural-emotional attitude, and the strength of the operation's success in this regard is shown by the semiotic afterlife granted the album's packaging (even if the chamber jazz contained within can now sound archaic). The trailer for *Ascenseur pour l'échafaud*'s 2005 Rialto Pictures rerelease advertises the "birth of the New Wave" and then "birth of the cool" using the name-checked album's distinctive white, red and black color scheme and typography.[22] The title sequence of the highly successful television period drama *Mad Men* (2007–) similarly co-opts the record's graphics to set up its portrayal of a golden age of cool consumption. Davis's 1950s recordings have been granted entrée to all kinds of venues by virtue of their often-reserved tone and discreet dynamic range: "[t]his is a period classic, like a '58 Impala," wrote Fred Bouchard in a 1990 *Down Beat* review of *Ascenseur*'s soundtrack rerelease. "It's smoky, sexy. Great black-and-white backdrop for intimate *tete-a-tetes* [*sic*]."[23] Ashley Kahn's 2001 book-length study of Davis's *Kind of Blue*, the text an extended exercise in commodity fetishism, closes by comparing that record to an "evocative motif played on an unaccompanied bamboo flute . . . a vintage claret that, once tasted, can neither be forgotten nor precisely recalled . . . a recording of Ravel's *Concerto for Left Hand and Orchestra*": the markers of bourgeois discernment—one authentically ethnic, the others hailing from France, home of the connoisseur—are evoked in an operation of consumerist pseudohistory.[24] These are ideological lessons in a jazz past's "meanings," given by the culture industries that are forever reloading and reusing them—and using them in commercials, trailers and credit sequences at least as much as in fully fledged creative works or historical narratives.

Just like the music did, these signs collapse not just time but also space, local and international musical and cultural history merging into one. And even if a fragmentary French jazz past is rendered ever more complete with every symbolic repetition—this book might have been one more nail in its coffin—in their commercial and scholarly appearances these signs are still "making jazz in France." Perhaps jazz histories should delve further into the ways that the form's heritage circulates in these different, competing media. Whatever the efforts we've seen being made here, the music still echoes between the popular and the artistic, between the market and the university (those things presented as opposites, again the eyebrow raises); maybe thinking and writing about jazz history should mean tracking those movements, following jazz up from the south but also down fiber-optic cables, along a time line of glorious progress but also across the screens on which its degraded images flicker. There might not be much to choose between junk memory and technocratic history, a porkpie hat in a pop video or an earnest treatise on cultural discourse, but beyond all that there must be a jazz scholarship that reads like the music being lived out, in all its forms.

Notes

1. See Tyler Stovall, *Paris Noir: African Americans in the City of Light* (New York: Houghton Mifflin, 1996).

2. On the Ansermet text's republication, see Hugues Panassié, *Douze Années de jazz (1927–1938) : Souvenirs* (Paris: Corrêa, 1946), 268–69. The translated text itself is reprinted as "A 'Serious' Musician Takes Jazz Seriously," in *Keeping Time: Readings in Jazz History*, ed. Robert Walser (New York: Oxford University Press, 1999), 9–11.

3. George E. Lewis, *A Power Stronger than Itself: The AACM and American Experimental Music* (Chicago: University of Chicago Press, 2008), 228 and passim.

4. James Lincoln Collier, *The Reception of Jazz in America* (Brooklyn: Institute for Studies in American Music, 1988).

5. The term "postwar" is a slippery one. Some historians would limit that period to the latter 1940s and early 1950s, while others would allow it to extend far further: Tony Judt's doorstop study *Postwar: A History of Europe Since 1945* (London: Heinemann, 2005) spans from 1945 into the 21st century.

6. On ragtime, the cakewalk and early jazz in France—and these musics' complex reception—see Petrine Archer-Straw, *Negrophilia: Avant-Garde Paris and Black Culture in the 1920s* (London: Thames and Hudson, 2000); Jody Blake, *Le Tumulte noir: Modernist Art and Popular Entertainment in Jazz-Age Paris, 1900–1930* (University Park: Pennsylvania State University Press, 1999); Jeffrey H. Jackson, *Making Jazz French: Music and Modern Life in Interwar Paris* (Durham, NC: Duke University Press, 2003); Matthew F. Jordan, *Le Jazz: Jazz and French Cultural Identity* (Urbana: University of Illinois Press, 2010); William A. Shack, *Harlem in Montmartre: A Paris Jazz Story between the Great Wars* (Berkeley: University of California Press, 2001). Many of the scenes of this confused racial-cultural encounter were also played out in New York, in the wake of the Harlem Renaissance.

7. On jazz in Nice, the music's second French home during this period, see Jonathan Duclos-Arkilovitch, *Jazzin' riviera. 70 ans de jazz sur la Côte d'Azur* (Nice:

Rom Editions, 1997); on jazz in Marseille, see Michel Samson and Gilles Suzanne, *A Fond de cale. 1917–2011 un siècle de jazz à Marseille* (Marseille: Editions Wildproject, 2011).

8. Jeremy F. Lane, "'Rythme de travail, rythme de jazz:' Jazz, Primitivism, and *Machinisme* in Inter-War France," *Atlantic Studies* 4, no. 1 (2007): 111. This idea would prove durable, and not just the fantasy of white observers: see LeRoi Jones [Amiri Baraka], *Blues People* (New York: Morrow Quill, 1963), 29.

9. Matthew F. Jordan, "Amphibiologie: Ethnographic Surrealism in French Discourse in Jazz," *Journal of European Studies* 31 (2001): 173–74.

10. See Jordan, *Le Jazz*, 113–16, and 150ff.; Chris Goddard, *Jazz Away From Home* (London: Paddington Press, 1979). In Britain as in France and the United States, "symphonic" orchestras were seen as "civilizing" jazz. Catherine Parsonage, *The Evolution of Jazz in Britain, 1880–1935* (Aldershot: Ashgate, 2005), 173.

11. Much of the earlier writing of Hugues Panassié, explored in the next chapter, laments this fact. See also André Hodeir, *Le Jazz, cet inconnu* (Paris: Collection Harmoniques, 1945), 36–40.

12. Le Quintette du Hot-club de France had more commercial success in Britain and elsewhere in Europe. Charles Delaunay, *Django Reinhardt* (London: Jazz Book Club by arrangement with Cassell, 1963), 81.

13. See Anne Legrand, *Charles Delaunay et le jazz en France dans les années 30 et 40* (Paris: Editions du Layeur, 2009).

14. See Benjamin Givan, *The Music of Django Reinhardt* (Ann Arbor: University of Michigan Press, 2010).

15. Gérard Régnier, *Jazz et société sous l'Occupation* (Paris: L'Harmattan, 2009), 144, 122, passim. I am avoiding reference to the well-known but self-admittedly part-fictionalized book by Mike Zwerin, *La Tristesse de Saint-Louis: Swing under the Nazis* (London: Quartet, 1985).

16. Régnier, *Jazz et société*, 48, 62–63.

17. Régnier, *Jazz et société*, 175, 63, 153, 72–79.

18. Legrand, *Charles Delaunay*, 145.

19. Charles Delaunay, "Histoire du Hot-club de France," *Jazz hot* 27 (2° série, 1948): 16; Andy Fry, "'That Gypsy in France:' Django Reinhardt's Occupation Blouze," in *Jazz Worlds / World Jazz*, ed. Philip Bohlman and Goffredo Plastino (Chicago: University of Chicago Press, forthcoming), 6, 12.

20. André Cœuroy, *Histoire générale du jazz. Strette, hot, swing* (Paris: Editions Denoël, 1942), 24.

21. Cœuroy, *Histoire générale*, 29, 25–26, 54, 193.

22. See Jordan, *Le Jazz*, 185–232.

23. Hodeir, *Le Jazz*, passim.

24. See E. Taylor Atkins's monograph *Blue Nippon: Authenticating Jazz in Japan* (Durham, NC: Duke University Press, 2001) and his subsequent edited volume *Jazz Planet* (Jackson: University Press of Mississippi, 2003); Alyn Shipton, *A New History of Jazz*, 2nd ed. (London: Continuum, 2008); or Stefano Zenni, *Storia del Jazz. Una prospettiva globale* (Viterbo: Nuovi Equilibri, 2012).

25. This approach is not uncommon to studies of jazz outside the United States. See, for instance, Atkins, *Blue Nippon*. Musicological studies of any aspect of French

jazz are scant. Vincent Cotro's *Chants libres : le free jazz en France, 1960–1975* (Paris: Editions Outre Mesure) is a valuable if sometimes problematic exception to the "culturalist" rule, but one that explicitly excludes critical and sociocultural issues from its music-analytical project.

26. Examples are Stovall, *Paris Noir*; Lewis, *A Power Stronger than Itself*; the texts listed in note 6; and Andy Fry, *Paris Blues: African American Music and French Popular Culture, 1920–1960* (Chicago: University of Chicago Press, forthcoming).

27. Among the most ardent of these efforts are Cotro, *Chants libres*, 81–93, and Francis Gooding's scholarly liner notes to *The Best of Jef Gilson* (Jazzman, 2011).

28. On this growth, see Robert Gildea, *France since 1945* (Oxford and New York: Oxford University Press, 1996), especially 85–86.

29. Such as the interpolation of the song "Some of These Days" in *Nausea* (1938), and the embroidered 1947 report from New York published in English as "I Discovered Jazz in America," in *Riffs & Choruses: A New Jazz Anthology*, ed. Andrew Clark (London: Continuum, 2001), 51–53.

30. Circulations given in Jacques Lahitte, "Jazz-news," *Arts*, February 9, 1955, 4; Anon., "Avis," *Jazz* (Marseille) 22 (1960), 5.

31. The article is by Jacques Kergoet: *Les Cahiers du jazz* 5 (1961), 55–63.

32. Tournès provides a good survey of jazz coverage in the wider press. Ludovic Tournès, *New Orleans sur Seine* (Paris: Fayard, 1999), 195–206.

33. Tournès, *New Orleans sur Seine*, 216–21.

34. Tournès, *New Orleans sur Seine*, 205–10; Roscoe Seldon Suddarth, "French Stewardship of Jazz: The Case of France Musique and France Culture" (master's thesis, University of Maryland, 2008).

35. For a contemporary report on the economic difficulties of these 1950s festivals see Anon., "Résurrection des semaines du jazz à Cannes et Knokke," *Arts*, February 26, 1958, 8.

36. Régnier, *Jazz et société*, 55.

37. Peter Pullman, *Wail: The Life of Bud Powell* (self-published Kindle edition, 2012), location 8374; Jean Rochard, "Dolo Music," *Le Glob*, February 27, 2012, http://nato-glob.blogspot.co.uk/2012/02/dolo-music.html.

38. In August 1975 the cover of *Jazz magazine* (no. 235) was headlined "Femmes et problèmes du jazz"—a play on the title of a book by André Hodeir discussed in chapter 3—and contained interviews with musicians like Dee Dee Bridgewater; the magazine's March 1979 edition (no. 273) had British bassoonist Lindsay Cooper on the cover. An outlier was the July 1961 issue of *Jazz* (Marseille), a special issue (no. 25), titled "Jazz et les femmes," which featured a number of articles on American vocalists.

39. See Marie Buscatto, "Contributions of Ethnography to Gendered Sociology: The French Jazz World," *Qualitative Sociology Review* 3, no. 3 (2007): 47ff. Thanks to Steve Wilford for this reference.

Chapter Two

1. Ludovic Tournès, "L'Electrification des sensibilités musicales : le disque, l'enregistrement électrique et la mutation du paysage sonore en France (1925–1939)," *French Cultural Studies* 16 (2005): 145. See also Jackson, *Making Jazz French*,

passim; Matthew F. Jordan, "Discophilie or Discomanie?: The Cultural Politics of Living Room Listening," *French Cultural Studies* 16 (2005): 151–69.

2. Hugues Panassié, *Monsieur Jazz. Entretiens avec Pierre Casalta* (Paris: Stock, 1975), passim, 74.

3. The declaration is cited in Legrand, *Charles Delaunay*, 92.

4. Matthew F. Jordan, "Amphibiologie," 159–60. This notwithstanding the factual errors induced by Panassié's distance from the music's source: see Collier, *The Reception of Jazz*, 57–62.

5. Panassié thus shifted position somewhat between *Le Jazz hot* and *The Real Jazz*: see Hugues Panassié, *The Real Jazz*, trans. Anne Sorelle Williams (New York: Smith & Durrell, 1942), vii–viii.

6. Hugues Panassié, "Les Disques," *Jazz hot* 9 (1936): 18; "Les Disques," *Jazz hot* 24 (1938): 18; *The Real Jazz*, 81.

7. Ted Gioia, "Jazz and the Primitivist Myth," *Musical Quarterly* 73, no. 1 (1989): 130–43. For an example of Panassié's placement in jazz history, see Richard Hadlock, "The New Orleans Revival," in *The Oxford Companion to Jazz*, ed. Bill Kirchner (Oxford: Oxford University Press, 2000), 310.

8. Tournès, *New Orleans sur Seine*, 36, 55. Panassié's Hot-club associate Jacques Bureau—who would become a member of the Resistance—argued later in life that Panassié's links with such groups had always been fluid and that the critic was too much of an individualist to join anyone else's organization. Régnier, *Jazz et société*, 99.

9. Hugues Panassié, *Hot Jazz: The Guide to Swing Music*, trans. Lyle and Eleanor Dowling (London: Cassell, 1936), 20–21. This, like other quotations taken from texts available in English translation, I have taken from the English version, though originals have been consulted.

10. Jordan, "Amphibiologie," 164.

11. Cited in Archer-Straw, *Negrophilia*, 113–14. The "medicomoral" trope of primitive black music as (tropical) disease was already much in use in the United States: see Ronald Radano, *Lying up a Nation: Race and Black Music* (Chicago: University of Chicago Press, 2003), 235–36.

12. Philippe Gumplowicz, "Vers le droit de cité. Naissance de la critique de jazz, Paris 1930–34," in *Musiques et musiciens à Paris dans les années trente*, ed. Daniele Pistone (Paris: Honoré Champion, 2000), 397.

13. The quotation, from the writer Sem (1923), is cited in Jackson, *Making Jazz French*, 30.

14. The Belgian Robert Goffin, who had been writing considered pieces on jazz in the Franco-Belgian journal *Le Disque vert* since the early 1920s, was also a surrealist poet.

15. See Jordan, "Amphibiologie," and Lane, "Rythme de travail," 103–16.

16. Simon Frith, "Playing with Real Feeling—Jazz and Suburbia," in *Music for Pleasure: Essays in the Sociology of Pop* (Cambridge: Polity Press, 1988), 45–63; Parsonage, *The Evolution of Jazz in Britain*, 53–54, and passim; George McKay, *Circular Breathing: The Cultural Politics of Jazz in Britain* (Durham, NC: Duke University Press, 2005), 108.

17. Panassié, *Monsieur Jazz*, 29.

18. Panassié, *Monsieur Jazz*, 30.

19. Panassié, *Hot Jazz*, 2–3; 12–13; 280–82.

20. Louis Bayard, "Hot : phénomène universel," *Jazz hot* 28 (1938): 13.

21. On notation, see Panassié, *The Real Jazz*, 20.

22. Panassié, *The Real Jazz*, 29.

23. Thus joining the ranks of those who had, the world over, recognized the educational potential of the phonograph: see Mark Katz, *Capturing Sound: How Technology Has Changed Music* (Berkeley: University of California Press, 2004), 61–62.

24. Panassié performs his mime in the films *L'Aventure du jazz* (dir. Louis Panassié, 1972) and *Hugues Panassié, ou la passion du jazz* (dir. Jean Arnautu, Paul Paviot, 1974). It has not been possible to license an image from one of these films for this book.

25. Tournès, *New Orleans sur Seine*, 45.

26. Hugues Panassié, *Douze Années de jazz (1927–1938) : souvenirs* (Paris: Corrêa, 1946), 106; see also Hugues Panassié, *Histoire des disques Swing* (Geneva: Ch. Grasset, 1944), 65.

27. Tournès, *New Orleans sur Seine*, 79.

28. Panassié, *The Real Jazz*, 7–8.

29. Tournès, *New Orleans sur Seine*, 99.

30. See René Guénon, *The Crisis of the Modern World* (Delhi: Indica, 1999); Philippe Gumplowicz, "Musicographes réactionnaires des années 1930," *Le Mouvement social* 3, no. 208 (2004): 91–124.

31. Hugues Panassié, "Toujours le mal blanc," *Bulletin du Hot-club de France* 77 (1958), 3–8; *Monsieur Jazz*, 131.

32. Guénon, *The Crisis*, 15–16, 27.

33. Mark Sedgwick, *Against the Modern World: Traditionalism and the Secret Intellectual History of the Twentieth Century* (Oxford: Oxford University Press, 2004), 23–25.

34. George Boas, *Primitivism and Related Ideas in the Middle Ages* (Baltimore: Johns Hopkins University Press, 1997), 7, 8, 5.

35. Panassié, *The Real Jazz*, 6.

36. Panassié, *Douze Années*, 182.

37. Panassié, *The Real Jazz*, 228, 55.

38. Panassié, *The Real Jazz*, 54.

39. See Boas, *Primitivism*, 129–53; Ter Ellingson, *The Myth of the Noble Savage* (Berkeley: University of California Press, 2001); Jean-Jacques Rousseau, *Discourse on Inequality*, trans. Franklin Philip (Oxford: World's Classics, 1994), 55–58.

40. Denis-Constant Martin, "De l'Excursion à Harlem au débat sur les 'Noirs' : les terrains absents de la jazzologie française," *L'Homme* 158/159 (2001): 269, 268.

41. Panassié, *Monsieur Jazz*, 199, 210–11.

42. Boas, *Primitivism*, 25.

43. Georges Herment, "Hot—sixième sens," *Jazz hot* 9 (1936): 12.

44. Hugues Panassié, *Cinq Mois à New-York* (Paris: Corrêa, 1947), 133–35.

45. This experience gave rise to a number of others making the link between tempo and cosmic order before the event itself was related in *Cinq mois à New-York*. See for instance Panassié, *The Real Jazz*, 27.

46. Panassié, *Hot Jazz*, 284.

47. Panassié, *Cinq Mois*, 135–36.

48. Panassié, *Histoire des disques Swing*, 46–48. This notwithstanding the difference in late 1930s realizations of "swing" and the 1920s jazz that Panassié always valued most highly.

49. Panassié, *Histoire des disques Swing*, 48. This elaboration refers not to the Webb experience but to a similar moment in one of the recording sessions Panassié supervised during the New York trip.

50. See Panassié, *Cinq Mois*, for descriptions of sessions conducted by Count Basie, Fats Waller and others.

51. Tournès, "L'Electrification," 145.

52. Walter Benjamin, "The Work of Art in the Age of Mechanical Reproduction," in *Illuminations*, ed. Hannah Arendt, trans. Harry Zohn (London: Pimlico, 1999), 211–44; Tournès, "L'Electrification," 147.

53. Panassié, *Histoire des disques Swing*, 49.

54. Panassié, *The Real Jazz*, 203; *Douze Années*, 171.

55. For a rather more detailed reading of Benjamin and Panassié's competing theories, see Tom Perchard, "Hugues Panassié Contra Walter Benjamin: Bodies, Masses and the Iconic Jazz Recording in Mid-Century France," *Popular Music and Society* 35, no. 3 (2012): 375–98.

56. Charles Delaunay, *De la vie et du jazz* (Paris: Editions Hot Jazz, 1939), 13.

57. See the 1940 letter to *Down Beat* reprinted as Charles Delaunay, "From Somewhere in France," in *Keeping Time*, ed. Walser, 129–31.

58. Hodeir, *Le Jazz*, 17.

59. See Panassié, *Monsieur Jazz*, 177–78, where Panassié also protests that he harbored Jews during the occupation.

60. See Christian Faure, *Le Projet culturel de Vichy* (Lyon: Presses Universitaires de Lyon, 1989), 142–55.

61. Tournès, *New Orleans sur Seine*, 96.

62. Charles Delaunay, "Vrai jazz ? ," *Jazz hot* 5 (2° série, 1946): 9.

63. Tournès, *New Orleans sur Seine*, 106ff. Delaunay's federation would be short lived.

64. Alyn Shipton, "The New Orleans Revival in Britain and France," in *Eurojazzland: Jazz and European Sources, Dynamics, and Contexts*, ed. Luca Cerchiari, Laurent Cugny, and Franz Kerschbaumer (Lebanon, NH: Northeastern University Press, 2012), 253–74.

65. Legrand, *Charles Delaunay*, 115.

66. See Bernard Gendron, "'Moldy Figs' and Modernists: Jazz at War (1942–1946)," in *Jazz among the Discourses*, ed. Krin Gabbard (Durham, NC: Duke University Press, 1995), 31–56. As Andy Fry points out, an old jazz primitivism attended Bechet's French reception even in the 1950s. Fry, "Remembrance of Jazz Past: Sidney Bechet in France," in *The Oxford Handbook to the New Cultural History of Music*, ed. Jane Fulcher (New York: Oxford University Press, 2012), 316–17.

67. Both purist and constructivist tendencies were embodied in Panassié's Swing discs: in his book on the sessions, *Histoire des disques Swing*, the critic rhapsodized over, for example, Tommy Ladnier's distillation of authentic, King Oliver–period jazz trumpet, while overlooking the more contemporary context in which it appeared.

68. In the studio at least, the clarinet was largely abandoned upon Bechet's move to France.

69. Fry, "Remembrance of Jazz Past," 315.

70. Fry, "Remembrance of Jazz Past," 317.

71. Fry, "Remembrance of Jazz Past," 316.

72. Fry, "Remembrance of Jazz Past," 319.

73. See, for example, André Hodeir, "Letter on Evolutionism and the Role of Criticism," in *Toward Jazz*, trans. Noël Burch (London: Jazz Book Club, by arrangement with Grove Press, 1965), 38.

74. Tournès cites a 1957 *Figaro* article to this effect. Tournès, *New Orleans sur Seine*, 337.

75. Raymond Mouly, "Les Musiciens français à l'honneur sur Europe 1," *Jazz magazine* 48 (1959): 14–15.

76. Perhaps the adolescent need to report oneself skewed these figures. Anon., "Qui êtes-vous ? ," *Jazz* 51 (1959): 17–18.

77. Anon., "Referendum 70," *Jazz hot* 258 (1970): 6–7. A good number of musicians eventually identified with bebop, free jazz and free improvisation began by playing in the New Orleans style, in France and elsewhere—Bobby Jaspar, Barney Wilen, François Tusques, Henri Texier and Daunik Lazro were among them.

78. Irakli is cited at "Musiciens," Hot-club de France, http://www.hot-club.asso. fr/musicos/iraklibio.htm; Gérard Conte, "Irakli : la première partie du concert a confirmé sa classe," *Jazz hot* 211 (1965): 9.

79. Cited in Pierre Cressant, "Jean-Claude Albert-Weil et la 'Transculture'," *Jazz hot* 239 (1968): 28.

80. Hans Belting, Likeness and Presence: *A History of the Image Before the Era of Art*, trans. Edmund Jephcott (Chicago: The University of Chicago Press, 1994), 150; 27–28. The process that Benjamin attributed to the technological reproduction of the 19th century had occurred hundreds of years earlier, and yet aura had not been removed from the equation so much as recast. For a critique of Benjamin's art history narrative, see Paul Mattick, "Mechanical Reproduction in the Age of Art," *Theory, Culture & Society* 10 (1993): 127–47.

81. Belting, *Likeness and Presence*, 140, and passim.

82. André Hodeir, *Hommes et problèmes du jazz* (Paris: Au Portulan, Chez Flammarion, 1954), 341.

83. Panassié, *Cinq Mois*, 46.

84. See Tournès, *New Orleans sur Seine*, 108.

85. *Le Bulletin du Hot-club de France* 2 (1950): 1; Panassié, *Cinq Mois*, 132. On Panassié's ex-Vichy associates, see Tournès, *New Orleans sur Seine*, 192–93.

86. This phrase comes from a 25th anniversary chronology of the HCF printed in *Le Bulletin du Hot-club de France* 72 (1957): 6. In true "Vichy syndrome" style, the chronology jumps without comment from April 1937, and Panassié's first conférence-audition at the Sorbonne, directly to Rex Stewart's tour of December 1947.

87. Panassié, *Douze Années*, 182.

88. Pierre Bourdieu and Jean-Claude Passeron, *Reproduction in Education, Society and Culture*, 2nd ed. (London: Sage Publications, 1990), 20, 56–63, 20, 64, 15.

89. The HCF had received charitable status in 1952. See *Le Bulletin du Hot-club de France* 15 (1952): 2, and no. 25 (1953): 2.

90. *Le Bulletin du Hot-club de France* 19 (1952): 3.

91. *Le Bulletin du Hot-club de France* 20 (1952): 5–6.

92. *Le Bulletin du Hot-club de France* 126 (1963): 4.

93. It's not the case that this canon is absolutely static. Compensating for New Orleans's receding heyday, through the 1950s and '60s an increasing number of what would later be called blues and roots appear in the review pages (Memphis Slim reviewed over sixty times). R&B, especially its jazzier side, also qualifies for entry: Jimmy Smith and Earl Bostic are each reviewed almost fifty times, Aretha Franklin and Chuck Berry around twenty, James Brown four times. For Panassié all these forms represented the popular, improvisational, habit-based expression that he venerated. It's less the inclusions that define the doctrine than the exclusions.

94. See the last *Bulletin* Panassié edited before his sudden death, 243 (1974); see also 188 (1969).

95. See the examples in *Le Bulletin du Hot-club de France* 3 (1950).

96. *Le Bulletin du Hot-club de France* 44 (1955): 36. The prize in this instance was, unsurprisingly, a Louis Armstrong disc. For such a "pedagogical" review, see *Le Bulletin du Hot-club de France* 77 (1958): 12–14.

97. *Le Bulletin du Hot-club de France* 8 (1951): 19.

98. Though in the next issue members are admonished for not having responded: *Le Bulletin du Hot-club de France* 16 (1952): 2.

99. *Le Bulletin du Hot-club de France* 18 (1952): 2.

100. *Le Bulletin du Hot-club de France* 53 (1955): 36.

101. Hodeir, *Hommes et problèmes*, 333.

102. Boris Vian, "Revue de presse," *Jazz hot* 119 (1957): 28.

103. The Parti Communiste Français, for example, counted 29,000 members in 1933 and 288,000 by the end of 1936. Julian Jackson, *The Popular Front in France: Defending Democracy, 1934–8* (Cambridge: Cambridge University Press, 1988), 219–20.

104. Jackson, *The Popular Front in France*, 218, 285.

105. James Clifford, "Histories of the Tribal and the Modern," in *The Predicament of Culture: Twentieth-Century Ethnography, Literature, and Art* (Cambridge, MA: Harvard University Press, 1988), 195–96.

106. Elsewhere I have argued that this is no less an interesting proposition for historians than a body of work that would seek to engage African American music according to its "own terms" (perhaps also characterized, imagined). Tom Perchard, "Tradition, Modernity and the Supernatural Swing: Re-Reading "Primitivism," in Hugues Panassié's Writing on Jazz," *Popular Music* 3, no. 1 (2011): 25–45.

107. *Le Bulletin du Hot-club de France* 186 (1969): 24.

Chapter Three

1. Their group also included Hubert Fol, alto sax, André Persiany, piano, and Emmanuel Soudieux, bass.

2. On this impact see Boris Vian, "Dizzy Gillespie in Paris," in *Round About Close to Midnight: The Jazz Writings of Boris Vian*, ed. and trans. Mike Zwerin (London and New York: Quartet, 1988), 30–31 (originally published in *Combat*, February 19, 1948); Lucien Malson, "Jazz d'aujourd'hui : du swing sur du papier," *Jazz magazine* 53 (1959): 30. Gillespie's abuser is cited in his original language in Boris Vian, "La Liberté guide nos pas (air connu)," *Autres écrits sur le jazz* (Paris: Christian Bourgois Editeur, 1981),

261. A translation appears in Vian, *Round About Close to Midnight*, 33. The piece was originally published in *Combat*, March 28, 1948.

3. Tournès, "New Orleans sur Seine," 225, 227.

4. Tournès, "New Orleans sur Seine," 226–27.

5. "Bernard G.-R.," "Du Style New-Orleans au Be-Bop ! ," *Arts*, May 21, 1948, 7; Tournès, *New Orleans sur Seine*, 244, 257.

6. The releases *Bebop in Paris*, vols. 1 and 2 (Jazztime, 1992) give an excellent survey of this recording activity, and most of the music discussed here is contained in these collections.

7. See the Panassié-baiting side, "Assy Pan Assy": Hubert Fol and his Bebop Minstrels, with Nat Peck, trombone, Bernard Peiffer, piano, Jean Bouchety, bass, and Kenny Clarke, drums, October 29, 1949.

8. See "Lover Man," recorded by Hubert Fol et ses Minstrels: Hubert Fol, alto, Dick Collins, trumpet, Raymond Fol, piano, Alf Masselier, bass, and Richie Frost, drums, November 15, 1948.

9. Givan, *The Music of Django Reinhardt*, 176ff.

10. Givan, *The Music of Django Reinhardt*, 160–61.

11. Scott DeVeaux, *The Birth of Bebop: A Social and Musical History* (London: Picador, 1999), 95.

12. Likewise, Laurent Cugny has identified the guitarist's 1952 piece "Flèche d'or" as an example of modal jazz that anticipates the work of Miles Davis and others. Laurent Cugny, "Flèche d'or : pourquoi ne l'a-t-on pas entendu ? ," *Les Cahiers du jazz* 3 (nouvelle série, 2006): 82–87. See also Andrew Berish, "Negotiating 'A Blues Riff'": Listening for Django Reinhardt's Place in American Jazz," *Jazz Perspectives* 3, no. 3 (2009): 254.

13. Anon., "André Hodeir : je n'appartiens pas au 'troisième courant,'" *Jazz Hot* 162 (1961): 13. Though not signed, this piece was likely written by Lucien Malson.

14. Kenny Clarke and His Orchestra: Dick Collins, trumpet, Hubert Fol, alto, Jean-Claude Fohrenbach, tenor sax, Laurence, violin, Jacques Denjean, piano, Harry Montaggioni, guitar, Alf Masslier, bass, Clarke, drums, May 4, 1948.

15. Hodeir's early efforts aside, French bebop compositions were keen to signal their sources and work in quotations from the new bebop standards. "Sèvres-Babylone" and "Sweet and Bebop," recorded in July 1947 by Robert Mavounzy et son Orchestre, illustrate this tendency: the one is a pastiche bebop line that works in a quotation from "Salt Peanuts," the other provides a new line to the changes of "Sweet and Lovely" while openly citing the original melody.

16. Hodeir, *Le Jazz*, 169.

17. A discussion of this trend and the quandaries it presented can be found in Tom Perchard, *Lee Morgan: His Life, Music and Culture* (London: Equinox, 2006), 208–19.

18. Lucien Malson, "André Hodeir ou la recherche d'une esthétique," *Jazz magazine* 64 (1960): 31–32.

19. The "ballet for fish" description was Cousteau's own (as was related by Hodeir during his April 1956 appearance on the early French television program *A la recherche du jazz*: the film is held by the Institut National de l'Audiovisuel [INA]). Music from

both films mentioned here is available on André Hodeir, *The Vogue Sessions* (Sony BMG, 1999).

20. The several resultant Vogue single 78s were collected on the Blue Note 10-inch album *James Moody with Strings*.

21. Hodeir recalls this unhappy period in Patrice Caratini, "André Hodeir : 'excusez-moi, c'est le matin,'" *Jazz magazine* 417 (1992): 52; and Anon., "Je n'appartiens pas," 14.

22. Jean-Jacques Gaspard, "Jazz et musique concrète : une oeuvre d'André Hodeir," *Jazz Hot* 68 (1952): 19; Marc Battier, "André Hodeir et la réalisation de *Jazz et Jazz*," *Les Cahiers du Jazz* 3 (nouvelle série, 2006): 55–57; Richard F. Kuisel, *Seducing the French: The Dilemma of Americanization* (Berkeley: University of California Press, 1993), 28.

23. Jean-Louis Pautrot, "Introduction," in *The André Hodeir Jazz Reader*, ed. Pautrot (Ann Arbor: University of Michigan Press), 1–19; Caratini, "Excusez-moi," 53. The Modern Jazz Quartet's appearance at the notionally art-music-based Donaueschingen festival was so successful that jazz was excluded from then on. See Lewis, *A Power Stronger than Itself*, 248–49.

24. Pautrot, "Introduction," 5.

25. The piece's use of the tone row is illustrated in Nat Peck, "L'Oeuvre orchestrale d'André Hodeir," *Jazz Hot* 99 (1955): 8.

26. Anon., "Je n'appartiens pas," 14.

27. André Hodeir, "Vers un renouveau de la musique de jazz ? A propos des enregistrements de Dizzy Gillespie," *Jazz hot* 7 (2° série, 1946): 4–5, 7.

28. Unless noted, quotations here are taken from the 1956 English translation. André Hodeir, *Jazz: Its Evolution and Essence*, trans. David Noakes (London: Secker and Warburg, 1956), 13.

29. Hodeir, *Jazz: Its Evolution and Essence*, 19.

30. Hodeir, *Jazz: Its Evolution and Essence*, 63.

31. Hodeir, *Jazz: Its Evolution and Essence*, 77. This is the 1956 translation, but those tonal aspects are faithful to the French original. The remark comes at the beginning of the book's most impressive chapter, a study of Ellington's "Concerto for Cootie."

32. Panassié showed a particular distaste for Hodeir's modernist vocabulary of "disjunction," "conjunction," "discontinuity." This language he counterposed to an "entire metaphorical language [langage imagé] [that] has been created among jazzmen . . . The conformist critics, for their part, express themselves on jazz in the same manner as on European music." Hugues Panassié, *La Bataille du jazz* (Paris: Editions Albin Michel, 1965), 103.

33. Hodeir, *Jazz: Its Evolution and Essence*, 45.

34. Hodeir, *Jazz: Its Evolution and Essence*, 46.

35. On Malson's anti-racism see Tournès, *New Orleans sur Seine*, 258–59.

36. Hodeir, *Jazz: Its Evolution and Essence*, 234.

37. Hodeir, *Jazz: Its Evolution and Essence*, 156.

38. Hodeir, *Jazz: Its Evolution and Essence*, 236.

39. Hodeir, *Jazz: Its Evolution and Essence*, 234–35.

40. Hodeir's quasi-scientific vocabulary is here joined by quasi-scientific racialism: "It is the American Negroes who created jazz; and the number of them who are capa-

ble of complete neuro-muscular relaxation is very remarkable. This characteristic has been demonstrated in track and field events, where colored sprinters' and jumpers' ability to relax is regarded as the principal reason for their speed and agility." Hodeir, *Jazz: Its Evolution and Essence*, 207.

41. Hodeir, *Jazz: Its Evolution and Essence*, 240.

42. Tony Judt, *Marxism and the French Left: Studies in Labour and Politics in France, 1830–1981* (Oxford: Clarendon Press, 1986), 175.

43. Judt, *Marxism and the French Left*, 181.

44. If Hodeir wrote that black Americans showed a greater sense of swing that white players, he stopped well short of disqualifying nonblack players from either swinging or playing jazz in general.

45. Hodeir, *Jazz: Its Evolution and Essence*, 92.

46. Hodeir, *Jazz: Its Evolution and Essence*, 164.

47. Hodeir, *Jazz: Its Evolution and Essence*, 180–81.

48. Malson, "André Hodeir ou la recherche," 30, 31.

49. Wendell Otey, "Hodeir: Through His Own Glass. A Review of His LPs," *Jazz: A Quarterly of American Music* 2 (1959): 105. Axiomatic of the book's wary British reception is John Forrester, "An Academician Looks at Jazz: A Review of André Hodeir's *Jazz: Its Evolution and Essence*," *Jazz Monthly* 2, no. 6 (1956): 2, 3, 31.

50. John Gennari, *Blowin' Hot and Cool: Jazz and Its Critics* (Chicago: University of Chicago Press), 188–89.

51. LeRoi Jones, "Jazz and the White Critic," *Black Music* (Westport, CT: Greenwood Press, 1980), 14, 18.

52. For Hodeir's later reception, see Lee B. Brown, "The Theory of Jazz Music: 'It Don't Mean a Thing . . . ,'" *Journal of Aesthetics and Art Criticism* 49, no. 2 (1991): 115–27; Krin Gabbard, "Introduction: The Jazz Canon and its Consequences," in *Jazz among the Discourses*, ed. Gabbard (Durham, NC: Duke University Press, 1995), 1–28; Robert Walser, "Deep Jazz: Notes on Interiority, Race, and Criticism," in *Inventing the Psychological: Toward a Cultural History of Emotional Life in America*, ed. Joel Pfister and Nancy Schnog (New Haven, CT: Yale University Press, 1997), 280–85.

53. Tournès, *New Orleans sur Seine*, 255.

54. Wendell Otey, "Hodeir," 110.

55. André Hodeir, "Why Did Duke Ellington 'Remake' His Masterpiece?," in *Toward Jazz*, trans. Noël Burch (London: Jazz Book Club, by arrangement with Grove Press, 1965), 24–32. The suspicion here noted lingers throughout Hodeir's discussion of Ellington in *Hommes et problèmes*; in his last major work on jazz, Hodeir would articulate this idea clearly through the words of a fictional character (and alter ego). See Hodeir, *The Worlds of Jazz*, trans. Noël Burch (New York: Grove Press, 1972), 223.

56. "Il faut agrandir le jazz pour ne pas en sortir." Hodeir, *Hommes et problèmes*, 6.

57. Peck, "L'Oeuvre orchestrale," 8; Anon., "Je n'appartiens pas," 14.

58. Anon., "Je n'appartiens pas," 14.

59. André Clergeat, "André Hodeir aux U.S.A.," *Jazz Hot* 118 (1957): 16. Otey, "Hodeir," 107–8.

60. For Otey all this was "in many ways a daring attack on the boundaries of jazz." Otey, "Hodeir," 107–8; Anon., "Je n'appartiens pas," 15.

61. Reissued on Hodeir, *The Vogue Sessions*.

62. Particularly afflicted are "Saint-Tropez," "Criss Cross" and "Esquisse 1."

63. Reissued with the same title (Universal, 2001).

64. Compare these textures with the opening of "Farben," from Schoenberg's Five Orchestral Pieces (1909). These influences can be heard as well in "Tension-détente" (0:21 on).

65. An older tradition is alluded to in "Bicinium," a piece named after the pedagogical two-part studies of the Renaissance, in which Hodeir gives two (ever-changing) instruments their say in a complex, metrically shifting contrapuntal dialogue, this then fragmented into more Webernian pointillism as Jean Algedon's Lee Konitz–style alto solo unfolds.

66. This developing and successful approach was briefly blown off course by Hodeir's discovery of Thelonious Monk, especially the pianist's solo of fragments on "Bags' Groove," which, recorded with Miles Davis in 1954 but only reaching France late in 1956, caused great excitement among the Parisian jazz élite: see André Hodeir, Nat Peck and Michel Fano, "Miles, Monk : sur deux grandes oeuvres du jazz d'aujourd'hui," *Jazz Hot* 116 (1956): 13–15, 26, 37. (A phrase in Monk's solo here seems to have directly inspired Hodeir's piece "On a Riff.") Halfway through preparing a sextet recording that would be made in winter 1956 under the nominal leadership of the returning Kenny Clarke, Hodeir was moved to abandon what he described as that "lyric," developmental style for an "abstract" approach—one in which music would not develop organically, but arrive in a series of "sounding figures which are mobile in space," this "an orchestral projection of what Monk does at the piano." But the "figures in space"—elements of "Bemsha Swing"'s theme, for instance, are chopped up, augmented, and, thinly orchestrated, are left to float unsupported—are rarely effective; where still in use, the "lyrical" style has for now degenerated into endless contrapuntal note-spinning that is extremely fatiguing to listen to, if not to compose (Hodeir admitted that he could easily have written 20-minute passages of this music). Clergeat, "André Hodeir aux U.S.A.," 17. For fatiguing counterpoint, see "Jeru" and "When Lights Are Low" on the resultant album, *Kenny Clarke's Sextet Plays André Hodeir* (Philips).

67. Clergeat, "André Hodeir aux U.S.A.," 15; Otey, "Hodeir," 106-7. The Americans—who include the relocated Belgian, Bobby Jaspar—handle the music with a much lighter touch than the original performers, and the repertoire is slightly expanded, notably by the eleven-minute "The Alphabet," written in New York as a feature for Annie Ross's scat vocal. The album was released by Savoy as *American Jazzmen Play André Hodeir's Essais*.

68. Clergeat, "André Hodeir aux U.S.A.," 16.

69. Hodeir, "Je n'appartiens pas," 16. Fano's film was *Chutes de pierres, danger de mort*, and Kyrou's, *Le Palais idéal*, was a documentary on Ferdinand Cheval's bricolage monument. Hodeir talks about large and small forms in Bernard Courouble, "Hodeir parse [*sic*]", *Jazz* (Marseille) 11 (1959): 12–13. Hodeir provides an analysis of three of the pieces from this period—"Le Désert," "Blues," the *Jazz cantata*—in his article "Trois Analyses," *Les Cahiers du jazz* 7 (1962): 35–94.

70. See M. J. Grant, *Serial Music, Serial Aesthetics: Compositional Theory in Post-War Europe* (Cambridge. Cambridge University Press, 2000).

71. Clergeat, "André Hodeir aux U.S.A.," 16. Writing in the 1990s—though hav-

ing been musically inactive since the 1970s and having remained faithful to his ideas of the late 1950s—Hodeir attempted a definition of such simulated improvisation as it appeared in his mature composition. It was, he wrote, "the reproduction, in written form, of an imaginary solo as one would wish it could have been played at the precise point in the work where the composer put it." André Hodeir, "Improvisation Simulation: Its Origins, Its Function in a Work of Jazz (Presentation)," in *The André Hodeir Jazz Reader*, ed. Pautrot, 265–66.

72. Hodeir, "Improvisation Simulation," 265–66. The showpiece for multitracked flute, "Flautando," was written for Roland Guiot in this way.

73. Jacques B. Hess, "Hodeir : la grande forme," *Jazz magazine* 197 (1972): 25.

74. (Legrand would die on the same day as Hodeir, November 1, 2011.) The *Jazz cantata*, a ten-minute work that mixes Stan Kenton anxiety, Gil Evans lushness and period vocalese, represented an advance to Hodeir, who said a couple of years later that he had "never been so close to attaining . . . this oneiric poetic, this sort of musical delirium and this tumultuous, continuous lyricism that I found in Charlie Parker." Anon., "Je n'appartiens pas," 16.

75. Jef Gilson, Sim Copans et al., "La Critique parisienne répond à dix questions : à propos de *Jazz et Jazz*," *Jazz hot* 163 (1961):18.

76. Hodeir, "Improvisation Simulation," 256.

77. André Hodeir, "Foreword," in *Toward Jazz*, trans. Noël Burch (London: Jazz Book Club, by arrangement with Grove Press, 1965), 7.

78. Pierre Boulez, "Aléa," in *Stocktakings from an Apprenticeship*, ed. Paule Thévenin, trans. Stephen Walsh (Oxford: Oxford University Press, 1991), 26–38; Boulez, "Sonate, que me veux-tu?," in *Orientations: Collected Writings*, ed. Jean-Jacques Nattiez, trans. Martin Cooper (London: Faber, 1986), 143–54; George E. Lewis, "Improvised Music after 1950: Afrological and Eurological Perspectives," *Black Music Research Journal* 16, no. 1 (1996): 91–122.

79. Karlheinz Stockhausen, *Towards a Cosmic Music: Texts by Karlheinz Stockhausen*, ed. Tim Nevill (Element Books, 1989), 39.

80. Pierre Boulez, "Possibly . . . ," in *Stocktakings*, 113. Other examples of this rhetoric abound; see Jacques Attali, *Noise: A Political Economy of Music*, trans. Brian Massumi (Manchester: Manchester University Press, 1985), 113.

81. André Hodeir, *La Musique depuis Debussy* (Paris: Presses Universitaires de France, 1961).

82. Malson, "André Hodeir ou la recherche," 43, 32, 33. Nietzsche is also alluded to in André Hodeir, "Comment peut-on écrire du Jazz?," *Jazz hot* 203 (1964): 32.

83. Malson, "Jazz d'aujourd'hui," 30.

84. Hodeir took pains to extricate himself from Merceron's attentions. Pierre Fargeton, personal communication with the author, May 2013.

85. Gérald Merceron, "Hodeir aux deux visages," *Jazz hot* 213 (1965): 24, 25.

86. A digest of such philosophical racism is Emmanuel Chukwudi Eze, ed., *Race and the Enlightenment: A Reader* (London: Blackwell, 1997).

87. Merceron, "Hodeir aux deux visages," 18. Apparently unaware of Merceron's background, the scholar-musician Stephen Lehman has criticized the Haitian's writing in these terms. Stephen Lehman, "I Love You with an Asterisk: African-American Experimental Music and the French Jazz Press, 1970–1980," *Critical Studies in Impro-*

visation / *Etudes critiques en improvisation* 1, no. 2 (2005): 38–53, http://www.criticalim prov.com/article/view/18.

88. Patrice Caratini, "Joyce par Hodeir par Caratini," *Jazz magazine* 413 (1992): 63.

89. The Nietzsche was Hodeir's own, but the British composer Constant Lambert had seen jazz's future in similar terms as early as 1934. Constant Lambert, *Music Ho! A Study of Music in Decline* (New York: Charles Scribner's Sons, 1934), 222.

90. This development was, of course, highly contested: see Brian Rigby, *Popular Culture in Modern France: A Study of Cultural Discourse* (London: Routledge, 1991).

91. Though one brief article assessed the contribution of jazz towards the rejuvenation of light music. Marc Pincherle, "Où va le jazz ? ," *Arts*, October 31, 1947, 8.

92. Claude Chamfray, "La Semaine du jazz," *Arts*, June 11, 1948, 7.

93. Boris Vian, "La Vie difficile du musicien du jazz," *Arts*, June 9, 1954, 3.

94. The first figure is derived from Lahitte, "Jazz News," 4; the second from Stanley Dance, "Lightly and Politely: Un Journaliste Fatigué qui Viellit Mal?," *Jazz Journal* 11, no. 9 (1958): 7.

95. Hodeir's fixation on aging suggests he had not escaped this waning of passion.

96. Hodeir, *Jazz: Its Evolution and Essence*, 13; Vian, "La Vie difficile," 3; Lucien Malson, "Le Jazz ne doit plus rester une maladie de l'adolescence," *Arts*, July 6, 1960, 13; Lucien Malson, "Saxo et blousons noirs," *Arts*, September 7, 1960, 6.

97. Jacques B. Hess, "En 4 ans le jazz moderne a conquis les intellectuels," *Arts*, April 23, 1958, 9.

98. Hodeir, *"Foreword,"*, 8.

99. Hodeir, *"Foreword,"* 7.

100. Ténot's contribution, headed "Yes, because *le noir* plays with all his body," demonstrated the difficulty some progressive critics had in getting away from old racialized models; an anti-essentialist Hess used Lester Young and Miles Davis to coolly subvert primitivist stereotypes and insist that musical skills were cultivated, not inborn. Frank Ténot and Jacques B. Hess, "Le Jazz est-il toujours un art nègre ? ," *Arts*, August 4, 1954, 5.

101. In particular, see Hodeir, Peck and Fano, "Miles, Monk."

102. André Hodeir, "Monk or the Misunderstanding," in *The Thelonious Monk Reader*, ed. Rob Van der Bliek (New York: Oxford University Press, 2001), 129, 125.

103. Robin D. G. Kelley locates the first signs of a critical backlash against Monk the supposed automaton in late 1959. Robin D. G. Kelley, *Thelonious Monk: The Life and Times of an American Original* (New York: Free Press, 2009), 283.

104. Raymond Mouly et al., "Monk Newport Cannonball Mahalia," *Jazz magazine* 71 (1961): 25.

105. Delorme in J.-J. Gaspard et al., "En butte à Monk," *Jazz hot* 197 (1964): 22.

106. Claude Lenissois, "Monk toujours," *Jazz hot* 208 (1965): 3, 5.

107. Philippe Kœchlin, "New thing et Messengers," *Jazz hot* 208 (1965): 3, 5; Philippe Constantin, "Courrier des lecteurs," *Jazz hot* 241 (1968): 5.

108. Lenissois, "Monk toujours," 5.

109. Michel Claude Jalard, "Thelonious Monk à l'heure du simulacra," *Jazz magazine* 105 (1964): 28.

110. Jalard, "Thelonious Monk à l'heure du simulacra," 28–29.

111. Jalard, "Thelonious Monk à l'heure du simulacra," 29.

112. Jalard, "Thelonious Monk à l'heure du simulacra," 29.

113. Jalard, "Thelonious Monk à l'heure du simulacra," 29.

114. Jalard, "Thelonious Monk à l'heure du simulacra," 29. Some of the 1964 performances are captured on Thelonious Monk, *Live in Paris Vol. 1* and *Vol. 2* (Explore, 2007).

115. Pierre Klossowski, "A Propos du simulacre dans la communication de Georges Bataille," *Critique* 195/196 (1963): 742–50. Deleuze's simulacrum is much more positively conceived: see Gilles Deleuze, "The Simulacrum and Ancient Philosophy," in *The Logic of Sense*, ed. Constantin V. Boundas, trans. Mark Lester and Charles Stivale (London: Athlone Press, 1990), 253–79.

116. Jean Baudrillard, "The Precession of Simulacra," in *Simulations*, trans. Paul Foss et al. (Cambridge, MA: Semiotext[e], 1983), 4.

117. In circular fashion, the simulacrum displaces reality by a hyperbolic version of itself. Jean Baudrillard, "The Implosion of Meaning in the Media," in *Simulacra and Simulation*, trans. Sheila Faria Glaser (Ann Arbor: University of Michigan Press, 1994), 81.

118. Baudrillard, "The Precession of Simulacra," 5.

119. Baudrillard, "The Precession of Simulacra," 6.

120. Boris Vian, "Nice, Jazz Capital of the World: Hearing Double," in *Round About Close to Midnight*, 35–36, 52–53. Hodeir used the same phonographic image to make the same point about Joe Williams in a piece originally published in *Jazz hot* in 1957 and reprinted as "Basie's Way," in *Toward Jazz*, trans. Noël Burch (London: Jazz Book Club, by arrangement with Grove Press, 1965), 115.

121. Raymond Horricks, "Thelonious Monk: Two Sides of an Enigmatic Musician," *Jazz Monthly* 2 (1956): 8.

122. Charles Timbrell, *French Pianism: An Historical Perspective* (White Plains, NY: Pro/Am Music Resources, 1992), 16.

123. Konrad Wolff, *The Teaching of Artur Schnabel: A Guide to Interpretation* (London: Faber and Faber, 1972), 25, 20.

124. Bruno Monsaingeon, *Sviatoslav Richter: Notebooks and Conversations*, trans. Stewart Spencer (London: Faber and Faber, 2001), 142, 153, 143, 153. These 20th century masters of 19th century music recall E.T.A. Hoffman's much reprinted 1813 injunction against interpretation, cited in an insightful article that covers some of this ground: Jairo Moreno, "Body 'n' Soul?: Voice and Movement in Keith Jarrett's Pianism," *The Musical Quarterly* 83, no. 1 (1999): 85. See Bruce Ellis Benson, *The Improvisation of Musical Dialogue* (Cambridge: Cambridge University Press, 2003), for further examples and discussion of the *Werktreue*.

125. Foucault and Derrida, French intellectual celebrities then in the making, had already begun to critique this anciently rooted, Western "logocentrism": see Moreno, "Body 'n' Soul?"

126. I am grateful to Anthony Pryer for this coining.

127. Les Tomkins, "Thelonious Speaking," *Crescendo* (May 1965): 11.

128. François Postif, "'Round 'bout Sphere," *Jazz hot* 186 (1963): 25.

129. Jalard, "Thelonious Monk," 29. Whitney Balliett made the same observation

about Monk's valedictory 1975 Newport appearance. See Benjamin Givan, "Thelonious Monk's Pianism," *Journal of Musicology* 26, no. 3 (2009): 412.

130. Monk cited in Postif, "'Round 'bout Sphere," 39.

131. Panassié cited this statement as an example of modernist stupidity: Panassié, *La Bataille du Jazz*, 111.

132. Perhaps even the kind of entertainer described by Philip Larkin in 1965, "a funny-hat man to whom it would be idle to ascribe profundity." Larkin, "The Parker Legend," in *All What Jazz: A Record Diary* (London: Faber and Faber, 1985), 136. Raymond Horricks dismissed Monk's first Paris performance as "[a]n act in the good old vaudeville tradition." Horricks, "Thelonious Monk," 8.

133. Untraced Théâtre de la Mutualité concert film fragment, http://uk.youtube.com/watch?v=Rf6ksjTplwo. Thanks to Chris Sheridan for his assistance of my unsuccessful efforts to locate full versions of this and other unissued TV recordings from Monk's 1966 European tour. For further details of these, see Chris Sheridan, *Brilliant Corners: A Bio-Discography of Thelonious Monk* (Westport, CT: Greenwood Press, 2001).

134. Philippe Nahman and Pierre Lattes, "Monk à Paris," *Jazz hot* 220 (1966): 5.

135. On the studio recording of Lulu, Butch Warren played bass. Monk had made a previous attempt to record the song during a 1956 Columbia session, for some reason abandoning the effort on that occasion.

136. If the following analyses seem to overlook the performance contributions of Monk's band members, see the extended version of this investigation: Tom Perchard, "Thelonious Monk Meets the French Critics: Art and Entertainment, Improvisation, and Its Simulacrum," *Jazz Perspectives* 5, no. 1 (2011): 61–94. The four recordings are taken from performances in Paris, March 20, 1966, found on Thelonious Monk, *The Paris Concert* (Charly, 2003); Oslo, April 15, 1966, found on the DVD Thelonious Monk, *Live in '66* (Jazz Icons, 2006); Copenhagen, April 17, 1966, also found on *Live in '66*; and Manchester, April 29, 1966, found on Thelonious Monk, S/T (Tempo di Jazz, 1991). The transcriptions are enharmonically spelled with as much consistency as is practical.

137. Paul Berliner, *Thinking in Jazz: The Infinite Art of Improvisation* (Chicago: University of Chicago Press, 1994), 1.

138. Monk can be heard forming these pathways (on another song) in a home practice tape released as *The Transformer* (Explore, 2007). The terms "path" and "pathway" are suggested by David Sudnow's *Ways of the Hand: A Rewritten Account* (Cambridge, MA: MIT Press, 2001), passim.

139. The approximation is usually one of accent and weight; sometimes (not shown in my examples here), it's also one of pitch. In his excellent article on Monk's piano playing, Benjamin Givan similarly remarks that the cross-hand technique of these passages irregularizes the force and articulation of the upper register notes. Givan, "Thelonious Monk's Pianism," 438.

140. Gunther Schuller noted in the late 1950s that Monk incorporated such "accidents" of fingering into his style. See Givan, "Thelonious Monk's Pianism," 421.

141. A similar attitude can be seen in examples below, in which Monk's more-or-less repetitive left-hand chord voicings are varied not by different conception—or even, in a sense, by different execution—but by hand weighting that emphasizes some notes over others as the particular instance of their playing seems to demand.

Alexander Hawkins refers to Monk's technique thus facilitating "two levels of intentionality" (personal communication, November 2009).

142. For transcribed examples see Perchard, "Thelonious Monk," 84.

143. Compare the 1957 recording of "Rhythm-A-Ning" on *Art Blakey's Jazz Messengers with Thelonious Monk* (Atlantic, 1999) with versions recorded at the Five Spot in the autumn of 1958 (*Live in New York, Vol. 1*, Explore, 2007), in Paris, 1964 (*Live in Paris Vol. 2*, Explore, 2007) and Manchester, 1966 (*Thelonious Monk*, Tempo di Jazz, 1991); taken in order, these and other recordings of this song show these quasi-textual elements becoming gradually more numerous and often more "fixed."

144. Thelonious Monk, *Solo Monk* (Columbia, 2003).

145. See Kelley, *Thelonious Monk*, 27, 54.

146. Anon., "Thelonious Monk: Thelonious; Suburban Eyes," in *The Thelonious Monk Reader*, ed. Van der Bliek, 31.

147. As on "Bluehawk."

148. For instance, in his 1963 *Jazz Gehört und Gesehen* performance. See Kelley, *Thelonious Monk*, 333.

149. Kelley, *Thelonious Monk*, 103.

150. Thelonious Monk, *It's Monk's Time* (Columbia, 1964).

151. These characteristics can be found in Waller's 1935 recording of "Lulu's Back in Town," and in James P. Johnson's piano solo "Toddlin'" (recorded in August 1923), parts of which bear striking resemblance to the later Warren and Dubin piece.

152. Monk cited by Delorme in Gaspard et al., "En butte à Monk," 22. Paul S. Machlin, *Stride: The Music of Fats Waller* (London: Macmillan Press, 1985), 13.

153. See Kelley, *Thelonious Monk*, 135, 253, 261.

154. James A. Snead, "Repetition as a Figure of Black Culture," in *Black Literature and Black Literary Theory*, ed. Henry Louis Gates Jr. (New York and London: Routledge, 1984), 59–79. (For the sake of argument I am glossing over the problems inherent in Snead's totalizing polemic.) I don't argue that "text" and "repetition" define *everything* (of the comparatively little) that Monk recorded after 1965–66; but the bathetic *Monk's Blues* (1968), his last Columbia album, has Monk refusing to stray from the melody for long (and, in "Monk's Point," making use of repetition to an almost obsessive extent), while the pianist's final sessions, made in London in 1971, have an exhausted Monk reprising the solo stride routine he had first put on record in 1965.

155. See Anon, "Le Jazz Group de Paris à Donaueschingen," *Jazz Hot* 121 (1957): 24; J. Gerloff, "Beim NDR: André Hodeir," *Jazz Podium* 8, no. 12 (1959): 278; Anon., "Le Jazz Groupe à Hambourg," *Jazz Hot* 150 (1960): 26. The Groupe gave a swan song fifteenth-anniversary concert broadcast at the ORTF in 1969.

156. Tournès, *New Orleans sur Seine*, 274.

157. This music was eventually recorded by Solal's big band in 1984. Anon., "'Première' du groupe Hodeir-Solal," *Jazz hot* 186 (1963): 15; Jean Tronchot and Claude Lenissois, "Bravo, Hodeir ! ," *Jazz hot* 198 (1964): 16; Michel Delorme, "Lloyd, Hodeir et le free," *Jazz hot* 226 (1966): 28–29.

158. Hess, "Hodeir," 24.

159. See Clergeat, "André Hodeir aux U.S.A.," 16; Hess, "Hodeir," 24; André Hodeir, "To Hear All About 'Anna Livia,'" *International Jazz Archives Journal* 1, no. 3 (1995): 28.

160. Hodeir, "To Hear," 29–30; Hess, "Hodeir," 24.

161. Hess, "Hodeir," 25.

162. At 4:42 in the recording on *Martial Solal et son orchestre jouent André Hodeir* (Carlyne Music, 1984).

163. The titles given here follow those given on the Caratini recording: in the score, sections are only numbered.

164. Hodeir discusses aspects of this section in "To Hear," 30–32. The recording is André Hodeir, direction musicale Patrice Caratini, *Anna Livia Plurabelle* (Label Bleu, 1994). The score is André Hodeir, *Anna Livia Plurabelle* (MJQ Music, 1967)

165. Alain Gerber, "*Anna Livia Plurabelle*; 'Jazz Cantata' d'André Hodeir," *Jazz magazine* 191 (1971): 6; Gérald Merceron, "Sur une oeuvre de André Hodeir. Anna Livia Plurabelle : plaidoyer pour une cause insolite," *Jazz hot* 266 (1970): 26, 27.

166. Many of Hodeir's objections to free jazz—and its political intent and interpretation—are contained in Lucien Malson, "Neuf entretiens sur le jazz neuf," *Les Cahiers du jazz* 16/17 (1968): 1–60.

167. Philippe Kœchlin, "Hodeir 66," *Jazz hot* 225 (1966): 24.

168. Alain Gerber listed the authors pastiched: "Michel Butor, Alain Robbe-Grillet, Michel Foucault, Samuel Beckett, James Joyce, Jorge Luis Borges, Marcel Proust, André Pieyre de Mandiargues, and, without doubt, many others I haven't been able to recognise'" Gerber, "André Hodeir et ses mondes du jazz," *Jazz magazine* 186 (1971): 30–33, 47–50, 32. The book more than deserved the *Jazz hot* reviewer's alternate title, "Antimemoirs of a Paranoid Musician." Gérard Noel, "Des Démons d'Hodeir . . . au monde du jazz," *Jazz hot* 272 (1971): 14–15.

169. Gilson, Copans et al., "La Critique parisienne," 16.

170. Pierre Fargeton, "'Et je me suis aperçu que j'étais seul !.' Un entretien avec André Hodeir," *Les Cahiers du jazz* 1 (nouvelle série, 2004): 135.

171. Fargeton, "'Et je me suis aperçu,'" 132.

172. See Pierre Bourdieu, *Photography: A Middle-Brow Art*, trans. Shaun Whiteside (Palo Alto, CA: Stanford University Press, 1990), 95–97. This judgment has also been noted by Eric Drott, among others.

Chapter Four

1. Hodeir, *Jazz: Its Evolution and Essence*, 118.

2. The saxophonists who had, in the latter 1940s, made up Woody Herman's "Four Brothers" were tenors Stan Getz, Herbie Steward, Zoot Sims and the baritone Serge Chaloff. On this style in France, see Henri Olier, "Panorama des ténors modernes en France," *Jazz hot* 93 (1954): 38.

3. See, for example, his late playing on Chet Baker, *The Italian Sessions* (Bluebird, 1990).

4. Peter N. Stearns, *American Cool: Constructing a Twentieth-Century Emotional Style* (New York: New York University Press, 1994).

5. Scott Saul, *Freedom Is, Freedom Ain't: Jazz and the Making of the Sixties* (Cambridge, MA: Harvard University Press, 2005): 29–31, 48, 65. These arguments were selective: the new civil rights protesters in no way satisfied this generational description.

6. Saul, *Freedom Is, Freedom Ain't*, 52, 53, 54.

7. Saul, *Freedom Is, Freedom Ain't*, 51–53. On the mid-century successes and failures of existentialism and its stars in the United States, see George Cotkin, *Existential America* (Baltimore: Johns Hopkins University Press, 2003).

8. Richard Ivan Jobs, *Riding the New Wave: Youth and the Rejuvenation of France after the Second World War* (Palo Alto, CA: Stanford University Press, 2007): 142, 147. In her 1958 generational portrait *La Nouvelle vague*, Françoise Giroud presented as remarkable that, in contrast to surveys from earlier eras, only 6 percent of the young people questioned would be willing to die for their country; 42 percent could imagine no cause for which they would imperil themselves. Françoise Giroud, *La Nouvelle vague* (Paris: Gallimard, 1958), 14–15.

9. Tournès counts thirty-one jazz-soundtracked French feature films between 1957 and 1960, and there are likely more. Tournès, *New Orleans sur Seine*, 327.

10. See Alan Stanbridge, "From the Margins to the Mainstream: Jazz, Social Relations, and Discourses of Value," *Critical Studies in Improvisation / Etudes critiques en improvisation* 4, no. 1 (2008): 1–18, http://www.criticalimprov.com/article/view/361.

11. The Prix Louis Delluc was awarded for best film of 1957, the year of *Ascenseur*'s production, but the film was released in France in January 1958. It appeared across Europe over the next couple of years (in the United Kingdom entitled *Lift to the Scaffold*) and in the United States in summer 1961 (as *Elevator to the Gallows* or *Frantic*).

12. Raymond Borde, "*Ascenseur pour l'échafaud*, de Louis Malle," *Les Temps modernes*, April-May 1958, 1908, 1909, 1010.

13. For other reviews see Pierre Billard, Louis Malle *: le rebelle solitaire* (Paris: Plon, 2003), 167-68.

14. Borde, "*Ascenseur*," 1909–10.

15. Borde, "*Ascenseur*," 1910.

16. Hodeir, *Jazz: Its Evolution and Essence*, 118.

17. Philip French with Louis Malle, *Malle on Malle* (London: Faber and Faber, 1993), 1.

18. Hugo Frey, *Louis Malle* (Manchester: Manchester University Press, 2004), 6–7.

19. Cited in Frey, *Louis Malle*, 76.

20. Frey, *Louis Malle*, 78. See also Hugo Frey, "Louis Malle and the 1950s: Ambiguities, Friendships and Legacies," *South Central Review* 23, no. 2 (2006): 34.

21. Frey, "Louis Malle and the 1950s," 25–26. Giroud's *La Nouvelle vague* includes the extended testimonies of numerous young people: one, a self-proclaimed fascist, rambles on in exactly these terms. Giroud, *La Nouvelle vague*, 44–47.

22. French, *Louis Malle*, 32; Frey, *Louis Malle*, 12–14.

23. Frey, "Louis Malle and the 1950s," 28.

24. Jim Hillier, ed., *Cahiers du Cinéma: Volume 1, The 1950s* (London: Routledge & Kegan Paul, 1985), 251–52.

25. Hillier, *Cahiers*, 214.

26. Frey, *Louis Malle*, 3.

27. Hillier, *Cahiers*, 74. That New Wave leftism must not be overstated: Hugo Frey writes of "François Truffaut's early links to Lucien Rebatet" and "Claude Chabrol's collaboration with the reactionary scriptwriter, Paul Gégauff." Frey, "Louis Malle and the 1950s," 30.

28. French, *Louis Malle*, 31–32.

29. Malle told Philip French that "there was a rebellion of the technicians at the lab after they had seen the dailies. They went to the producer and said, 'You must not let Malle and [director of photography] Decaë destroy Jeanne Moreau.' They were horrified." French, *Louis Malle*, 12.

30. Louis Malle, "Le Problème de la musique de film," *Jazz hot* 115 (1960): 15.

31. See Ken Vail, *Miles' Diary: The Life of Miles Davis 1947–1961* (London: Sanctuary Publishing, 1996).

32. John Szwed, *So What: The Life of Miles Davis* (London: Arrow, 2003), 152. A bootleg recording of the quintet's concert in Amsterdam shows Davis in fluid form, the rhythm section performing adequately (though in his accompanying the young Urtreger is submissively overresponsive to the Americans' suggestions), Wilen full of sound but somewhat stilted in phrasing.

33. French, *Louis Malle*, 18–19.

34. Andrea Pejrolo, "The Origins of Modal Jazz in the Music of Miles Davis: A Complete Transcription and Linear/Harmonic Analysis of *Ascenseur pour l'échafaud (Lift to the Scaffold)*—1957" (PhD dissertation, New York University, 2001), 219.

35. Billard, *Louis Malle*, 165; Szwed, *So What*, 151.

36. Miles Davis and Quincy Troupe, *Miles: The Autobiography* (London: Picador, 1989), 207.

37. Romano's account is cited in Szwed, *So What*, 153.

38. Malle is cited in French, *Louis Malle*, 19. For an example of such confusion, see Colin Nettlebeck, *Dancing with De Beauvoir: Jazz and the French (Melbourne: Melbourne University Press, 2005)*, 168. Urtreger's words come from an interview included on a DVD release of the film, titled here *Lift to the Scaffold* (Optimum World, 2007).

39. Exact times differ, but the principle is confirmed by Urtreger and Michelot in Pejrolo, "The Origins," 221, 236. The press conference, cocktails and lamps are only found in Barney Wilen's account of the evening, given very shortly after the recording session to the student newsletter *Marseille-Université*, and republished as "Ascenseur pour l'échafaud," *Jazz* (Marseille) 25 (1958): 4.

40. As reported by Urtreger in the Optimum World DVD interview.

41. Pejrolo, "The Origins," 223.

42. Szwed, *So What*, 153; Jack Chambers, *Milestones: The Music and Times of Miles Davis* (New York: Da Capo Press, 1998), 266.

43. This was recounted by Hodeir on the television program *A la recherche du jazz*, screened on April 24, 1956 (and held by the INA). The film itself, which I have not been able to trace, is variously listed as *Neiges* and *La Neige*.

44. Szwed, *So What*, 154–55.

45. Michelot cited in Szwed, *So What*, 155.

46. Malle, "Le Problème," 14, 15.

47. Royal S. Brown, *Overtones and Undertones: Reading Film Music* (Berkeley: University of California Press, 1994), 186; French, *Louis Malle*, 19.

48. " Sur l'autoroute" is based on "Sweet Georgia Brown," though Davis asked René Urtreger not to play on this piece so it would be less identifiable as the standard from which it had evolved (Pejrolo, "The Origins," 226). In the motel music Davis's

group plays a fast blues, in his solo the trumpeter deemphasizing the chord changes in favor of a continually mixolydian line (see Pejrolo, "The Origins," 101).

49. Szwed, *So What*, 154. Later, as Louis and Véronique escape Paris in the stolen car, the soundtrack dips ironically as the girl turns the radio down.

50. Pejrolo identifies these as Phrygian on F in "L'Assassinat de Carala" and "Julien dans l'ascenseur"; "Visite du vigile" has several modal areas: D Phrygian, Eb Lydian, D Locrian, D Locrian/Ionian. Pejrolo, "The Origins," 189, 192.

51. Szwed, *So What*, 151. In 1957 Davis had begun a relationship with Beverly Bentley—to whom, indeed, the trumpeter had made his comment on Moreau's arhythmic walk—and she had appeared in Kazan's *A Face in the Crowd* (1957).

52. See Annette Davison, *Alex North's A Streetcar Named Desire: A Film Score Guide* (Lanham, MD: Scarecrow Press, 2009).

53. Pejrolo, "The Origins," 130–31, 167.

54. Pejrolo, "The Origins," 81.

55. Pejrolo, "The Origins," 220, 120.

56. Eric Rohmer, "Premier accessit : *Ascenseur pour l'échafaud*," *Cahiers du cinéma* 80 (1958): 59–60.

57. Nathan Southern with Jacques Weissgerber, *The Films of Louis Malle: A Critical Analysis* (Jefferson, NC, and London: McFarland, 2006), 37.

58. On the one occasion this is not the case, it is hidden in an ensemble, shouting public domain blues figures with Wilen during the motel party.

59. Full takes available on the soundtrack rerelease (Fontana, 1988) show that Davis did make a very small amount of use of the mute on some of the Florence music, but this has been removed from the final cut, the open horn / voice correspondence further strengthened in postproduction. Note that the titling and sequencing of tracks on this "full" (but actually incomplete) reissue is a mess; my discussion above refers to music as heard in the film itself rather than on this release.

60. Nettlebeck, *Dancing*, 170. Likewise Krin Gabbard suggests that "the music for *Lift to the Scaffold* is best understood as part of a movie and not as stand-alone music." Krin Gabbard, "Miles from Home: Miles Davis and the Movies," *The Source / Jazz Research Journal* 1, no. 1 (2004): 29.

61. André Bazin, "The Evolution of the Language of Cinema," in *What Is Cinema*, ed. and trans. Hugh Gray (Berkeley: University of California Press, 2004), 33–34.

62. See Bazin, "The Evolution of the Language of Cinema," 24.

63. Bazin, "The Evolution of the Language of Cinema," 25, 34–36.

64. Malle, "Le Problème," 15.

65. André Bazin, "The Ontology of the Photographic Image," in *What Is Cinema*, 10.

66. Bazin, "The Ontology," 14.

67. Frey, *Louis Malle*, 56 (translation slightly altered).

68. Malle, "Le Problème," 14.

69. This film is included in another DVD release of the film, this time under the name *Elevator to the Gallows* (Criterion, 2006).

70. Boris Vian, liner notes to Miles Davis: *Ascenseur pour l'échafaud* (Fontana, 1988). Vian's mention of the painter's "touch" is almost certainly a reference to a celebrated

1945 essay on Cézanne by Vian's friend Merleau-Ponty. See Maurice Merleau-Ponty, ed. Thomas Baldwin, trans. Hubert L. Dreyfus and Patricia Allen Dreyfus, "Cézanne's Doubt," in *Maurice Merleau-Ponty: Basic Writings* (London: Routledge, 2004), 272–90.

71. Cited in Pejrolo, "The Origins," 225.

72. Mary Caulfield, "Miles Davis, *Ascenseur pour L'Echafaud,*" *Mojo blog*, March 3, 2011, http://www.mojo4music.com/blog/2011/03/miles_davis_1.html (minor typographical corrections have been made here).

73. Anon, "De A à W," *Positif* 28 (1958), 56.

74. Peter Watrous tells the same story in the *New York Times* in 1989, as does the paper's Alix Browne nearly twenty years later (by which time *Ascenseur* has become "a compulsory course in cool"); in a 2007 issue of the *Observer* the obligatory tropes are deployed by Nick James in a list of the "Fifty Greatest Film Soundtracks" (*Ascenseur* was no. 10); in the *Guardian* in 2008 David Thompson, brimming with irony, nevertheless dabbles with the same signifiers as he compiles a list of great jazz films. Peter Watrous, "Things Happened when Jazz Got on Screen," *New York Times*, April 23, 1989, http://www.nytimes.com/1989/04/23/movies/recordings-things-happened-when-jazz-got-on-screen.html?src=pm; Alix Browne, "Required Viewing: *Elevator to the Gallows,*" *New York Times*, July 9, 2008, http://tmagazine.blogs.nytimes.com/2008/07/09/required-viewing-elevator-to-the-gallows/?scp=1&sq=Required%20Viewing%20|%20%E2%80%98Elevator%20to%20the%20Gallows%E2%80%99%20Design%20By%20ALIX%20BROWNE&st=cse; David Thompson, "Shooting from the Hip," *Guardian*, November 7, 2008, http://www.guardian.co.uk/film/2008/nov/07/jazz-film; Nick James et al., "The 50 Greatest Film Soundtracks," *Observer*, March 18, 2007, http://www.guardian.co.uk/music/2007/mar/18/features.musicmonthly14. For a "jazz history" telling, see Nettlebeck, *Dancing*, op cit.

75. Delaunay, *De la vie*, 71.

76. All of this "presence" was dependent on reproduction technology, as Simon Frith has pointed out: "[T]he microphone had the same function as the close-up in film history—it made stars knowable, by shifting the conventions of personality, making singers sound sexy in new ways, giving men a new prominence in big bands, and moving the focus from the song to the singer." Simon Frith, "Art versus Technology: the Strange Case of Popular Music," *Media, Culture and Society* 8 (1986): 270.

77. Southern, *The Films of Louis Malle*, 40–41, 39.

78. Frey notes that this ambivalence, on view throughout his oeuvre, functioned as a form of control: "Malle's technique of implicitly saying everything (condemning and forgiving: presenting two mutually exclusive political these simultaneously in the same film) is a position of great power and authority." Frey, *Louis Malle*, 101.

79. Marc Vernet, "The Look at the Camera," *Cinema Journal* 28, no. 2 (1989): 48–63.

80. See Jean-Louis Baudry, "Ideological Effects of the Basic Cinematic Apparatus," in *Narrative, Apparatus, Ideology: A Film Reader*, ed. Philip Rosen (New York: Columbia University Press, 1986), 286–98; and, in the same volume, both Baudry's "The Apparatus: Metapsychological Approaches to the Impression of Reality in the Cinema," 299–318, and Jean-Louis Comolli, "Technique and Ideology: Camera, Perspective, Depth of Field [Parts 3 and 4]," 421–43.

81. The key theoretical equipment in these discussions was the psychoanalytic theory of Jacques Lacan.

82. Mulvey structures her argument around Lacan's (now-ubiquitous) formulation of what that theorist called the "mirror stage." Laura Mulvey, "Visual Pleasure and Narrative Cinema," in *The Sexual Subject: A* Screen *Reader in Sexuality*, ed. Mandy Merck (London and New York: Routledge, 1992), 22–34.

83. For a summary of the reception of Mulvey's piece, and a further example of its challenging and extension, see Clifford T. Manlove, "Visual 'Drive' and Cinematic Narrative: Reading Gaze Theory in Lacan, Hitchcock, and Mulvey," *Cinema Journal* 46. no. 3 (2007), 83–108.

84. Mulvey, "Visual Pleasure," 27.

85. Mulvey, "Visual Pleasure," 29.

86. Mulvey, "Visual Pleasure," 28.

87. Kaja Silverman, *The Acoustic Mirror: The Female Voice in Psychoanalysis and Cinema* (Hoboken: Wiley and Sons, 1988), 45.

88. Silverman, *The Acoustic Mirror*, 63.

89. Silverman, *The Acoustic Mirror*, 67. Davis, of course, has become known for his controlling misogyny, but he was always known for his understanding of the power of the look, and the look's denial. This was the man who famously refused to be subject to the one-way audience gaze, turning his back to onlookers as he played or else theatrically scrutinizing them from the stage; the man who, in a newsreel film of his arrival in Paris in 1963, can be seen examining the assembled fan and press photographers from behind dark glasses, brandishing a camera, filming the filmers. This film is in the archive of the INA.

90. This concern she identifies as particularly masculine. See Silverman, *The Acoustic Mirror*, 2.

91. Silverman, *The Acoustic Mirror*, 9.

92. I am not foregrounding the Lacanian origins of the post-Bazin work described here, but for theoretical discussions of the ways that selfhood, and voice, are defined through others, see Jacques Lacan, *The Four Fundamental Concepts of Psycho-Analysis* (London: Penguin, 1979), 203–15; Mladen Dolar, *A Voice and Nothing More* (Cambridge, MA: MIT Press, 2006), 73–74, 102–3.

93. Louis Malle noted this as early as 1960: Malle, "Le Problème," 14. See also Ashley Kahn, *Kind of Blue: The Making of the Miles Davis Masterpiece* (London: Granta, 2001), 64–65.

94. Davis and Troupe, *Miles*, 231–32. Though the passage in which these claims are made has a ring of authenticity about it, it's worth restating that this autobiography was a highly mediated production.

95. Ulanov's words here may be the source of what seems to be a misquotation constantly repeated, in which Miles plays "like a man walking on eggshells." Ulanov cited in Howard Brofsky, "Miles Davis and 'My Funny Valentine': The Evolution of a Solo," *Black Music Research Journal* 3 (1983): 24.

96. Charles Fox, *The Jazz Scene* (London: Hamlyn, 1972), 106. Whitney Balliett, "Young Werther," *Dinosaurs in the Morning: 41 Pieces on Jazz* (London: Phoenix House, 1962), 142. I was directed to these appraisals by Chambers, *Milestones*, 364.

97. Watrous, "Things Happened."

98. Though, along these lines, Ian Carr rightly notes that with the soundtrack Davis "became aware of the tragic character of his music, which, until then, had been

only dimly expressed." Ian Carr, *Miles Davis: The Definitive Biography* (London: HarperCollins, 1982), 87.

99. Kuisel, *Seducing the French*, 31ff. On the growth of French postwar consumerism, see Michael Seidman, *The Imaginary Revolution: Parisian Students and Workers in 1968* (New York and Oxford: Berghahn Books, 2004), 233; Kuisel, *Seducing the French*, 150.

100. Kristin Ross, *Fast Cars, Clean Bodies: Decolonization and the Reordering of French Culture* (Cambridge, MA: MIT Press, 1995), 38.

101. Ross, *Fast Cars*, 44.

102. Jones, *Blues People*, 213.

103. Anti-American feeling was not just a leftist phenomenon: in the late-1960s diplomatic relations between the two countries were fraught, French forces having withdrawn from NATO and demanded the removal of all U.S. military from French soil in 1966. Kuisel, *Seducing the French*, 139–40.

104. See Jean-Philippe Mathy, *Extrême-Occident: French Intellectuals and America* (Chicago: University of Chicago Press, 1993).

105. Rigby, *Popular Culture*, 81, 68, and passim.

Chapter Five

1. The phone call is described in Armand Migiani, Barney Wilen and Michel de Villers, "Tribune Libre : Armand Migiani, Barney Wilen et Michel de Villers ne sont pas contents," *Jazz hot* 133 (1958): 37; the New York episode is addressed in detail later; the African activities were described by Patrick Wilen and Caroline de Bendern, author's interviews, February 25 and March 22, 2012, respectively.

2. Cited in Mike Zwerin, "If You're Good at It, Do It," *Culture Kiosk*, June 4, 1998, http://www.culturekiosque.com/jazz/miles/rhemile10.htm.

3. Marcel Romano, "Barney Wilen," *Jazz hot* 122 (1957): 16; Pierre Lapijover, "Jazzman et français. Barney Wilen," *Jazz hot* 355 (1978): 30.

4. Lucas, "Le Myth," 29.

5. On Mr. Sperry, see Raymond Mouly, "Barney Wilen ou la persévérance," *Jazz magazine* 67 (1961): 19.

6. Mouly, "La Persévérance," 19; Wilen cited in Lapijover, "Jazzman," 30.

7. On the Belgian orchestra, see Lapijover, "Jazzman," 30. The ephiphany is recounted in Romano, "Barney Wilen," 16, and Lapijover, "Jazzman," 30. Wilen is cited in the latter.

8. Romano, "Barney Wilen," 16.

9. Philippe Carles and Jean-Louis Comolli, "Entretien avec Barney Wilen. Portrait d'un fantôme," *Jazz magazine* 127 (1966): 30; Lapijover, "Jazzman," 32.

10. Romano, "Barney Wilen," 16; Lapijover, "Jazzman," 32; Henri Olier, "La Cave du Hot-club de Nice," *Jazz hot* 92 (1954): 39.

11. Henri Olier, "Panorama," 38.

12. Wilen would also take gigs with Allen Eager (November 1956), J. J. Johnson (October 1957) and others, including Bud Powell and Clark Terry. Anon., "Barney Wilen a repris le collier," *Jazz magazine* 22 (1956): 12; André Hodeir, "Au Club Saint-Germain," *Arts*, October 23, 1957, 6.

13. Romano, "Barney Wilen," 16; Olier, "La Cave," 39.

14. Lapijover, "Jazzman," 32. Wilen found time during the summer of 1955 to play on the south coast with Henri Renaud's group. See Jean-Pierre Clemencet, "Barney Wilen," *Jazz bulletin* 13 (1957): 3.

15. Romano, "Barney Wilen," 17.

16. Anonymous, "Barney rencontrera enfin Miles Davis," *Jazz magazine* 29 (1957): 17; Anon., "Barney Wilen aux Etats-Unis," *Jazz hot* 118 (1957): 25; Anon., "Barney Wilen et les Jazz Messengers lauréats de l'Académie du Jazz," *Jazz hot* 123 (1957): 25.

17. Lapijover, "Jazzman," 32.

18. Romano, "Barney Wilen," 17.

19. Anon., "Barney rencontrera," 17.

20. Marcel Romano, "Blow, Barney, Blow," *Jazz hot* 122 (1957): 19.

21. Romano, "Barney Wilen," 17. Romano suggested that this was a wider trend, giving René Urtreger and the drummer Charles Saudrais as other examples.

22. Guy Kopelowicz, "Barney Wilen sur la salette. Sonny Rollins n'a peur de rien ! ," *Jazz magazine* 33 (1957): 30.

23. Barney Wilen, "Sonny Rollins apprécié par Barney Wilen," *Jazz hot* 117 (1957): 27. See also Barney Wilen, "Charlie Parker à travers les disques," *Jazz hot* 159 (1957): 12–13.

24. Bibi Rovère plays bass on both sides; on side 1, Maurice Vander plays piano and Al Levitt, drums.

25. It's possible that this is a false impression given by studio recordings. But a similar manner is presented by the Wilen recorded live at the Newport Jazz Festival and at Club Saint-Germain in 1959.

26. Romano is cited in Philippe Carles's liner notes to the reissue of *Barney* (BMG, 1997).

27. Romano, "Blow, Barney, Blow ! ," 19.

28. Jean-Louis Ginibre, "Pièges pour Barney," *Jazz magazine* 144 (1967): 29.

29. These are "Ménilmontant," "Que reste-t-il de nos amours ? ," "J'ai ta main," and "La Route enchantée."

30. The *Témoin dans la ville* group featured Duke Jordan, Paul Rovère and Kenny Clarke; the Swiss drummer Daniel Humair, recently arrived in Paris, replaced Clarke for the recording of *Barney*, the other musicians remaining.

31. Philippe Carles, liner notes to the 1997 reissue of *Barney*.

32. Wilen's ballad feature on the soundtrack, "Prelude in Blue," is taken at a mid-tempo bounce and, no less anachronistically, on a creamy soprano saxophone. Wilen had taken to the instrument—in advance of its adoption by John Coltrane—thinking that "there was something else to do with it besides what Bechet had done." Carles and Comolli, "Entretien," 30.

33. Mouly, "Les Musiciens français à l'honneur sur Europe 1," 14–15. Mouly, "La Persévérance," 19.

34. Carles and Comolli, "Entretien," 32.

35. This information is from Patrick Wilen (author's interview, February 26, 2012).

36. This information comes from the author's interview with Jacques Thollot, March 22, 2012. On December 15, 1962, Wilen did play in Paris: at La Nuit de jazz, a

concert featuring a number of French stars, all of whom were discussed in *Jazz hot*'s review of the event apart, oddly, from the saxophonist. Philippe Kœchlin and Jean Tronchot, "La Nuit de jazz," *Jazz hot* 183 (1963): 14–17.

37. Roger Luccioni, Alain Delaye and Florimond Delannoy, "Dix jours de folie," *Jazz hip* 32 (1963): 32–34.

38. Delaye, Delannay and Luccioni, "Dix jours," 33.

39. Delaye, Delannay and Luccioni, "Dix jours," 33–34; Carles and Comolli, "Entretien," 30.

40. Philippe Kœchlin, "Barney l'exilé : ma direction, c'est le classique," *Jazz hot* 196 (1964): 13.

41. This argument ran through, for instance, A. B. Spellman's book *Four Lives in the Bebop Business* (New York: Pantheon Books, 1966).

42. Kœchlin, "Barney l'exilé," 13.

43. Kœchlin, "Barney l'exilé," 13.

44. Kœchlin, "Barney l'exilé," 13; Carles and Comolli, "Entretien," 34.

45. Carles and Comolli, "Entretien," 32.

46. Carles and Comolli, "Entretien," 32.

47. Tusques, whose words might be taken with a pinch of salt, is cited in Jedediah Sklower, *Free jazz, la catastrophe féconde* (Paris: L'Harmattan, 2006), 148, 155.

48. Though present in Europe in 1962–63, neither Albert Ayler nor Cecil Taylor made it beyond Scandinavia on those occasions. Coleman was, nevertheless, regarded by many French musicians as their primary influence in moving towards free jazz: see Cotro, *Chants libres*, 54.

49. Yves Buin, "Michel Portal : un choix courageux," *Jazz hot* 218 (1966): 18.

50. Sklower, *Free jazz*, 149–50, 151. Other venues hosting the developing free jazz were clustered around the 5th arrondissement, on Paris's Left Bank: Le Caméléon, Le Lucernaire, Le Jazz Blues Museum, Gill's Club, the Requin Chagrin. And although concerts often took place at halls like the Mutualité and the Centre Culturel Américain, even the biggest American free jazz names only very occasionally performed at Paris's biggest halls, the Salle Pleyel and the ORTF. Cotro, *Chants libres*, 67.

51. Yves Buin "Le Rêve et la liberté," *Jazz hot* 216 (1966): 17.

52. Aside from the official Cherry recordings noted above, this method—and a performance announced from the stage as a "cocktail composition"—can be heard on the three volumes of Danish radio broadcasts released as *Live at Café Montmartre 1966* (ESP, 2007).

53. Cotro provides a transcription of the theme: *Chants libres*, 98.

54. Sklower, *Free jazz*, 157.

55. Occasionally joining these core players were a number of those other Parisians who had played with Don Cherry during his recent visits: Karl Berger, Beb Guérin, Bernard Vitet and Michel Portal. Though Delorme's report on the Requin gig (cited in the next note) suggests that Texier was the group's regular bassist, Jacques Thollot remembered Texier being present less often that the other players named here. Thollot also argued that the work done at the Requin was a continuation rather than a totally new departure, he and Wilen having been playing together regularly over the preceding two years. Author's interview, March 22, 2012.

56. Michel Delorme, "Le Retour de Barney Wilen," *Jazz hot* 214 (1965): 8.

57. "Sagittaire" recalls Coltrane's then-recent music, for instance; "Lion," Coleman's.

58. See John Schott, "We Are Revealing a Hand That Will Later Reveal Us: Notes on Form and Harmony in Coltrane's Work," in *Arcana: Musicians on Music*, ed. John Zorn (New York: Granary Books / Hips Road, 2000), 345–66. Coltrane is cited on p. 350.

59. Coltrane's fullest exploration of the augmented scale is made on a recording of the piece "One Down, One Up" (1965).

60. See "Verseau," 0:50.

61. "Les Sorcières," 5:50.

62. Though "Les Sorcières" also introduces another brief glimpse of the European free improvisation to come, a layered, heterophonic group improvisation emerging out of the piece's semi-modal theme.

63. Again Wilen's treatment of this scale suggests Coltrane's "augmented" materials: Wilen often concentrates on the fragment G-F♯-D♯-D, the top of an augmented scale on G, though also of a much more standard harmonic minor—either way, this allows Wilen to access the flavor of some of Coltrane's lines.

64. Sklower, *Free jazz*, 122–23.

65. Guy Kopelowicz, "Autumn in New York. Voyage au cœur de la New Thing," *Jazz hot* 214 (1965): 28–31; "Autumn in New York II," *Jazz hot* 215 (1965): 39–43; "Autumn in New York III," *Jazz hot* 216 (1966): 21–25. Kopelowicz provided another such piece two years later, "Impressions de New York," *Jazz hot* 238 (1968): 19–22. Another significant article series was the two-part Archie Shepp feature by Guy Kopelowicz and François Postif, "Archie Shepp ou la marée qui monte," *Jazz hot* 210 (1965): 22–26, and 211 (1965): 38–41.

66. On the jazz body, see especially part 2. Michel Le Bris and Bruno Vincent, "La Tête, le cœur et le pied," *Jazz hot* 232 (1967): 15–17; 233 (1967): 15–16; 234 (1967): 23–31. On Bourdieu et al. see Eric Drott, *Music and the Elusive Revolution: Cultural Politics and Political Culture in France, 1968–1981* (Berkeley: University of California Press, 2011), 122.

67. Eric Plaisance, "Idéologie et esthétique à propos du free jazz," *Les Cahiers du jazz* 15 (1967): 6–23; this in turn was countered by Yves Buin, "La Nuit noire," *Jazz hot* 236 (1967): 23. See also Drott, *Music*, 124–25.

68. Drott, *Music*, 121.

69. Robert Aldrich, *Greater France: A History of French Overseas Expansion* (Basingstoke: Palgrave, 1996), 265, 270, 5.

70. Aldrich, *Greater France*, 28ff.

71. Aldrich, *Greater France*, 266. New, Cold War interests played a major part in the colonial conflicts.

72. Kristin Ross, *May '68 and Its Afterlives* (Chicago: University of Chicago Press, 2002), 80–81. Drott, *Music*, 121.

73. Ross, *May '68*, 84.

74. Guy Kopelowicz, "Le Nouveau jazz et la réalité américaine," *Jazz hot* 231 (1967): 18–23.

75. Annette Lena, "Révolution culturelle à Harlem," *Jazz hot* 249 (1969): 17. Eric Plaisance, "Jazz, racisme et sexualité," *Les Cahiers du jazz* 18 (1970): 8–15.

76. Michel Le Bris (uncredited). 1969. "A propos d'un certain S.O.S.," *Jazz hot* 252 (1969): 47. Hess's original piece was "Hess-o-Hess," *Jazz magazine* 167 (1969): 5.

77. Le Bris, "A propos," 47.

78. Philippe Carles and Jean-Louis Comolli, *Free Jazz / Black Power* (Paris: Editions Champ Libre, 1971).

79. Cecil Taylor, Anthony Braxton and Clifford Thornton made relatively brief visits; the Art Ensemble of Chicago stayed for a period of some months; Sunny Murray, Alan Silva, Frank Wright and Marion Brown moved to Paris for the medium or long term. Later, players including Archie Shepp and David Murray would move to the city. Radical black politics also made occasional touchdowns in Paris: see Stovall, *Paris Noir*, 268–71. July 1969 also saw Cecil Taylor perform at the Fondation Maeght near Nice (Albert Ayler and Sun Ra would play there a year later); in August, Archie Shepp, Alan Silva, Grachan Moncur III and a host of other African American musicians and intellectuals would descend on Algiers for the First Pan-African Cultural Festival.

80. Anthony Braxton, "Le Jazz est une musique dangereuse," *Jazz magazine* 205 (1972): 12–17; see also Lewis, *A Power Stronger than Itself*, 226.

81. For a French intellectual coterie at least, the plight of black America—so familiar to music fans versed in the cry of the blues—had long been given an internationalist interpretation by those many African and African American writers and thinkers who, making Paris their home in the 1940s and '50s, played roles in the anti-colonial movements. See Stovall, *Paris Noir*, 195–96.

82. See Drott, *Music*, 138.

83. Philippe Constantin, "Entretien : Michel Portal," *Jazz hot* 241 (1968): 15.

84. Carles and Comolli, *Free Jazz / Black Power*, 59, 71.

85. See Cotro, *Chants libres*, 58, where Thollot is cited. Cotro also suggests (p. 157) that the polyinstrumentalism of Joachim Kühn, Portal, Thollot, Romano, Jenny-Clark and others was a way to get away from conventional expression and "academic" standards of facility and beauty.

86. The "Paix au Vietnam et égalité raciale aux USA" concert of March 1966, featuring the singer Collete Magny, Claude Nougaro, and a François Tusques group including Vitet, Portal and Wilen, was apparently better received than what was reported by *Jazz hot* as a desultory rerun in early summer 1967. Then, Tusques, Portal, Beb Guérin, Jenny-Clark, Thollot and others performed against Vietnam to a Mutualité crowd small enough to lead the reviewer to throw up his hands at the hopelessness of it all. Anonymous, untitled news item, *Jazz hot* 220 (1966): 9; Daniel Berger, "Paix au Vietnam-Mutualité," *Jazz hot* 234 (1967): 5.

87. Wilen echoed Michel Portal, cited earlier, and in so doing showed no little blindness to local realities of race: "[Free] is jazz's only hope. People sometimes ask if I'm going in the same direction. In fact, my music couldn't be that similar because in France we aren't confronted by the same racial problems. We don't really have a race problem." Ginibre, "Pièges pour Barney," 29.

88. Cited in Philippe Carles, "Noir sur blanc," *Jazz magazine* 141 (1967): 15.

89. Ginibre, "Pièges pour Barney," 28.

90. Ginibre, "Pièges pour Barney," 29.

91. Michel Le Bris, "Barney Wilen : ma direction c'est le rock . . . ," *Jazz hot* 245 (1968): 28.

92. The 1964 recording and subsequent radio performance are reported in Le Bris, "Ma Direction," 28. The radio broadcast referred to is likely the spring 1967 ORTF concert reported by Michel Delorme, "Don Cherry Barney Wilen," *Jazz hot* 230 (1967): 10. Both pieces shared the name *Grand Prix Formule 1*. The ORTF performance featured Tusques and Joel Vandrogenbruck, pianos, Jenny-Clark and Guérin, basses, Thollot and Eddy Gaumont, drums. The tragic May 1967 race later described yet to take place, the piece was dedicated to Louis Chiron. Delorme reports being highly impressed by the performance.

93. Le Bris, "Ma Direction," 28.

94. Le Bris, "Ma Direction," 28; Cotro, *Chants libres*, 243–44.

95. J.-P. Binchet, "Autojazz," *Jazz magazine* 149 (1967): 22.

96. The unadorned, tonal simplicity of some of these lyrical figures also recalls Ayler's folk-like tunes.

97. Both the idea and the field recordings were reused for 1993's live recording *Le Grand cirque* (Nato).

98. Le Bris, "Ma Direction," 29.

99. Lapijover, "Jazzman," 34.

100. For a long examination of such convergences, see Denis Lémery, "Les Présents conjugués," *Jazz magazine* 165 (1969): 34–48.

101. Drott, *Music*, 206.

102. Drott, *Music*, 203–4.

103. Roger Luccioni, "Editorial," *Jazz hip* 35 (1964): 9. The numbers in any case were healthy rather than huge: the Marseille record shop had sold thirty-five jazz records during each of jazz's best days, Luccioni wrote.

104. Drott, *Music*, 192.

105. At Amougies, Pink Floyd and Soft Machine appeared alongside the Art Ensemble, Don Cherry, Archie Shepp and others. Like most ambitious festivals of the time the event was an organizational disaster. See Drott, *Music*, 113; Paul Alessandrini and Guy Le Querrec, "Freepop," *Jazz magazine* 173 (1969): 30. The importance of Pop-Club was signaled to me by Jacques Oger. Author's interview, March 14, 2012.

106. Wilen, cited in Le Bris, "Ma Direction," 28.

107. Wilen, cited in Le Bris, "Ma Direction," 28.

108. Drott, *Music*, 90.

109. Alan Heineman, "Barney Wilen," *Down Beat* 36/23 (1969): 24. The group was sometimes greeted with equal disdain by jazz audiences, as happened at September 1968's Lugano jazz festival. Le Bris, "Ma Direction," 28.

110. Seidman, *The Imaginary Revolution*, 5; Ross, *May '68*, 182–83, and passim. This interpretation was endorsed by Nicolas Sarkozy during his successful presidential campaign of 2007.

111. Ross, *May '68*, 26, and passim.

112. Seidman, *The Imaginary Revolution*, 10; Ross, *May '68*, 1ff.

113. Seidman, *The Imaginary Revolution*: 17–52.

114. A number of the student leaders to emerge during May and June reported

having been politicized by France's appallingly bloody battle to hold on to its last great imperial possession, by the hushed-up police massacre of hundreds of peaceful Algerian protesters in Paris in October 1961, or by the police riot at Charonne métro station that killed nine French protesters early in 1962. Ross, *May '68*, 39–41. François Tusques, whose musical and political activities would further converge during 1968, reported the same experience. See Sklower, *Free jazz*, 171.

115. Ross, *May '68*, 90.

116. Seidman, *The Imaginary Revolution*, 117; Ross, *May '68*, 52.

117. Ross, *May '68*, 76.

118. Sklower, *Free jazz*, 179. Tournès, *New Orleans sur Seine*, 401–3.

119. Anonymous, "Les Musiciens et la révolution de mai," *Jazz hot* 242 (1968): 14–16. The unions were by no means universally respected or trusted by the workers they represented; see Ross, *May '68*, 32, passim.

120. Drott, *Music*, 40–50.

121. Seidman, *The Imaginary Revolution*, 76. See also Drott, *Music*, 2.

122. See Pascal Virot, "Des Milliers de personnes pour un hommage sans chaleur. Marchais, pour mémoire," *Liberation*, November 21, 1997, http://www.liberation.fr/politiques/0101229542-des-milliers-de-personnes-pour-un-hommage-sans-chaleur-marchais-pour-memoire.

123. Seidman, *The Imaginary Revolution*, 187.

124. Ross, *May '68*, 59. Stovall, *Paris Noir*, 283.

125. Seidman, *The Imaginary Revolution*, 220.

126. Seidman, *The Imaginary Revolution*, 197, 233.

127. See, for instance, Lucien Malson, "Courier des lecteurs," *Jazz hot* 222 (1966): 15; Philippe Constantin, "Courier des lecteurs," *Jazz hot* 242 (1968): 5.

128. The magazine's 1969 poll received only 262 answers, each category's vote being tripled to hide the public's failing interest. Sklower, *Free jazz*, 188. Sales recovered somewhat thereafter.

129. Carrière et al., "Editorial," *Jazz hot* 256 (1969): 7.

130. Ross, *May '68*, 97–98.

131. Ross, *May '68*, 99.

132. Denis Constant, "Free + rock + livre rouge," *Jazz hot* 164 (1969): 11.

133. Anon., "Les Femmes de mai," *Elle*, April 17, 2008, http://www.elle.fr/Societe/Les-enquetes/Les-femmes-de-mai-594937/Caroline-de-Bendern-egerie-malgre-elle-596137.

134. Delorme, "Le retour de Barney Wilen," 8–9.

135. Kieron Corless lists as the group's members the actors Pierre Clementi, Zouzou and Daniel Pommereulle, the painters Olivier Mosset and Frederic Pardo, and the director Philippe Garrel. Kieron Corless, "No Rest 'til Zanzibar," *Vertigo* 4, no. 3 (2002), http://www.vertigomagazine.co.uk/showarticle.php?sel=bac&siz=1&id=552. In Lapijover, "Jazzman," 34, Wilen records his gratitude towards Boissonnas's supporting of the trip.

136. In 1966, Wilen had recorded the music for Chris Marker's film *Si j'avais quatre dromadaires*; in 1989 he would contribute the music to *Les Baisers de secours*, directed by the onetime Zanzibar member Philippe Garrel. The soundtrack of an abandoned

1958 jazz film project was released in 2012 as Donald Byrd + Barney Wilen, *Jazz in Camera* (Sonorama).

137. J.-F. Hackenbush, "Barney Wilen part en Afrique," *Jazz hot* 249 (1969): 12.

138. Hackenbush, "Barney Wilen part en Afrique," 12.

139. Philippe Carles, "La Mission Barney," *Jazz magazine* 199 (1972): 12. Realizing that the images they had were inadequate, Wilen and Bendern made a shorter return visit before the end of 1971.

140. Carles, "La Mission Barney," 14.

141. This chronology is based on the accounts that Bendern gave to the author (interview, 22 March 2012) and for Stéphane Sinde for his 2008 Wilen documentary, *The Rest of Your Life*, and the 1972 *Jazz magazine* article cited earlier. There are some differences of detail between contemporary and later accounts.

142. Carles, "La Mission Barney," 14.

143. Carles, "La Mission Barney," 14.

144. On their second trip to Agadez in 1971, Wilen and Bendern had taken medicines, and this, too, was open to *Jazz magazine*'s question. "It was simply an issue of helping people who were sick but didn't have the means to take care of themselves," the saxophonist responded. Carles, "La Mission Barney," 12.

145. Carles, "La Mission Barney," 16.

146. Carles, "La Mission Barney," 15.

147. Carles, "La Mission Barney," 15.

148. See Michael Taussig, *Mimesis and Alterity: A Particular History of the Senses* (New York and London: Routledge, 1993), 241ff.

149. Carles, "La Mission Barney," 16.

150. Wilen is cited in Carles, "La Mission Barney," 15. Wilen's long solo on the title track merely demonstrates the pentatonic and blues scale ad nauseam—though it may be that this piece, like the album's other long tracks, harbors an intention to provide for trance-like deep listening rather than to create music that is actively engaging in the "Western" style. Three pop songs form the album's weakest moments. Here, Bendern and two other singers bash through long lyrics—concerning god and myth, the ills of colonialism, and a narrative of the original journey—which are hampered by trite melodies and grooves that remain very much of their time.

151. Lapijover, "Jazzman," 34.

152. "La Mission Barney," 15; Philippe Carles, "Barney Wilen Quartet / Michael Smith Trio," *Jazz magazine* 198 (1972): 31.

153. The information here is from the author's interview with Caroline de Bendern, March 22, 2012.

Chapter Six

1. Discussed in Tournès, *New Orleans sur Seine*, 258–59.

2. Anon, "André Hodeir," *Jazz Today* 2, no. 5 (1957): 9.

3. Lucien Malson, "François Jeanneau," *Arts*, March 16, 1960, 6; "René Urtreger," *Arts*, May 4, 1960, 6; "Michel de Villers," *Arts*, May 11, 1960, 5.

4. Anon, "5000 Jeunes passionnées de jazz repondent au référendum de *Arts*,"

Arts, March 23, 1960, 16. On French musicians in the polls, see Tournès, *New Orleans sur Seine*, 261.

5. Tournès, *New Orleans sur Seine*, 260.

6. Similarly, the historian's celebration of the arrival of several (Hot-club-trained) jazz specialists in the media industries of the 1950s—Vian, Ténot, Filipacchi—belies the fact that they were all soon bound to turn towards rock 'n' roll.

7. Nos. 22, 32 and 36, from 1960, 1963 and 1964, respectively.

8. Lucien Malson, Georges Arvanitas, Guy Lafitte, Michel de Villers, "Un Blanc vaut un noir," *Arts*, March 23, 1960, 14.

9. Martial Solal, Guy Pedersen et al., "Table ronde : le jazz français et ses problèmes," *Jazz hip* 32 (1963): 11.

10. Migiani, Wilen and Villers, "Tribune libre," 36–37. In 1965 Guy Lafitte, Michel Hausser, René Urtreger and others formed a section of the musician's union to campaign on this premise, described and discussed in Lucien Malson, Michel Hausser, René Urtreger, Siné, "L'Art et le métier," *Jazz hot* 217 (1966): 16–19.

11. Roger Luccioni, "Le Jazz français en danger ? ," *Jazz* (Marseille) 22 (1960): 8, 9.

12. "Kenny Clarke at the Salle Pleyel? That wouldn't work . . . it's not because he's French that the musician suffers, it's because he's always there." Lucien Malson, "Courrier des lecteurs," *Jazz hot* 224 (1966): 13. Bud Powell and Don Byas could play to near-empty clubs (as witnessed by Victor Schonfield. Private conversation, London, January 27, 2012).

13. Jef Gilson, Sim Copans et al., "La Critique parisienne répond a dix questions : à propos de *Jazz et Jazz*," *Jazz hot* 163 (1961): 17.

14. Gilson, Copans et al., "La Critique parisienne," 20.

15. For manufactured controversy, see André Hodeir, "Bataille à l'Académie du Jazz," *Arts*, July 3, 1957, 7.

16. Claude Lenissois and Jef Gilson described the association of the two players as a "commonplace" in 1963. Claude Lenissois and Jef Gilson, "Solal," *Jazz hot* 188 (1963): 26. One such historical appraisal is made by Ludovic Tournès, *New Orleans sur Seine*, 251.

17. Denis-Constant Martin and Olivier Roueff, *La France du Jazz* (Marseille: Editions Parenthèses, 2002), 86.

18. Martial Solal, *Ma Vie sur un tabouret* (Arles: Actes Sud, 2008), 30–39.

19. These 1965 pieces were collected on *Jazz à Gaveau et autres pièces (1959–66)* (Swing, 1997).

20. Solal, *Ma Vie*, 38.

21. See "18 + 1" and "Petite Poupée," both from 1962 and also included on *Jazz à Gaveau et autres pièces*.

22. Claude Lenissois and Jef Gilson, "Solal," 27.

23. Tournès, *New Orleans sur Seine*, 247, 248–49. Even in Solal's own output, the piece is unusual: a 1978 record for MPS, *Suite for Piano Trio* is somewhat misnamed.

24. Lenissois and Gilson, "Solal," 28. (The authors, of course, are here objecting to this common criticism.)

25. Hess' comment appears in Jacques B. Hess, Martial Solal, and Jean-Louis Chautemps, "Troix voix pour Hodeir," *Jazz magazine* 231 (1975): 28. For a later (and

insightful) example of Solal's sometimes ambivalent critical reception, see Ethan Iverson, "Philadelphia Story," *Do the Math*, April 10, 2011, http://dothemath.typepad.com/dtm/2011/04/philadelphia-story.html.

26. Which is not to say that he wasn't admired by musicians—he was, and rightly so.

27. The 2005 BBC documentary series *Jazz Britannia* (dir. Mike Connolly and Chris Rodley) hosted a number of these judgments.

28. Philippe Coulangeon, *Les Musiciens de jazz en France* (Paris. L'Harmattan, 1999), 39.

29. The first Cohelmec lineup comprised Jean Cohen (saxes), Dominique Elbaz (piano), François Mechali (bass) and Jean-Louis Mechali (drums). Flautist Evan Chandlee, guitarist Joseph Dejean and trumpeter Jean-François Canape were later members.

30. Denis Constant, "Cohelmec . . . kekcéksa," *Jazz magazine* 187 (1971): 20.

31. See Denis Constant, "Perception : 4 conceptions," *Jazz magazine* 190 (1971): 21.

32. Constant, "Cohelmec," 21.

33. Cotro, *Chants libres*, 192–93. This group, formed around 1968, had a number of personnel changes; central early members were Patricio Villarroel (piano), Michel Gladieux (bass), Jacques Mahieux (drums) and Jef Sicard (saxes). Guitarist Gérard Marais was among those who joined later. See Denis Constant, "Dharma," *Jazz magazine* 203 (1972): 15–17.

34. Cotro, *Chants libres*, 184, 193, 202. For a discussion of American jazz collectives, see Perchard, *Lee Morgan*, 194–207.

35. Cotro, *Chants libres*, 174. Other ensembles formed at this time included Bernard Lubat's Compagnie Lubat, Bernard Vitet and Jean-Jacques Birgé's Un Drame Musicale Instantané, Jean-Louis Chautemps' Rhizome (all 1976); Marseille's GRIM (Groupe de Recherche et d'Improvisation Musicales) was founded by Jean-Marc Montera, Lionel Dublanchet, David Rueff, André Jaume and Gérard Siracusa in 1978, and continued into the 21st century.

36. The group's album *Hippotigris Zebra Zebra* (Saravah, 1971) pits this late-Coltrane style alongside a later, more open free jazz improvisation and indeed an earlier, tumbling swing.

37. A good example of Davis pastiche is in "End, Starting," from *Snoopy's Time* (Société Française de Productions Phonographiques, 1970). "Coloristic" free jazz is heard on the Machi Oul Big Band album *Quetzalcoatl* (Palm, 1975).

38. A recording of the concert, the second half of which featured Steve Lacy's ensemble, is held by INA. Boutin's group would later move towards a rather odd jazz rock for its 1981 recording *Première ligne*.

39. Annecy Jazz Action, "Jazz en province : X-tet," *Jazz magazine* 219 (1974): 17; Denis Constant "Les Nouvelles aventures de l'X'tet," *Jazz magazine* 245 (1976): 25. Other countryside-dwelling groups of this period included Barney Wilen's *Moshi* band, and the Art Ensemble of Chicago, who lived in a farmhouse outside Paris. Micheline Graillier, interviewed in Sinde, *The Rest of Your Life*; Lewis, *A Power Stronger than Itself*, 224.

40. Anon., "Cohelmec," *Jazz magazine* 203 (1972): 14; Constant, "Dharma," 16, 15. This was Sicard's stated aim in particular.

41. Le Comice Khulturel Annecy Jazz Action, "Annecy Jazz Action," *Jazz hot* 300 (1973): 16.

42. Constant, "Dharma," 16.

43. Le Comice Khulturel Annecy Jazz Action, "Annecy Jazz Action," 16.

44. Le Comice Khulturel Annecy Jazz Action, "Annecy Jazz Action," 16.

45. Alain-René Hardy, "Les questions de Rouen Jazz Action," *Jazz magazine* 246 (1976): 16.

46. Le Comice Khulturel Annecy Jazz Action, "Annecy Jazz Action," 16–17. After Mitterrand's 1981 victory, the local jazz actions were grouped together more formally. See Sklower, *Free jazz*, 129.

47. ARFI's members made up several different ensembles—the Marvellous Band, Trace and, most notably, the Workshop de Lyon—as well as organizing performances, recording and pedagogy. See Jean-Marc Birraux, Serge Loupien and Françis Marmande, "A Lyon on improvise," *Jazz magazine* 283 (1980): 28–31; Alain-René Hardy, "Le Workshop de Lyon (interview aléatore)," *Jazz magazine* 256 (1977): 16–17, 39–41.

48. See Drott, *Music,* 234, and passim.

49. Rigby, *Popular Culture,* 133.

50. Drott, *Music,* 203–67.

51. Constant, "Dharma," 16; Annecy Jazz Action, "Jazz en province," 16; Alain-René Hardy, "Le Workshop de Lyon."

52. Annecy Jazz Action, "Jazz en province," 16.

53. Rouen Jazz Action, "Rouen Jazz Action," *Jazz magazine* 261 (1978): 31.

54. Gérard Rouy, "Dans le « désert culturel », Lille Jazz Action," *Jazz magazine* 244 (1976): 21.

55. Lapijover, "Jazzman," 30, 34; Sinde, *The Rest of Your Life.*

56. Eugen Weber, *Peasants into Frenchmen: The Modernization of Rural France, 1870–1914* (Palo Alto, CA: Stanford University Press, 1976), 303–38; Andy Green, *Education and State Formation: The Rise of Education Systems in England, France and the USA* (Basingstoke: Palgrave, 1991).

57. Gildea, *France since 1945,* 128–34; Thomas R. Christofferson, *The French Socialists in Power, 1981–1986: From Autogestion to Cohabitation* (Newark: University of Delaware Press, 1991), 55, 41.

58. Eric Drott, "The Nòva Cançon Occitana and the Internal Colonialism Thesis," *French Politics, Culture & Society* 29, no. 1 (2011): 1–23; Gildea, *France since 1945,* 130.

59. Philippe Carles, "Tusques : d'où viennent les sons justes ? ," *Jazz magazine* 202 (1972): 32–33.

60. Carles, "Tusques," 22.

61. Philippe Carles, "L'Intercommunal : jouer ce que vivent les gens," *Jazz magazine* 244 (1976): 16.

62. On "La Rencontre" ("The Meeting") and "Biniou koz free blues valse," respectively.

63. Serge Loupien, "François Tusques : pour une nouvelle musique bretonne," *Jazz magazine* 280 (1979): 30.

64. In particular the groups La Marmite Infernale and La Bête à Bon Dos.

65. In the 1980s the Front National grew in former regionalist hotspots as those local movements declined. Gildea, *France since 1945,* 134.

66. Jean-Pierre Patillot, "Bernard Lubat," *Jazz hot* 320 (1975): 11, 12, 13.

67. Cotro, *Chants libres*, 73–74; Sklower, *Free jazz*, 236.

68. Tournès, *New Orleans sur Seine*, 405–6.

69. See Laurent Goddet, "Châteauvallon," *Jazz hot* 331 (1976): 7; Tournès, *New Orleans sur Seine*, 407.

70. P-L Rossi, "Michel Polyvalent Portal," *Jazz magazine* 142 (1967): 24–25. Biographical detail here is also gleaned from Jean Delmas and Michel Lequime, "Portal en long, portal en travers," *Jazz hot* 296 (1973): 21; Cotro, *Chants libres*, 114.

71. On the Gilson albums Portal plays alto, on the Ponty, flute.

72. Yves Buin, "Michel Portal, un choix courageux," *Jazz hot* 218 (1966): 18; Rossi, "Michel Polyvalent Portal," 24.

73. Philippe Carles and Francis Marmande, "Michel Portal ou la parole au présent," *Jazz magazine* 210 (1973): 32.

74. Delmas and Lequime, "Portal en long," 21.

75. Portal also expressed reservations on the music's political intent. Drott, *Music*, 141.

76. Carles and Marmande, "Michel Portal ou la parole au présent," 12.

77. Lewis, "Improvised Music after 1950."

78. See Portal's comments in Delmas and Lequime, "Portal en long," 21.

79. Rossi, "Michel Polyvalent Portal," 25. Like those players cited earlier in the chapter, Portal also suggested that the music of Stockhausen and Varèse might form a model.

80. Delmas and Lequime, "Portal en long," 11.

81. Delmas and Lequime, "Portal en long," 9.

82. The "Unit" moniker would sometimes be applied to Portal's groups after this lineup disbanded a few years later, but only one commercial recording was released under the name.

83. Cited in Sklower, *Free jazz*, 107–8. Although Portal would go on to make a great number of studio recordings, he maintained this ambivalence throughout his career. See Vincent Bessières, "Je ne fais que passer," *Jazzman*, March 2007, 19–22.

84. Sklower, *Free jazz*, 108.

85. On its 2003 CD rerelease the album was retitled *Châteauvallon : 23 Août 1972*.

86. Anon., "Michel Portal face à face," *Jazz magazine* 290 (1980): 46.

87. Carles and Marmande, "Michel Portal ou la parole au present," 13. The 1976 recording was released by L'Escargot in 1979, under the names of all four musicians represented: Portal, Bernard Lubat, Beb Guérin and Léon Francioli.

88. Annecy Jazz Action, "Jazz en province," 16. "Europe is gaining importance in the world of jazz that it hasn't had before," Portal claimed proudly in 1973. Delmas and Lequime, "Portal en long," 11.

89. Tournès, *New Orleans sur Seine*, 406; Sklower, *Free jazz*, 213.

90. "European jazz," Portal said later, "I simply call 'music.' These are compositions that are more tinted by jazz colours than so-called 'contemporary' musics." Karine Vonna, "Michel Portal," *Jazz hot* 502 (1993): 35.

91. As do some of the signals themselves, like the one that marks the end of the first version of "No, no but it may be," from the 1972 Châteauvallon album.

92. Johansson's 1964 album *Jazz på svenska* (*Jazz in Swedish*, Heptagon) was a great

commercial success, and the pianist followed it with records that similarly reworked Russian and Hungarian folk material. On this trend, see E. Taylor Atkins, "Toward a Global History of Jazz," in Atkins, *Jazz Planet*, xix; and Atkins, *Blue Nippon*, 221ff and passim.

93. Delmas and Lequime, "Portal en long," 11. See also Vonna, "Michel Portal," 34.

94. Anon, "Michel Portal face à face," 46.

95. Carles and Francis, "Michel Portal ou la parole au present," 32.

96. Alain Gerber, "Retour au jazz," *Les Nouvelles littéraires*, September 22–29, 1977, 17.

97. For European label surveys, see Laurent Goddet, "ECM," *Jazz hot* 277 (1971): 24–5; Cardat-Schmitt, "Incus ICP Calig FMP Vogel etc.," *Jazz hot* 294 (1973): 12–15, and *Jazz hot* 295 (1973): 14–15; Gérard Rouy, "Incus ou la force tranquille," *Jazz magazine* 254 (1977): 20–21; Gérard Rouy, "Berlin Free Music Produktion," *Jazz magazine* 238 (1975): 12–15; Gérard Rouy, "Histoire d'Enja," *Jazz magazine* 252 (1977): 20. For surveys of non-American scenes, see Denis Constant, "Bruits de Londres," *Jazz magazine* 201 (1972): 18–21; Maurice Gourges, "Nouveau sons de Japon," *Jazz magazine* 221 (1974): 18–19; the various articles in the "Spécial France" edition of *Jazz magazine* 245 (1976); Gérard Rouy, "Nouveaux bruits de Londres," *Jazz magazine* 256 (1977): 26–27, 28, 41–42. Also see Didier Pennequin, Gérard Rouy, Alain Gerber, Philippe Carles, and Jean-Robert Masson, "Onze européens parlent de leur musique," *Jazz magazine* 220 (1974): 17–33.

98. Other terms, like "free music" and "free improvisation," were and (continue to be) used.

99. Author's personal correspondence with Gérard Rouy, August 2012.

100. See Anon., "En marge," *Jazz magazine* 233 (1975): 46.

101. On the financial difficulties of the improviser's life, see Alain Gerber, "Les Bruits de la vie de Berrocal," *Jazz magazine* 254 (1977): 36; Jean-Louis Chautemps, "Une Spécialité bien française : le jazz enchaîné," *Les Nouvelles littéraires*, September 22–29, 1977, 24.

102. Anon., "En marge," 33, 32, 34, 46. Similarly, in 1977 Philippe Carles would identify the new improvised music as a European analogue to the African American free jazz movement that had rejected bourgeois artistic and social practices. Philippe Carles, "Postfree," *Les Nouvelles littéraires*, September 22–29, 1977, 23.

103. For an example, see Serge Loupien, "Voix nouvelles : Daunik Lazro," *Jazz magazine* 269 (1978): 33.

104. 28 rue Dunois's concert programs are archived at http://www.dunoisjazz.info/PROGRAMME.htm.

105. Gerber, "Les Bruits," 35; Hardy, "Le Workshop de Lyon," 39, 40. Here, the workshop's members discussed their interest in and being influenced by various non-European musics other than African American jazz.

106. Loupien, "Voix nouvelles," 32. Lazro's most significant early association was with the Franco-American bassist Saheb Sarbib, in whose ensemble he (and François Jeanneau) played in the mid- and latter 1970s.

107. This was something of an illusion: the idiom-happy groups Alterations and British Summertime Ends, for instance, were as much a part of the British scene of

the 1980s as the "non-idiomatic" guitarist Derek Bailey. But it was the example of Bailey and players like him that largely defined "the" British approach, especially to those looking on from abroad.

108. In an article published that year in *Le Monde*. Cited in Cotro, *Chants libres*, 231.

109. For such a French historical evaluation, see Sklower, *Free jazz*, 248; for an American equivalent see the final episode of Ken Burns's PBS series *Jazz*, "A Masterpiece by Midnight" (2001), during which the "delta" image is employed.

110. Alain Gerber, "Total Issue vers quoi ? ," *Jazz magazine* 192 (1971): 14, 15.

111. Philippe Carles and Daniel Soutif, "Le Retour en solo d'Henri Texier," *Jazz magazine* 244 (1976): 19.

112. *Jazz hot* was notably more open to jazz fusion, and to non-jazz African American musics like soul and disco, than was its rival *Jazz magazine*.

113. Gildea, *France since 1945*, 98–102; Christofferson, *The French Socialists*, passim, 91.

114. Christofferson, *The French Socialists*, 90, 92.

115. Rigby, *Popular Culture*, 160.

116. Rigby, *Popular Culture*, 165, passim; Christofferson, *The French Socialists*, 91.

117. Coulangeon, *Les Musiciens*, 22–3.

118. Coulangeon, *Les Musiciens*, 25.

119. Archived at http://www.audiorama.org/planeta/index.html.

120. Tournès, *New Orleans sur Seine*, 236–37.

121. Tournès, *New Orleans sur Seine*, 416; Sklower, *Free jazz*, 65; Pierre Henri Ardonceau, "Une Ecole à Bordeaux : Sigma Jazz Focus," *Jazz magazine* 270 (1978): 31.

122. As related by one of those staff members, Martine Palmé. Interview with the author, Paris, March 27, 2012.

123. On this problem, see Coulangeon, *Les Musiciens*, 215; Patrice Caratini, "Faire le métier," http://www.caratini.com/page30/page34/metier.html.

124. These are *Orchestre National de Jazz 86*, directed by François Jeanneau, and *ONJ 87*, directed by Antoine Hervé (both Label Bleu). On the ONJ and high-culture "arrival," see Tournès, *New Orleans sur Seine*, 416–18; Sklower, *Free jazz*, 94–95. The financial (and sartorial) detail here is drawn from Nicolas Sokolowski, "ONJ : on jazze français ! ," *Jazz hot* 428 (1986): 13, 14, 15. Here, the orchestra's first director, François Jeanneau, says that musicians, contracted by the year, were paid 14,000 francs for 108 hours per month, and the director 23,000.

125. Coulangeon, *Les Musiciens*, 23.

126. Coulangeon, *Les Musiciens*, 25; Caratini, "Faire le métier."

127. Coulangeon, *Les Musiciens*, 26.

128. Coulangeon, *Les Musiciens*, 217, 215. Jazz recordings' market share was in any case small, hovering around 3 percent by the time of Coulangeon's study (11).

129. This term is Coulangeon's; Brierre's own is "detachment." Coulangeon, *Les Musiciens*, 21; Jean-Dominique Brierre, *Le Jazz français de 1900 à aujourd'hui* (Paris: Editions hors collection, 2000), 9.

130. Perchard, *Lee Morgan*, 36–52; Berliner, *Thinking in Jazz*, 52–55, and passim.

131. Malson, Arvanitas et al., "Un Blanc," 14.

132. Tom Perchard, "Writing Jazz Biography: Race, Research and Narrative Representation," *Popular Music History* 2/2 (2007): 119–45.

133. Mouly, "La Persévérance," 21.

134. Cotro, *Chants libres*, 227–28; Brierre, *Le Jazz français*, 9. I am using "fragrance" for Brierre's *parfum*.

135. Cited in Anya Suschitzky, "Debussy's Rameau: French Music and Its Others," *Musical Quarterly* 86, no. 3 (2002): 402, 412.

136. Clifford Geertz, "Deep-Play: Notes on the Balinese Cockfight," in *The Interpretation of Cultures* (London: Fontana, 1993), 448.

137. See, for a recent example, the comments made by Robert Glasper in the documentary *Icons among Us*, dir. Lars Larson, Michael Rivoira and Peter J. Vogt (Paradigm Studio, 2009).

138. Arnold Schoenberg, "Folk-Music and Art-Music," in *Style and Idea*, ed. Leonard Stein, trans. Leo Black (London: Faber and Faber, 1975), 168.

139. E. Taylor Atkins makes some of these arguments at greater length. Atkins, "Toward a Global History of Jazz," xi–xxvii.

Chapter Seven

1. The *bande dessinée* had long been a central fixture of French popular culture for adults as much as children, and under Jack Lang producers were further supported by the ministry of culture.

2. Following the collapse of his Nice jazz animation, Barney Wilen had launched a recording and production company with Caroline de Bendern, Quatre Aces. The project was a failure, and its tribulations led to the couple's separation; Wilen took up with one of the label's artists, the new wave chanteuse Marie Möör. Wilen's early 1980s was bitty and intermittent: he backed Möör, appeared alongside the electronic group Dièse 440, recorded a cameo for Stevie Nicks's 1985 album *Rock a Little*, and composed a piece for himself, guitarist Philippe Petit and orchestra for the inauguration of Nice's Acropolis exhibition center and concert hall.

3. Renault's "Papa and Nicole" commercials, which aired in the United Kingdom between 1991 and 1998, became pop-cultural fixtures: sketches unfolding in idyllic Provençal settings were soundtracked by jazz manouche jingles.

4. The film featured musicians like Herbie Hancock, Freddie Hubbard and Wayne Shorter in musical roles.

5. The complaint was made to his son, Patrick. Interview with the author, February 26, 2012.

6. Wilen's manager of the time, Martine Palmé, remembered how the saxophonist was "really very aware of the way he could work on his image, and he was much influenced in that by his experience with Miles [Davis] . . . refusing many interviews, not talking a lot to the promoters, always keeping a distance. He was very talented, in a way manipulative I would say, in that kind of attitude." Interview with the author, Paris, March 27, 2012.

7. Other examples of this vibrato and timbral play—and there are many—can be found throughout "Recado," from the trio record *Sanctuary* (IDA, 1991), and "No Problem '94" from *New York Romance* (Sunny Side, 1994); Wilen's similarly treated statement of "I Loves You Porgy," from *Talisman* (IDA, 1994), is one of the highlights of his recorded life's work.

8. Pascal Ory, *L'Entre-deux-Mai : histoire culturelle de la France, mai 1968-mai 1981* (Paris: Editions de Seuil, 1983), 118–27. See also Dudley Andrew and Steven Ungar, *Popular Front Paris and the Poetics of Culture* (Cambridge, MA, and London: Belknap Press of Harvard University Press, 2005), 17, 5; Naomi Greene, *Landscapes of Loss: The National Past in Postwar French Cinema* (Princeton, NJ: Princeton University Press, 1999), 9–10.

9. Nor was it confined to France, as American films like *The Sting (1973) and Ragtime* (1981) showed.

10. Stovall, *Paris Noir*, 285–86.

11. The trumpeter Randy Sandke developed related projects in the United States.

12. Burns, "A Masterpiece by Midnight."

13. Later, after his winning the 1993 Thelonious Monk International Piano Competition, Jacky Terrasson would also come to international prominence.

14. Gérald Arnaud, "En arrière, tout ! ," *Jazz hot* 416 (1984): 5; Michel-Claude Jalard, *Le Jazz est-il encore possible ?* (Marseille: Editions Parenthèses, 1986).

15. Pierre Nora, "Between Memory and History: Les Lieux de Mémoire," *Representations* 26 (1989): 9. As noted, in Britain Raphael Samuel was another important pioneer in this field; in France, Nora's project was contemporaneous with books like Jacques Le Goff, *History and Memory*, trans. Steven Rendall and Elizabeth Claman (New York: Columbia University Press, 1992).

16. As Benjamin Givan points out, Reinhardt's memorialization makes him "a notable exception to the distinctive Manouche ritual of erasing concrete signs of the dead by destroying their belongings and refraining from mentioning their names or commemorating them publically." Givan, *The Music of Django Reinhardt*, 6.

17. André Chastel, trans. Nancy Turpin, "The Notion of Patrimony," in *Rethinking France: Les Lieux de Mémoire. Volume 3: Legacies*, ed. Pierre Nora (Chicago: Chicago University Press, 2009), 39, 40. The historical process and dynamic that Chastel describes here has been seen in numerous other countries.

18. Ross, *Fast Cars*, 151, passim.

19. Jerome de Groot, *Consuming History: Historians and Heritage in Contemporary Popular Culture* (London: Routledge, 2008), 10.

20. Jim McGuigan, *Cool Capitalism* (London: Pluto Press, 2009), 95.

21. See, among other examples, Robin D. G. Kelley, "Miles Davis: The Chameleon of Cool; A Jazz Genius in the Guise of a Hustler," *New York Times*, May 13, 2001, http://www.nytimes.com/2001/05/13/arts/miles-davis-the-chameleon-of-cool-a-jazz-genius-in-the-guise-of-a-hustler.html.

22. The trailer is included on a further DVD release of *Ascenseur pour l'échafaud* (Arte Video, 2005).

23. Fred Bouchard, "Miles Davis: Ascenseur pour l'échafaud (Lift to the Scaffold) / Aura," *Down Beat* 57, no. 2 (1990): 34.

24. Kahn, *Kind of Blue*, 200.

Index

Wooding, Sam, 3
Woods, Phil, 55
Workshop de Lyon. *See* Free Jazz Workshop de Lyon
World War II. *See* German occupation of France during World War II

X-tet, 199–200, 202

Yerba Buena Jazz Band, 41

Young, La Monte, 174
Young, Lester, 8, 78, 112, 235
Young, Trummy, 83

Zanzibar group, 183
Zao, 222
Zappa, Frank, 177, 222
Zazous, 7
Zodiac (Barney Wilen), 159 60, 162
Zorn, John, 219